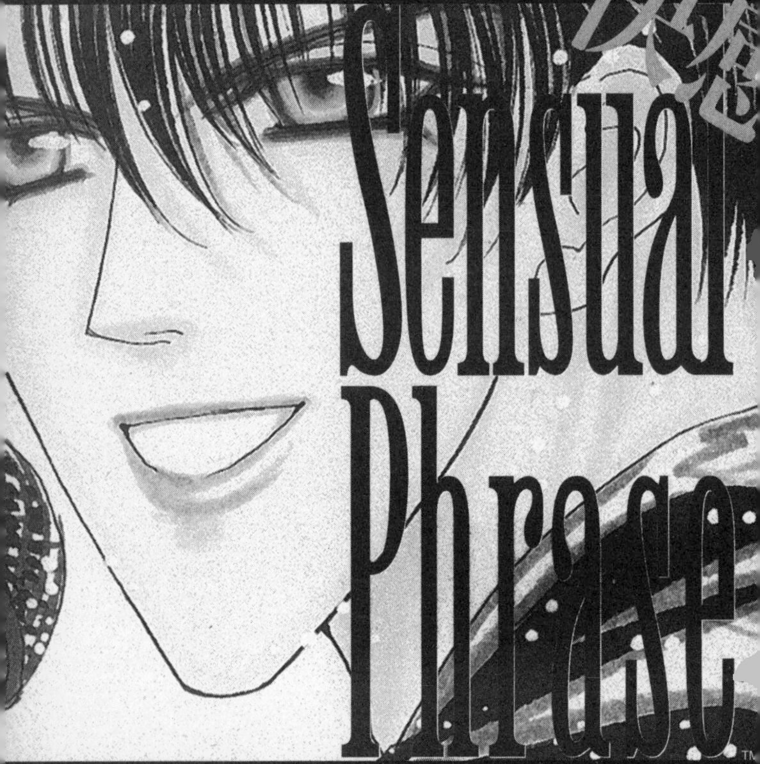

快感 Sensual Phrase™

Story and Art by Mayu Shinjo

vol.9

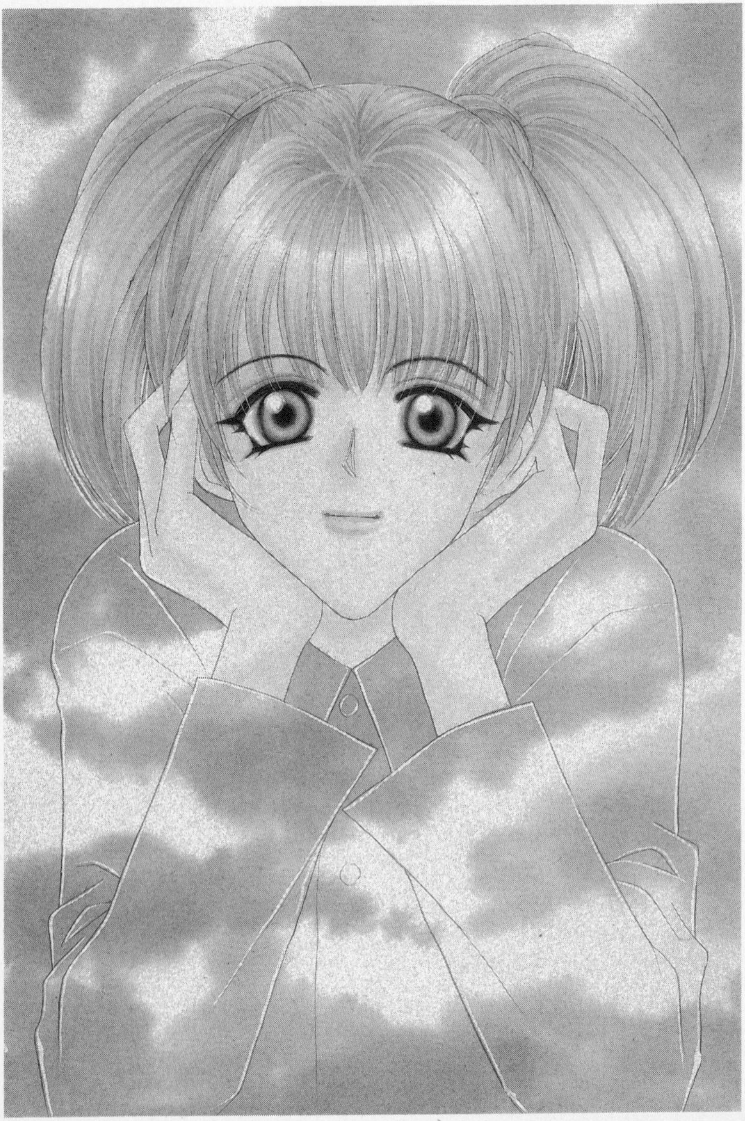

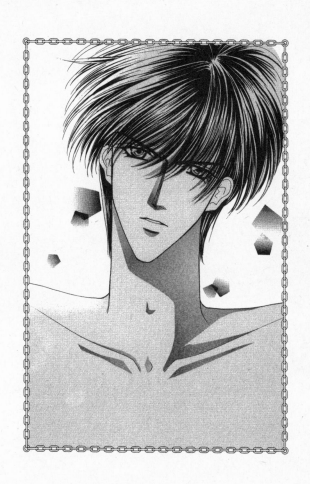

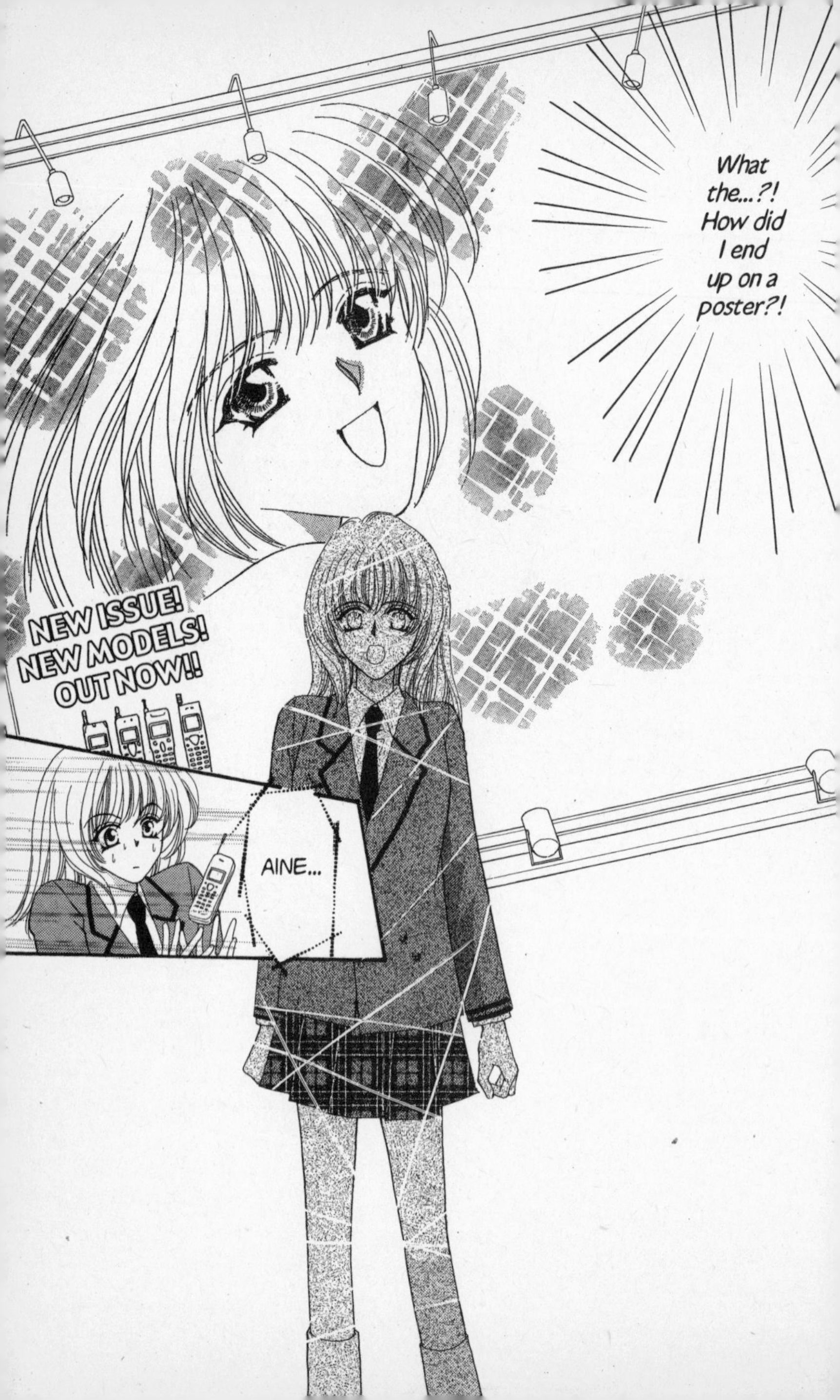
What the...?! How did I end up on a poster?!
NEW ISSUE! NEW MODELS! OUT NOW!!
AINE...

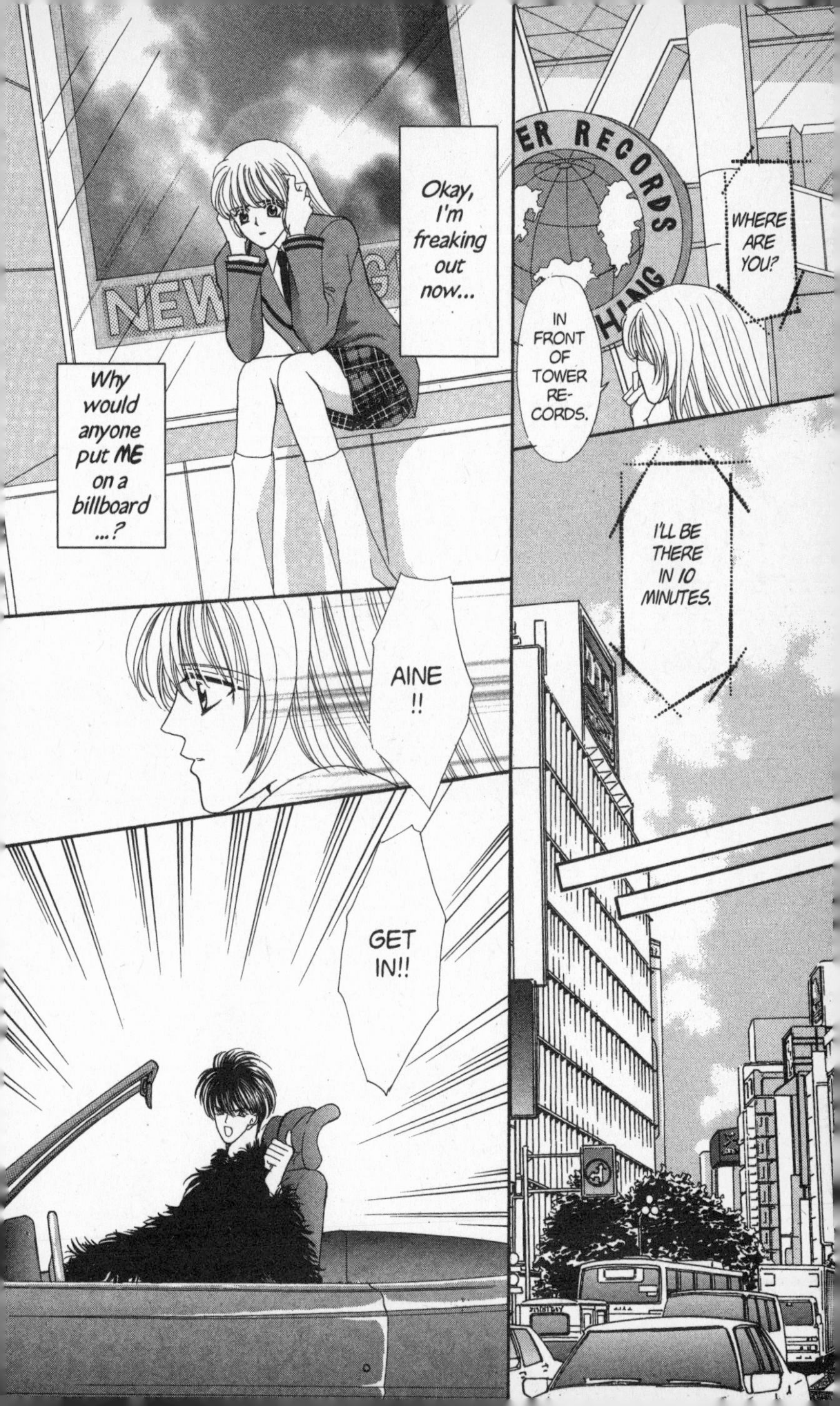
WHERE ARE YOU?
IN FRONT OF TOWER RE-CORDS.
I'LL BE THERE IN 10 MINUTES.
Okay, I'm freaking out now...
Why would anyone put ME on a billboard ...?
AINE !!
GET IN!!

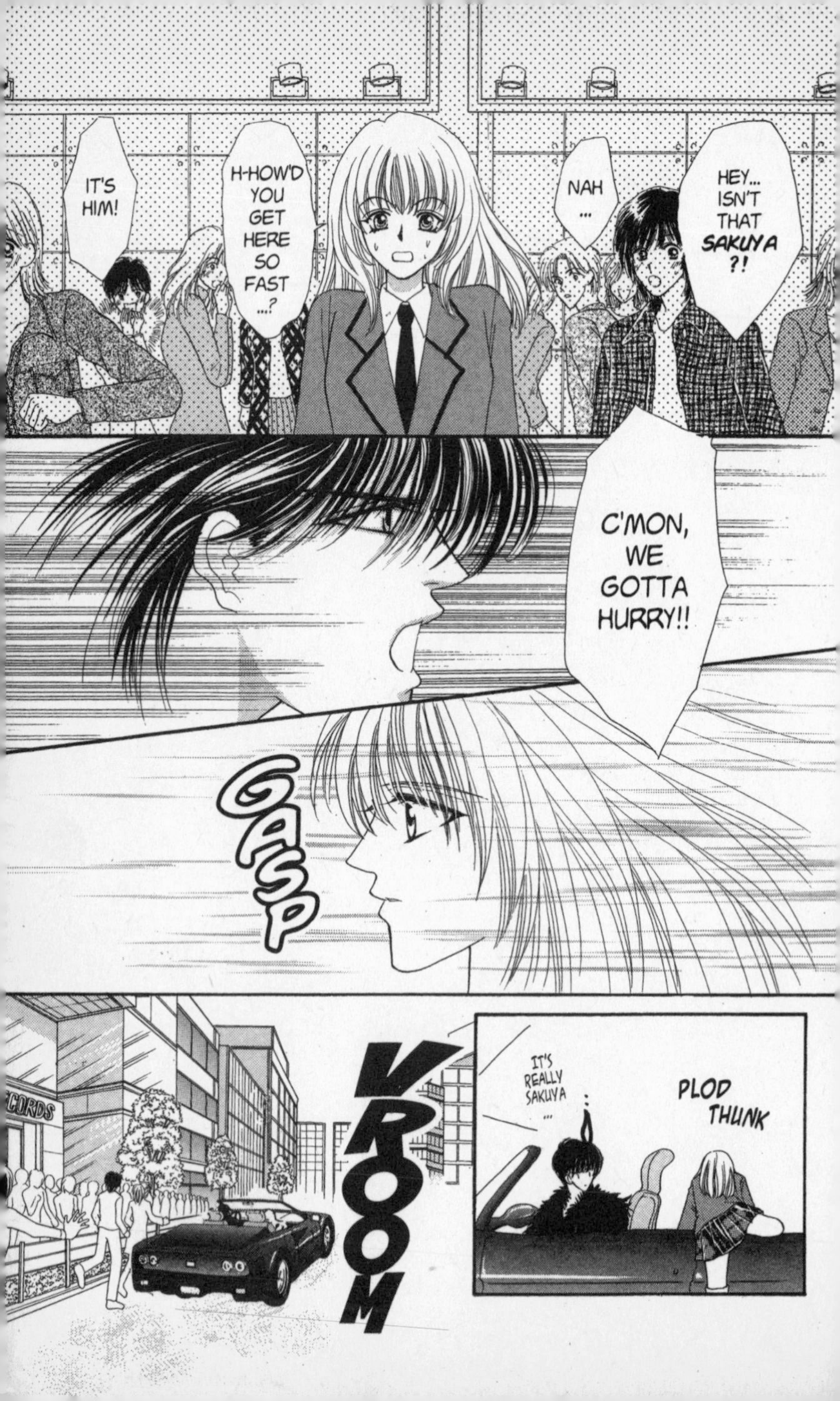
HEY... ISN'T THAT SAKUYA ?!
NAH ...
H-HOW'D YOU GET HERE SO FAST ...?
IT'S HIM!
C'MON, WE GOTTA HURRY!!
GASP
IT'S REALLY SAKUYA ...
PLOD THUNK
VROOM

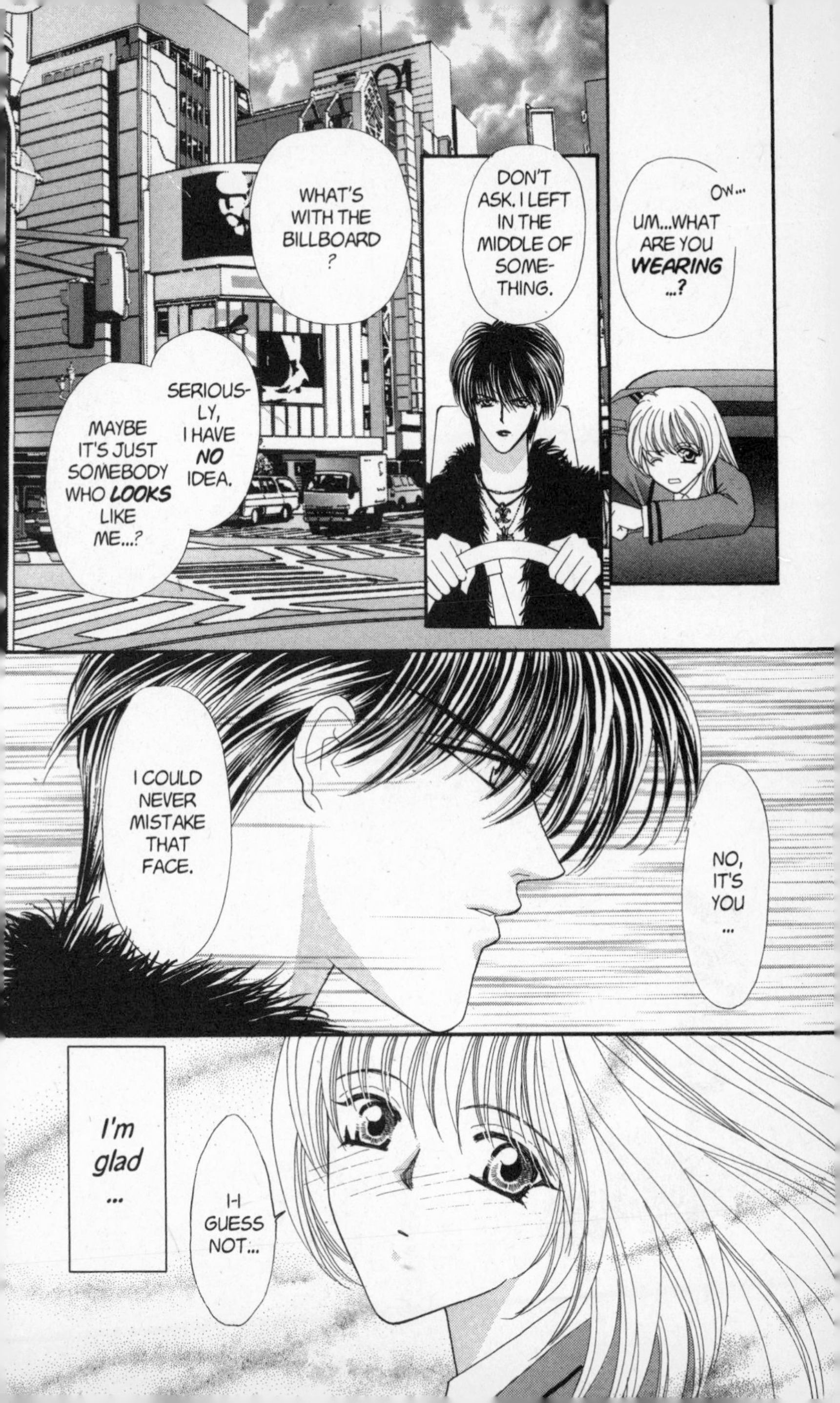
OW...
UM...WHAT ARE YOU *WEARING* ...?
DON'T ASK. I LEFT IN THE MIDDLE OF SOME-THING.
WHAT'S WITH THE BILLBOARD ?
SERIOUS-LY, I HAVE *NO* IDEA.
MAYBE IT'S JUST SOMEBODY WHO *LOOKS* LIKE ME...?
NO, IT'S YOU ...
I COULD NEVER MISTAKE THAT FACE.
I-I GUESS NOT...
I'm glad ...

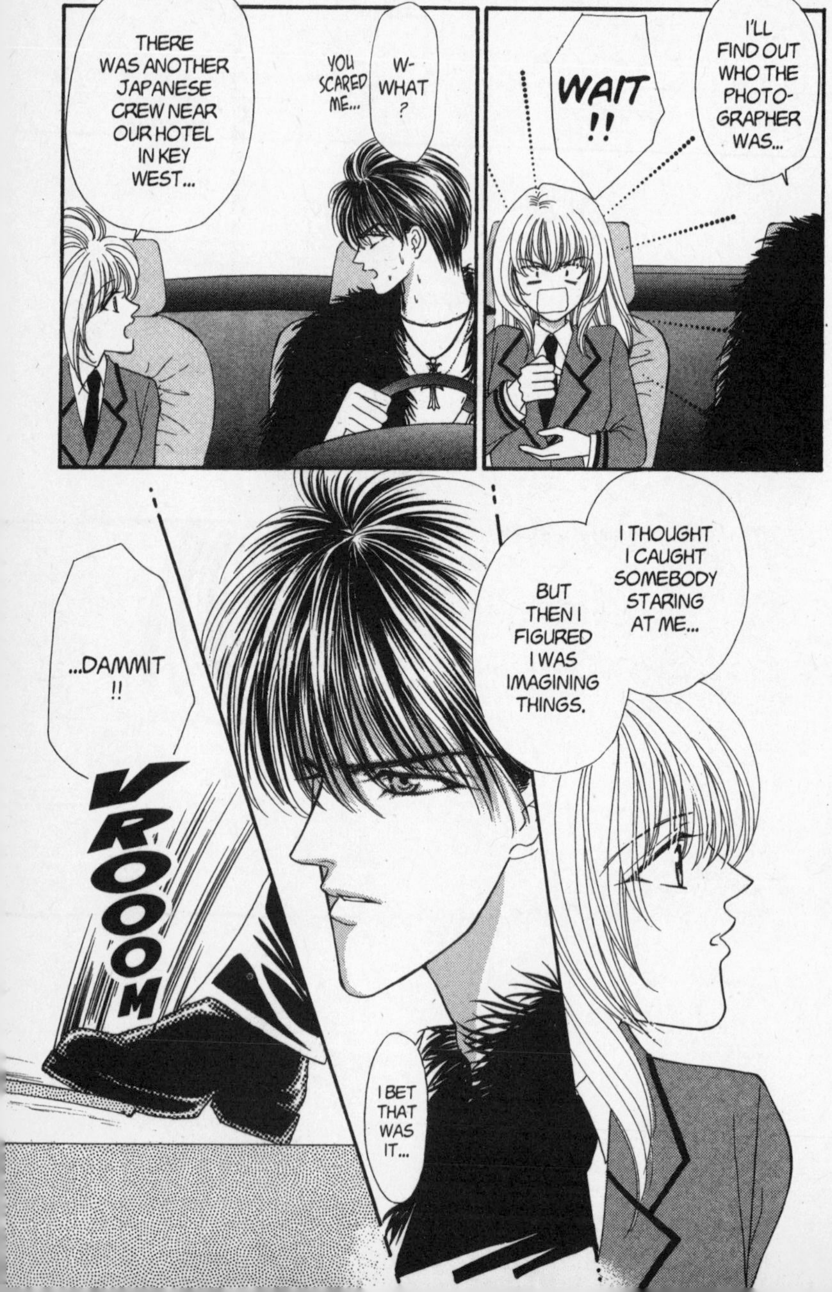
I'LL FIND OUT WHO THE PHOTO-GRAPHER WAS...
WAIT!!
W-WHAT?
YOU SCARED ME...
THERE WAS ANOTHER JAPANESE CREW NEAR OUR HOTEL IN KEY WEST...
I THOUGHT I CAUGHT SOMEBODY STARING AT ME...
BUT THEN I FIGURED I WAS IMAGINING THINGS.
...DAMMIT!!
VROOOM
I BET THAT WAS IT...

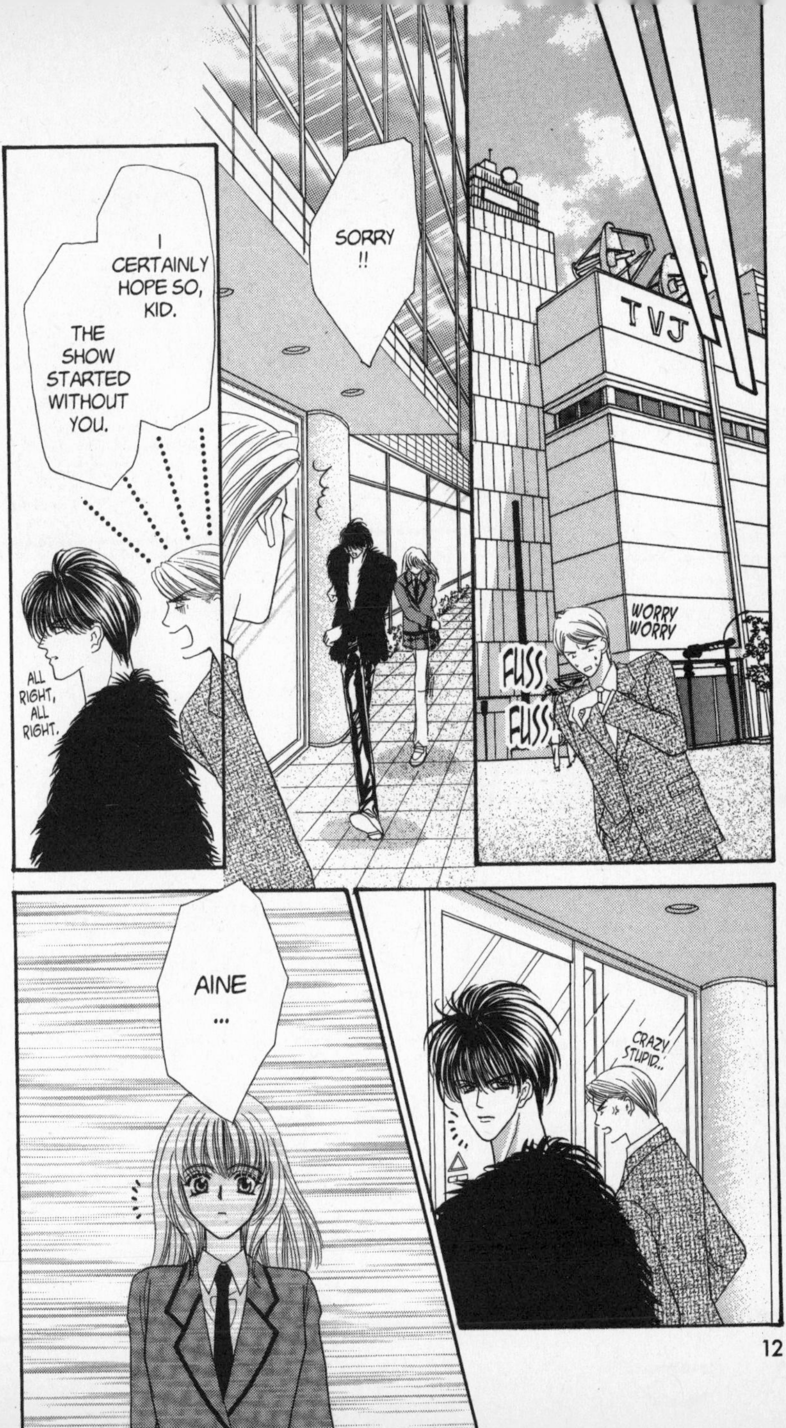
TVJ
WORRY WORRY
FUSS FUSS
SORRY !!
I CERTAINLY HOPE SO, KID.
THE SHOW STARTED WITHOUT YOU.
ALL RIGHT, ALL RIGHT.
CRAZY STUPID...
AINE ...

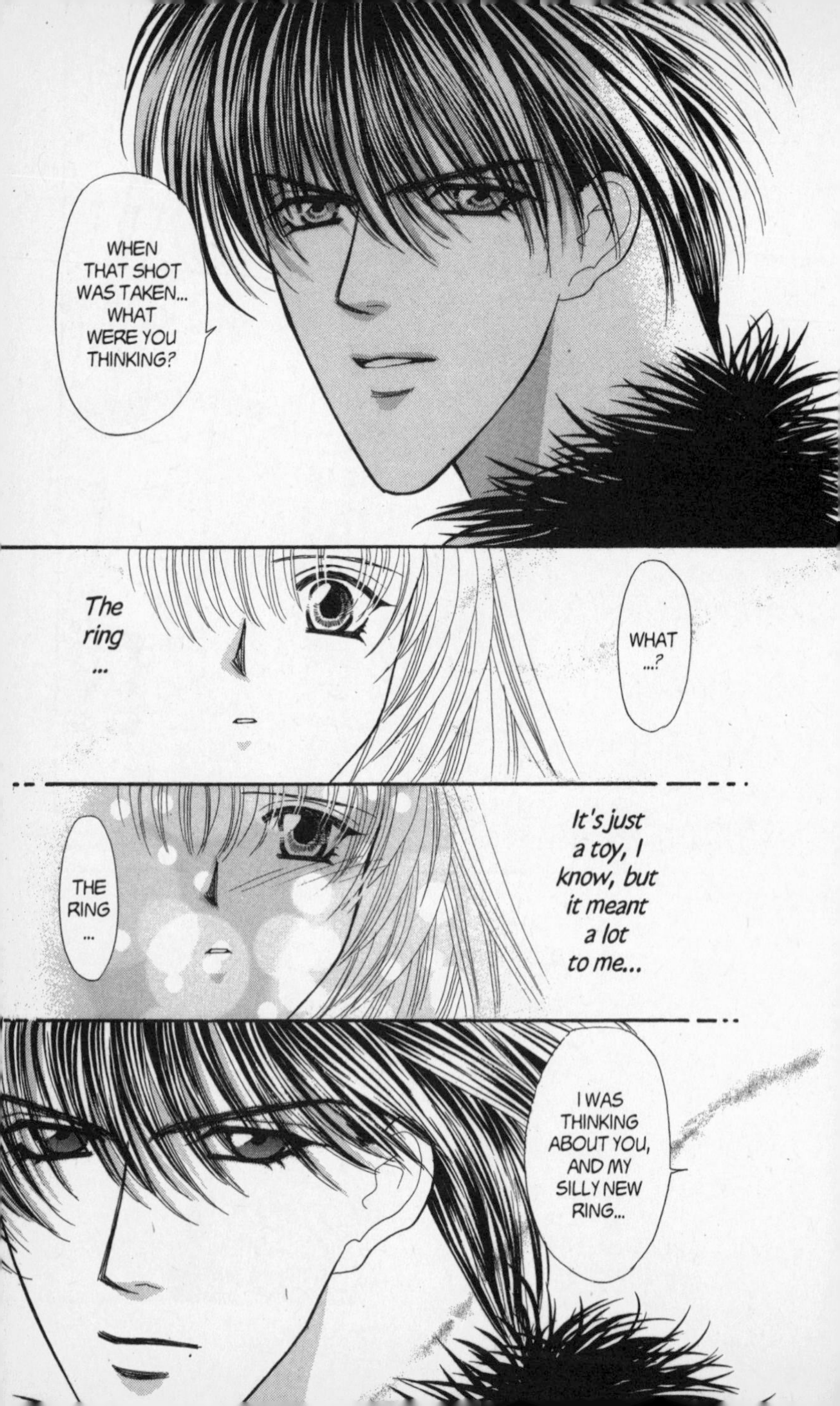

WHEN THAT SHOT WAS TAKEN... WHAT WERE YOU THINKING?
WHAT ...?
The ring ...
It's just a toy, I know, but it meant a lot to me...
THE RING ...
I WAS THINKING ABOUT YOU, AND MY SILLY NEW RING...

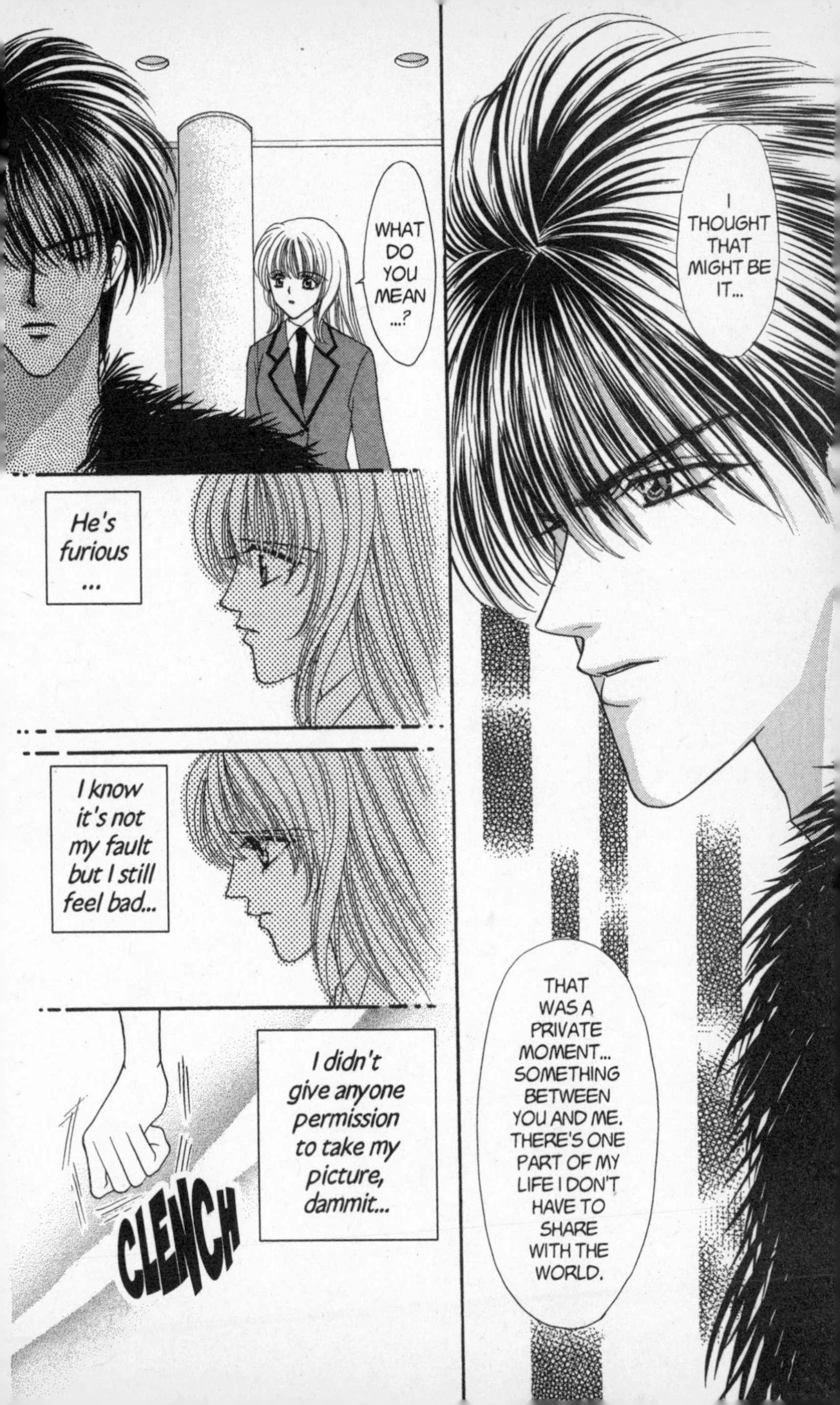
I THOUGHT THAT MIGHT BE IT...
THAT WAS A PRIVATE MOMENT... SOMETHING BETWEEN YOU AND ME. THERE'S ONE PART OF MY LIFE I DON'T HAVE TO SHARE WITH THE WORLD.
WHAT DO YOU MEAN ...?
He's furious ...
I know it's not my fault but I still feel bad...
I didn't give anyone permission to take my picture, dammit...
CLENCH

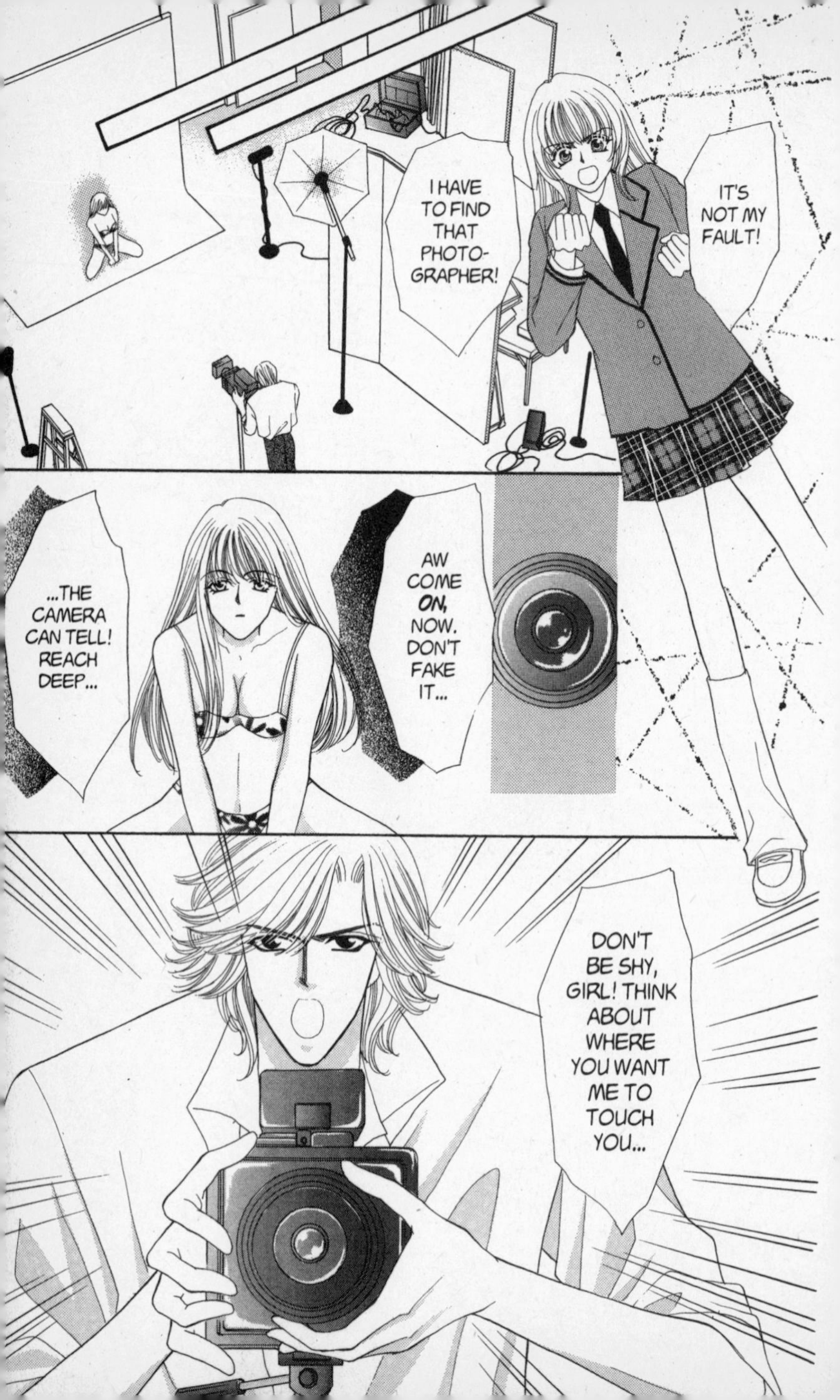
IT'S NOT MY FAULT!
I HAVE TO FIND THAT PHOTO-GRAPHER!
AW COME *ON,* NOW. DON'T FAKE IT...
...THE CAMERA CAN TELL! REACH DEEP...
DON'T BE SHY, GIRL! THINK ABOUT WHERE YOU WANT ME TO TOUCH YOU...

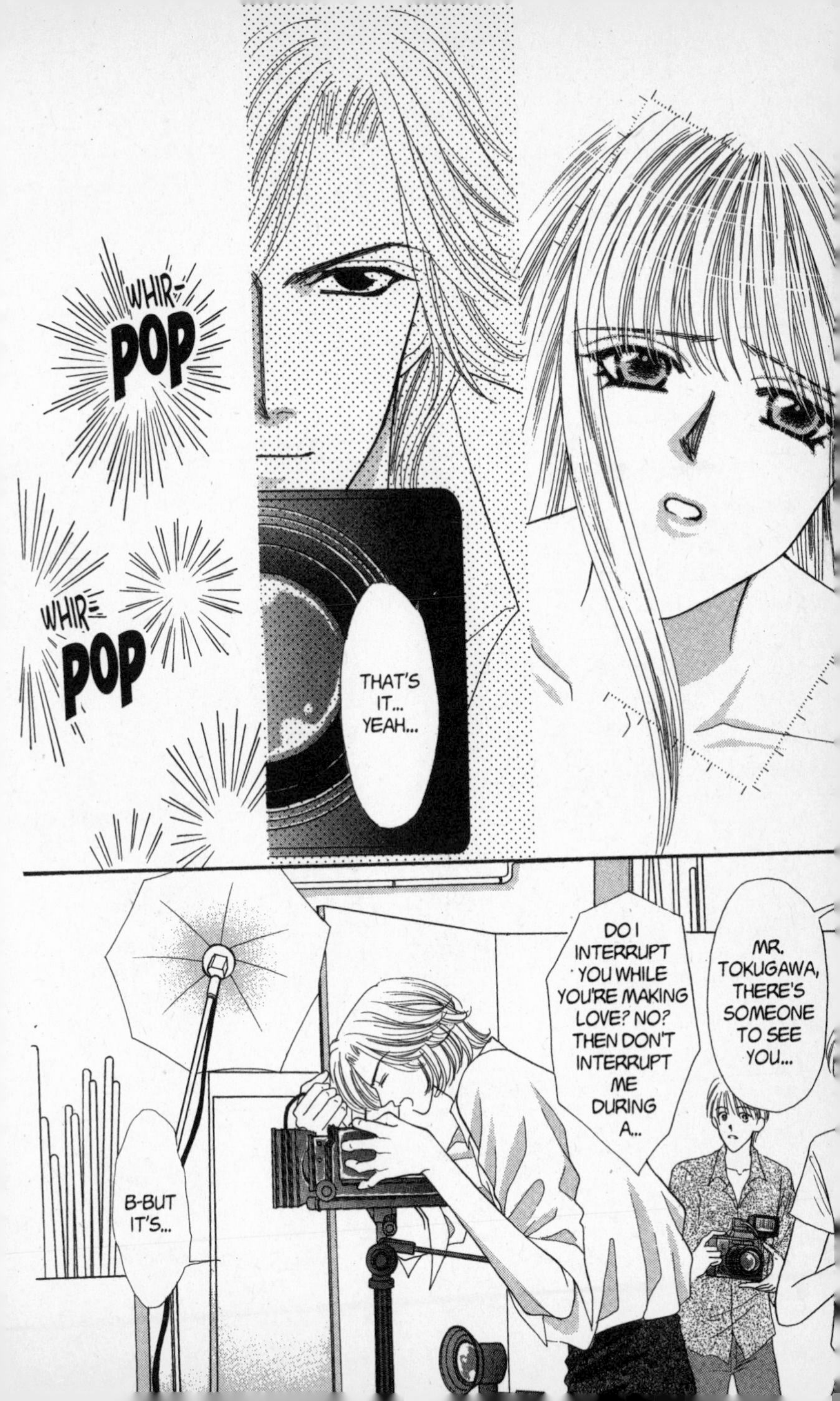
THAT'S IT... YEAH...
WHIR-POP
WHIR-POP
MR. TOKUGAWA, THERE'S SOMEONE TO SEE YOU...
DO I INTERRUPT YOU WHILE YOU'RE MAKING LOVE? NO? THEN DON'T INTERRUPT ME DURING A...
B-BUT IT'S...

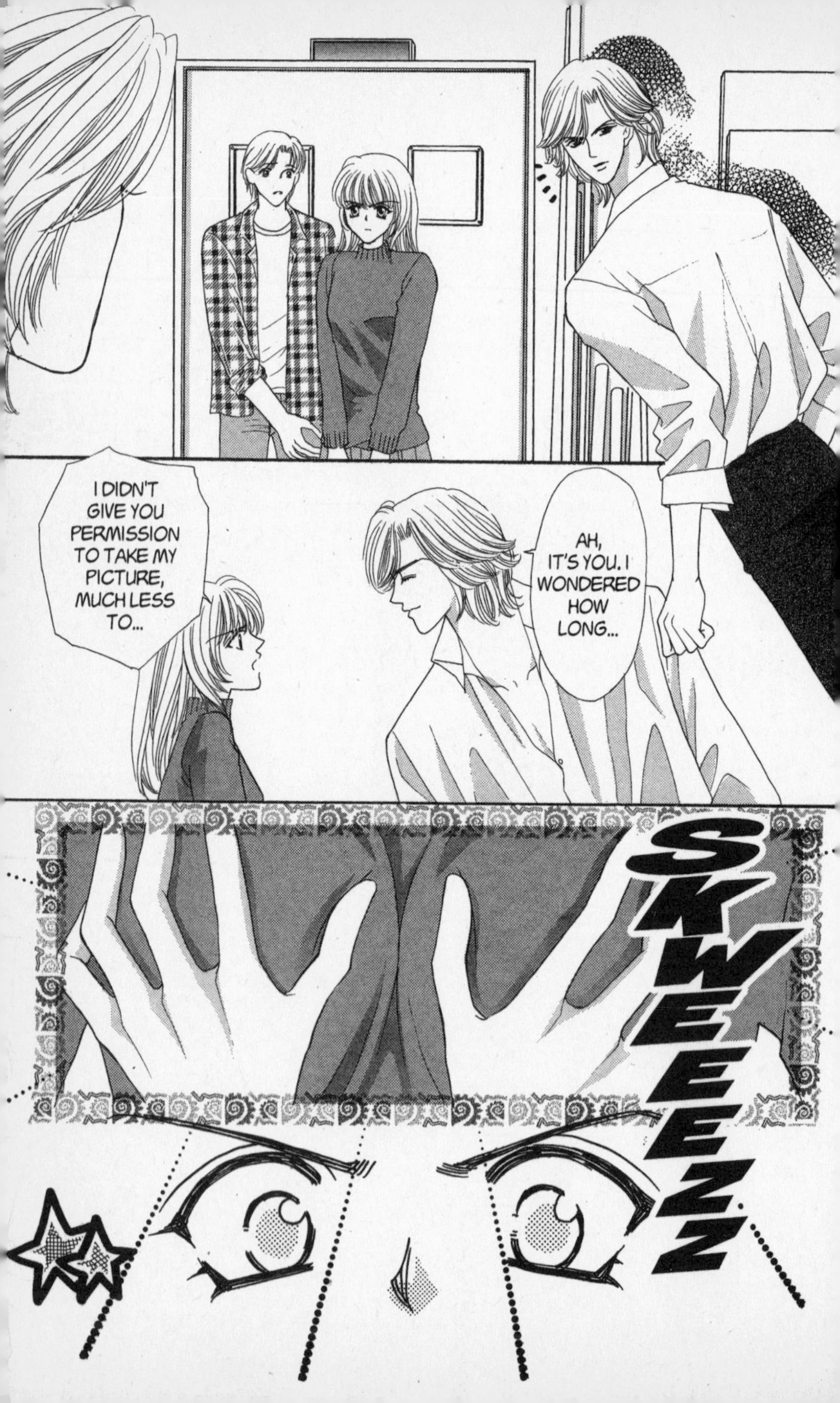
AH, IT'S YOU. I WONDERED HOW LONG...
I DIDN'T GIVE YOU PERMISSION TO TAKE MY PICTURE, MUCH LESS TO...
SKWEEZZ

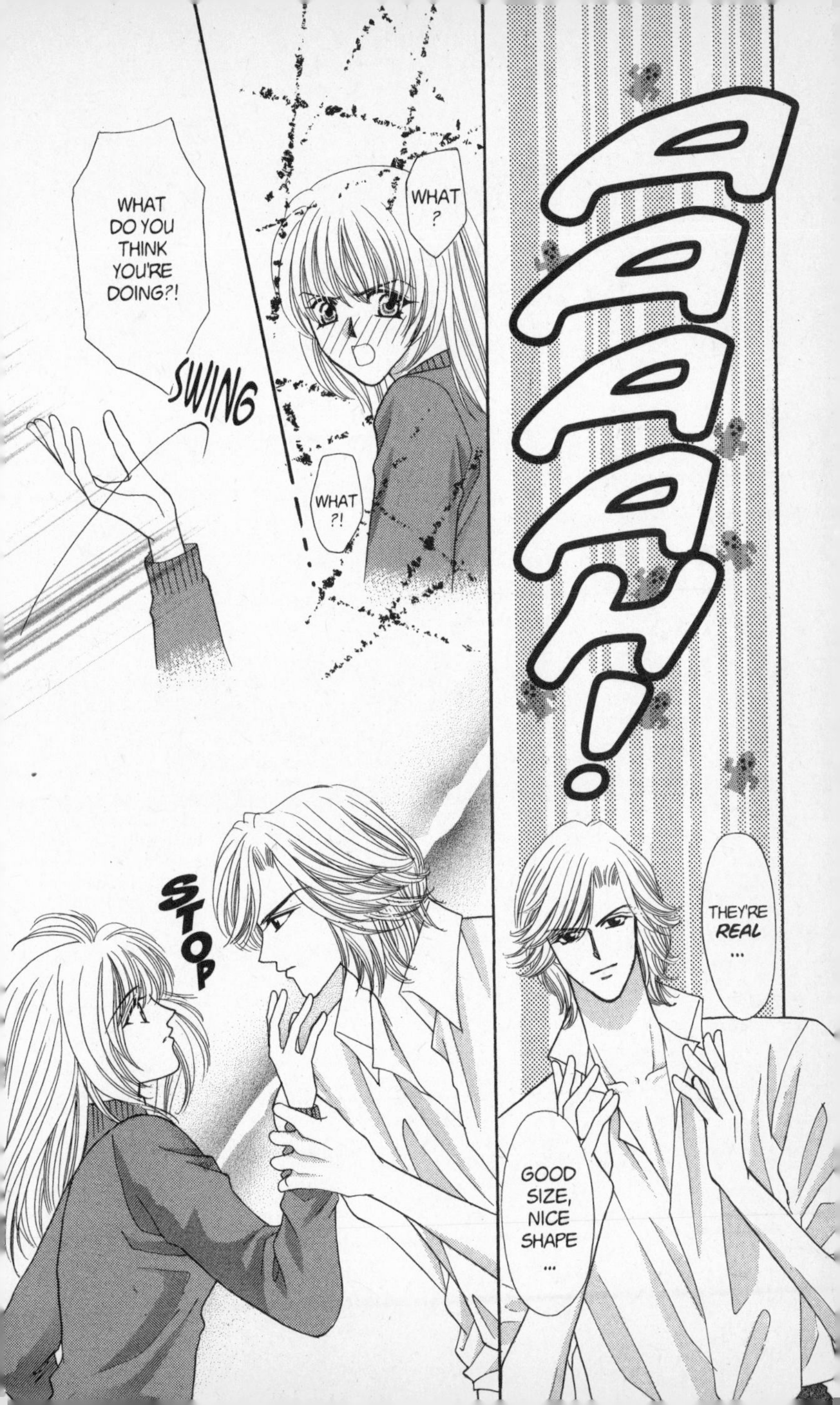
AAAAAH!
THEY'RE *REAL* ...
GOOD SIZE, NICE SHAPE ...
WHAT ?
WHAT ?!
WHAT DO YOU THINK YOU'RE DOING?!
SWING
STOP

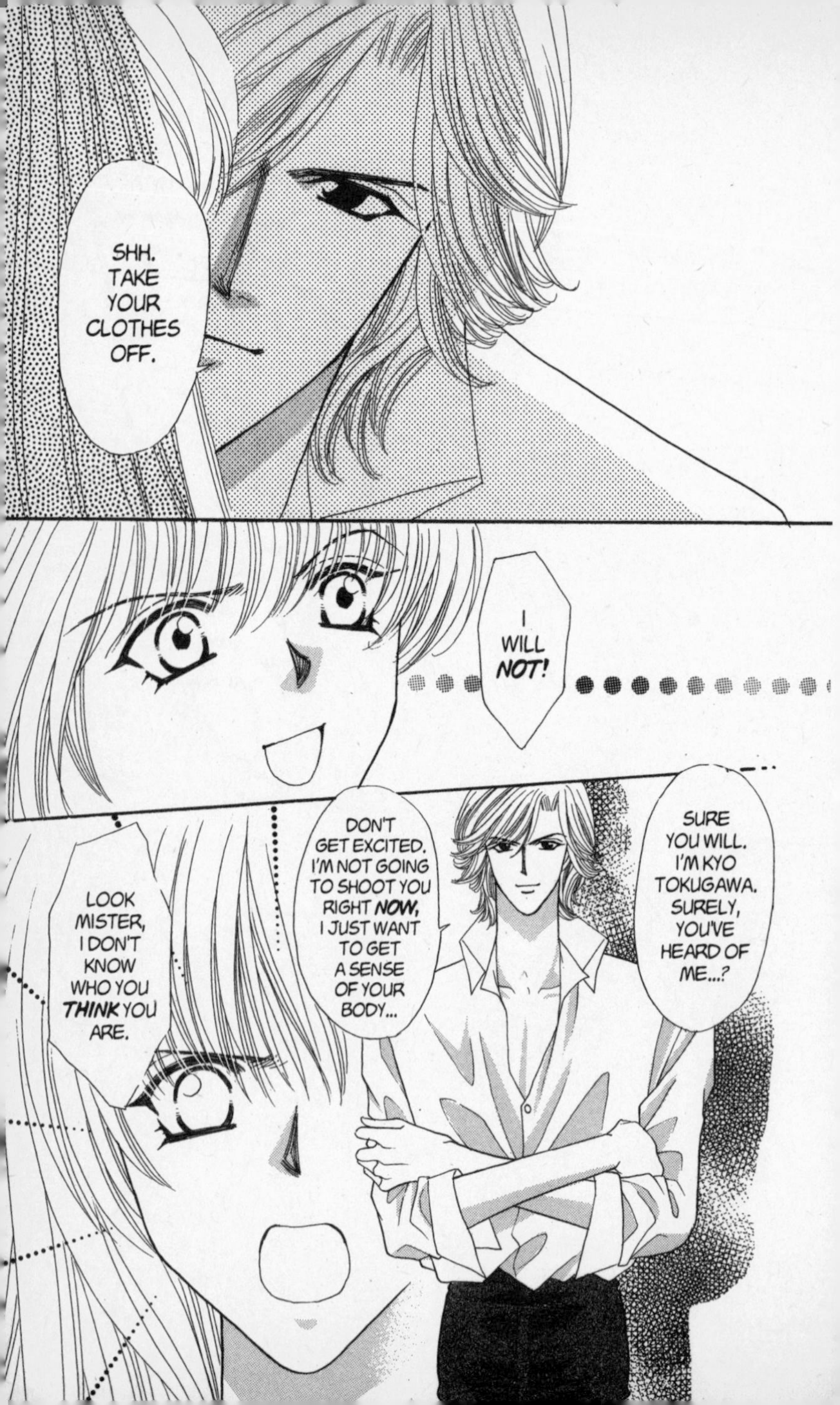
SHH. TAKE YOUR CLOTHES OFF.
I WILL *NOT*!
SURE YOU WILL. I'M KYO TOKUGAWA. SURELY, YOU'VE HEARD OF ME...?
DON'T GET EXCITED. I'M NOT GOING TO SHOOT YOU RIGHT *NOW*, I JUST WANT TO GET A SENSE OF YOUR BODY...
LOOK MISTER, I DON'T KNOW WHO YOU *THINK* YOU ARE.

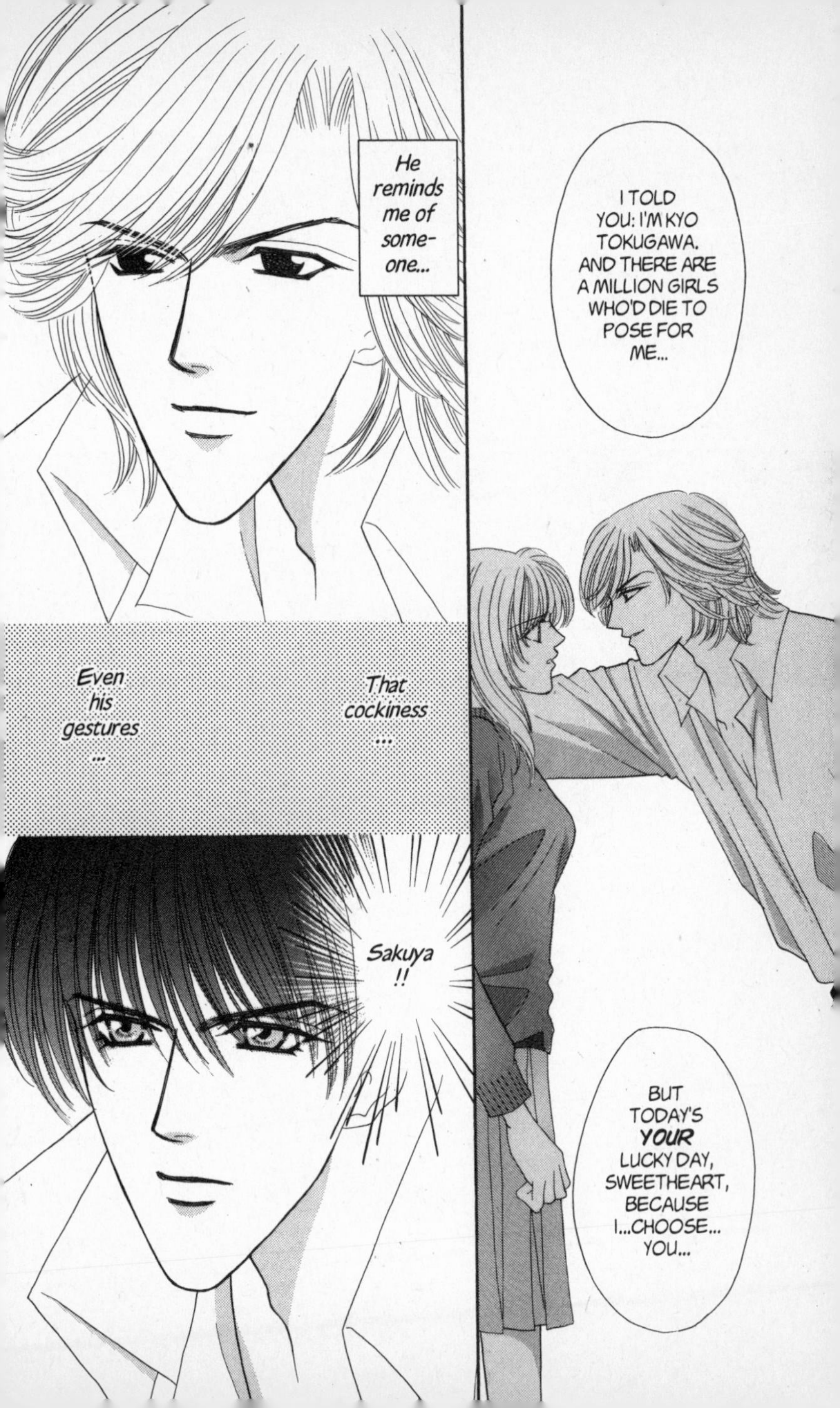

I TOLD YOU: I'M KYO TOKUGAWA. AND THERE ARE A MILLION GIRLS WHO'D DIE TO POSE FOR ME...
BUT TODAY'S **YOUR** LUCKY DAY, SWEETHEART, BECAUSE I...CHOOSE... YOU...
He reminds me of some-one...
That cockiness ...
Even his gestures ...
Sakuya !!

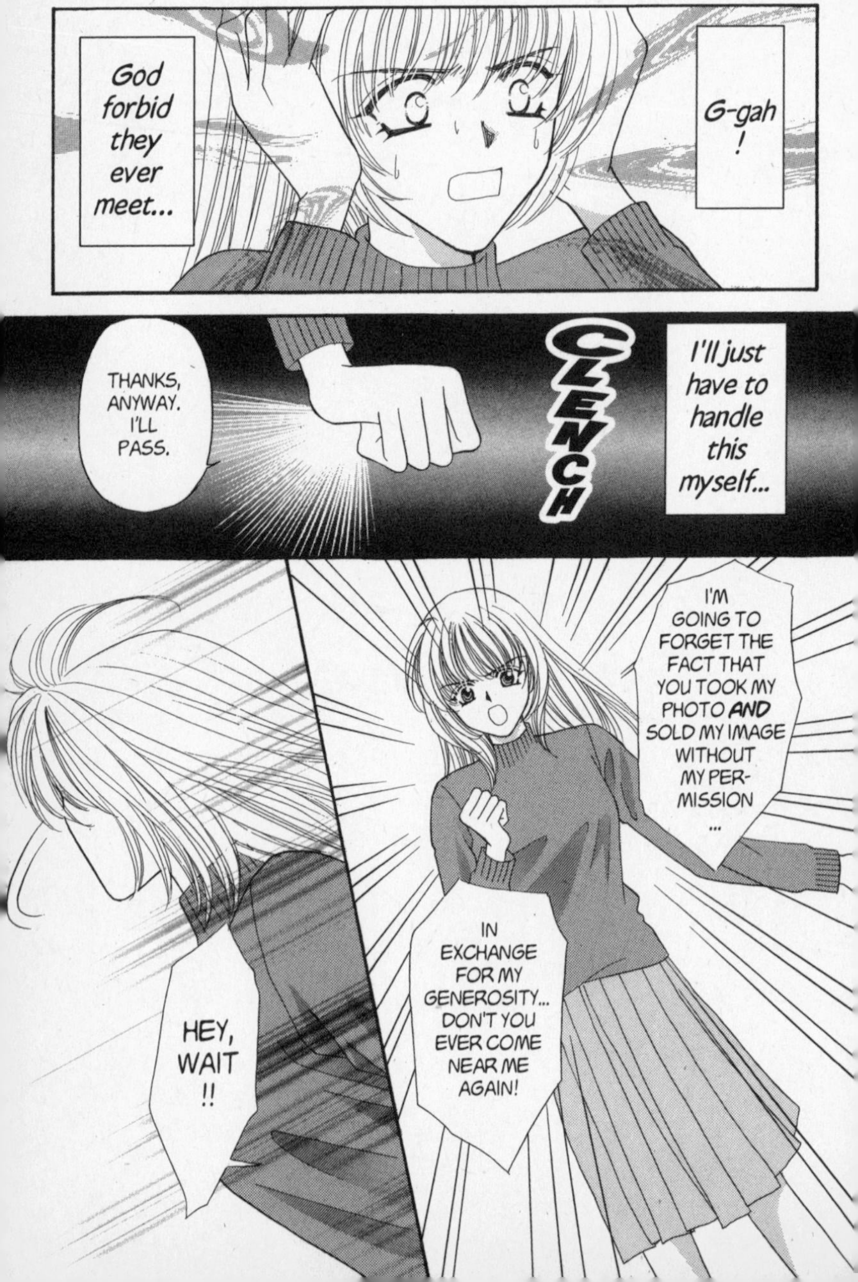
G-gah!
God forbid they ever meet...
I'll just have to handle this myself...
CLENCH
THANKS, ANYWAY. I'LL PASS.
I'M GOING TO FORGET THE FACT THAT YOU TOOK MY PHOTO **AND** SOLD MY IMAGE WITHOUT MY PER-MISSION...
IN EXCHANGE FOR MY GENEROSITY... DON'T YOU EVER COME NEAR ME AGAIN!
HEY, WAIT!!

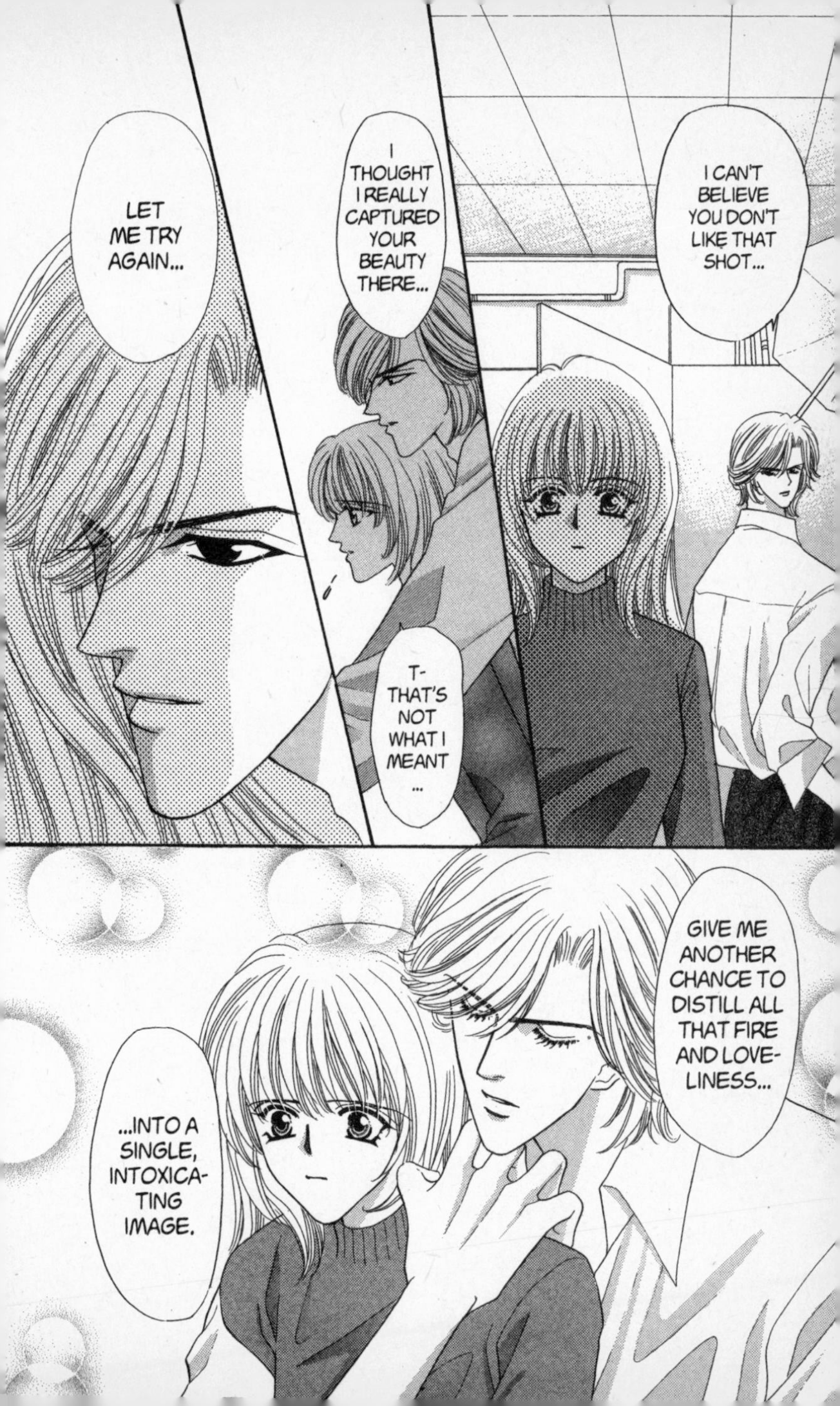
I CAN'T BELIEVE YOU DON'T LIKE THAT SHOT...
I THOUGHT I REALLY CAPTURED YOUR BEAUTY THERE...
T-THAT'S NOT WHAT I MEANT...
LET ME TRY AGAIN...
GIVE ME ANOTHER CHANCE TO DISTILL ALL THAT FIRE AND LOVE-LINESS...
...INTO A SINGLE, INTOXICA-TING IMAGE.

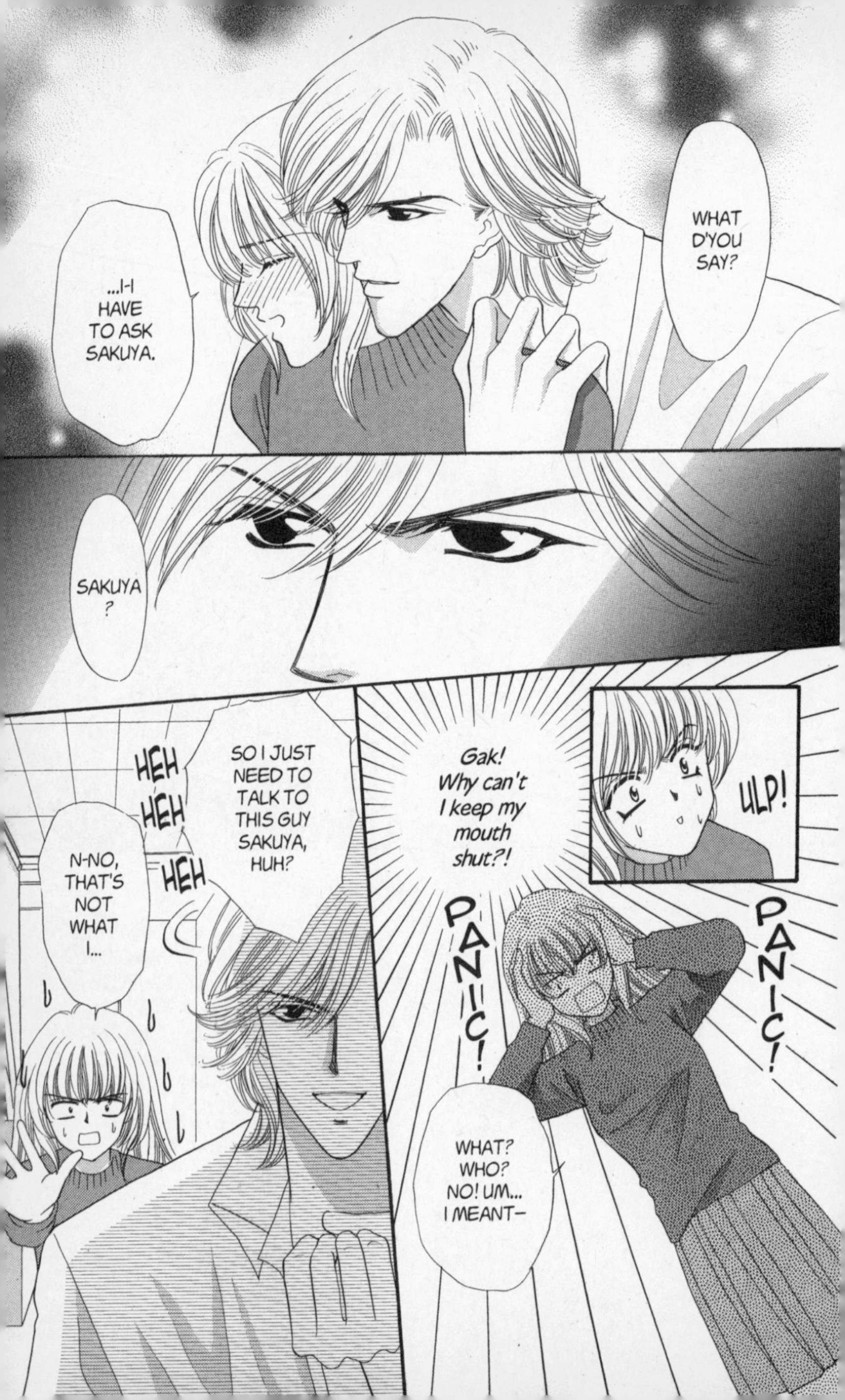
WHAT D'YOU SAY?
...I-I HAVE TO ASK SAKUYA.
SAKUYA?
ULP!
Gak! Why can't I keep my mouth shut?!
PANIC!
PANIC!
WHAT? WHO? NO! UM... I MEANT–
SO I JUST NEED TO TALK TO THIS GUY SAKUYA, HUH?
HEH HEH HEH
N-NO, THAT'S NOT WHAT I...

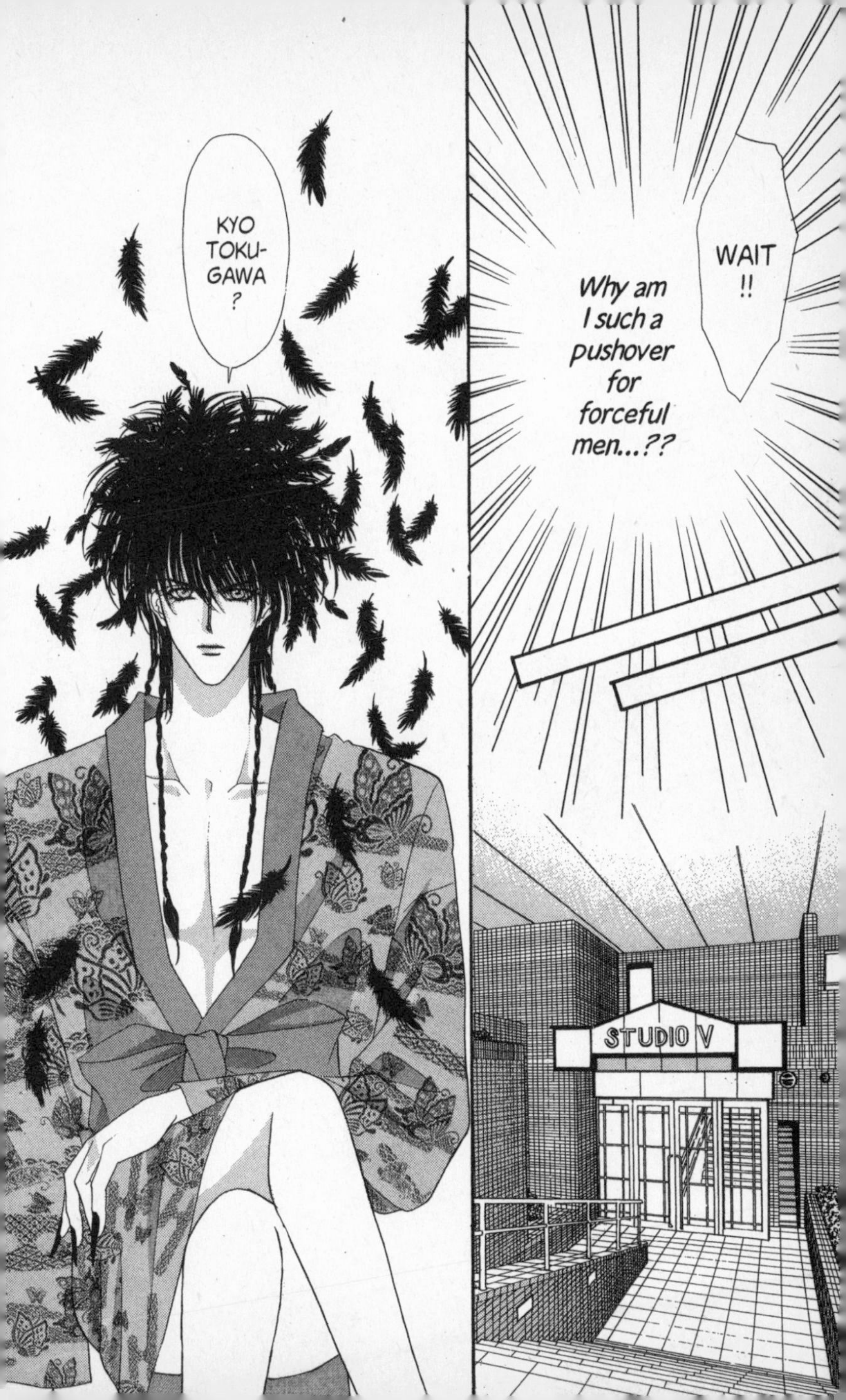
WAIT !!
Why am I such a pushover for forceful men...??
STUDIO V
KYO TOKU-GAWA ?

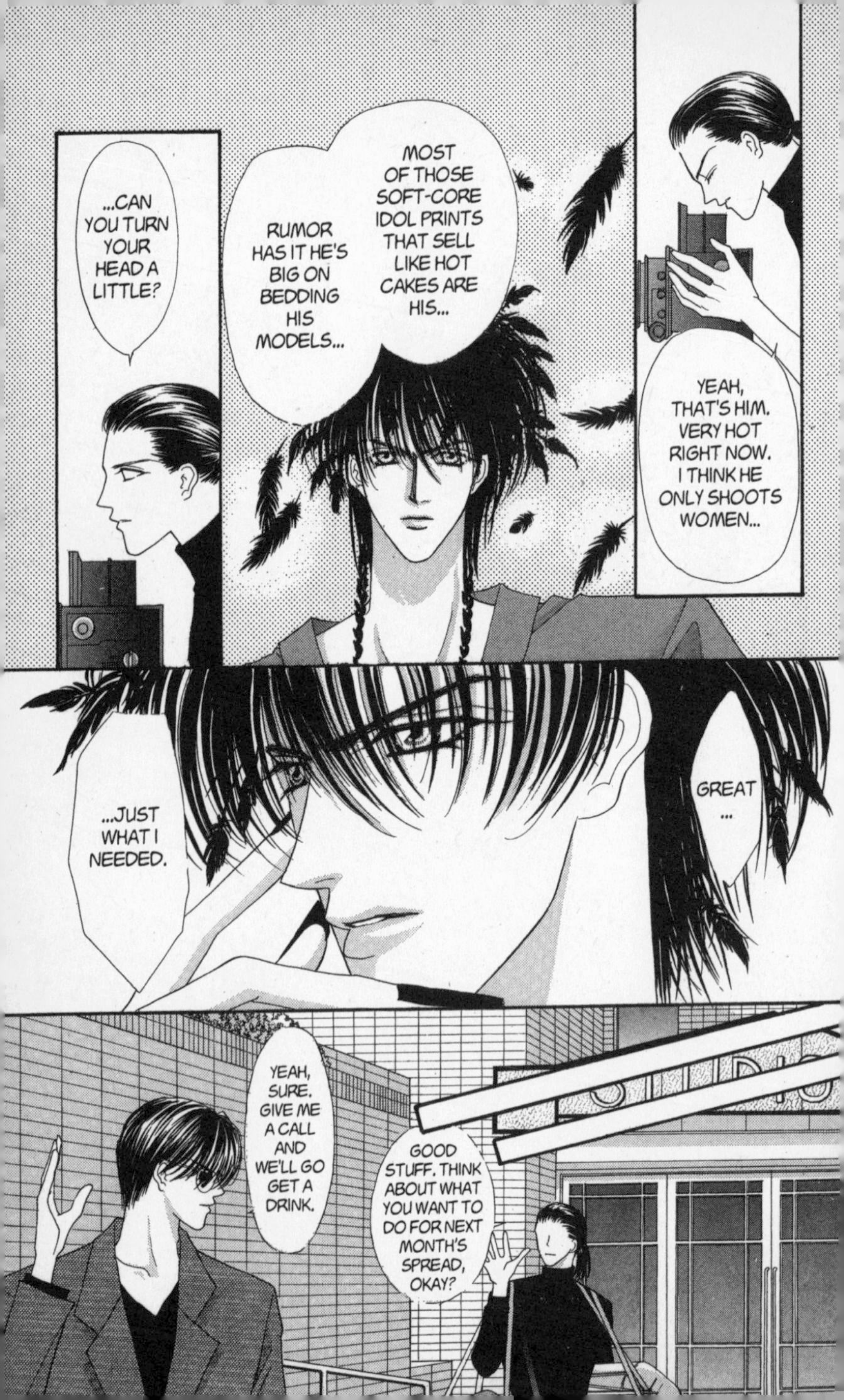
YEAH, THAT'S HIM. VERY HOT RIGHT NOW. I THINK HE ONLY SHOOTS WOMEN...
MOST OF THOSE SOFT-CORE IDOL PRINTS THAT SELL LIKE HOT CAKES ARE HIS...
RUMOR HAS IT HE'S BIG ON BEDDING HIS MODELS...
...CAN YOU TURN YOUR HEAD A LITTLE?
GREAT ...
...JUST WHAT I NEEDED.
GOOD STUFF. THINK ABOUT WHAT YOU WANT TO DO FOR NEXT MONTH'S SPREAD, OKAY?
YEAH, SURE. GIVE ME A CALL AND WE'LL GO GET A DRINK.

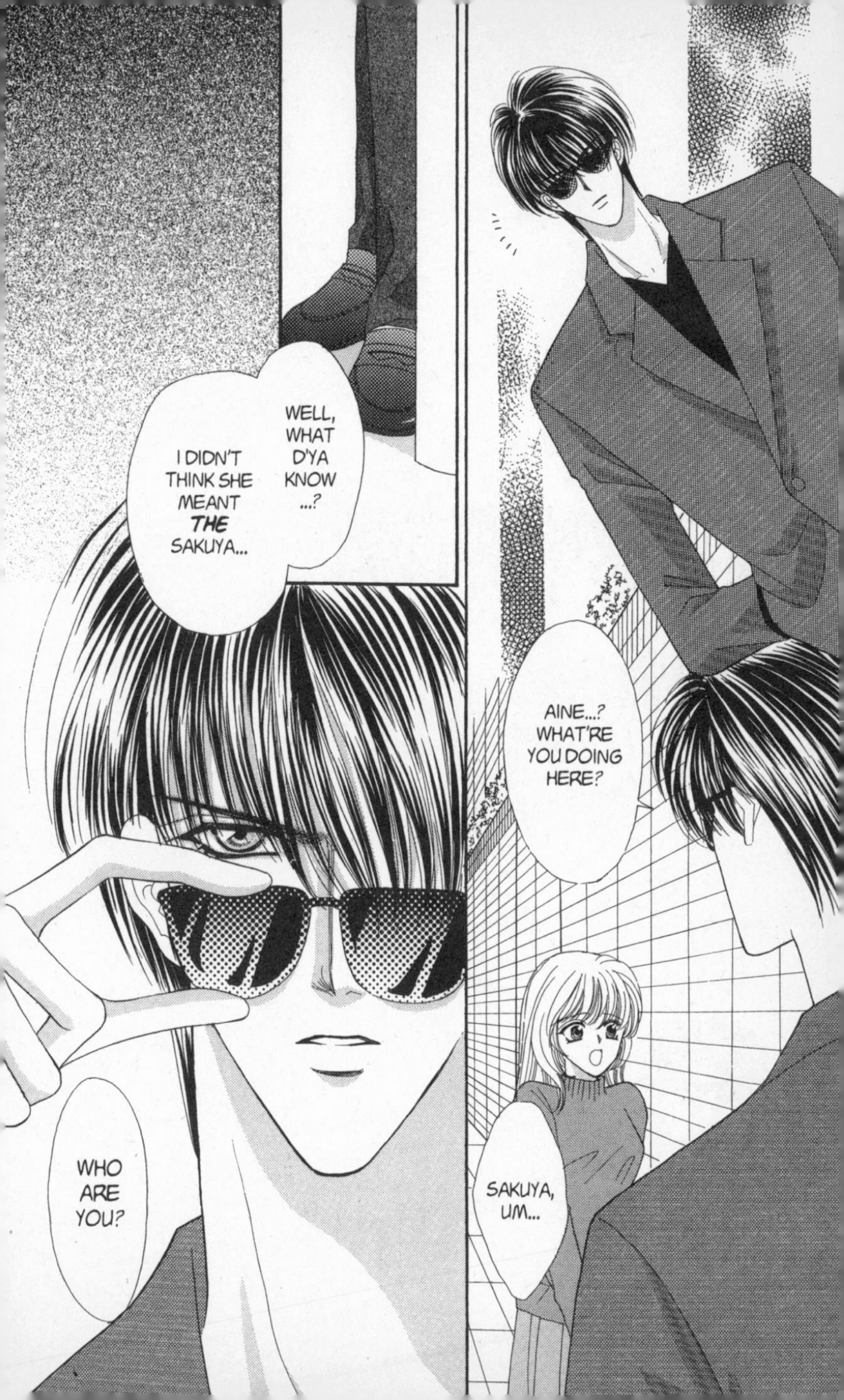
AINE...? WHAT'RE YOU DOING HERE?
SAKUYA, UM...
WELL, WHAT D'YA KNOW ...?
I DIDN'T THINK SHE MEANT **THE** SAKUYA...
WHO ARE YOU?

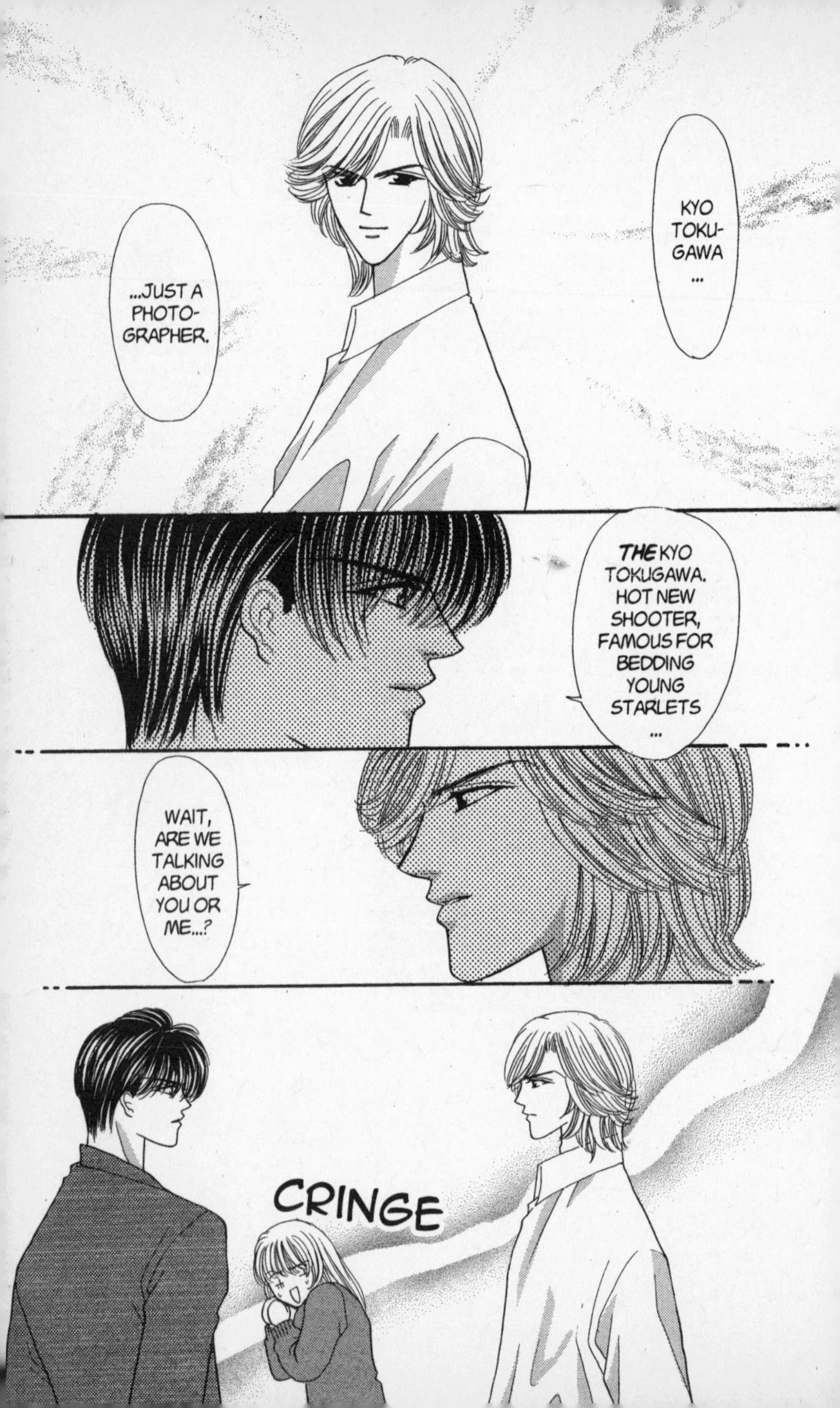
KYO TOKUGAWA ...
...JUST A PHOTOGRAPHER.
THE KYO TOKUGAWA. HOT NEW SHOOTER, FAMOUS FOR BEDDING YOUNG STARLETS ...
WAIT, ARE WE TALKING ABOUT YOU OR ME...?
CRINGE

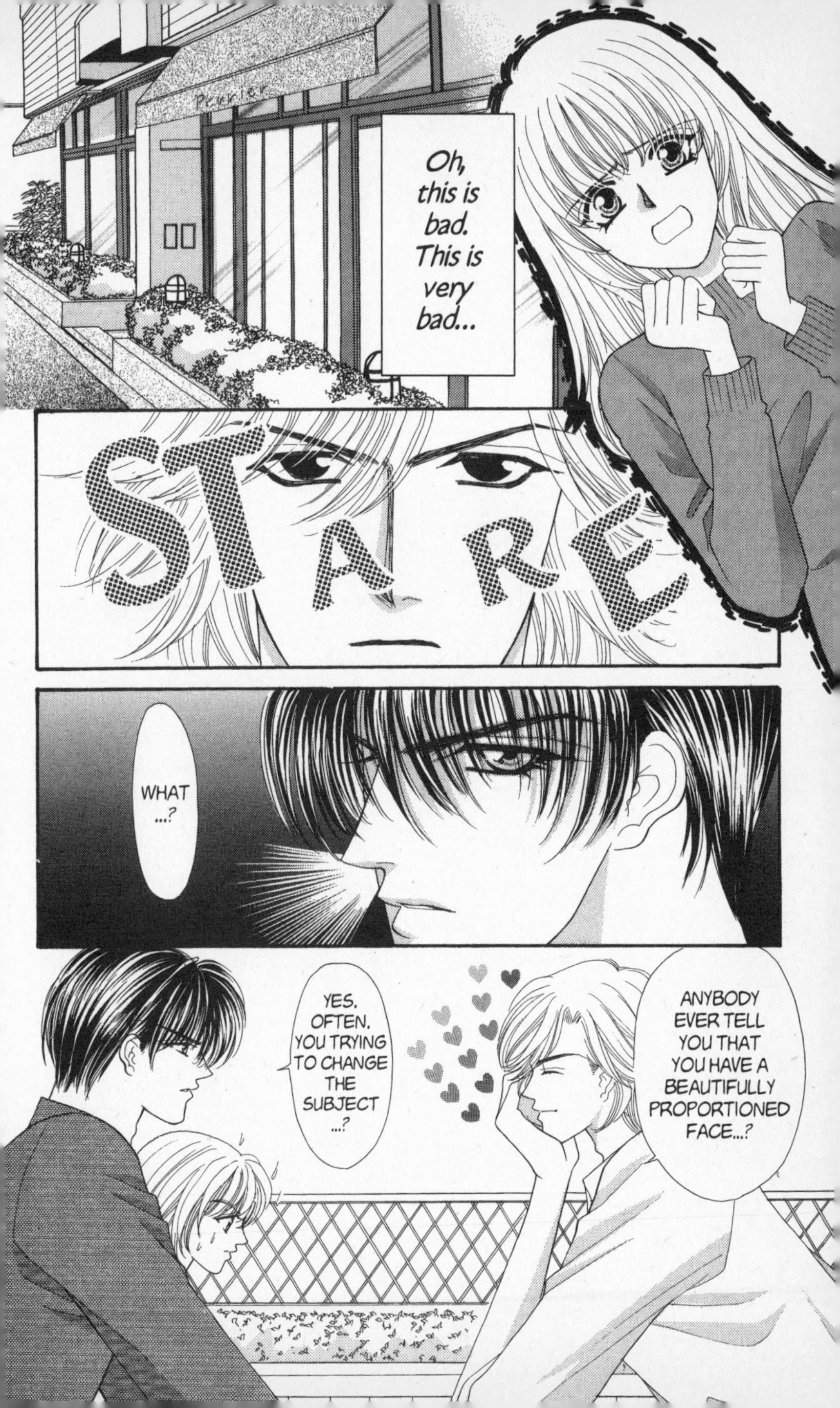
Oh, this is bad. This is very bad...
STARE
WHAT ...?
ANYBODY EVER TELL YOU THAT YOU HAVE A BEAUTIFULLY PROPORTIONED FACE...?
YES. OFTEN. YOU TRYING TO CHANGE THE SUBJECT ...?

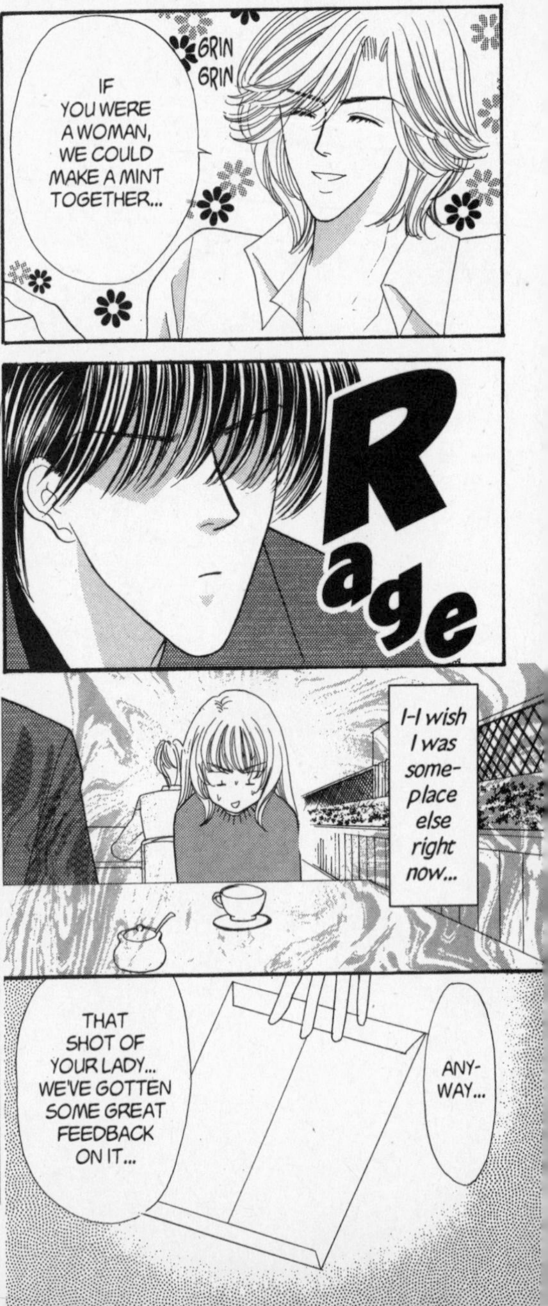
GRIN GRIN
IF YOU WERE A WOMAN, WE COULD MAKE A MINT TOGETHER...
Rage
I-I wish I was some-place else right now...
ANY-WAY...
THAT SHOT OF YOUR LADY... WE'VE GOTTEN SOME GREAT FEEDBACK ON IT...

Hello! Mayu Shinjo, here.

By the time you hold this volume in your hands, the anime should be on the air. Unbelievable, isn't it? I'm so excited. I sat in on a casting session for some of the voiceover actors the other day – there were some amazingly talented people there. I'm sure glad I wasn't the one who had to make the final choices!

(Oh, you'll get a kick out of this: the day of that casting session, I was already running about 15 minutes late because of traffic, when, to make matters worse, I got lost and I ended up driving through some teeny tiny alley, scratching my car—three times! When I finally arrived I was an hour late and my car looked like I'd driven through a mine field!)

Anyway, the actors have all been cast and while there are still a few decisions left to be made, by the time you're reading this everything should be finalized. (Duh, right? I mean, if it's on the air already...!)

(Oh, hey: I saw Glay at the dome. They change their set list all the time, so it seems like no matter how often I see them, there's always something new. I think 'Burst' is my favorite to see them do live and they haven't been performing it lately. They brought it back out for the dome show, thank heaven. How were the shows you guys went to?)

So anyway, when the anime project was first announced, it seemed like everyone fell into one of two categories: either they were super-psyched about it, or they were convinced it was a horrible idea and it would end up ruining the book. After all, it's impossible to make an anime that's 100% faithful to the manga, you know?

To be continued

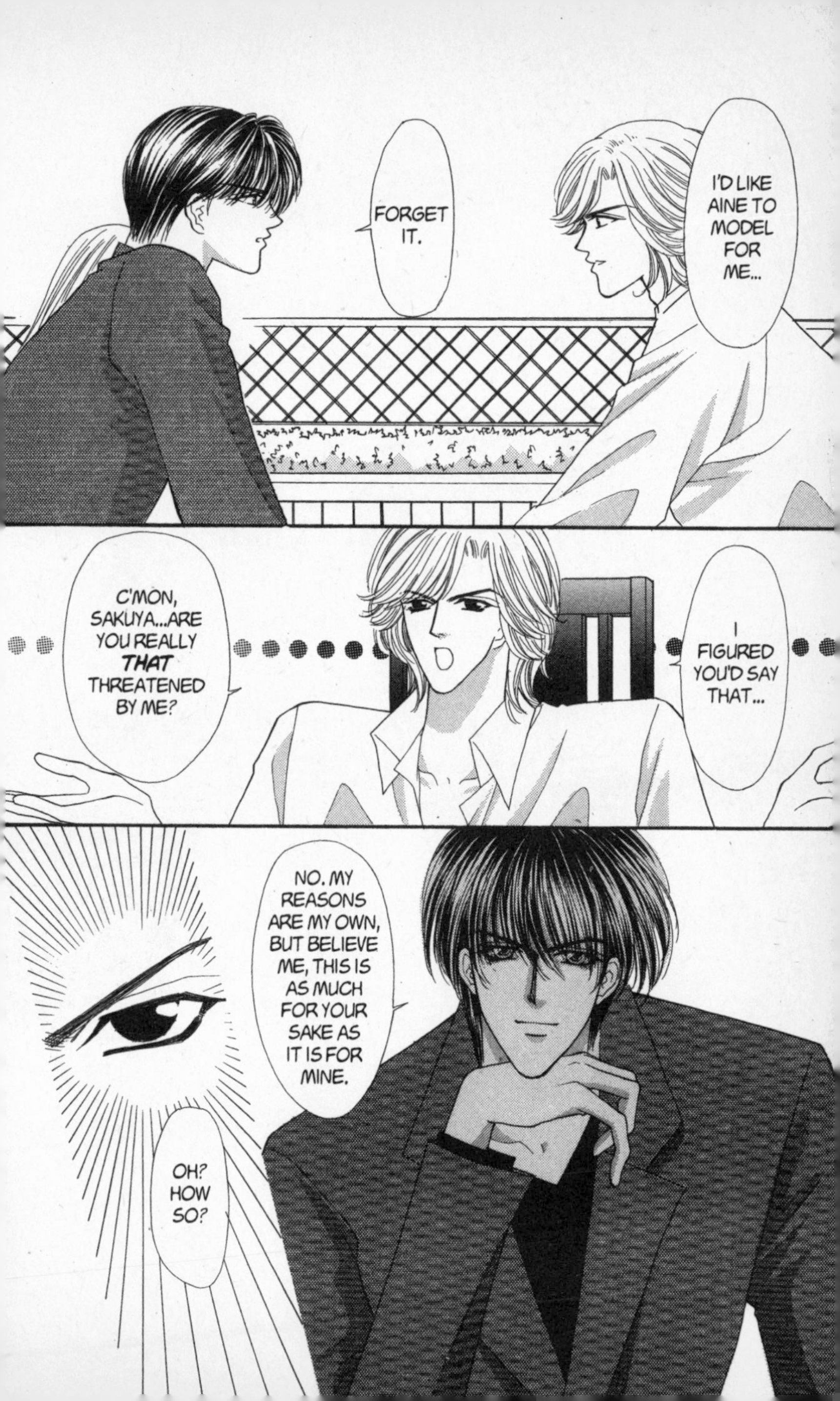
I'D LIKE AINE TO MODEL FOR ME...
FORGET IT.
I FIGURED YOU'D SAY THAT...
C'MON, SAKUYA...ARE YOU REALLY **THAT** THREATENED BY ME?
NO. MY REASONS ARE MY OWN, BUT BELIEVE ME, THIS IS AS MUCH FOR YOUR SAKE AS IT IS FOR MINE.
OH? HOW SO?

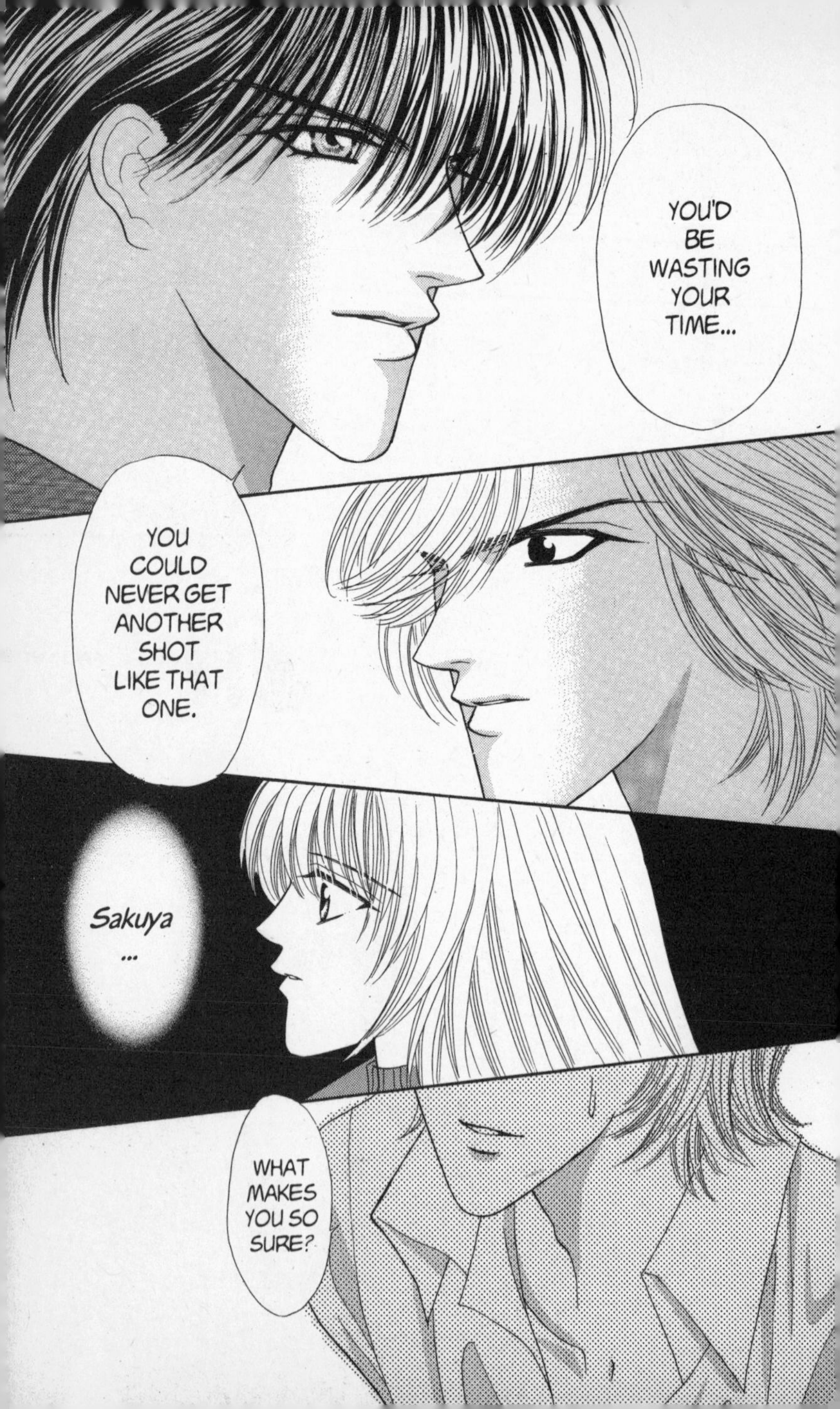
YOU'D BE WASTING YOUR TIME...
YOU COULD NEVER GET ANOTHER SHOT LIKE THAT ONE.
Sakuya ...
WHAT MAKES YOU SO SURE?

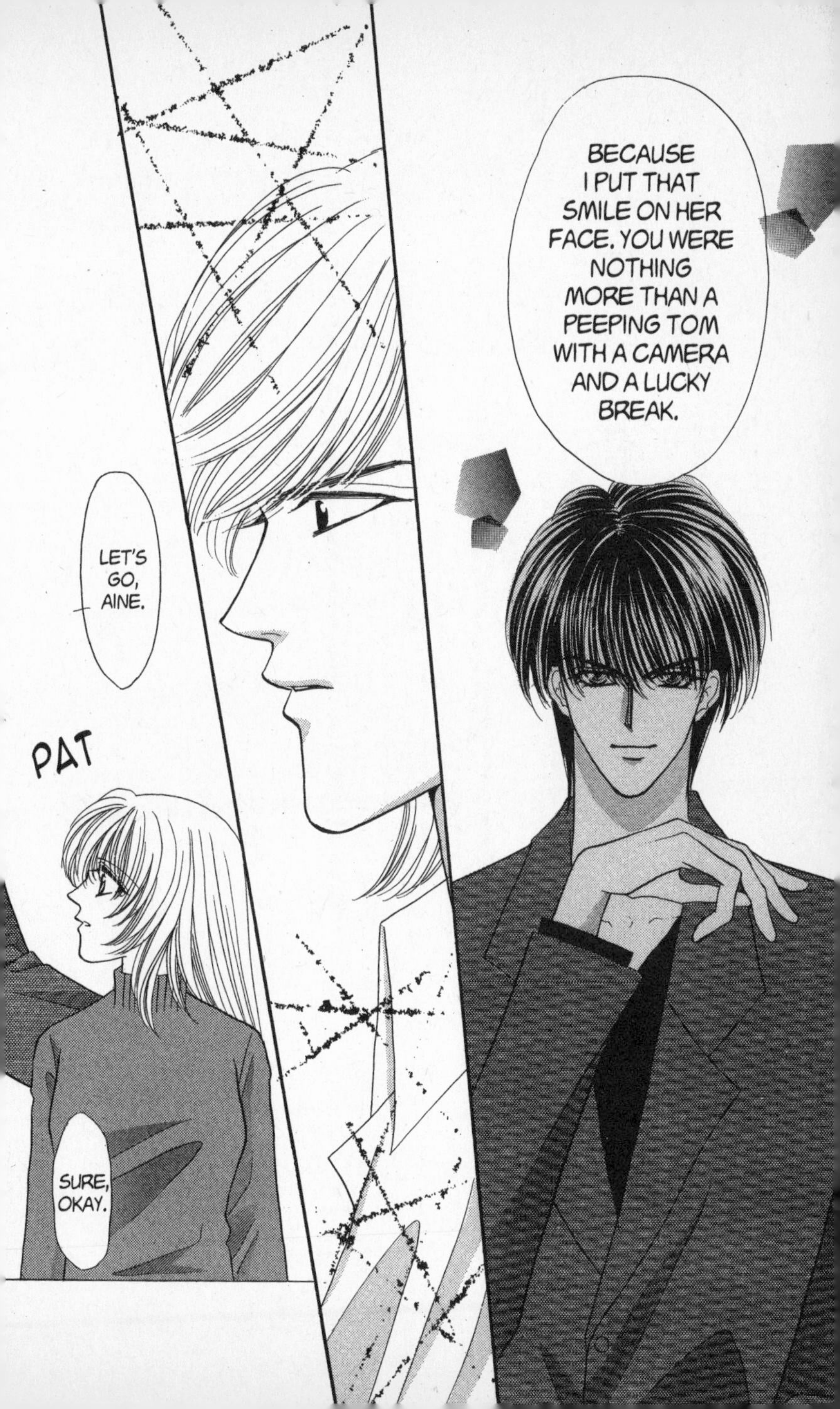
BECAUSE I PUT THAT SMILE ON HER FACE. YOU WERE NOTHING MORE THAN A PEEPING TOM WITH A CAMERA AND A LUCKY BREAK.
LET'S GO, AINE.
PAT
SURE, OKAY.

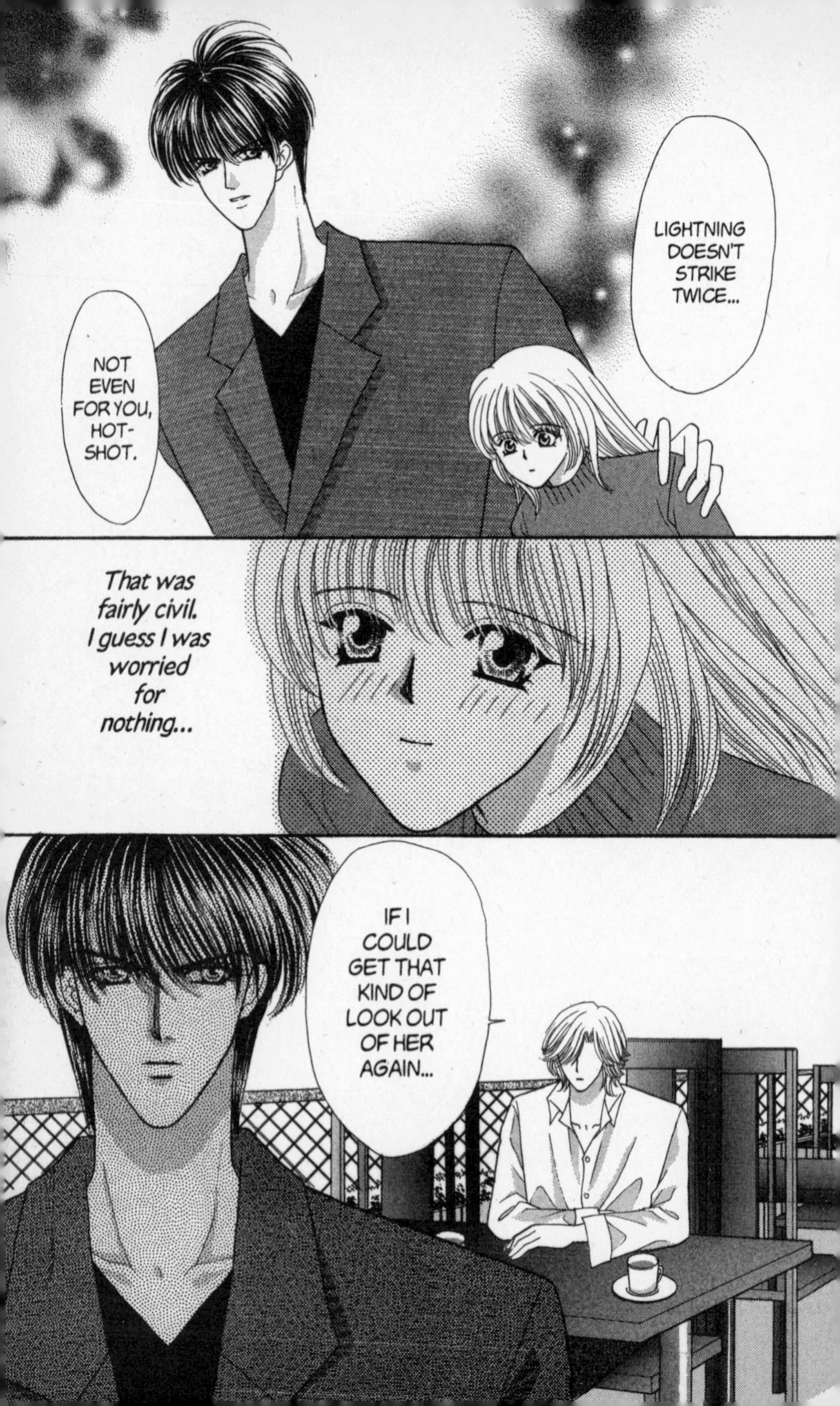
LIGHTNING DOESN'T STRIKE TWICE...
NOT EVEN FOR YOU, HOT-SHOT.
That was fairly civil. I guess I was worried for nothing...
IF I COULD GET THAT KIND OF LOOK OUT OF HER AGAIN...

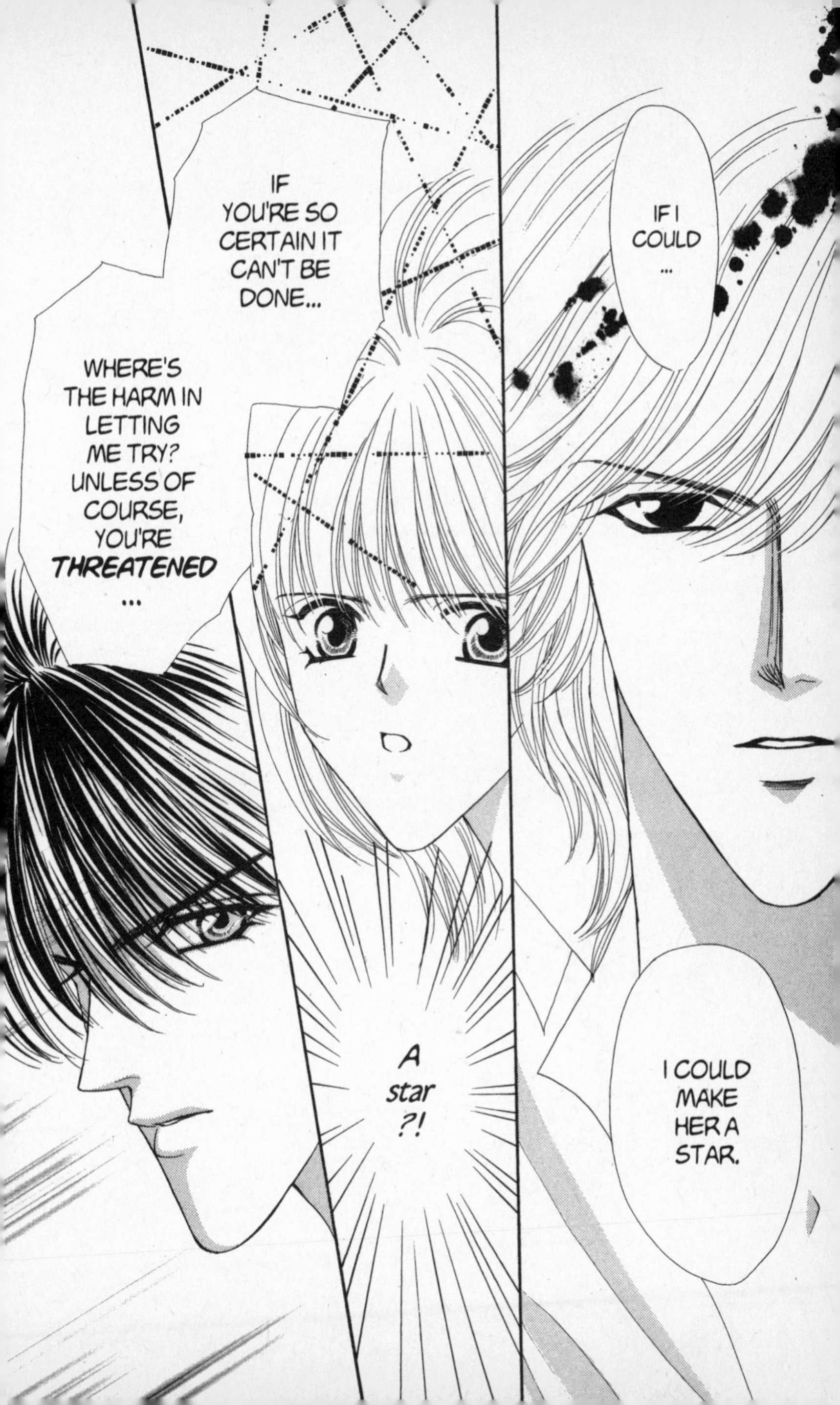
IF I COULD ...
I COULD MAKE HER A STAR.
A star ?!
IF YOU'RE SO CERTAIN IT CAN'T BE DONE...
WHERE'S THE HARM IN LETTING ME TRY? UNLESS OF COURSE, YOU'RE *THREATENED* ...

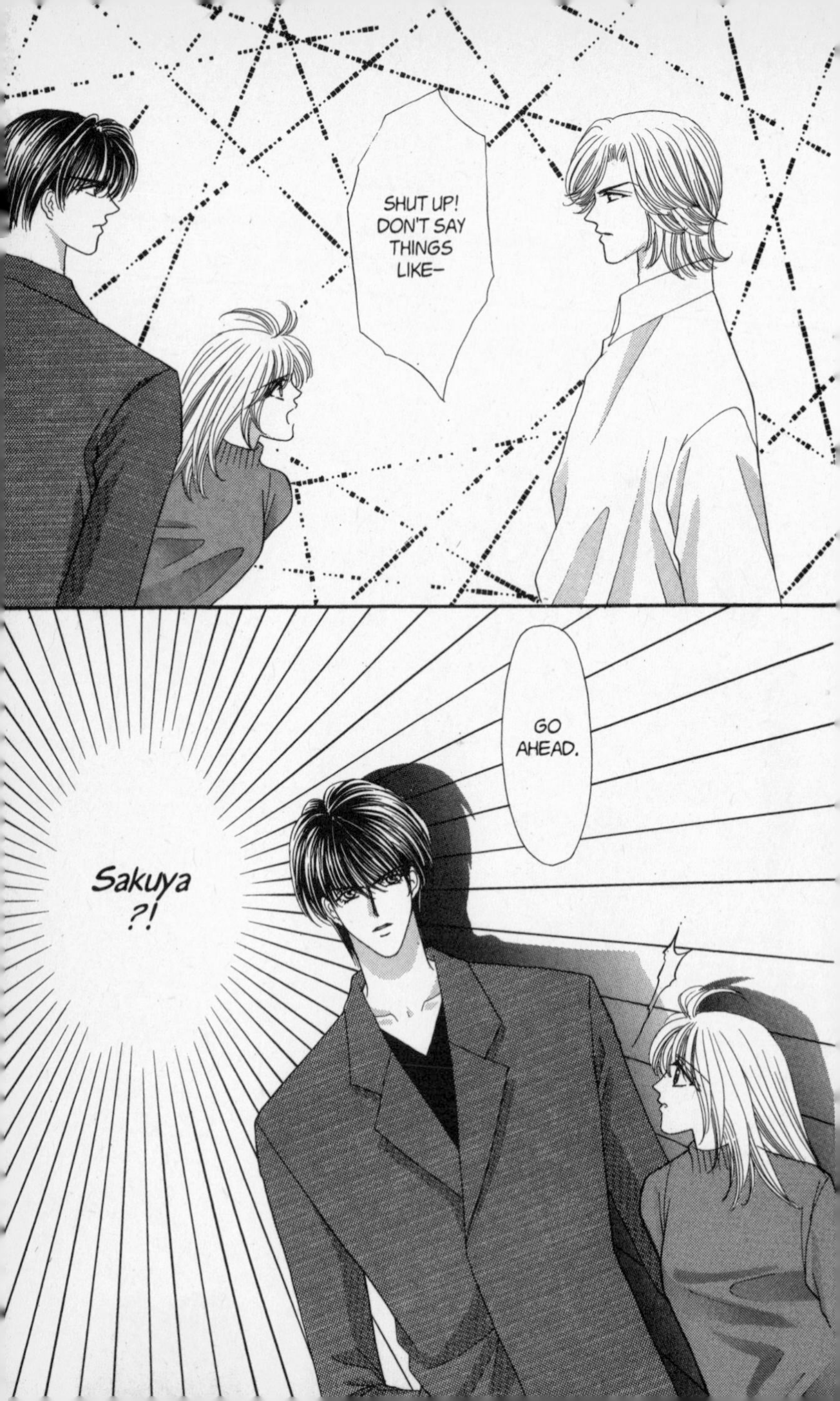
SHUT UP! DON'T SAY THINGS LIKE–
GO AHEAD.
Sakuya ?!

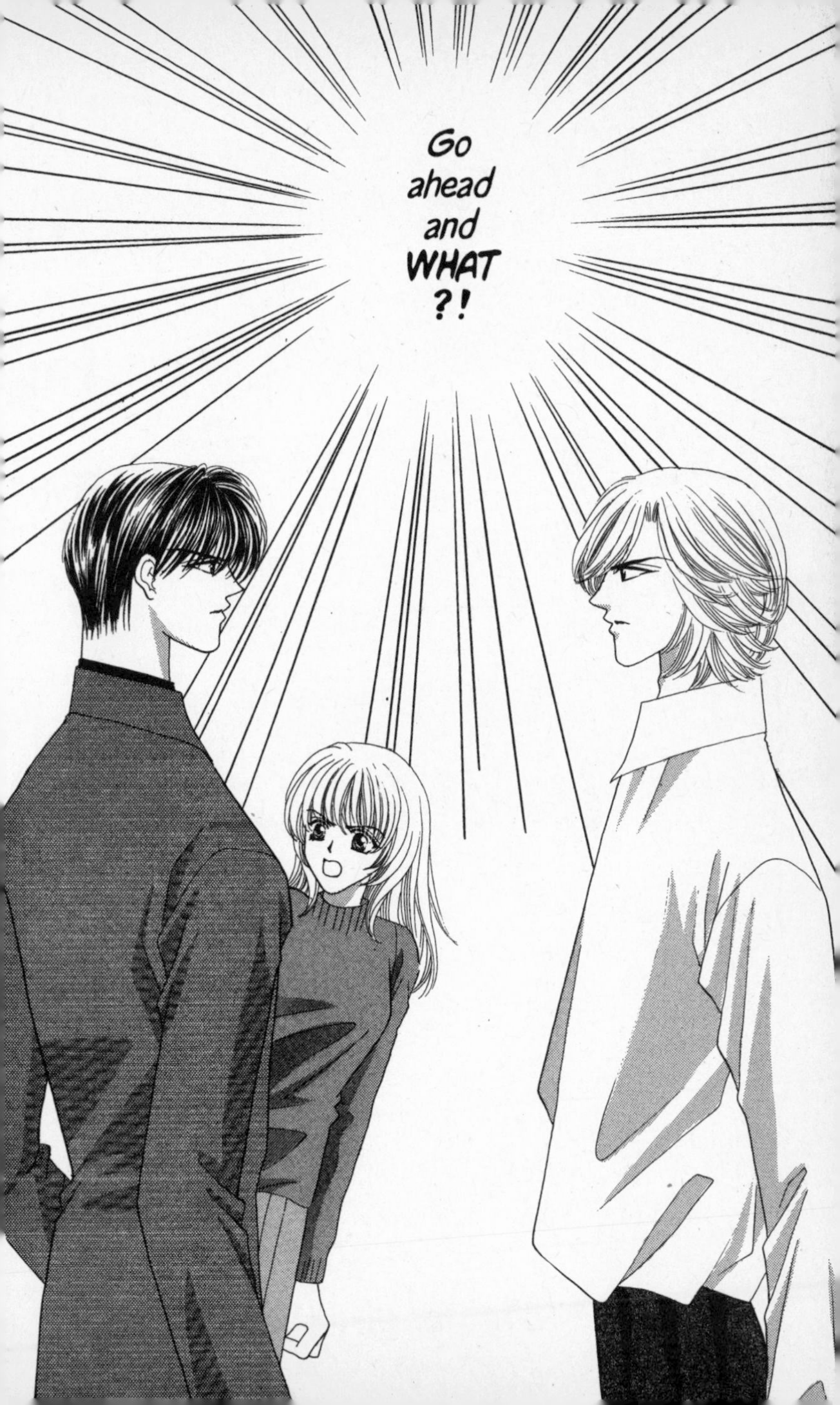
Go ahead and WHAT?!

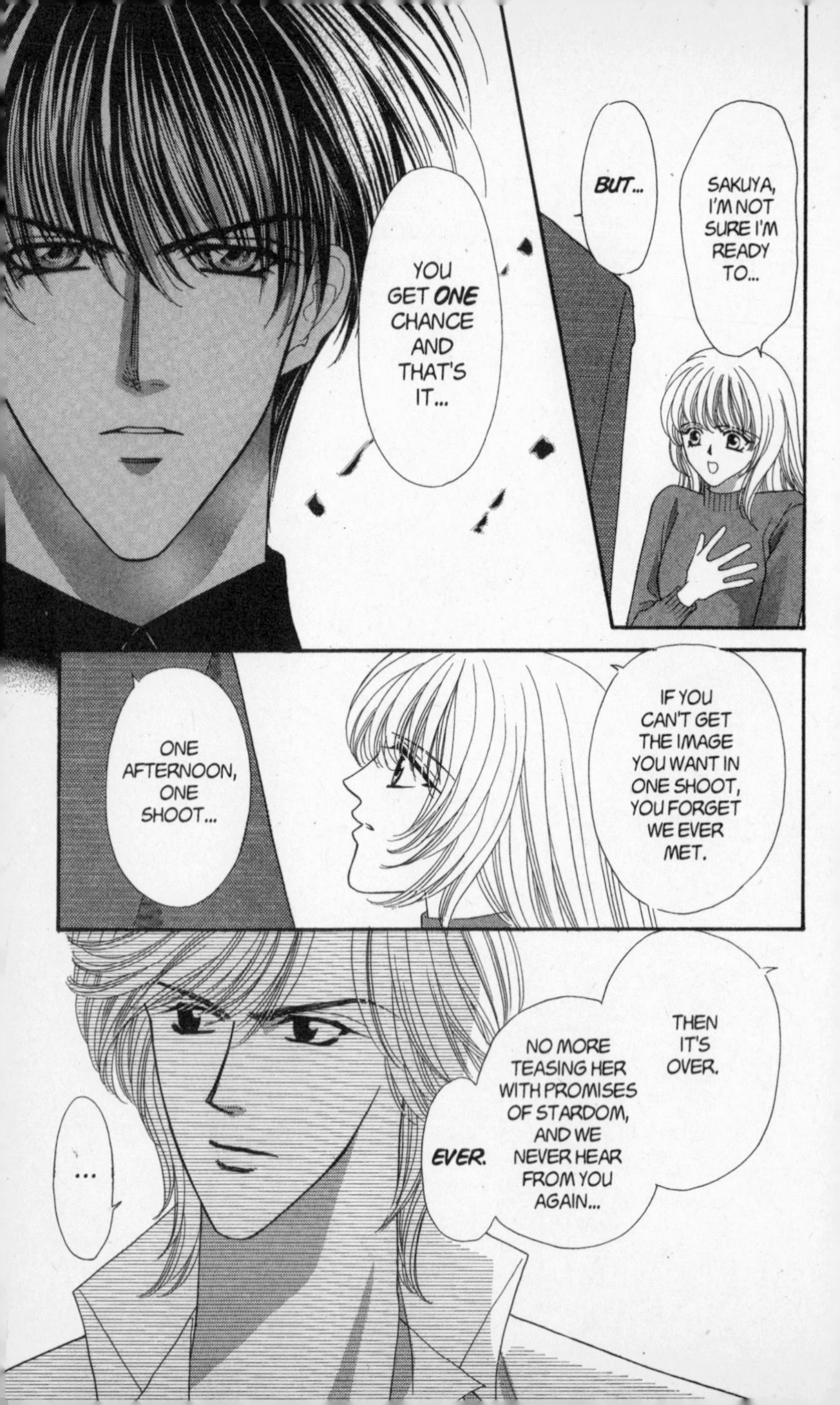
SAKUYA, I'M NOT SURE I'M READY TO...
BUT...
YOU GET ONE CHANCE AND THAT'S IT...
IF YOU CAN'T GET THE IMAGE YOU WANT IN ONE SHOOT, YOU FORGET WE EVER MET.
ONE AFTERNOON, ONE SHOOT...
THEN IT'S OVER.
NO MORE TEASING HER WITH PROMISES OF STARDOM, AND WE NEVER HEAR FROM YOU AGAIN...
EVER.
...

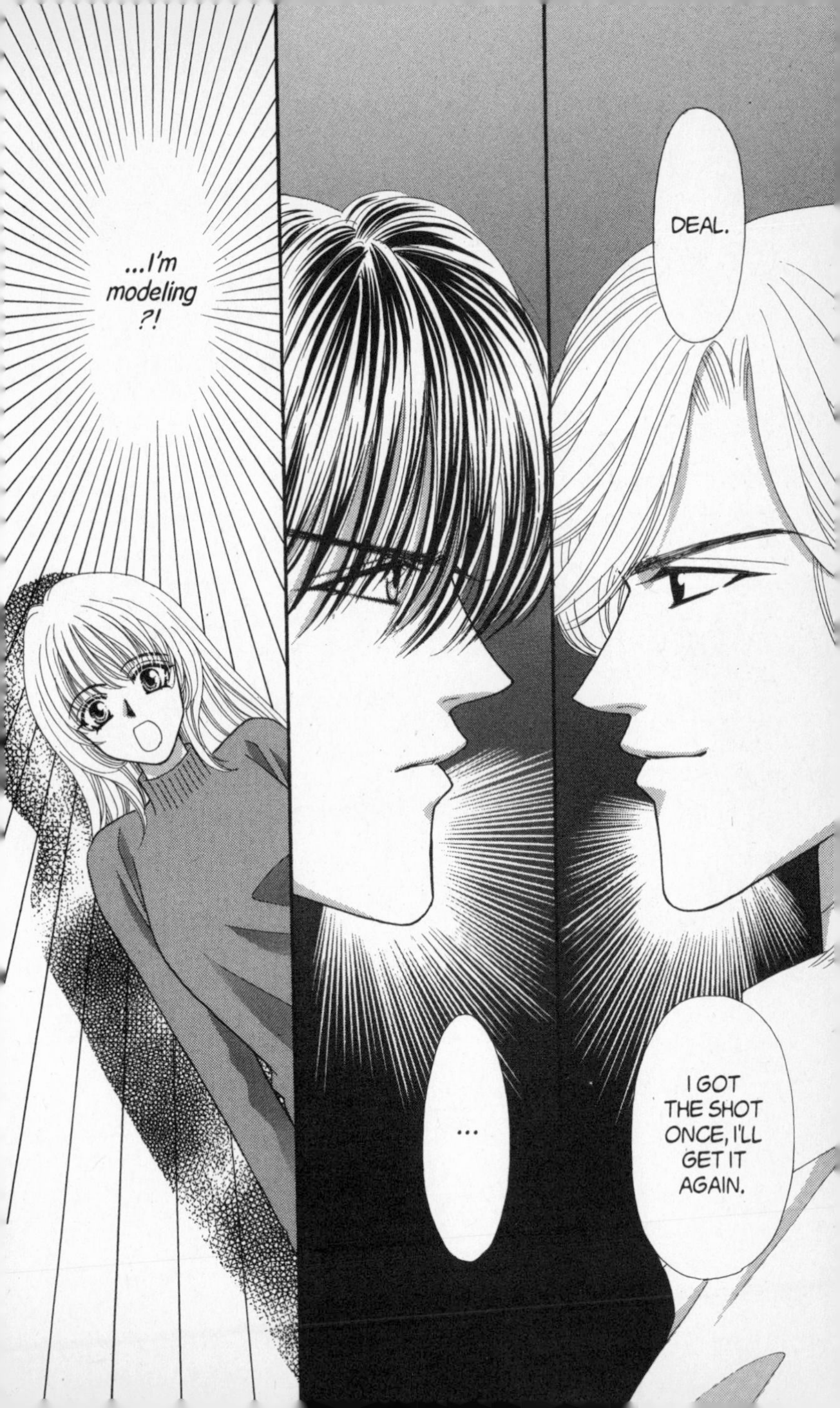
DEAL.
I GOT THE SHOT ONCE, I'LL GET IT AGAIN.
...
...I'm modeling ?!

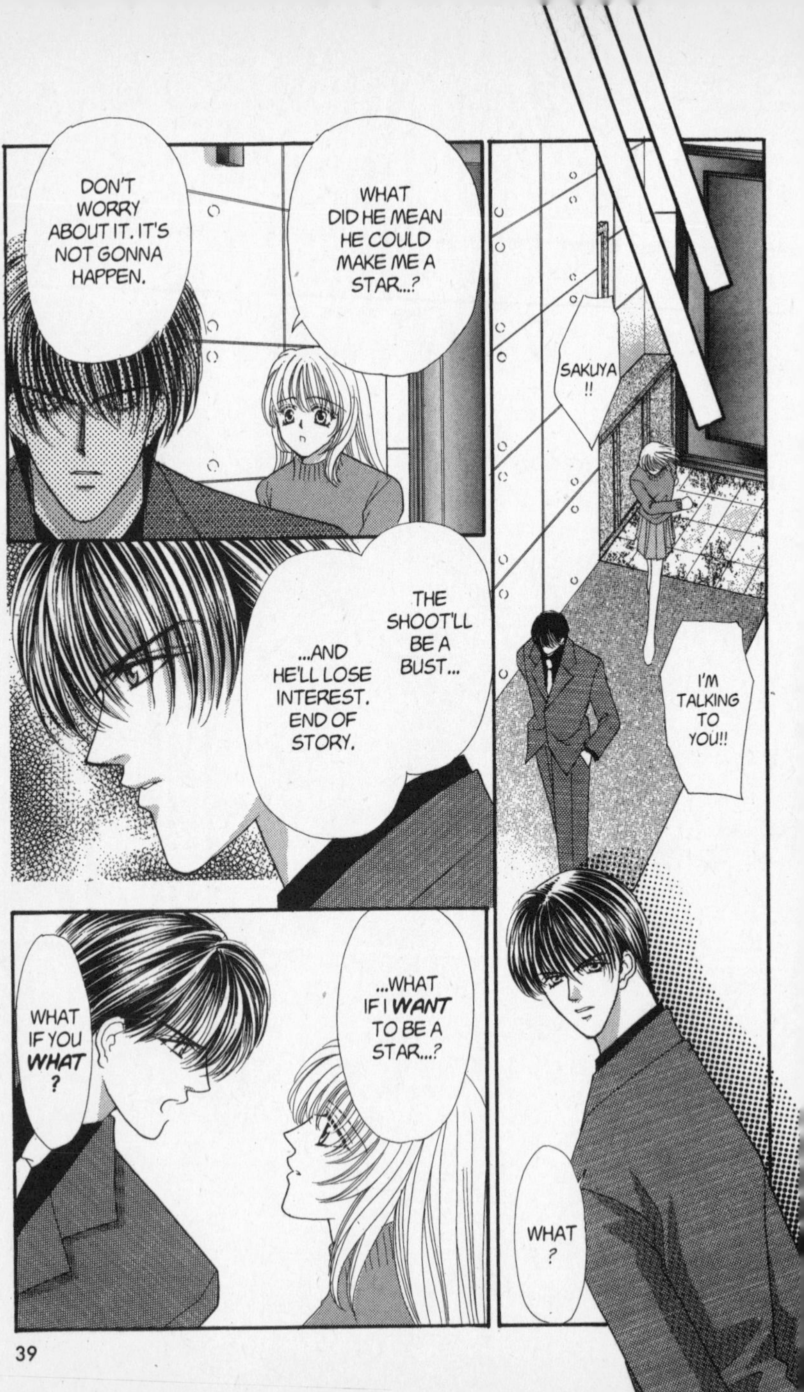
SAKUYA !!
I'M TALKING TO YOU!!
WHAT ?
WHAT DID HE MEAN HE COULD MAKE ME A STAR...?
DON'T WORRY ABOUT IT. IT'S NOT GONNA HAPPEN.
THE SHOOT'LL BE A BUST...
...AND HE'LL LOSE INTEREST. END OF STORY.
...WHAT IF I ***WANT*** TO BE A STAR...?
WHAT IF YOU ***WHAT*** ?

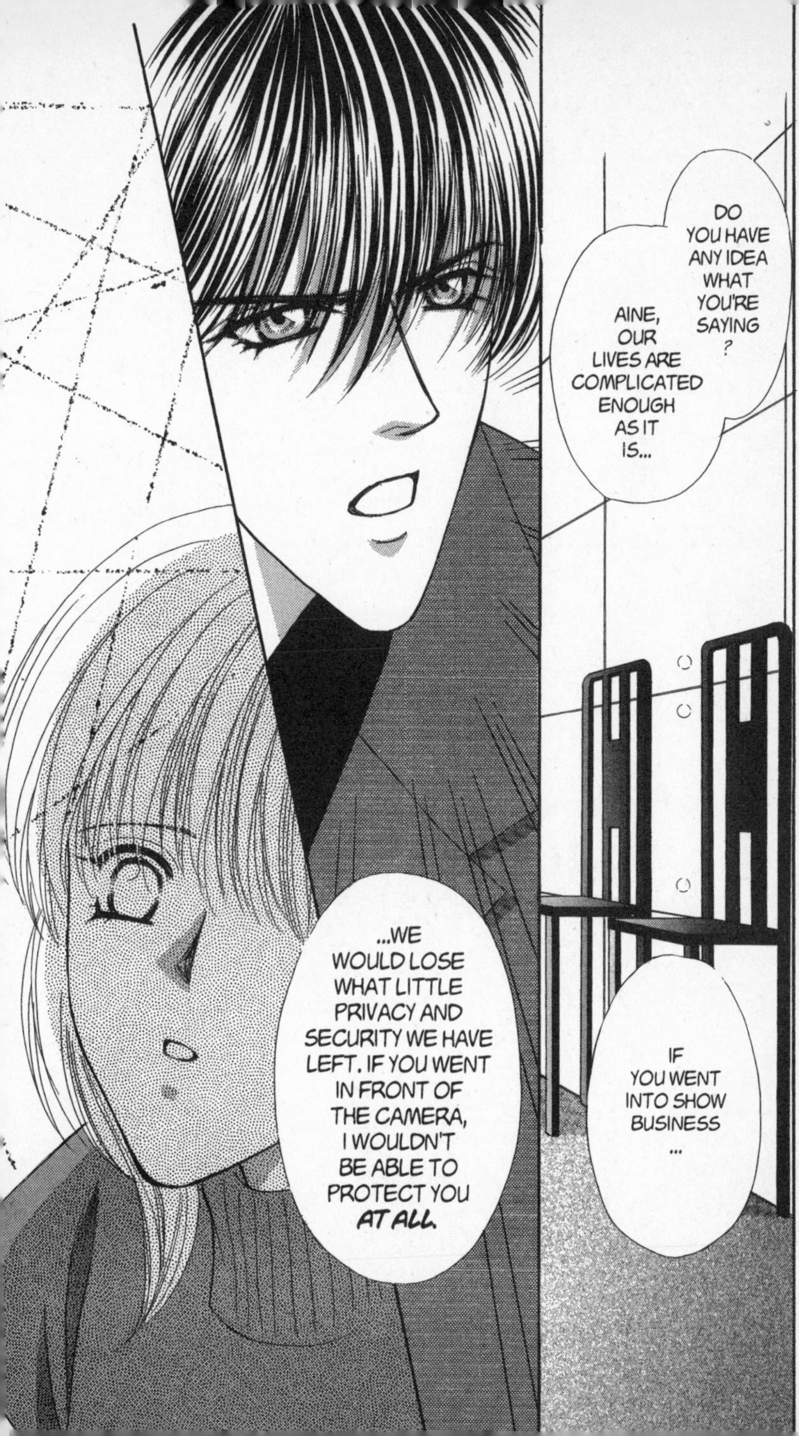
DO YOU HAVE ANY IDEA WHAT YOU'RE SAYING?
AINE, OUR LIVES ARE COMPLICATED ENOUGH AS IT IS...
IF YOU WENT INTO SHOW BUSINESS...
...WE WOULD LOSE WHAT LITTLE PRIVACY AND SECURITY WE HAVE LEFT. IF YOU WENT IN FRONT OF THE CAMERA, I WOULDN'T BE ABLE TO PROTECT YOU AT ALL.

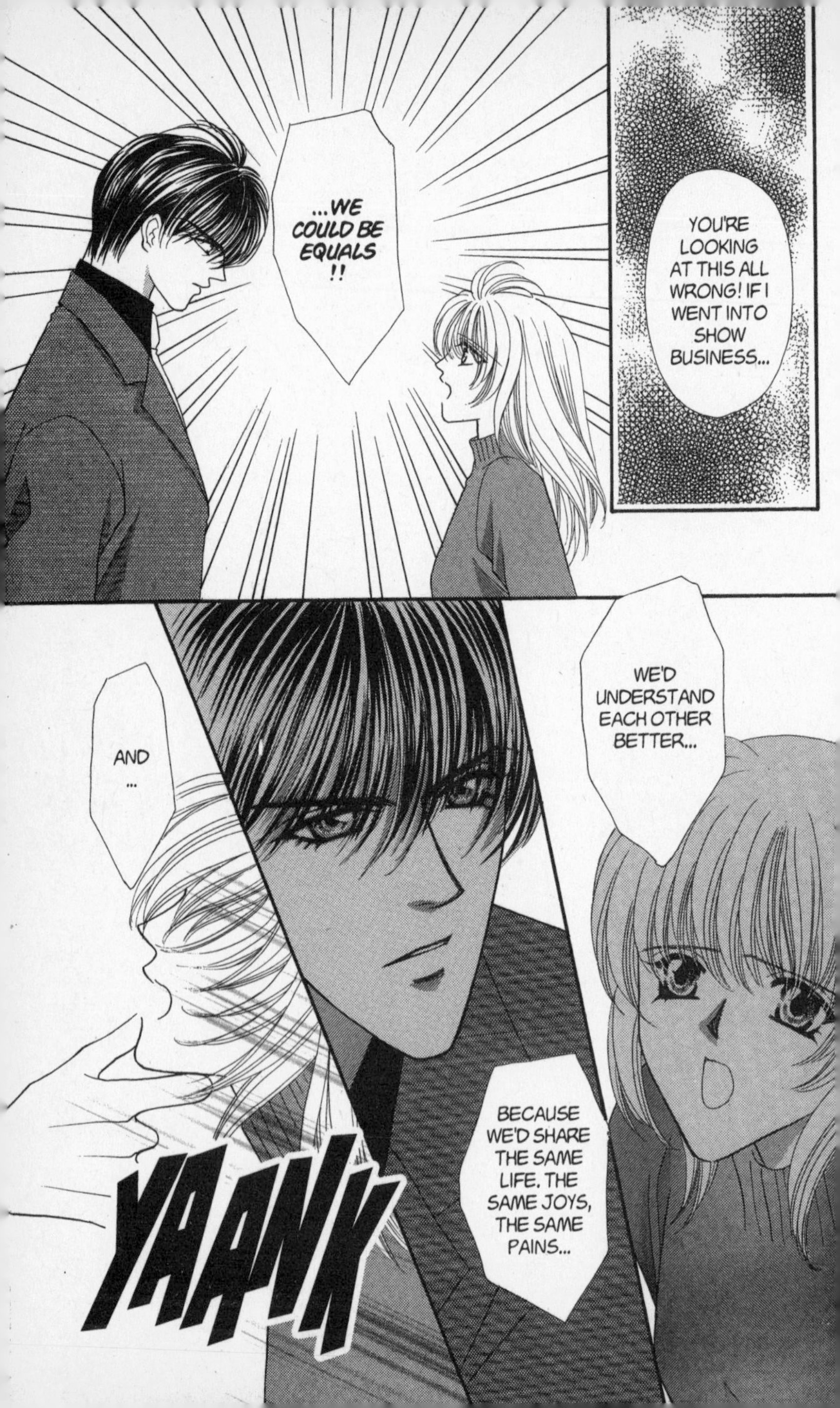
YOU'RE LOOKING AT THIS ALL WRONG! IF I WENT INTO SHOW BUSINESS...
...WE COULD BE EQUALS !!
WE'D UNDERSTAND EACH OTHER BETTER...
BECAUSE WE'D SHARE THE SAME LIFE. THE SAME JOYS, THE SAME PAINS...
AND ...
YAANK

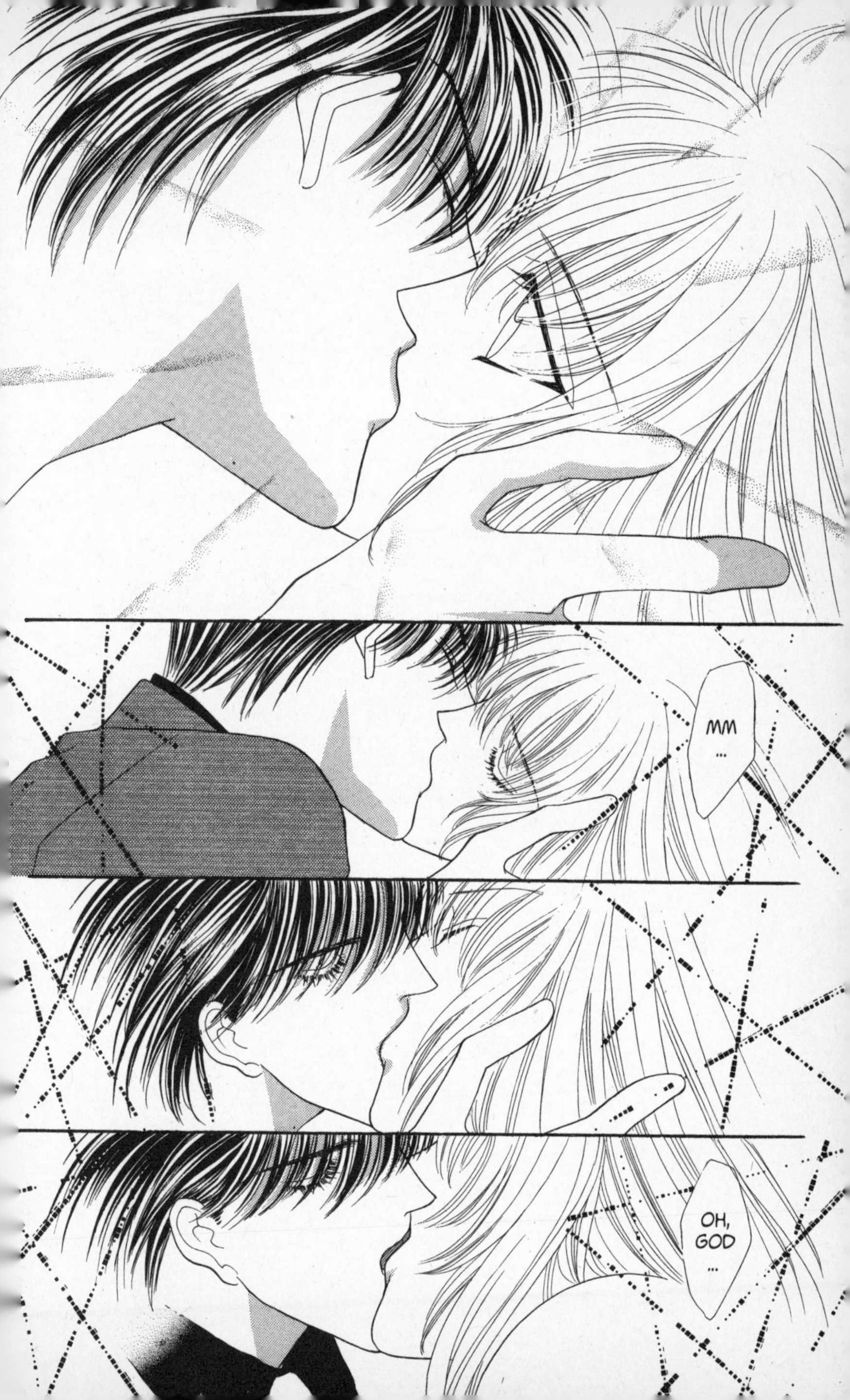
MM ...
OH, GOD ...

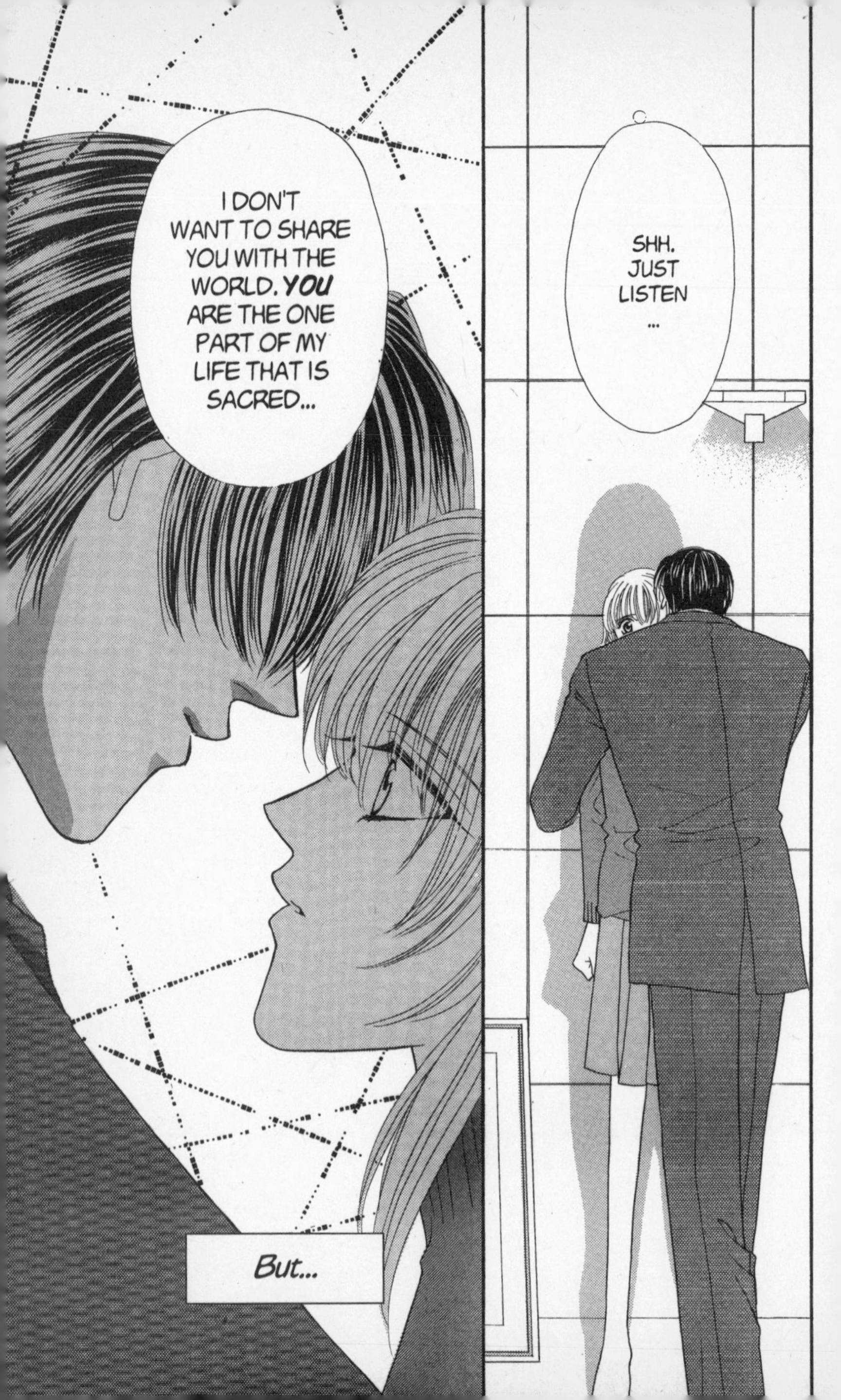
SHH. JUST LISTEN ...
I DON'T WANT TO SHARE YOU WITH THE WORLD. ***YOU*** ARE THE ONE PART OF MY LIFE THAT IS SACRED...
But...

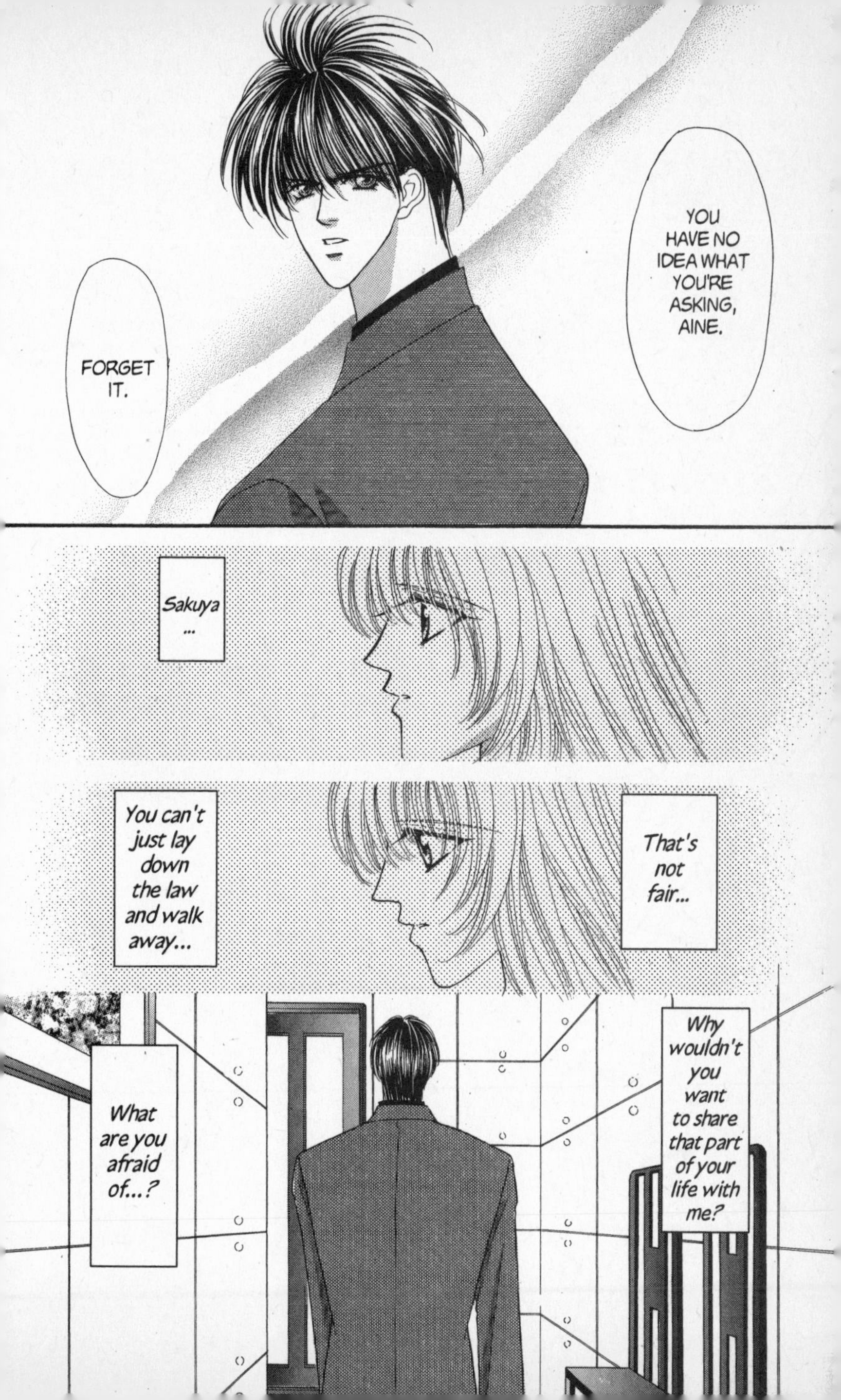
YOU HAVE NO IDEA WHAT YOU'RE ASKING, AINE.
FORGET IT.
Sakuya ...
That's not fair...
You can't just lay down the law and walk away...
Why wouldn't you want to share that part of your life with me?
What are you afraid of...?

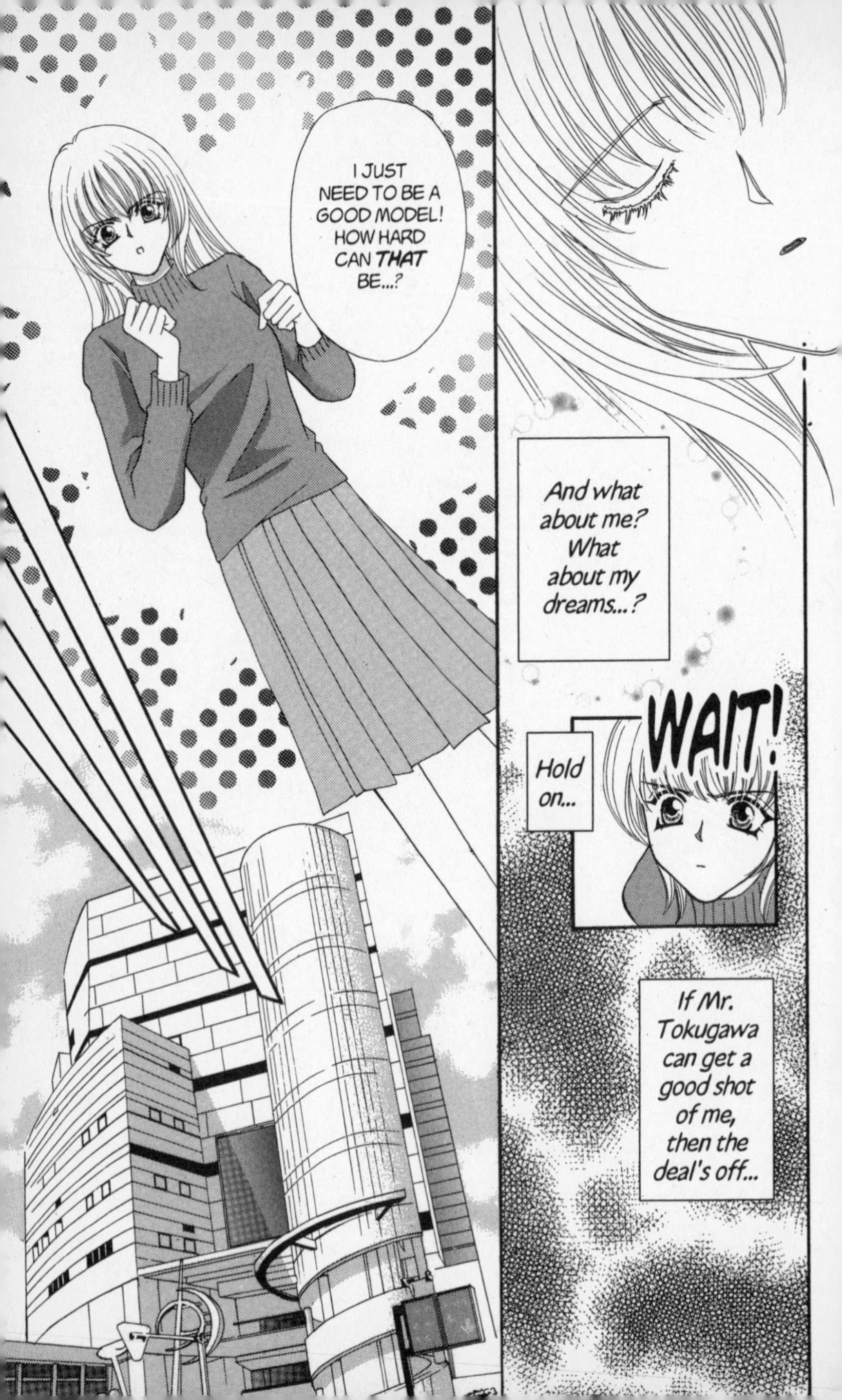
And what about me? What about my dreams...?
Hold on...
WAIT!
If Mr. Tokugawa can get a good shot of me, then the deal's off...
I JUST NEED TO BE A GOOD MODEL! HOW HARD CAN *THAT* BE...?

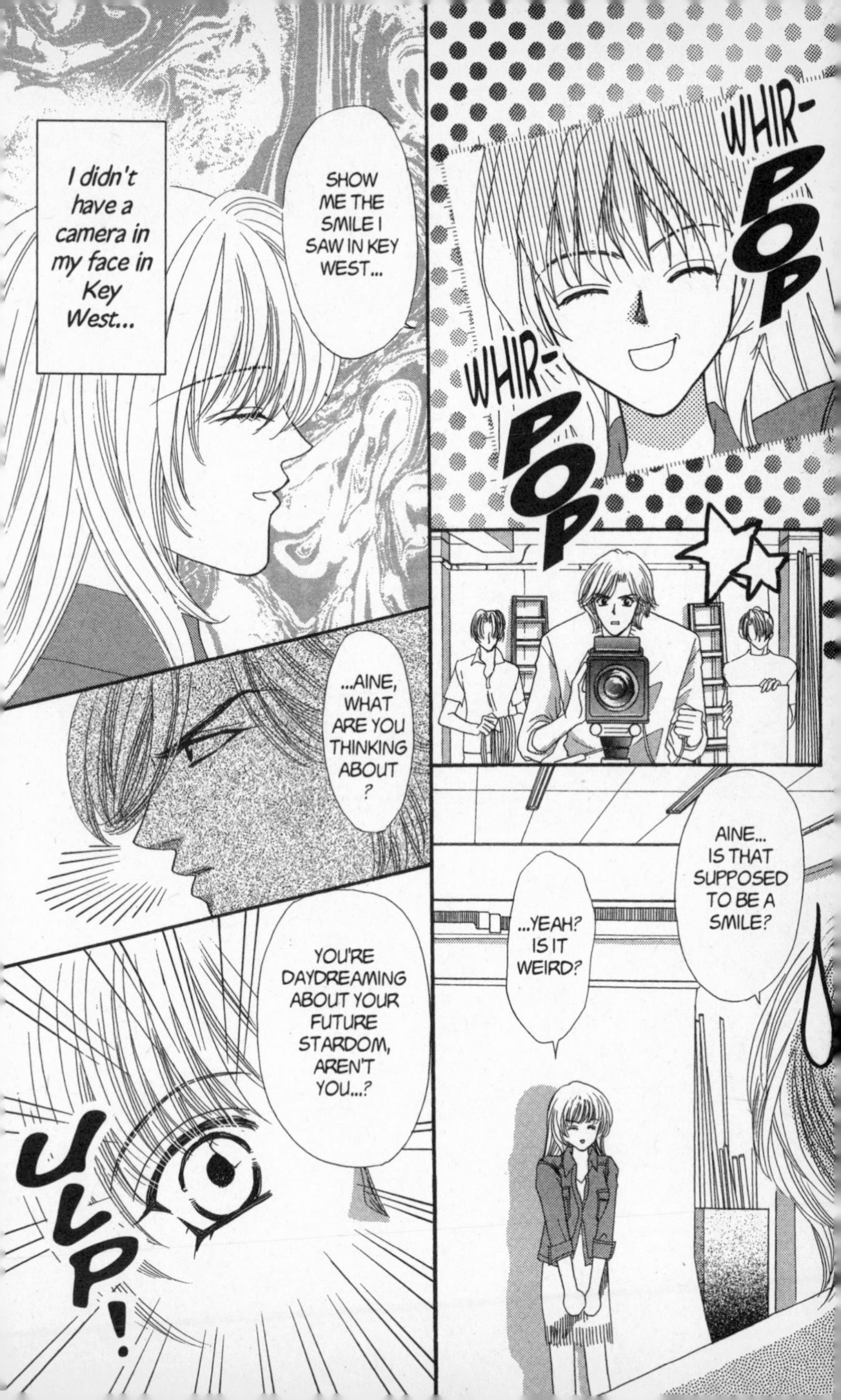

WHIR-POP
WHIR-POP
AINE... IS THAT SUPPOSED TO BE A SMILE?
...YEAH? IS IT WEIRD?
SHOW ME THE SMILE I SAW IN KEY WEST...
I didn't have a camera in my face in Key West...
...AINE, WHAT ARE YOU THINKING ABOUT?
YOU'RE DAYDREAMING ABOUT YOUR FUTURE STARDOM, AREN'T YOU...?
ULP!

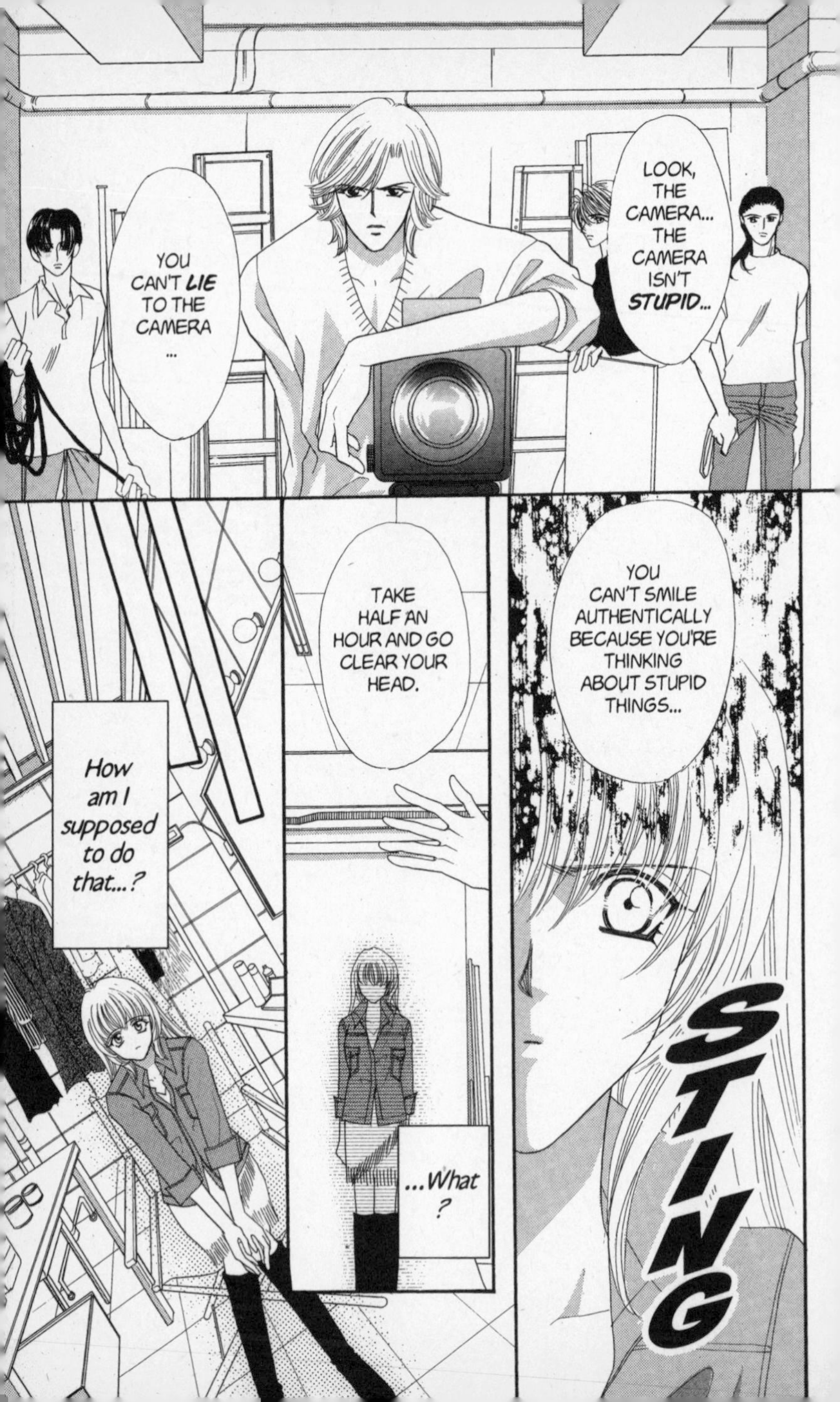
LOOK, THE CAMERA... THE CAMERA ISN'T STUPID...
YOU CAN'T LIE TO THE CAMERA ...
YOU CAN'T SMILE AUTHENTICALLY BECAUSE YOU'RE THINKING ABOUT STUPID THINGS...
STING
TAKE HALF AN HOUR AND GO CLEAR YOUR HEAD.
...What?
How am I supposed to do that...?

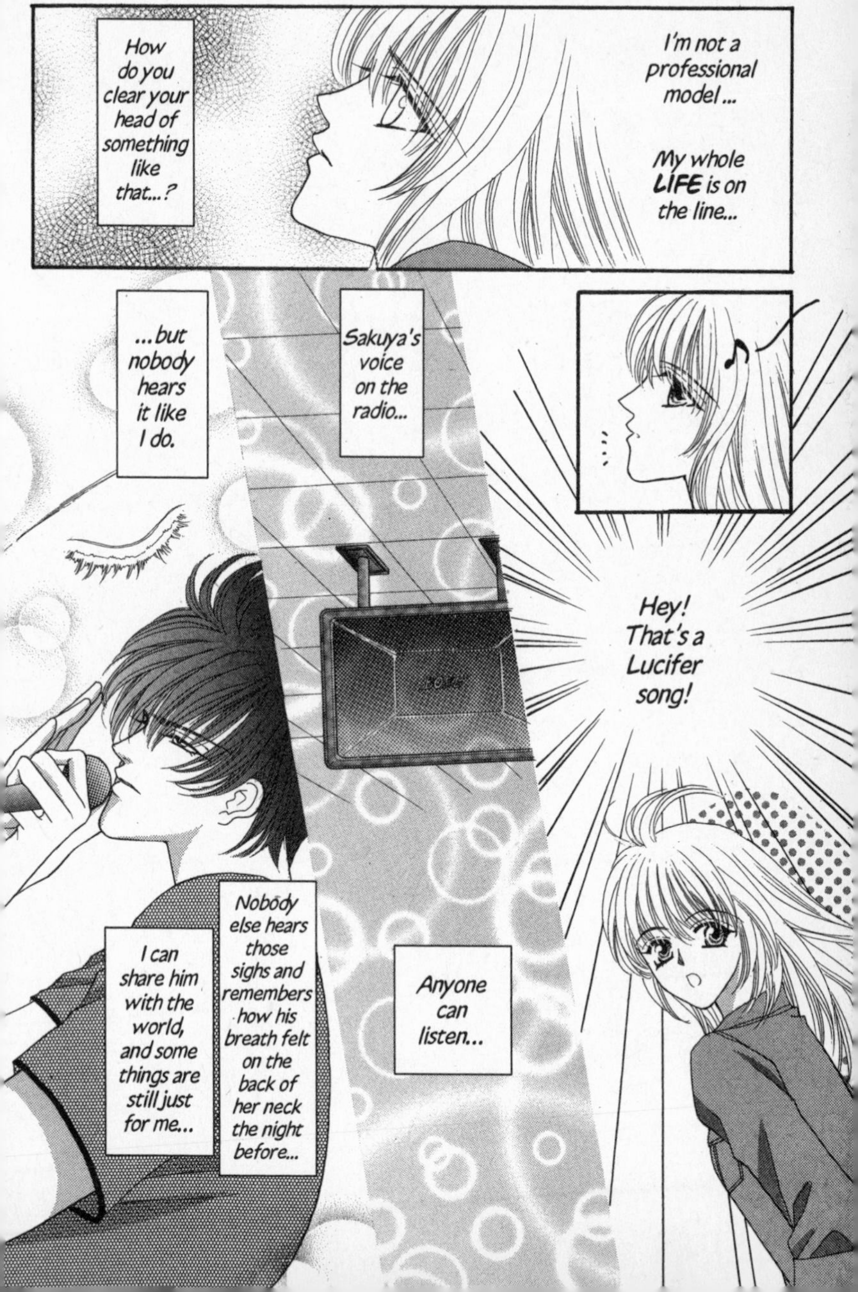
I'm not a professional model...
My whole LIFE is on the line...
How do you clear your head of something like that...?
Hey! That's a Lucifer song!
Sakuya's voice on the radio...
...but nobody hears it like I do.
Anyone can listen...
Nobody else hears those sighs and remembers how his breath felt on the back of her neck the night before...
I can share him with the world, and some things are still just for me...

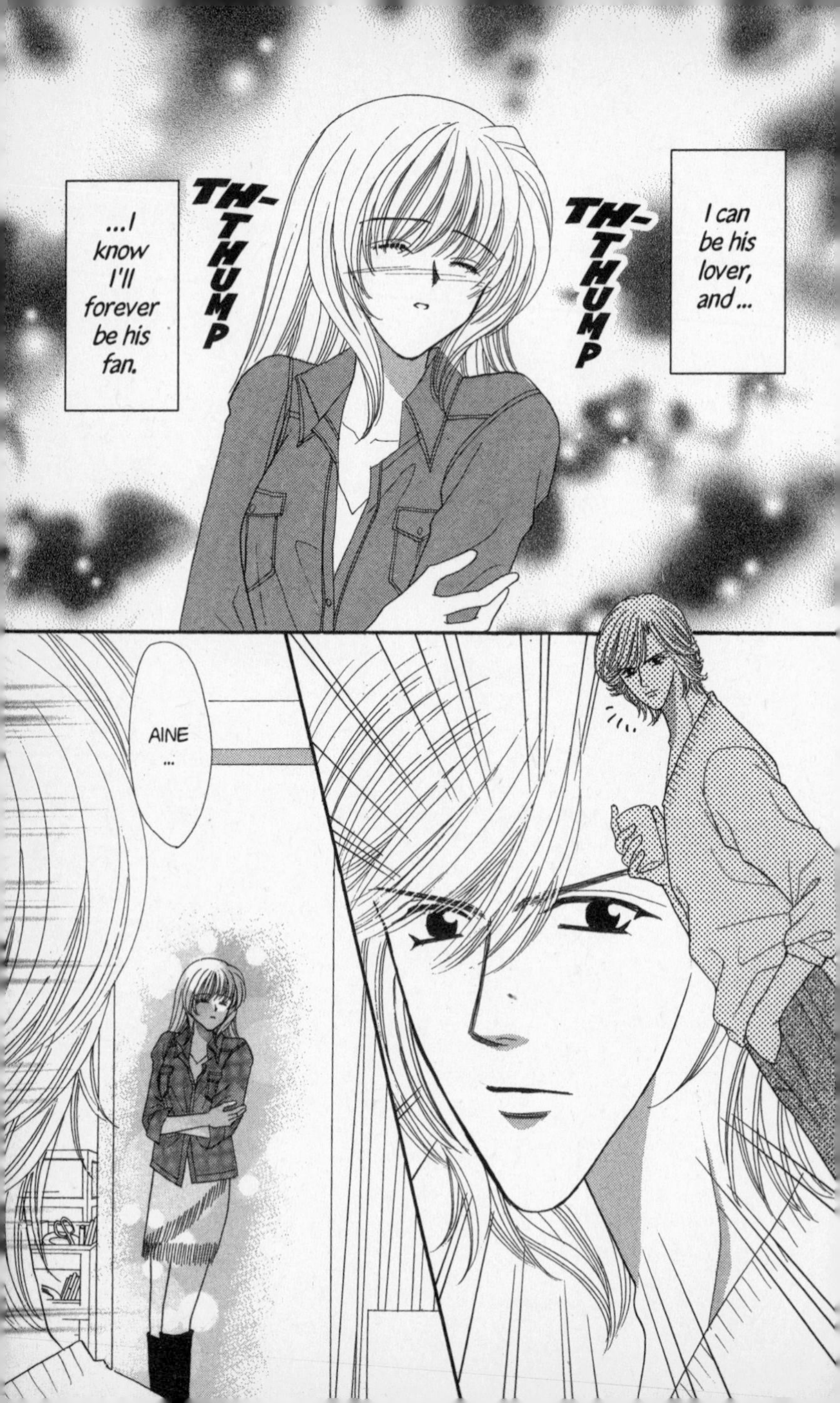

I can be his lover, and...
TH-THUMP
TH-THUMP
...I know I'll forever be his fan.
AINE ...

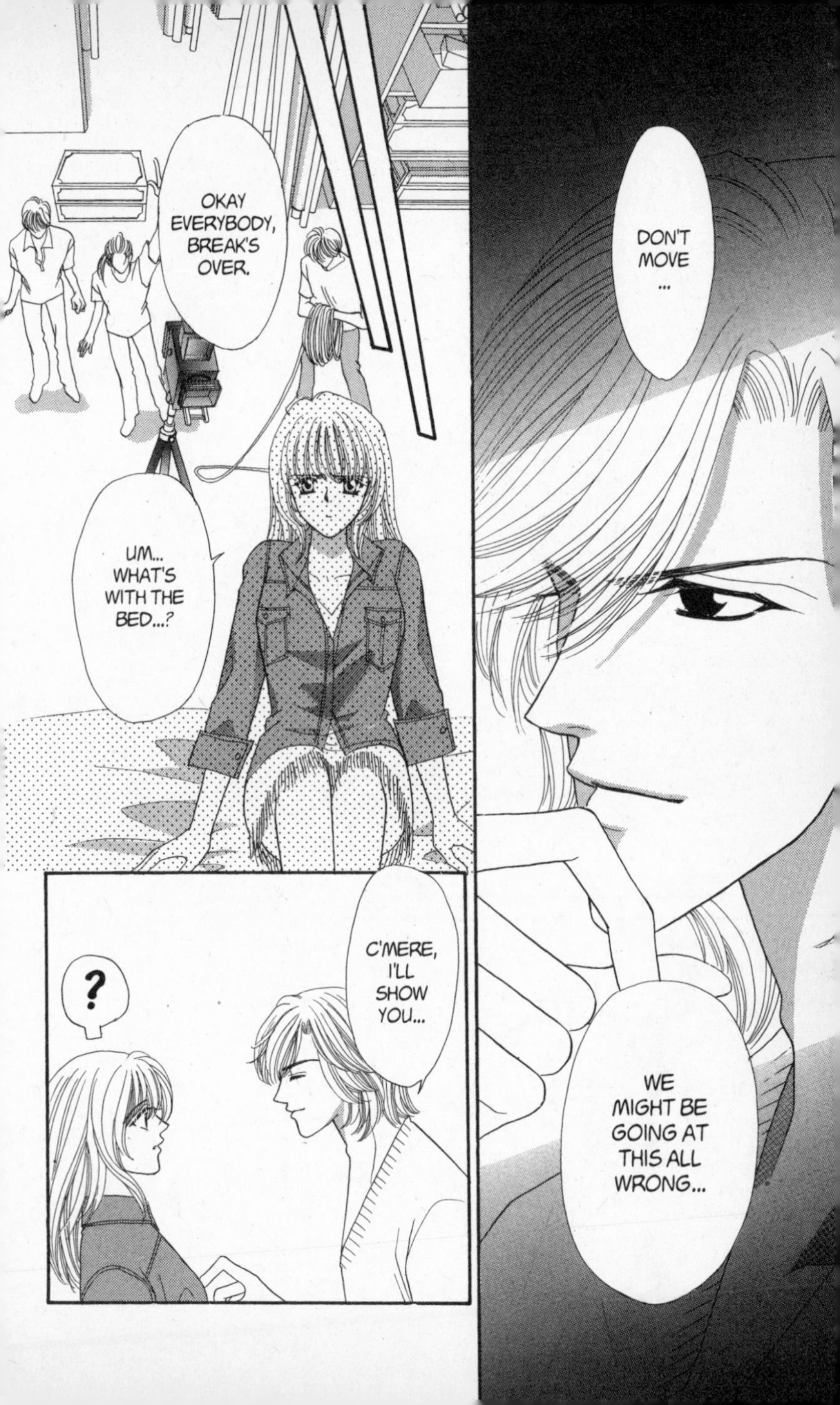
DON'T MOVE ...
WE MIGHT BE GOING AT THIS ALL WRONG...
OKAY EVERYBODY, BREAK'S OVER.
UM... WHAT'S WITH THE BED...?
C'MERE, I'LL SHOW YOU...
?

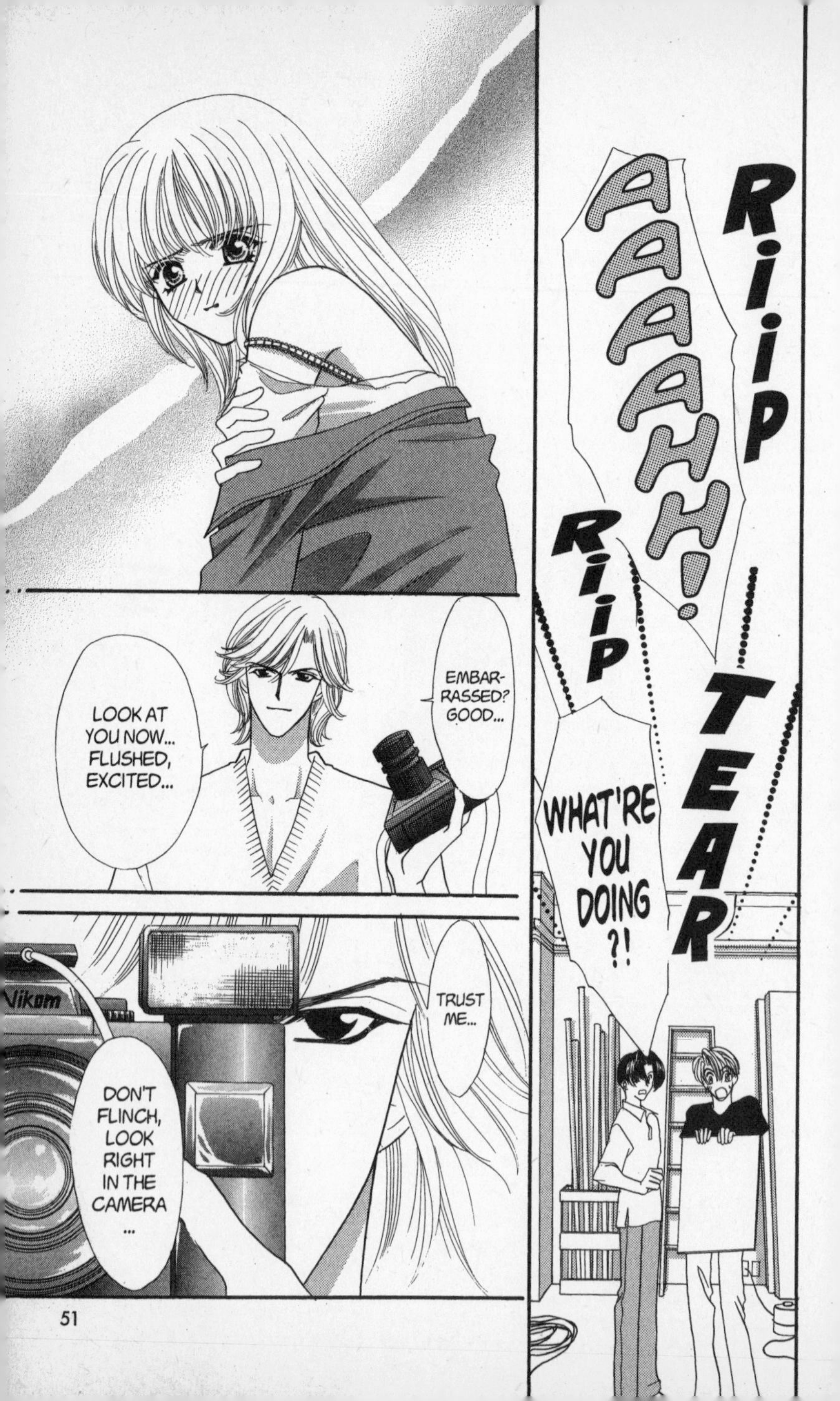
RIIP
AAAAHH!
RIIP
TEAR
WHAT'RE YOU DOING ?!
EMBAR-RASSED? GOOD...
LOOK AT YOU NOW... FLUSHED, EXCITED...
TRUST ME...
DON'T FLINCH, LOOK RIGHT IN THE CAMERA ...

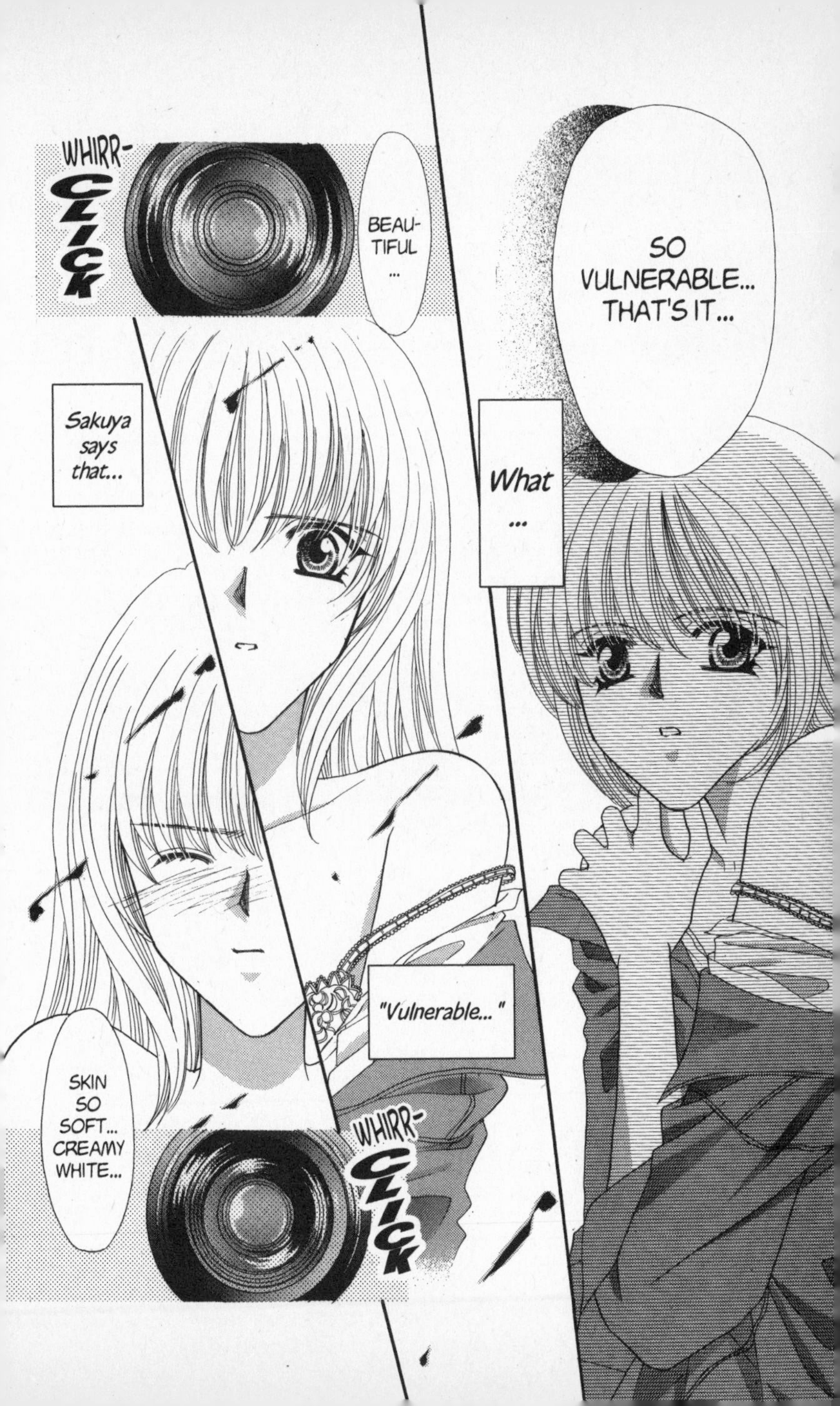
SO VULNERABLE... THAT'S IT...
What ...
BEAU-TIFUL ...
WHIRR-CLICK
Sakuya says that...
"Vulnerable..."
SKIN SO SOFT... CREAMY WHITE...
WHIRR-CLICK

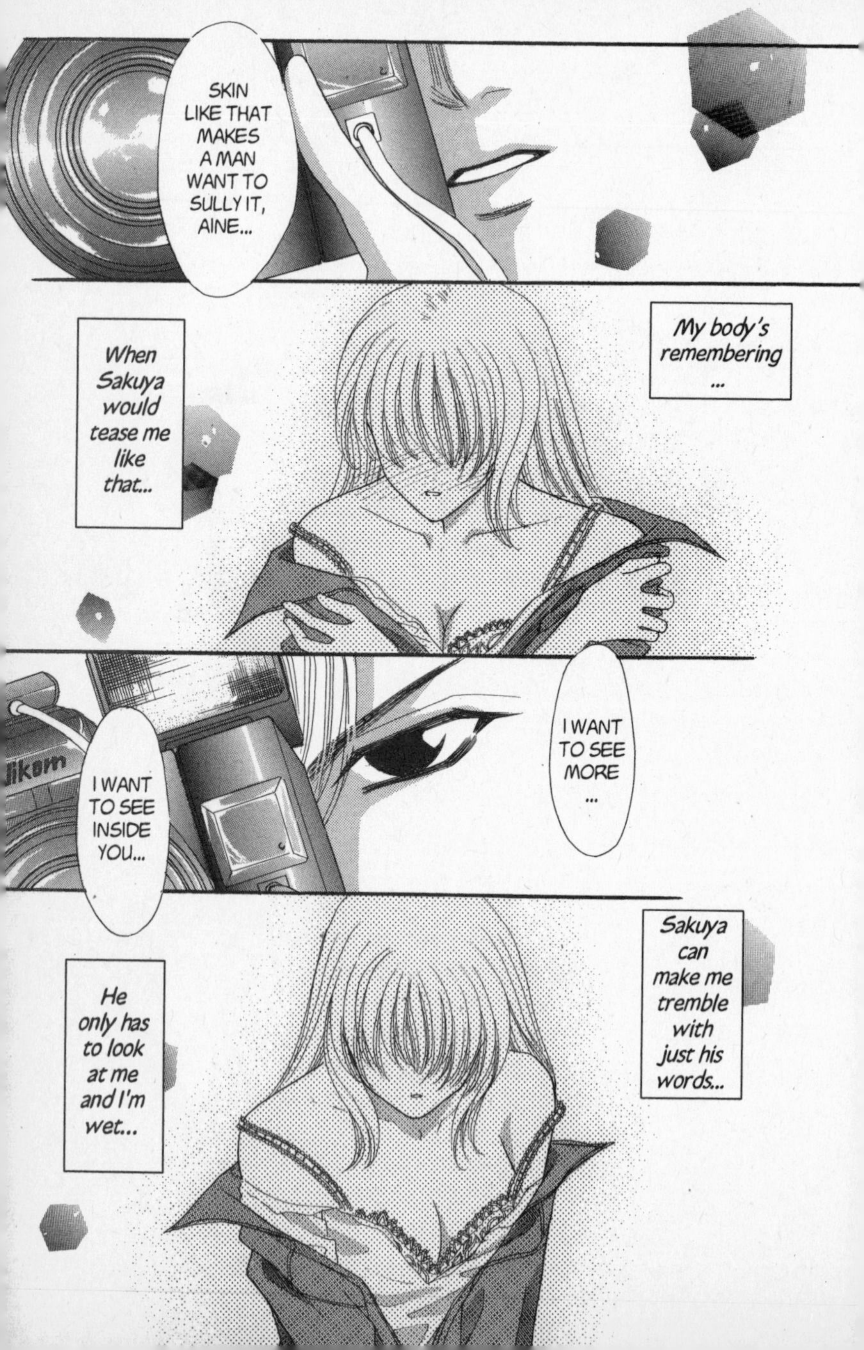
SKIN LIKE THAT MAKES A MAN WANT TO SULLY IT, AINE...
My body's remembering ...
When Sakuya would tease me like that...
I WANT TO SEE MORE ...
I WANT TO SEE INSIDE YOU...
Sakuya can make me tremble with just his words...
He only has to look at me and I'm wet...

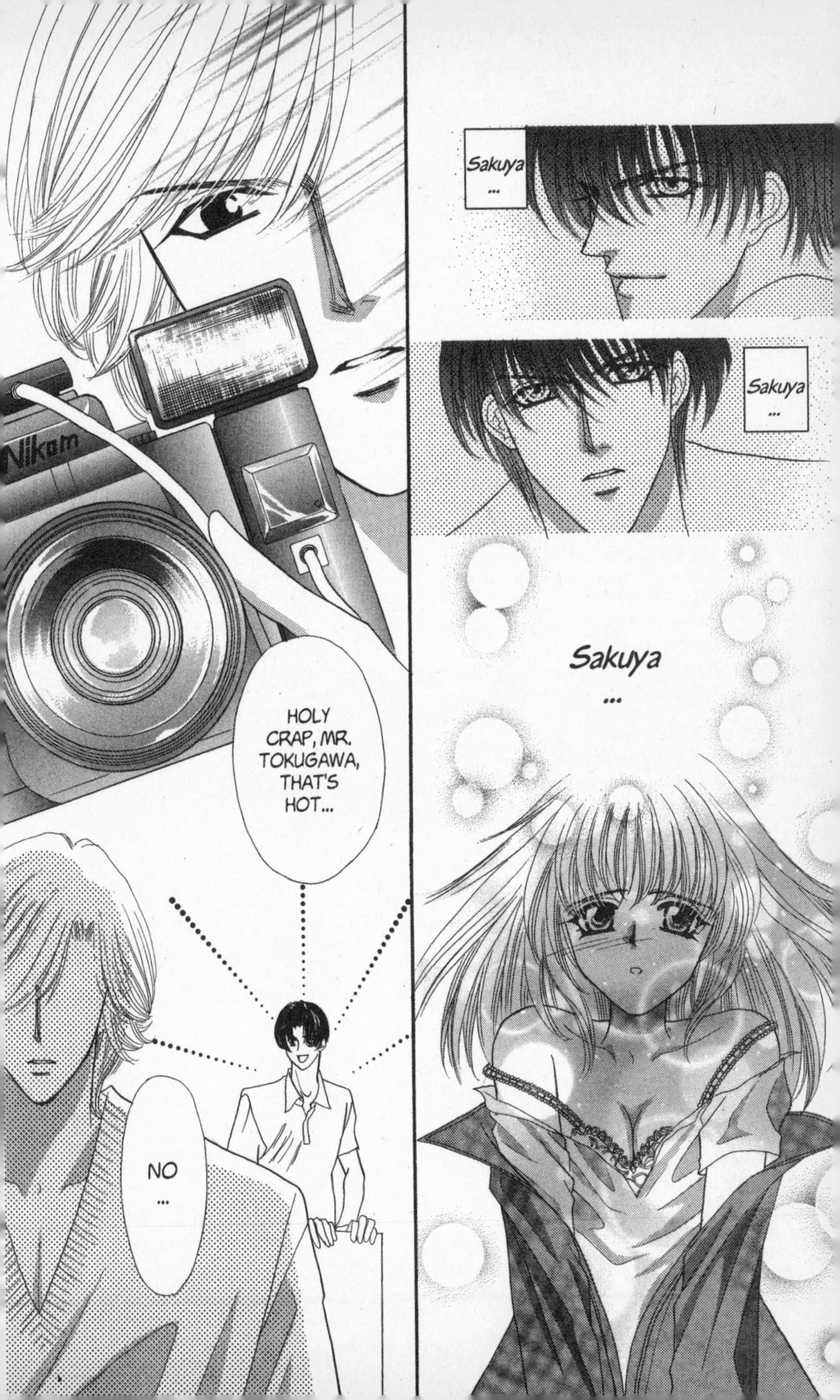

Sakuya ...
Sakuya ...
Sakuya ...
HOLY CRAP, MR. TOKUGAWA, THAT'S HOT...
NO ...

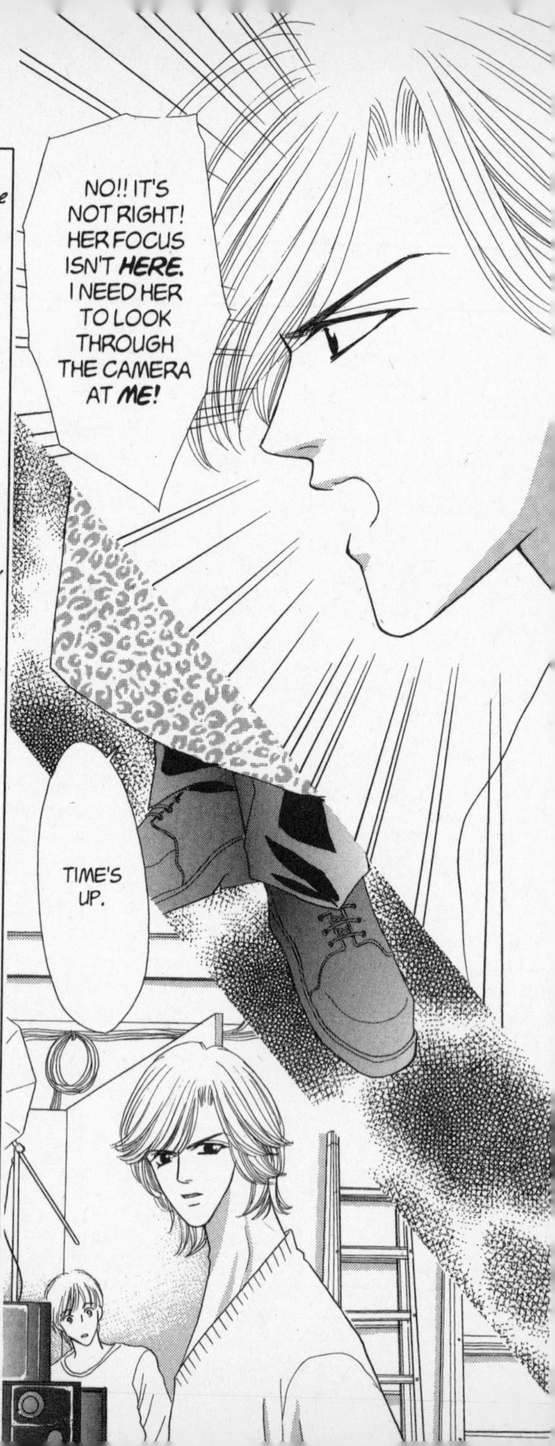
NO!! IT'S NOT RIGHT! HER FOCUS ISN'T ***HERE.*** I NEED HER TO LOOK THROUGH THE CAMERA AT ***ME!***
TIME'S UP.

...but the Sensual Phrase anime doesn't try to cover the same ground as the manga! It's a separate thing, a side-story - one compliments the other, but they both stand alone. Make sense?

I look forward to hearing what you think, so keep sending in those letters.

Oh yeah!! I want to recommend an artist here, too: Sex Machine Guns!! Their videos are cool and hilarious-funny lyrics, catchy melodies and solid musicianship– all my assistants are into them (okay, except for one)! They're so cool!! I really want to see them live--!! Check 'em out!! (Personally, I like TEKKEN II and Sakurajima!)

Have you noticed that the band boom has quieted down recently? Things were moving at a crazy pace there for a while. I mean, the Glay guys are already old pros! That was the sense I got from their dome show, anyway. I mean, their shows have become really high-tech. Sets, and props, and special effects–there's even a computerized Kei character that appears in the middle of the show to introduce the band. I can't be the only person who thought it looked like Sonoko Suzuki... Anyway, it's amazing how they've evolved. Next up: Okinawa!! The Hokkaido dates were all sold out. I was pretty bummed. Those of you who get to go, send me details!

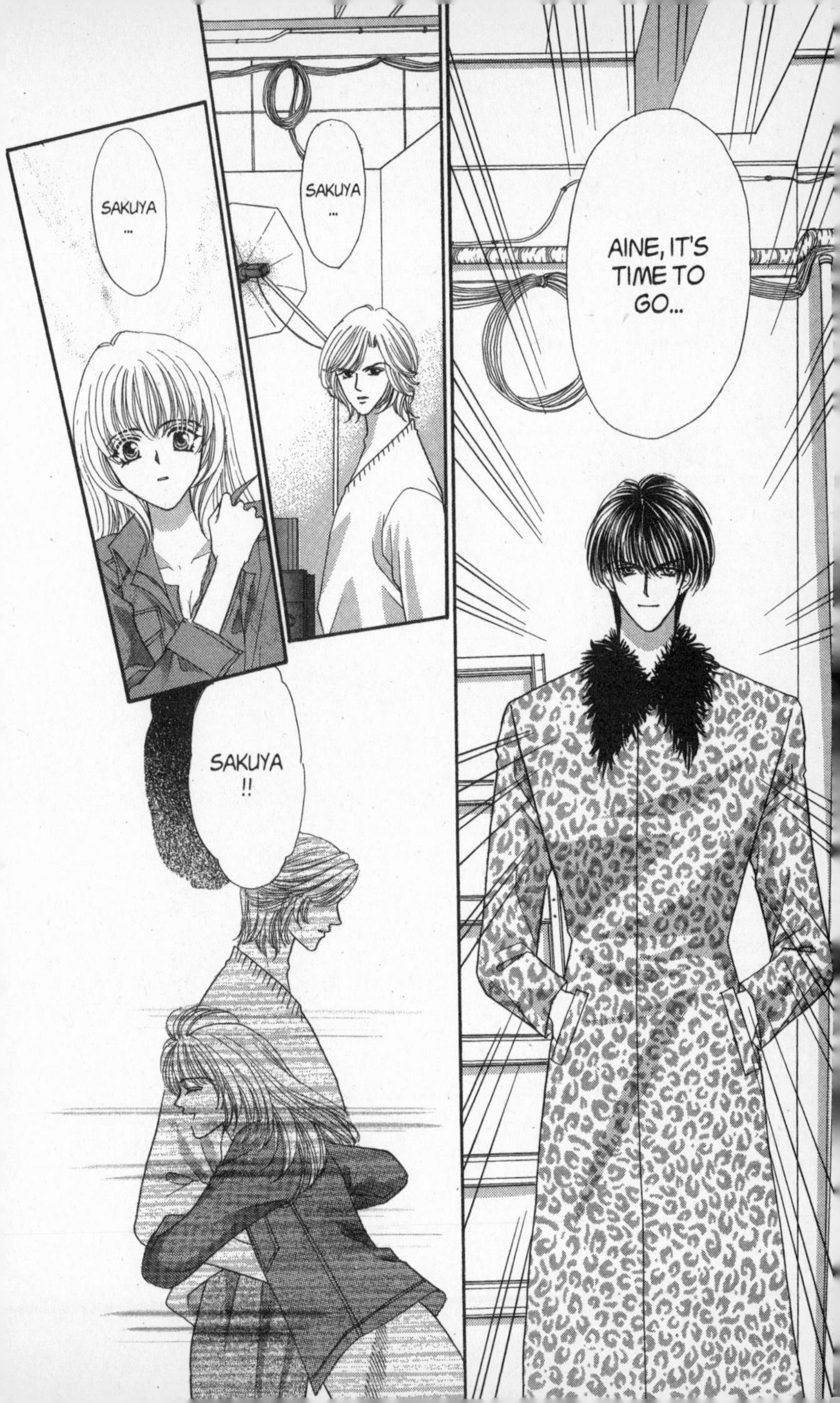
AINE, IT'S TIME TO GO...
SAKUYA ...
SAKUYA ...
SAKUYA !!

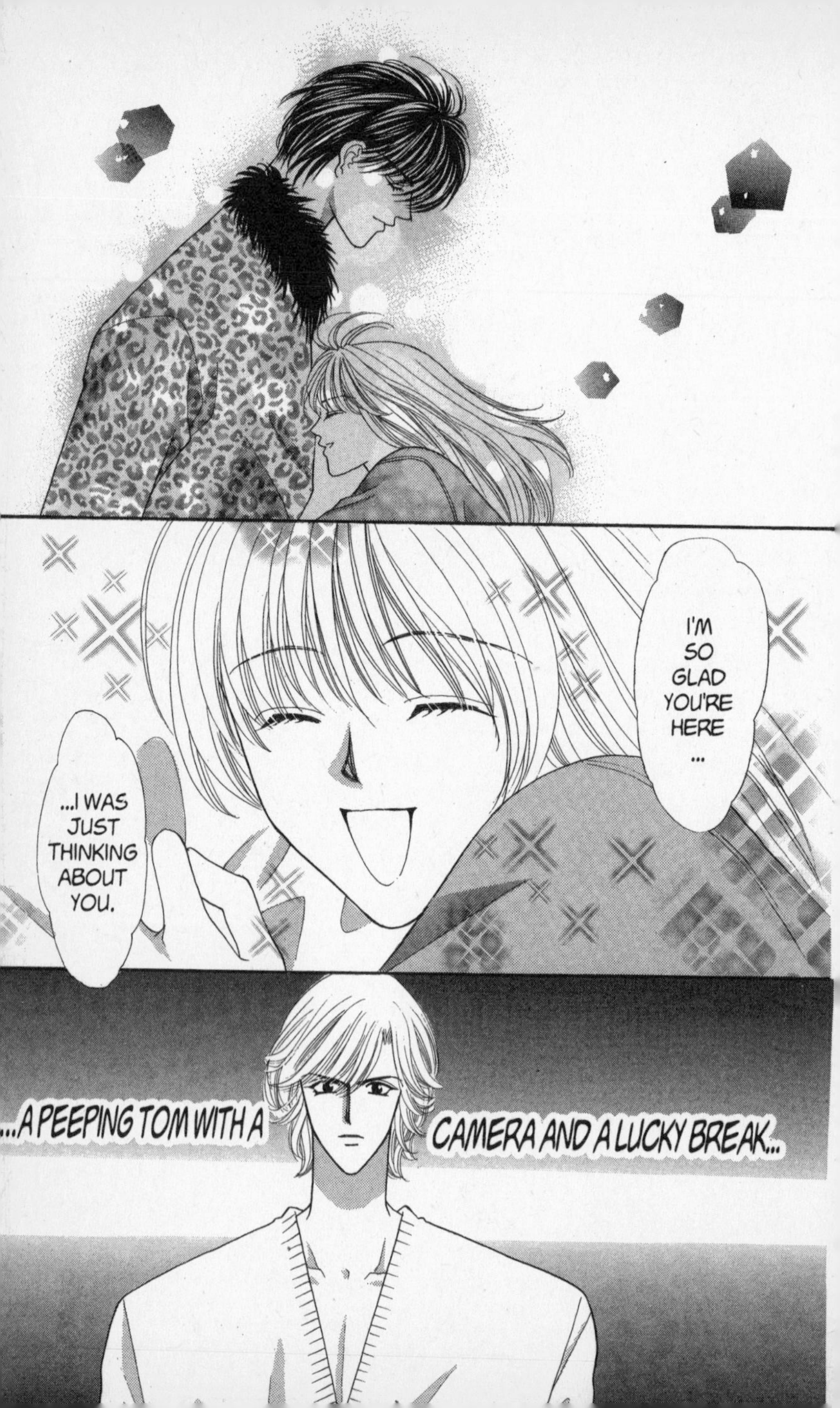
I'M SO GLAD YOU'RE HERE ...
...I WAS JUST THINKING ABOUT YOU.
...A PEEPING TOM WITH A
CAMERA AND A LUCKY BREAK...

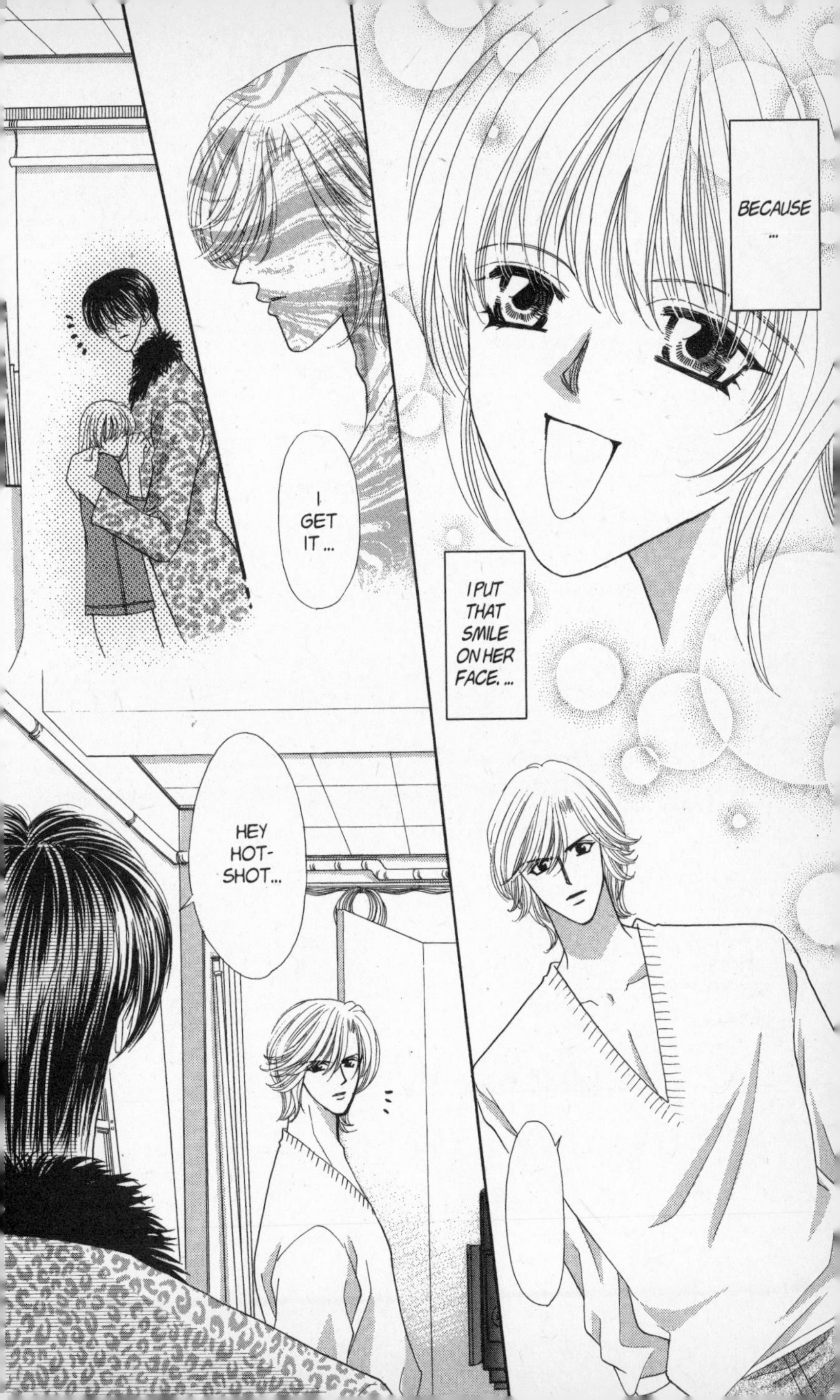
BECAUSE ...
I PUT THAT SMILE ON HER FACE. ...
I GET IT ...
HEY HOT-SHOT...

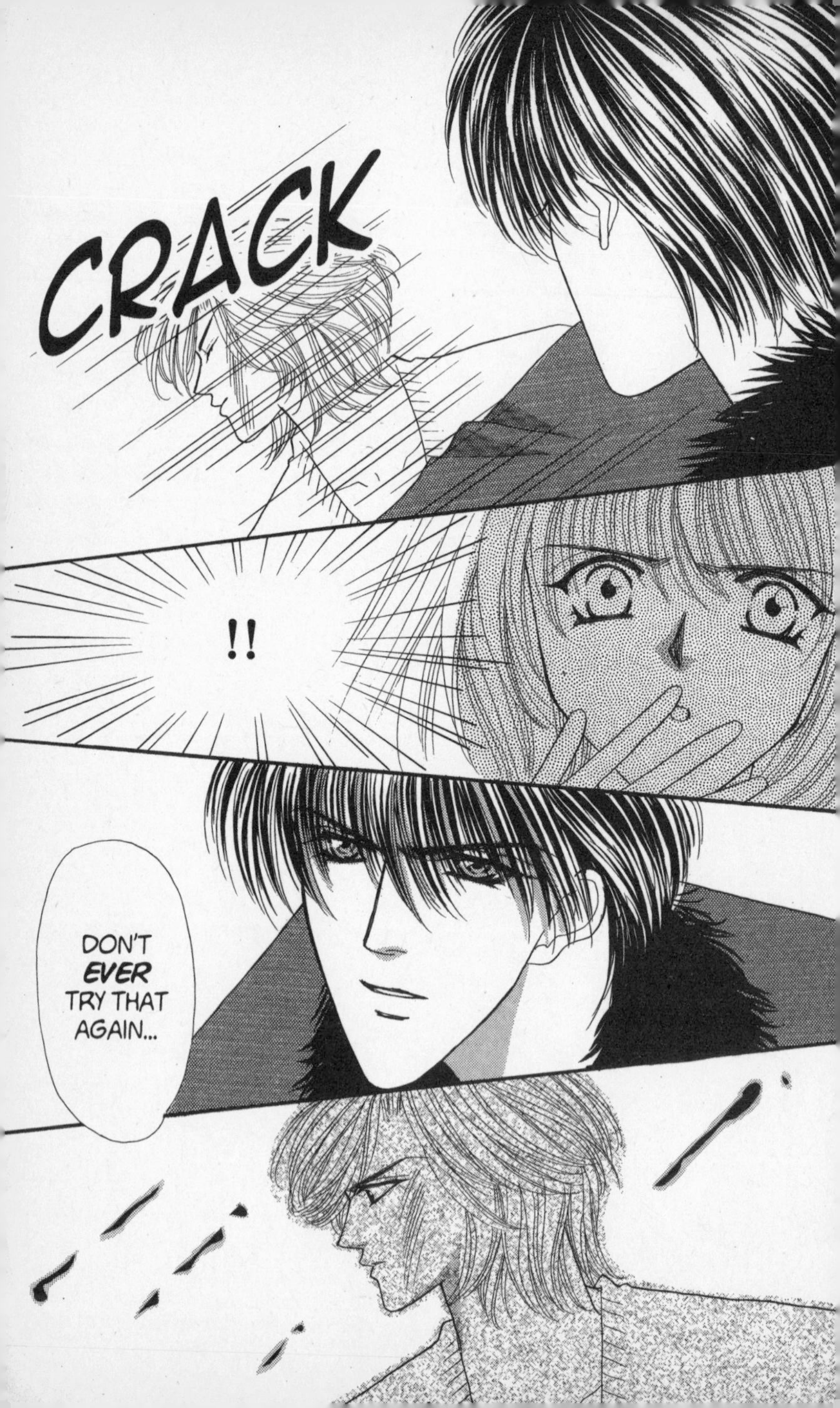
CRACK
!!
DON'T *EVER* TRY THAT AGAIN...

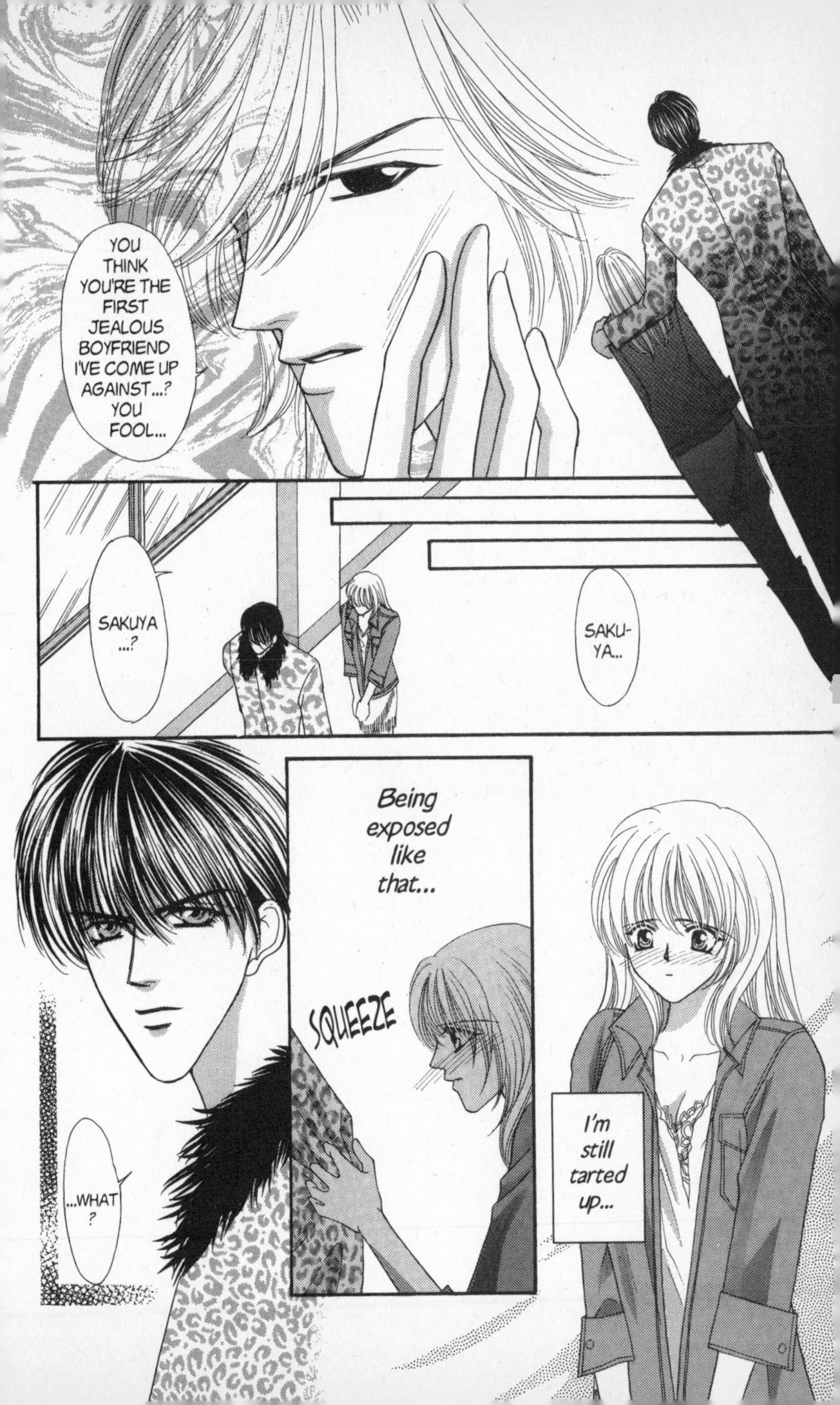
YOU THINK YOU'RE THE FIRST JEALOUS BOYFRIEND I'VE COME UP AGAINST...? YOU FOOL...
SAKU-YA...
SAKUYA ...?
I'm still tarted up...
Being exposed like that...
SQUEEZE
...WHAT ?

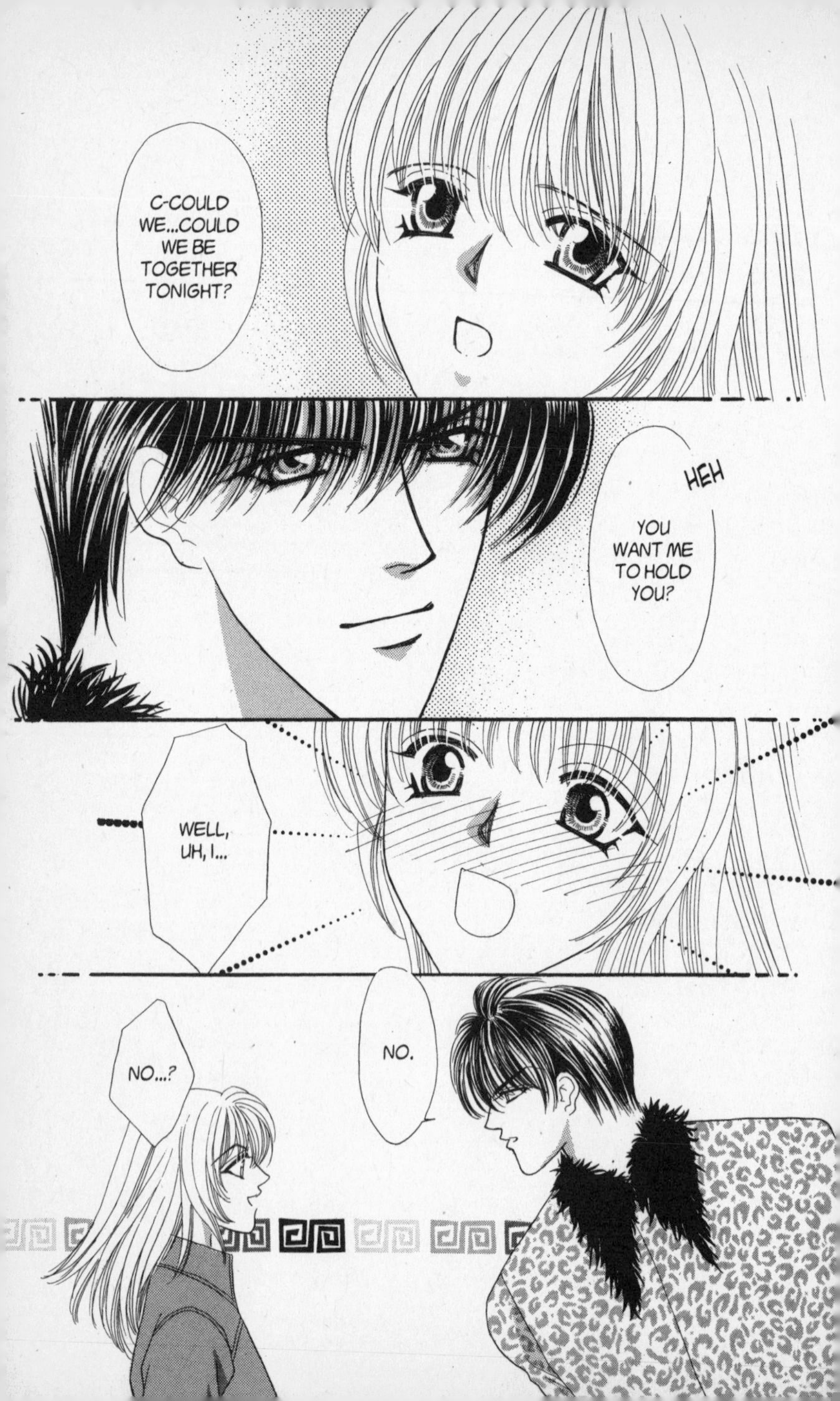

C-COULD WE...COULD WE BE TOGETHER TONIGHT?
HEH
YOU WANT ME TO HOLD YOU?
WELL, UH, I...
NO.
NO...?

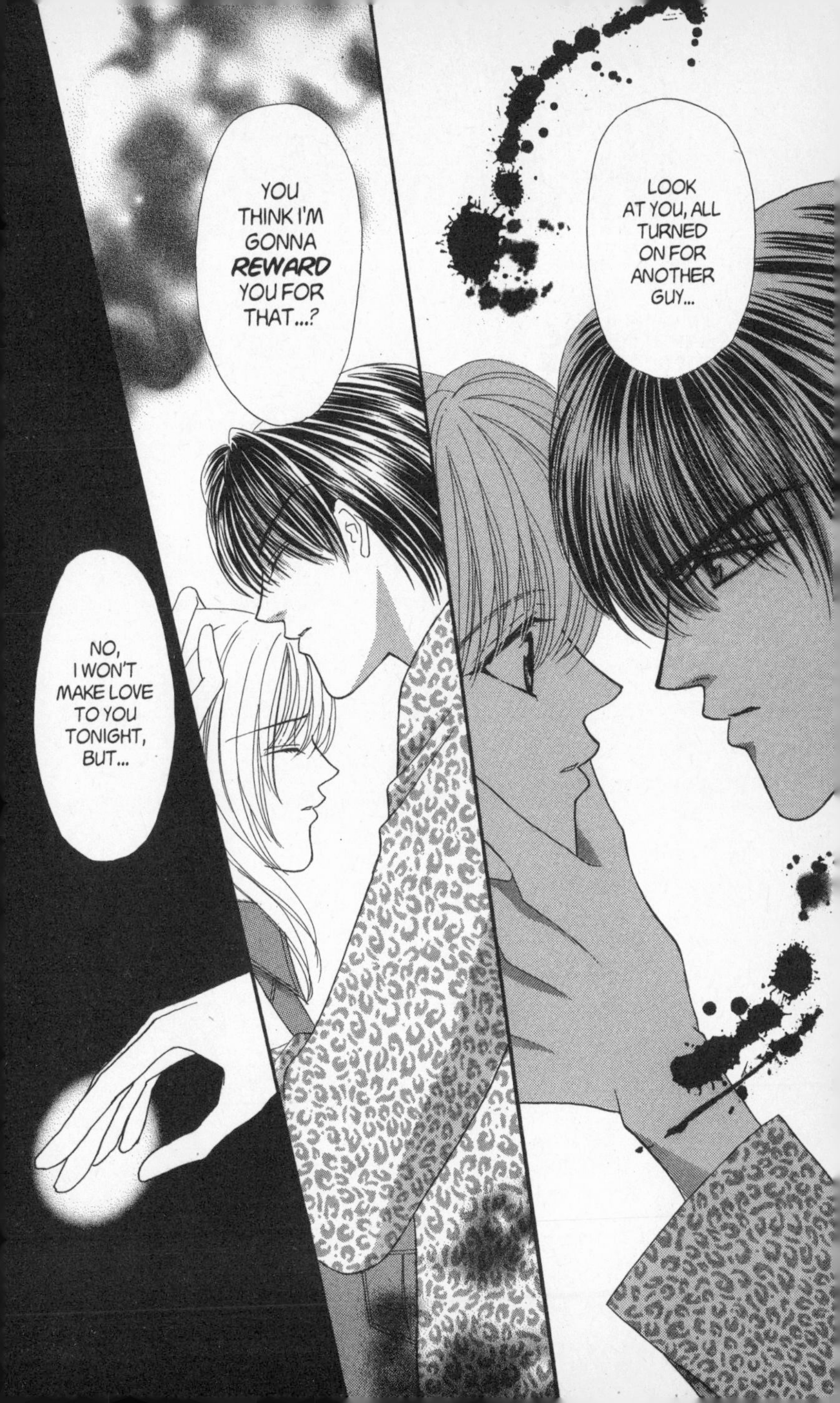
LOOK AT YOU, ALL TURNED ON FOR ANOTHER GUY...
YOU THINK I'M GONNA **REWARD** YOU FOR THAT...?
NO, I WON'T MAKE LOVE TO YOU TONIGHT, BUT...

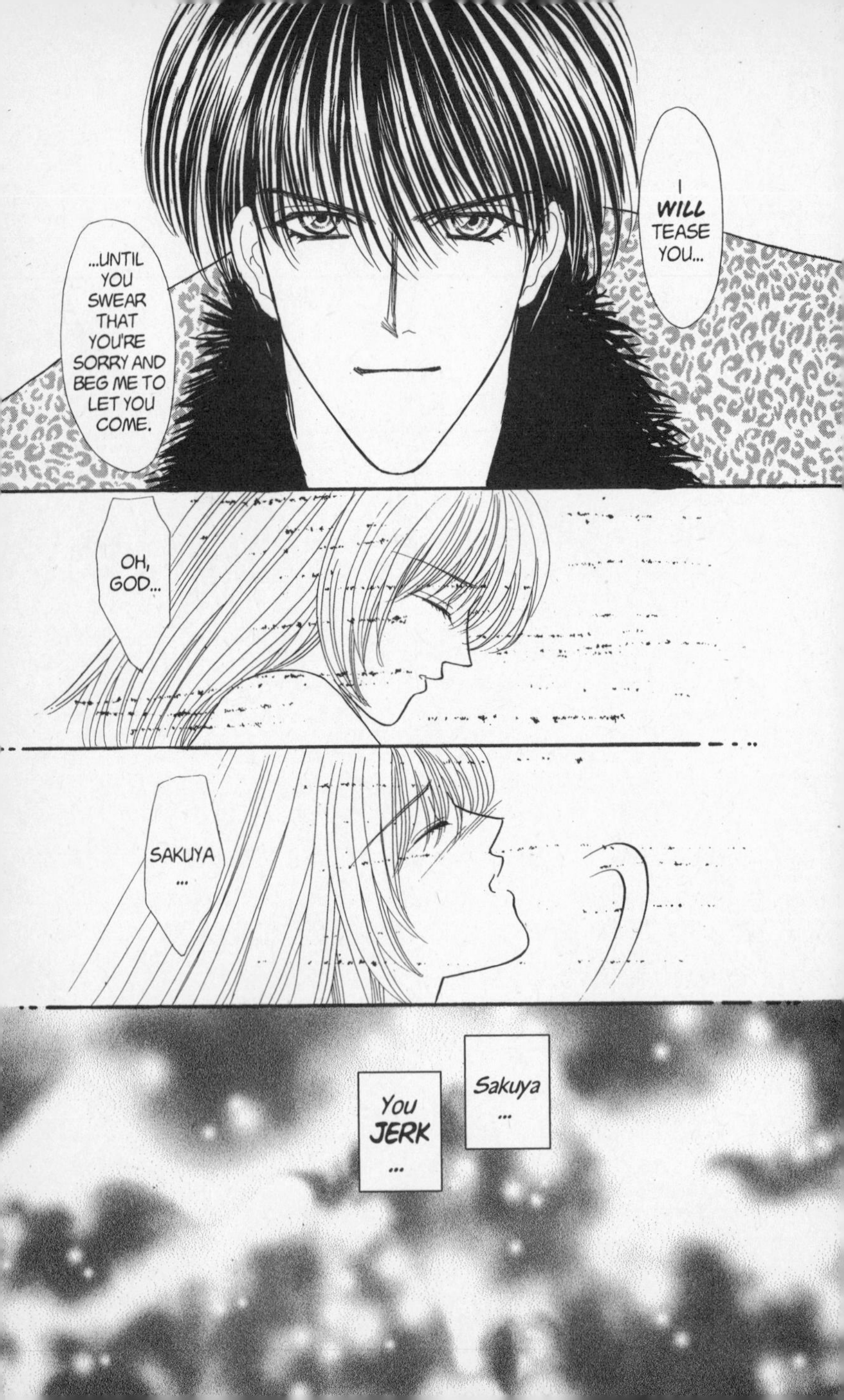
I WILL TEASE YOU...
...UNTIL YOU SWEAR THAT YOU'RE SORRY AND BEG ME TO LET YOU COME.
OH, GOD...
SAKUYA ...
Sakuya ...
You JERK ...

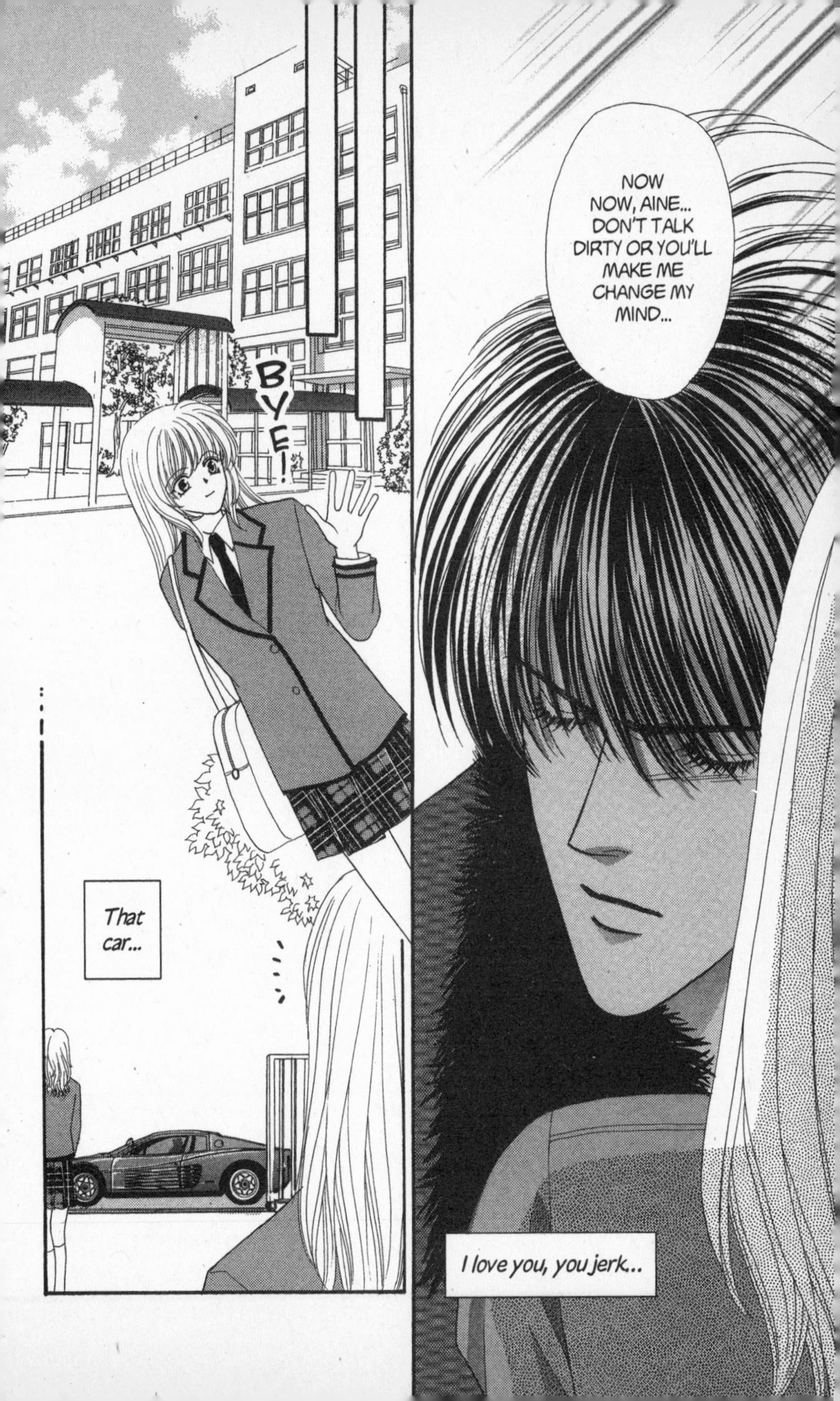

NOW NOW, AINE... DON'T TALK DIRTY OR YOU'LL MAKE ME CHANGE MY MIND...
I love you, you jerk...
BYE!
That car...

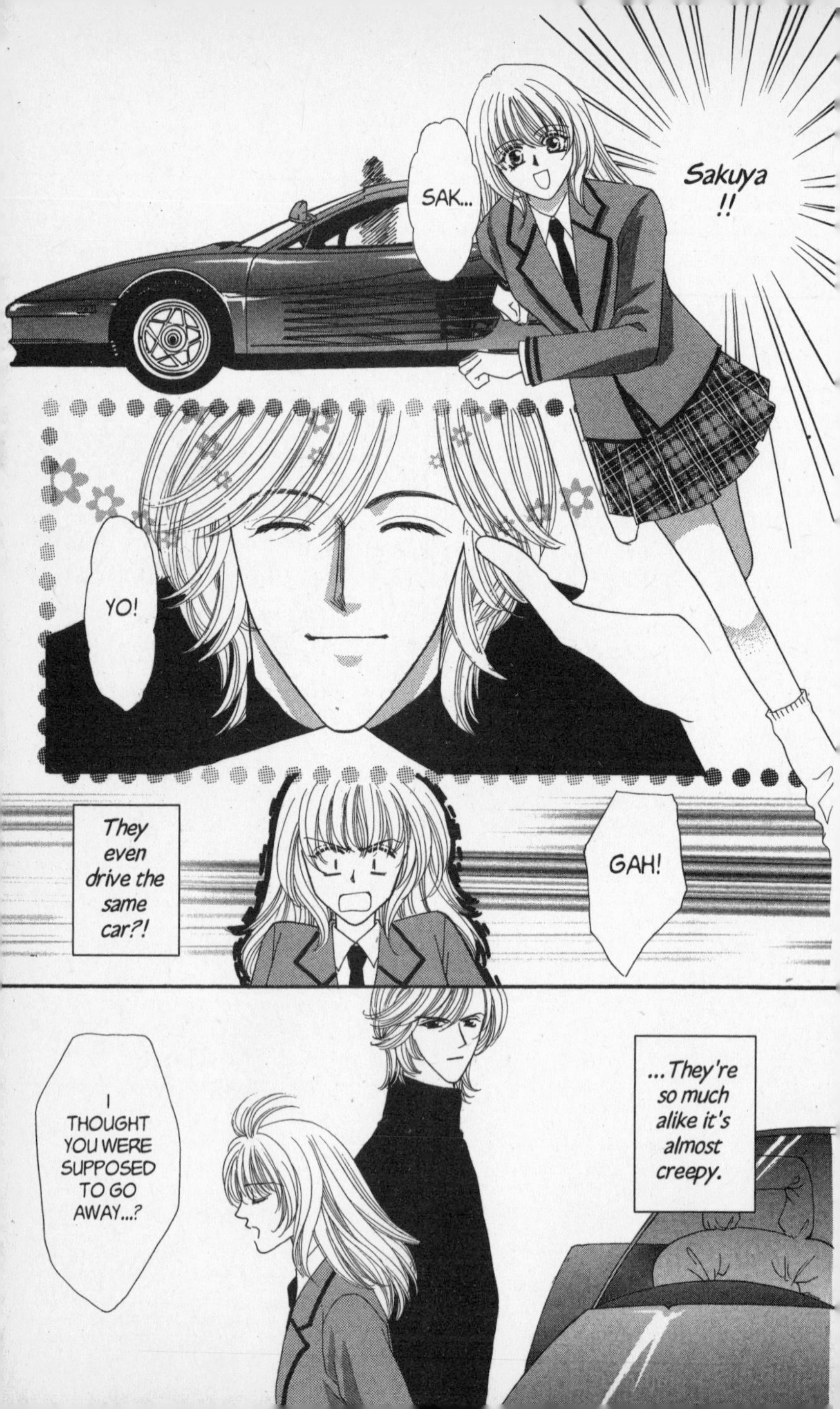
Sakuya !!
SAK...
YO!
GAH!
They even drive the same car?!
...They're so much alike it's almost creepy.
I THOUGHT YOU WERE SUPPOSED TO GO AWAY...?

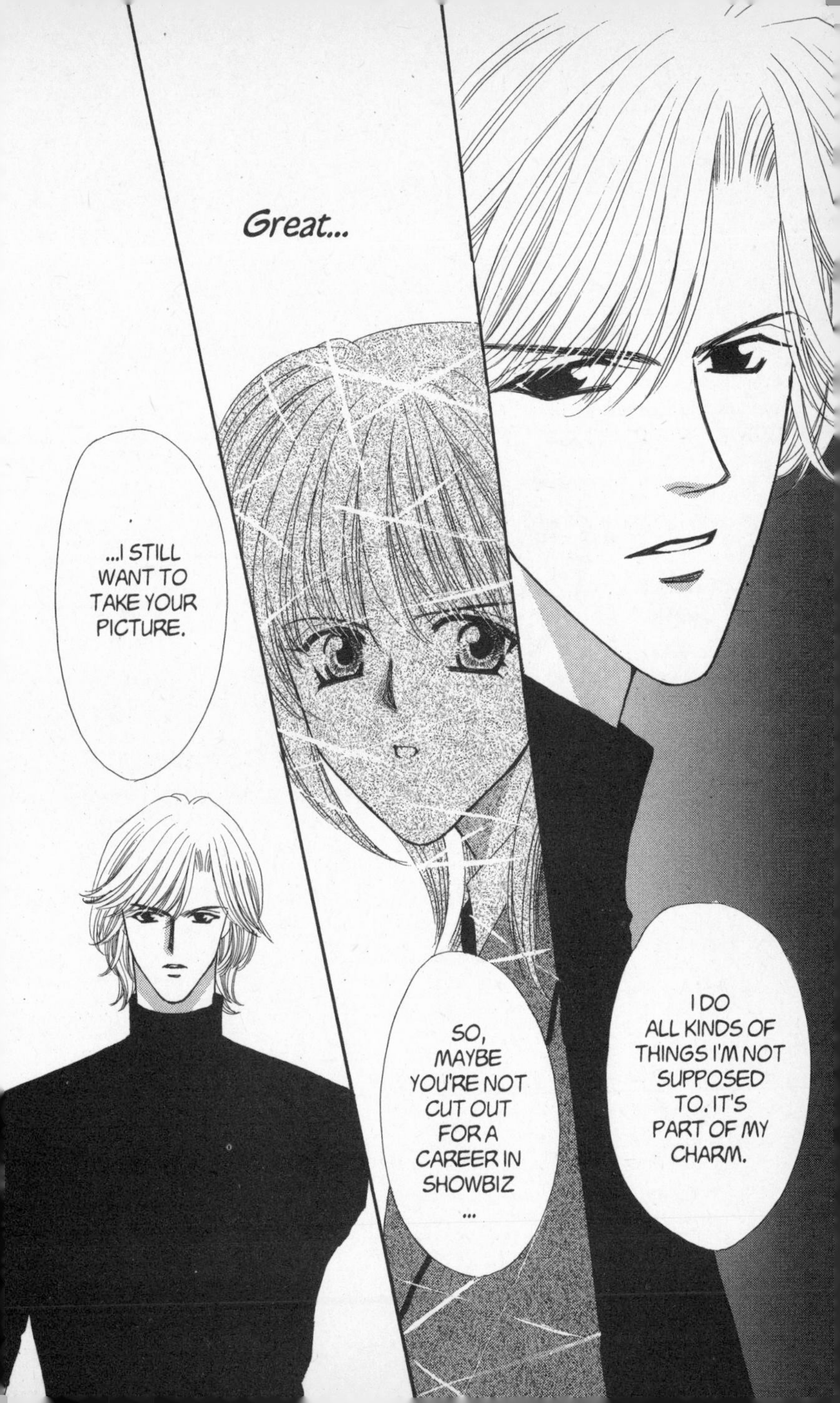
I DO ALL KINDS OF THINGS I'M NOT SUPPOSED TO. IT'S PART OF MY CHARM.
Great...
SO, MAYBE YOU'RE NOT CUT OUT FOR A CAREER IN SHOWBIZ ...
...I STILL WANT TO TAKE YOUR PICTURE.

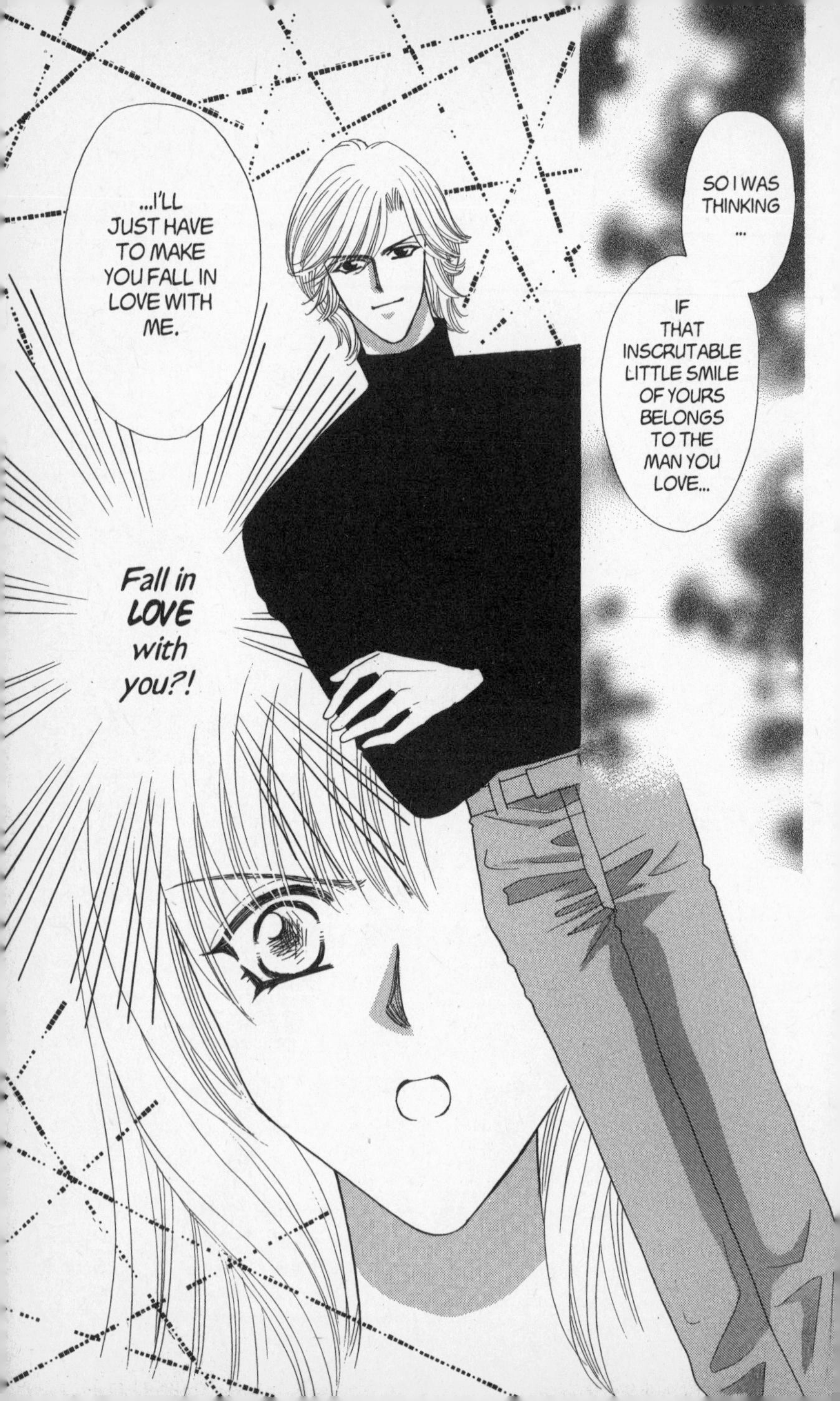
SO I WAS THINKING ...
IF THAT INSCRUTABLE LITTLE SMILE OF YOURS BELONGS TO THE MAN YOU LOVE...
...I'LL JUST HAVE TO MAKE YOU FALL IN LOVE WITH ME.
Fall in LOVE with you?!

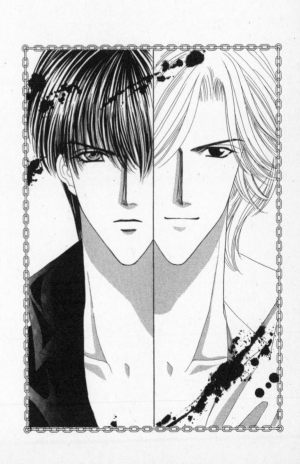

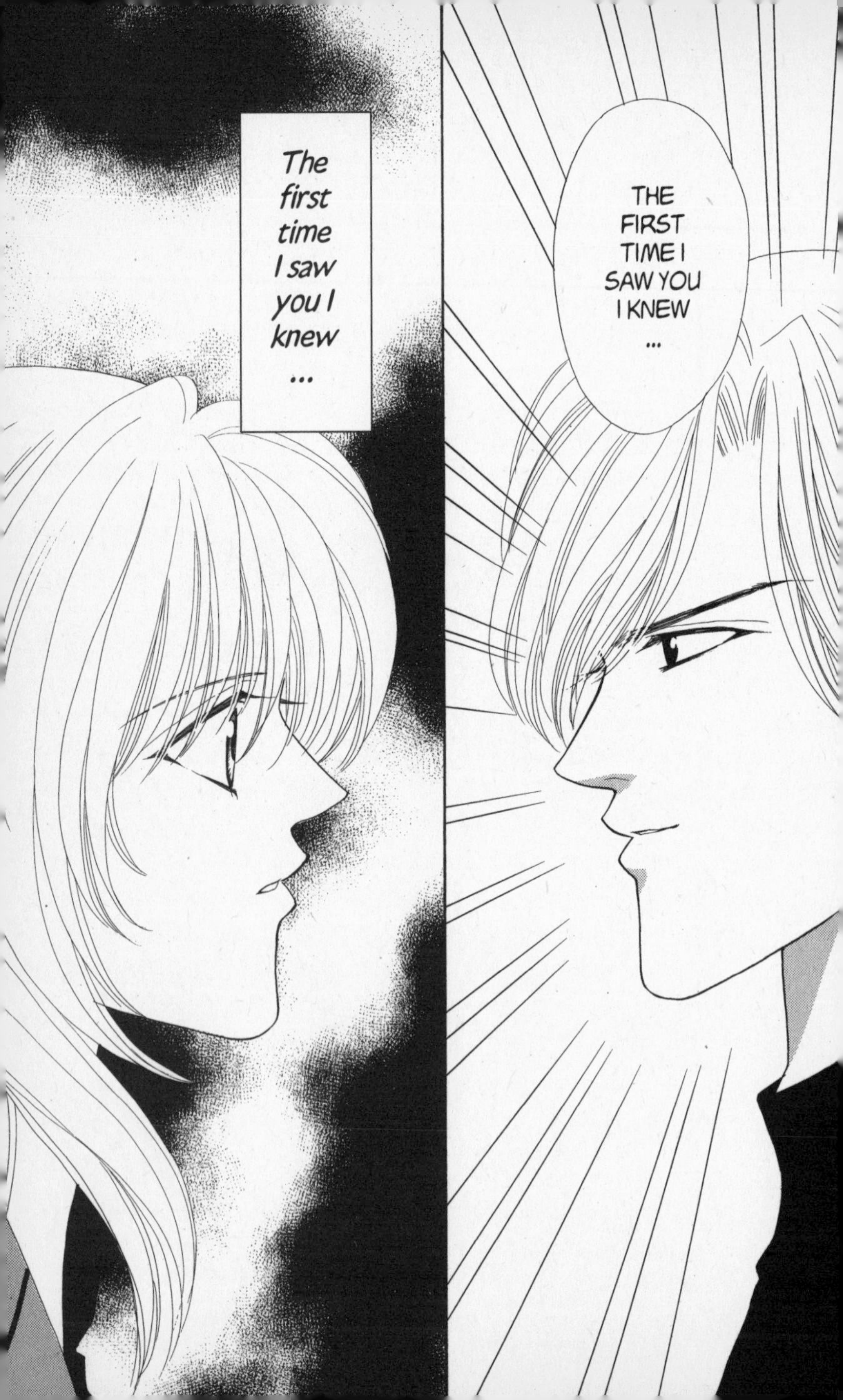
THE FIRST TIME I SAW YOU I KNEW ...
The first time I saw you I knew ...

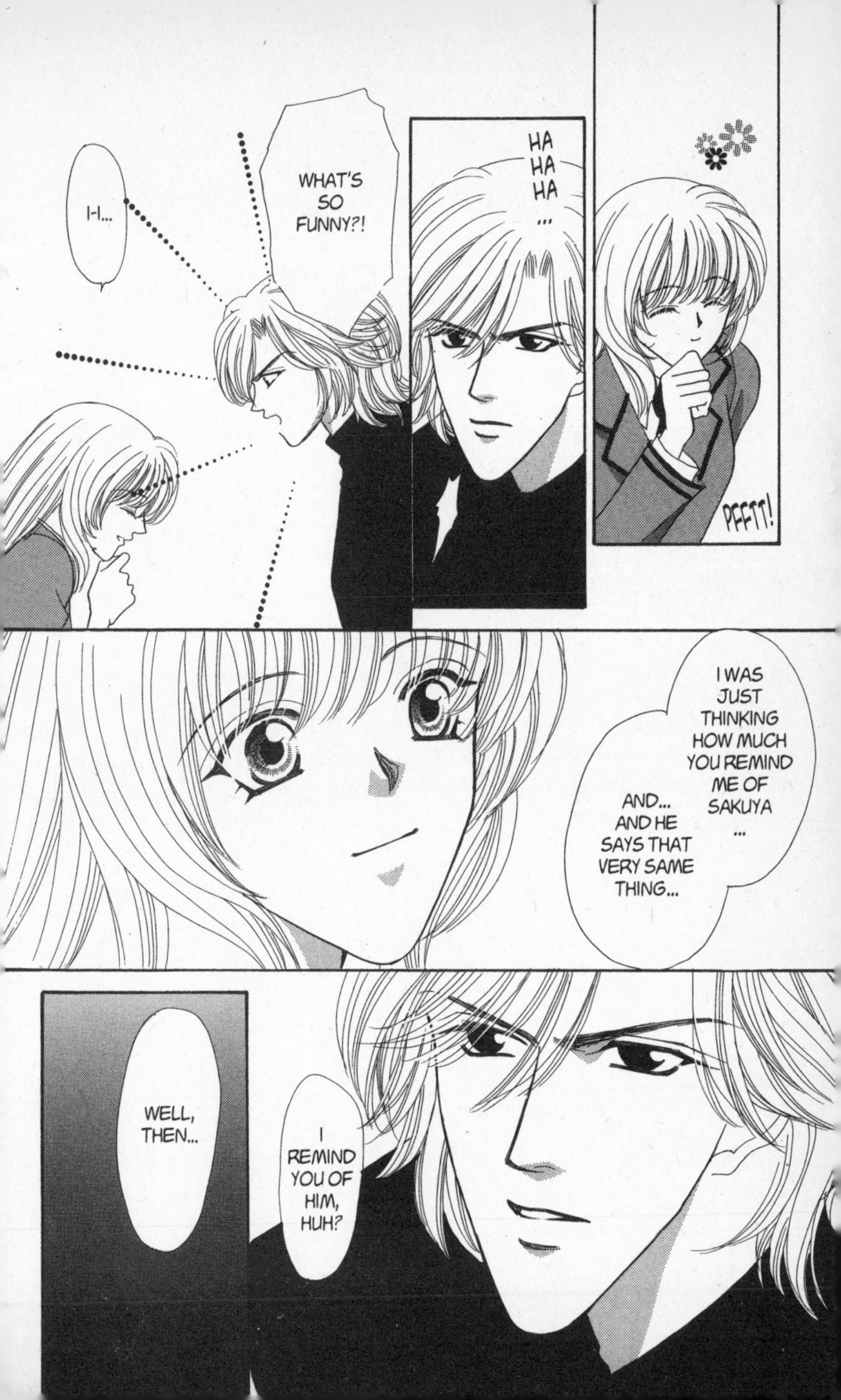
PFFTT!
HA HA HA ...
WHAT'S SO FUNNY?!
I-I...
I WAS JUST THINKING HOW MUCH YOU REMIND ME OF SAKUYA ...
AND... AND HE SAYS THAT VERY SAME THING...
I REMIND YOU OF HIM, HUH?
WELL, THEN...

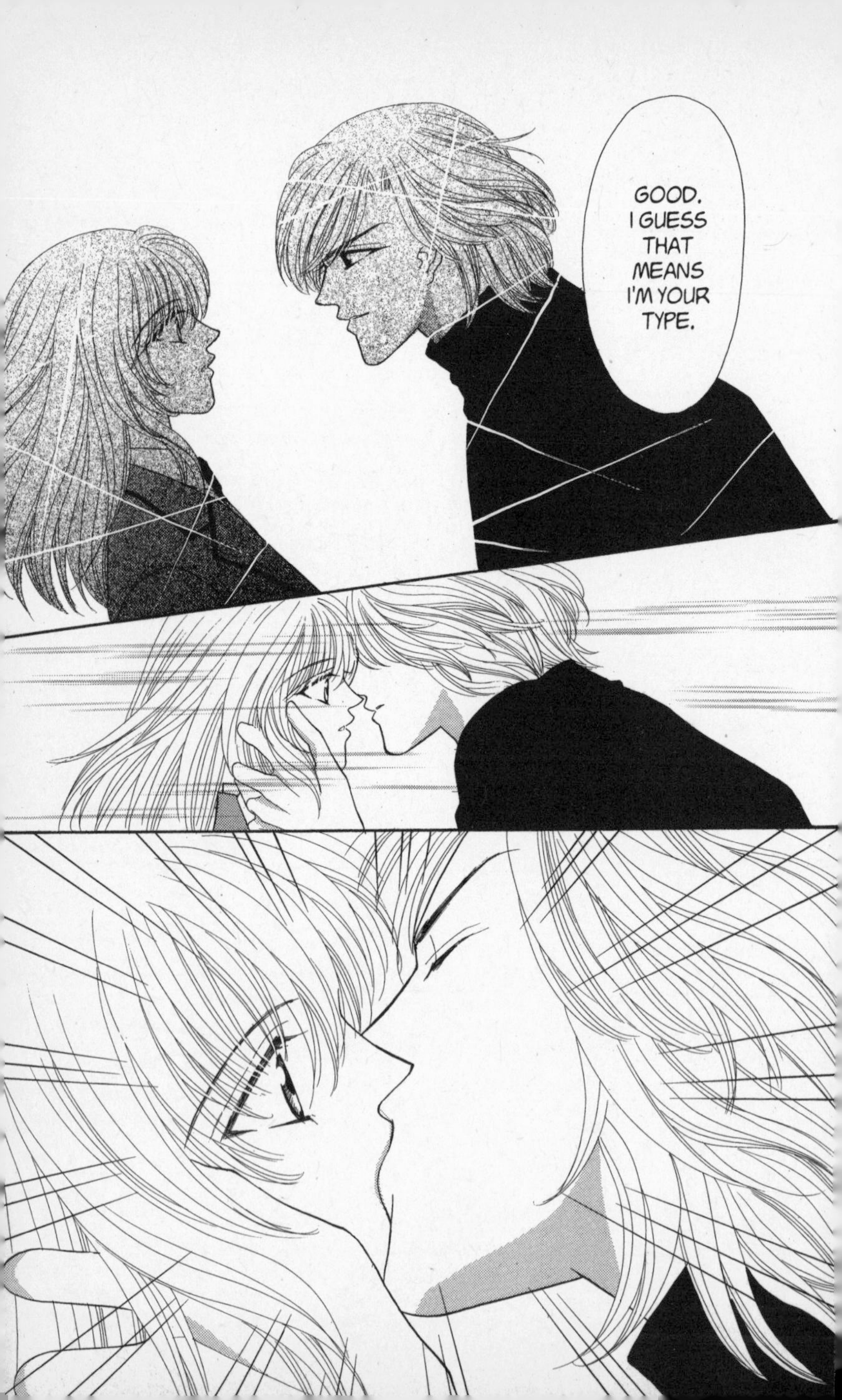
GOOD. I GUESS THAT MEANS I'M YOUR TYPE.

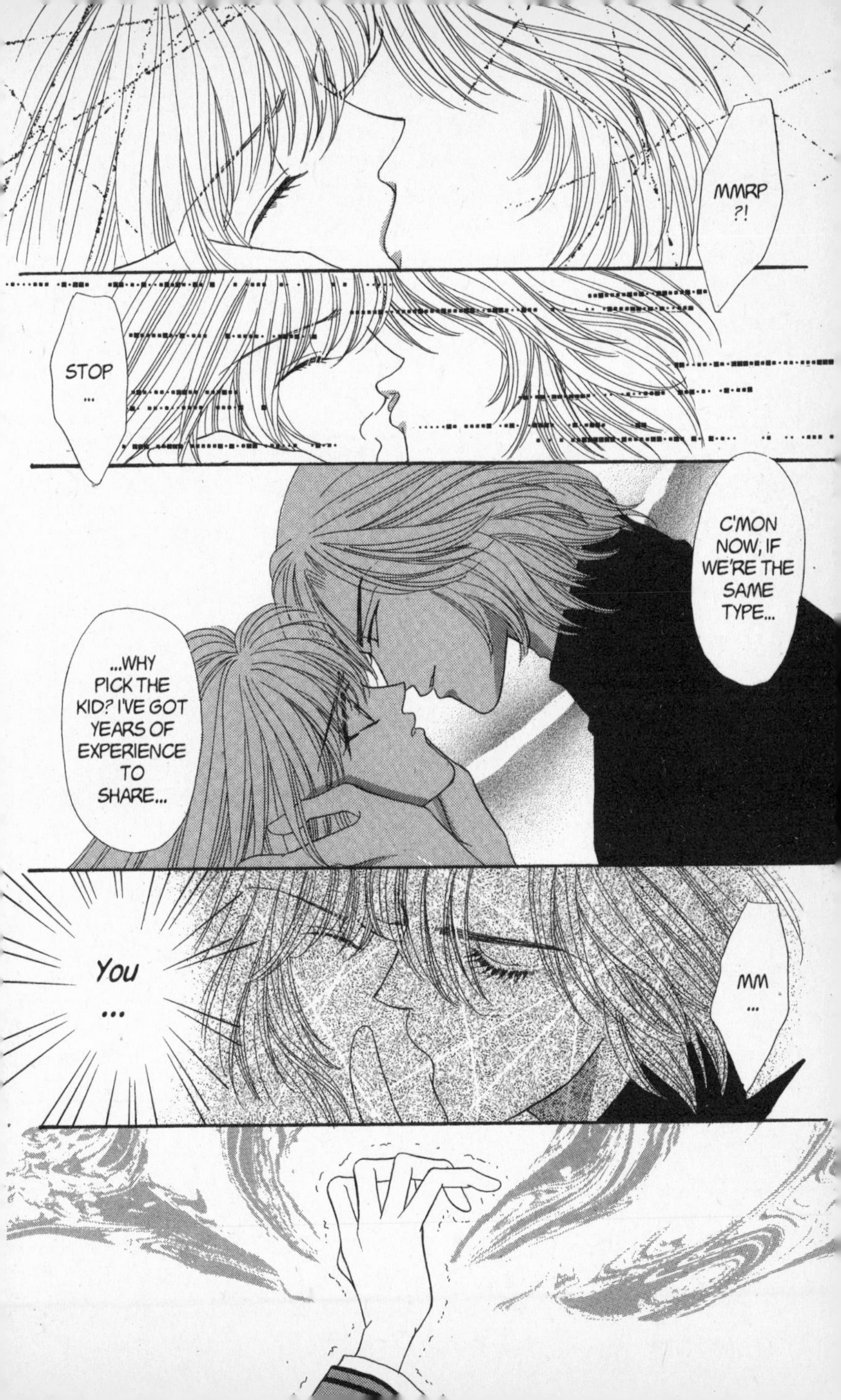
MMRP ?!
STOP ...
C'MON NOW, IF WE'RE THE SAME TYPE...
...WHY PICK THE KID? I'VE GOT YEARS OF EXPERIENCE TO SHARE...
MM ...
You ...

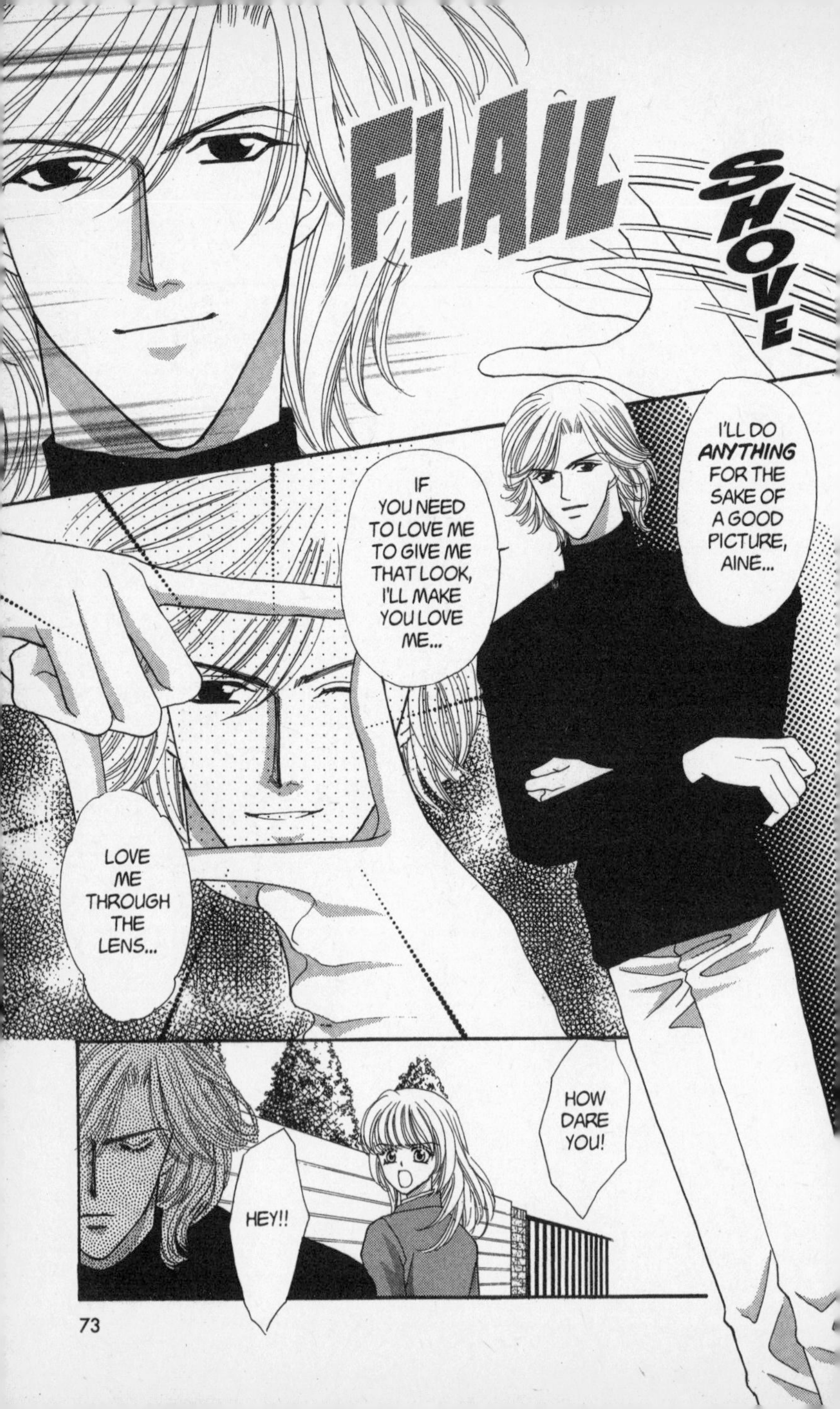
SHOVE
FLAIL
I'LL DO ANYTHING FOR THE SAKE OF A GOOD PICTURE, AINE...
IF YOU NEED TO LOVE ME TO GIVE ME THAT LOOK, I'LL MAKE YOU LOVE ME...
LOVE ME THROUGH THE LENS...
HOW DARE YOU!
HEY!!

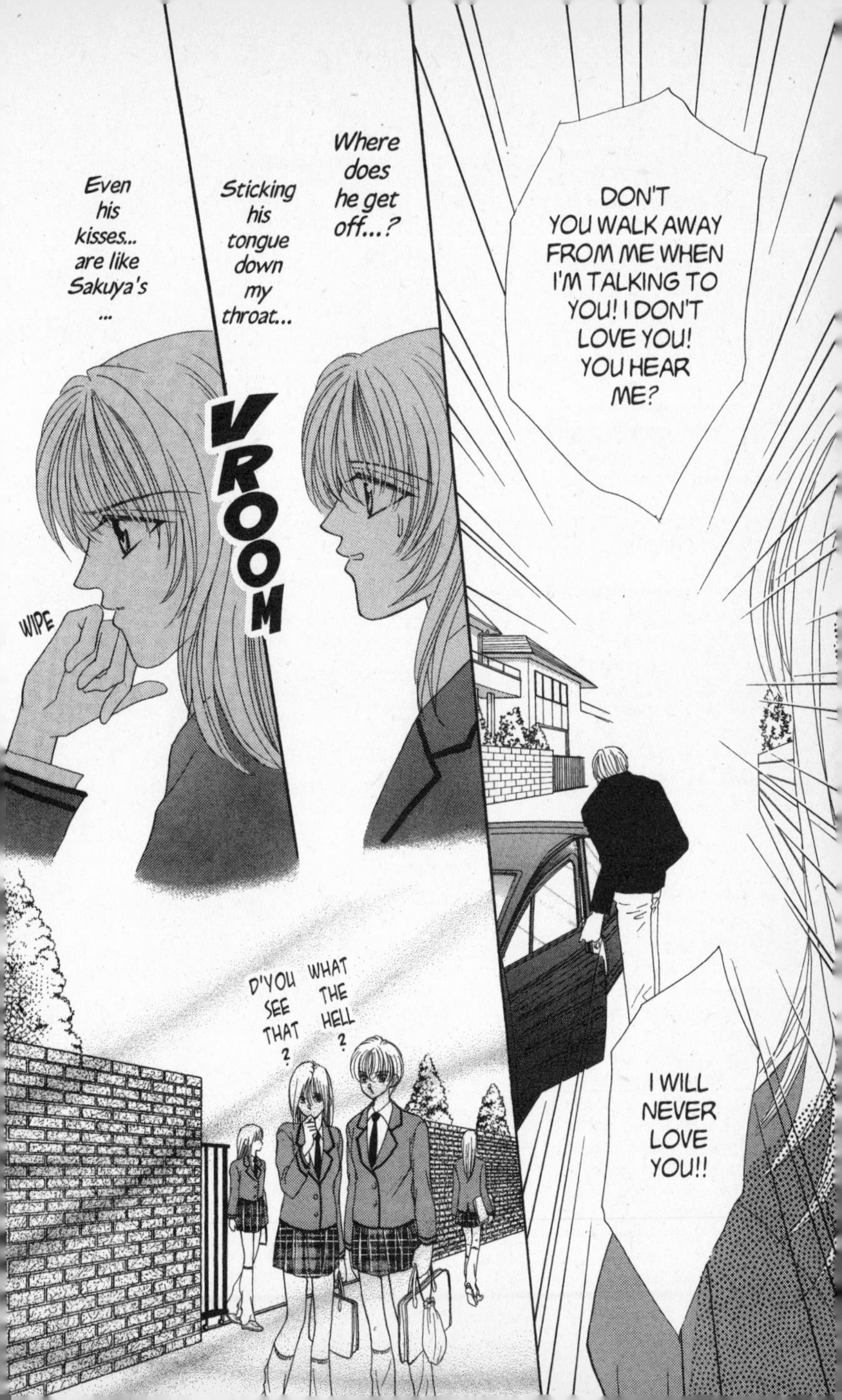
DON'T YOU WALK AWAY FROM ME WHEN I'M TALKING TO YOU! I DON'T LOVE YOU! YOU HEAR ME?
I WILL NEVER LOVE YOU!!
Where does he get off...?
Sticking his tongue down my throat...
VROOM
Even his kisses... are like Sakuya's ...
WIPE
WHAT THE HELL?
D'YOU SEE THAT?

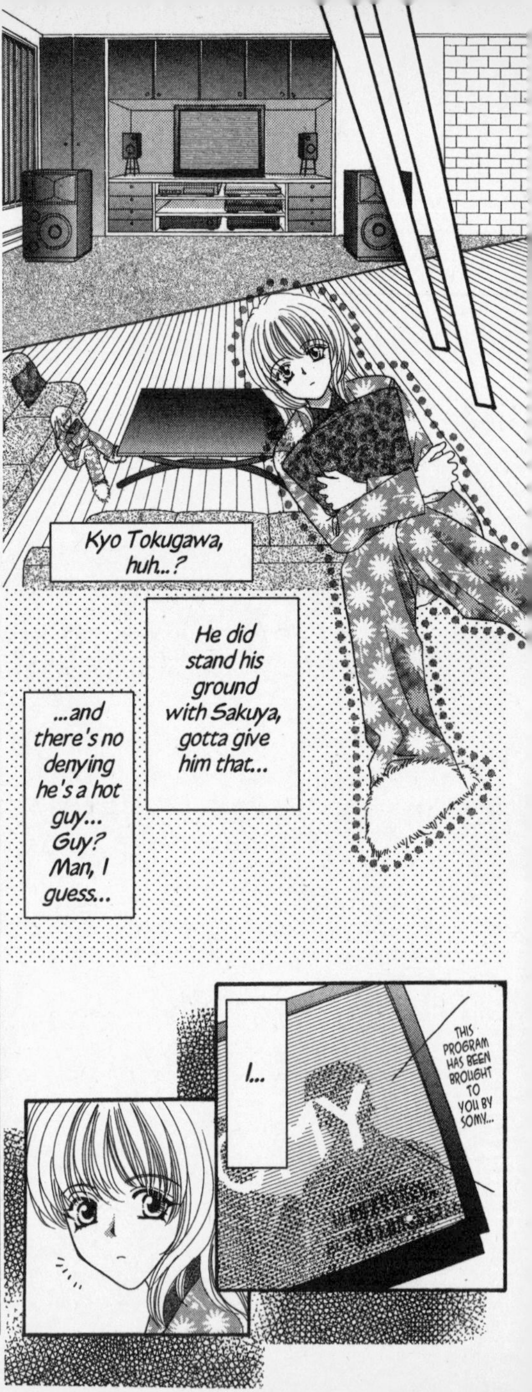

Kyo Tokugawa, huh...?
He did stand his ground with Sakuya, gotta give him that...
...and there's no denying he's a hot guy... Guy? Man, I guess...
THIS PROGRAM HAS BEEN BROUGHT TO YOU BY SOMY...
I...

The Seven Mysteries of Sensual Phrase

Okay, I confess: I've made a few, er, miscalculations that have resulted in some confusion. Let's clear the air here and now, shall we?

(1) AINE'S CLASS STARTED AS JUNIOR CLASS A, BUT NOW IT'S JUNIOR CLASS 5...?
Sorry, my bad... It'll be Junior class 5 from now on.

(2) AYAKO SAKURA AND SAKUYA'S AGE DIFFERENCE CHANGES...?
They should be eight years apart. So: if Sakuya is 17 right now, that makes Ayako 25.

(3) THE HICKEY THAT TOMOYUKI GIVES AINE CHANGES LOCATIONS...?
What? You mean you've never heard of a traveling hickey...? Yeah, okay, you got me. Sorry. I was out of it. It should have been on her left side the whole time.

Okay, I'm sure there are many more "mysteries" in Sensual Phrase, but I have a suggestion: don't look for mistakes! Just have a laugh, forgive me and move on!

About my BMer:
Okay, I've tooootally been into cars lately. I've been meeting people on the Internet and in person for the sole purpose of talking about cars. Most of them are men. (Heh!) I've modified all sorts of parts of my car (My car's name is "Terurin"). There's even a store in Yokohama that specializes in BMW parts - we get together there and chat or just shop. A BMW is a deep car, my friends. And hey - my driving has improved!

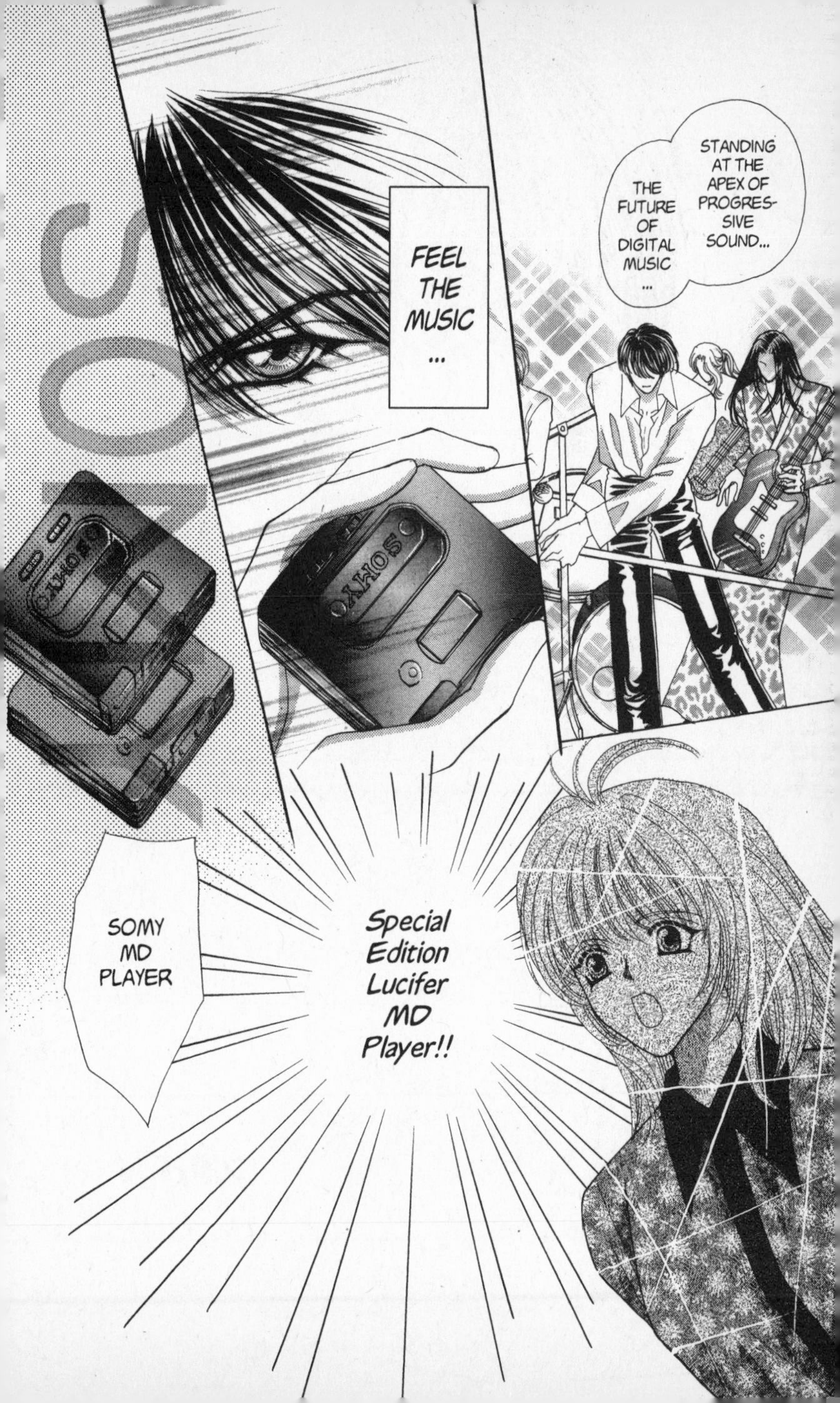
STANDING AT THE APEX OF PROGRES- SIVE SOUND...
THE FUTURE OF DIGITAL MUSIC ...
FEEL THE MUSIC ...
Special Edition Lucifer MD Player!!
SOMY MD PLAYER

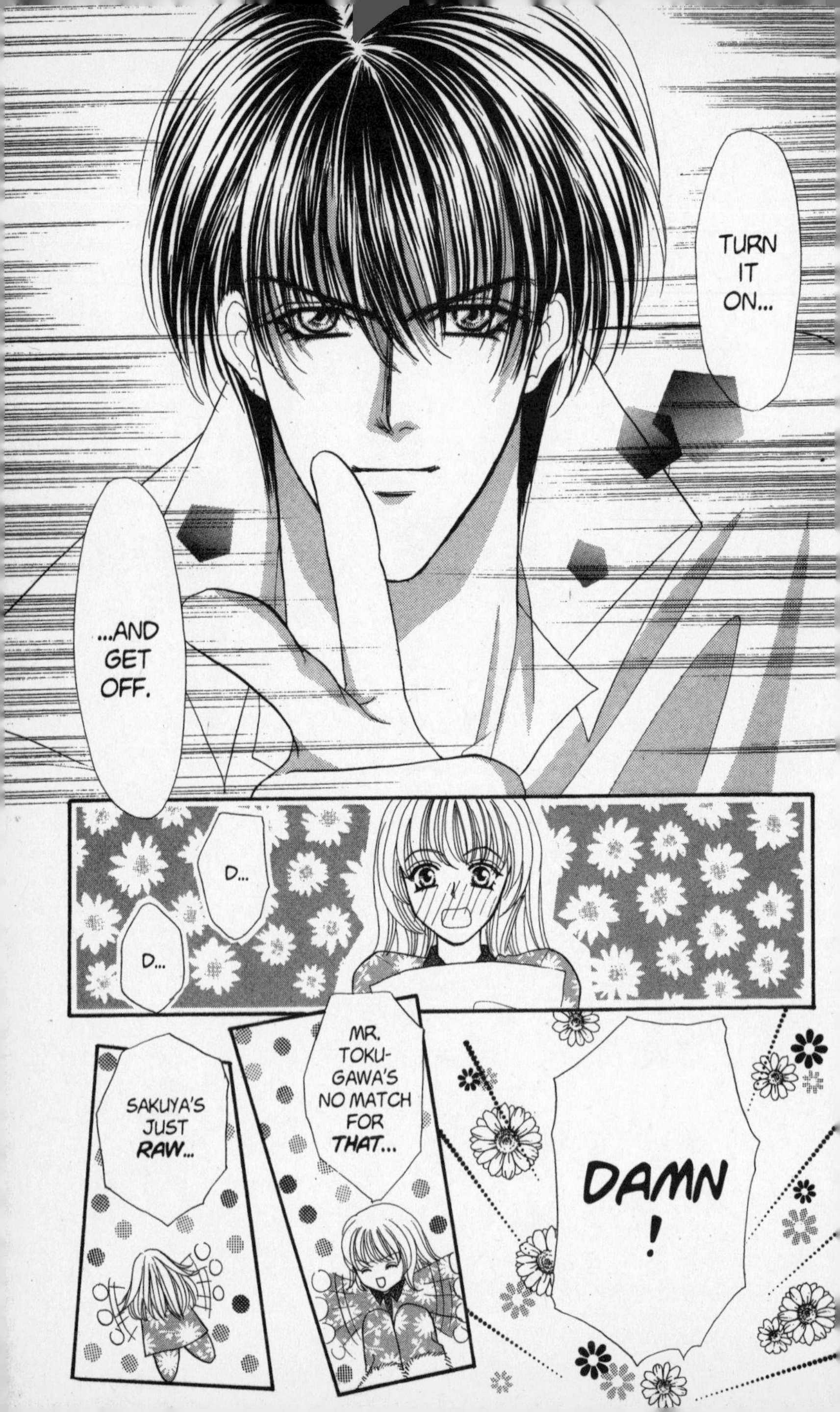
TURN IT ON...
...AND GET OFF.
D...
D...
DAMN!
MR. TOKU-GAWA'S NO MATCH FOR THAT...
SAKUYA'S JUST RAW...

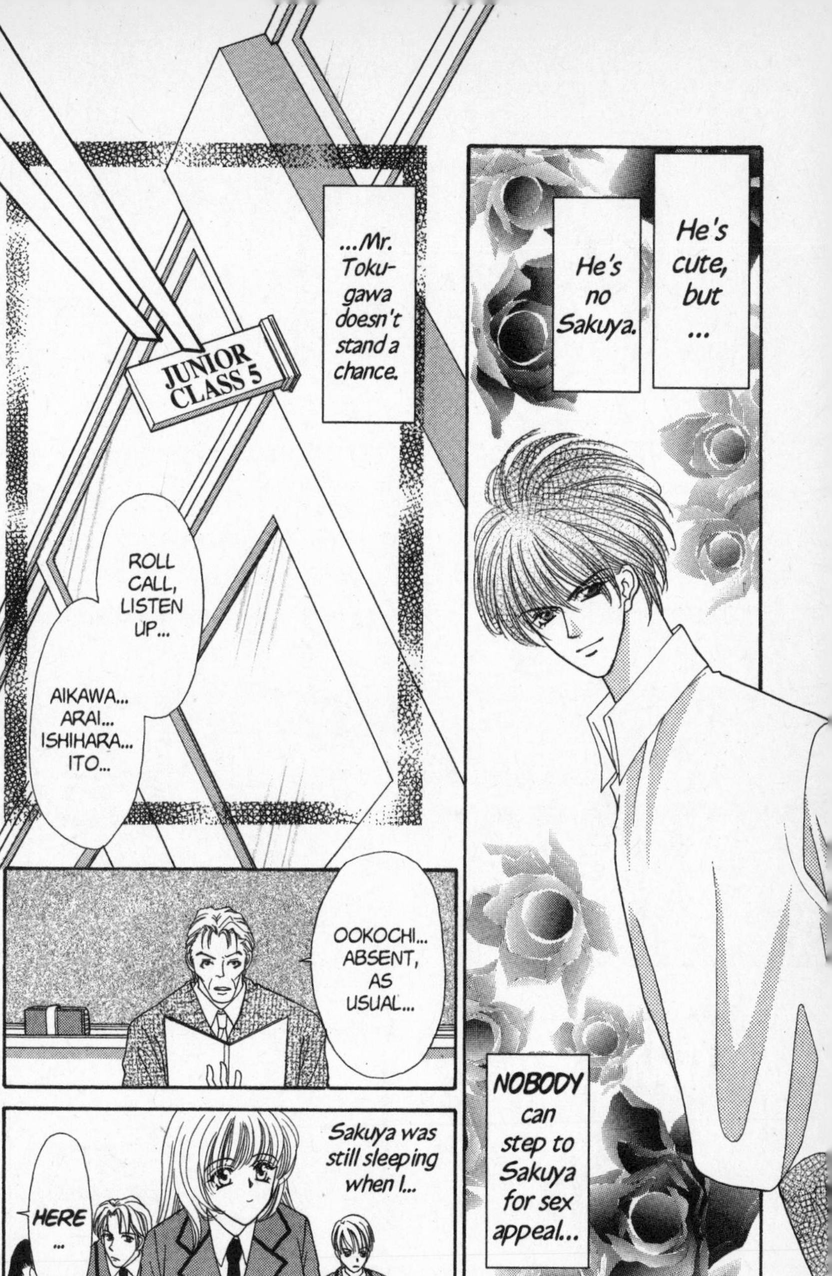
He's cute, but ...
He's no Sakuya.
NOBODY can step to Sakuya for sex appeal...
...Mr. Toku-gawa doesn't stand a chance.
JUNIOR CLASS 5
ROLL CALL, LISTEN UP...
AIKAWA... ARAI... ISHIHARA... ITO...
OOKOCHI... ABSENT, AS USUAL...
Sakuya was still sleeping when I...
HERE ...

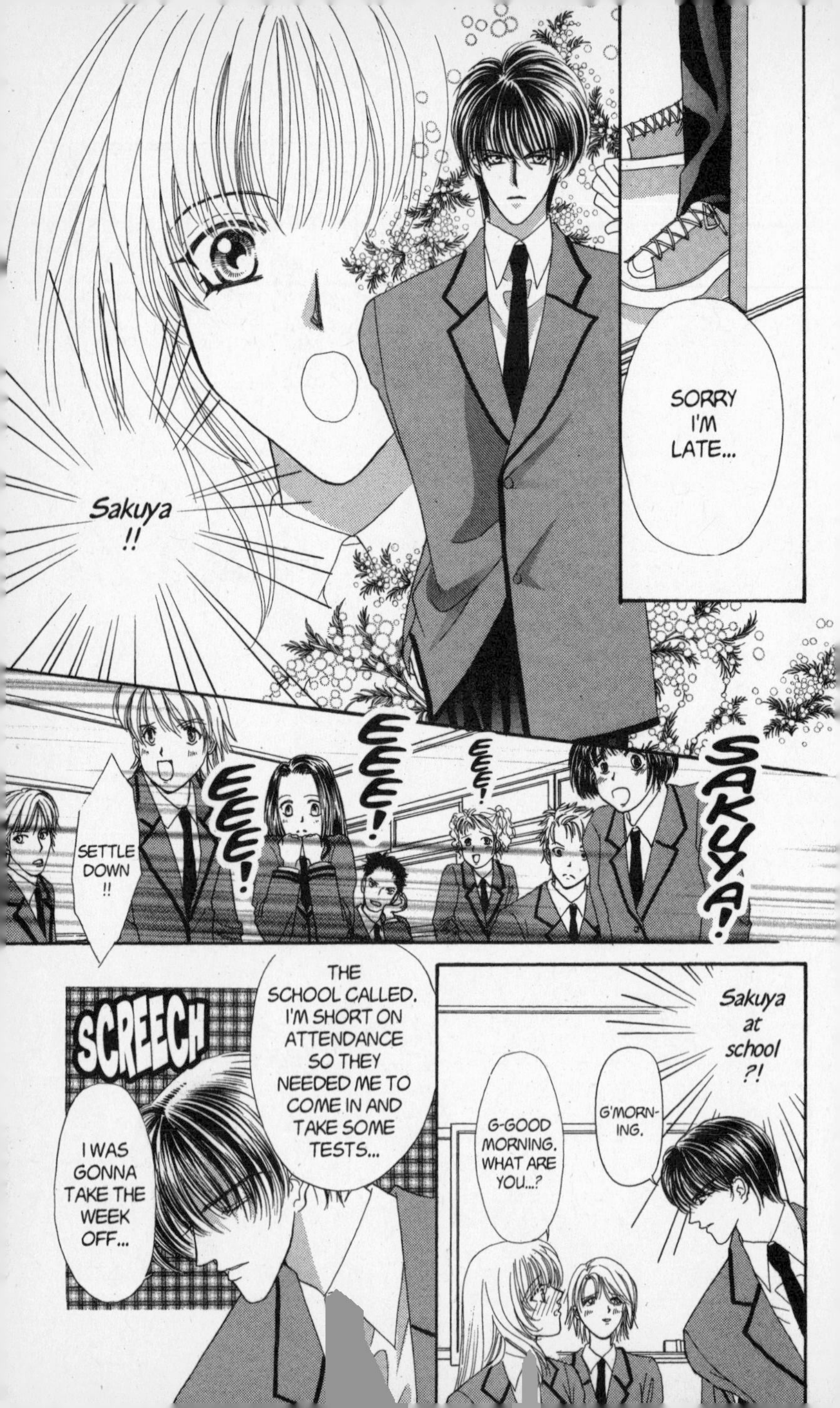
SORRY I'M LATE...
Sakuya !!
SAKUYA!
EEE!
EEE!
EEE!
SETTLE DOWN !!
Sakuya at school ?!
G'MORNING.
G-GOOD MORNING. WHAT ARE YOU...?
THE SCHOOL CALLED. I'M SHORT ON ATTENDANCE SO THEY NEEDED ME TO COME IN AND TAKE SOME TESTS...
SCREECH
I WAS GONNA TAKE THE WEEK OFF...

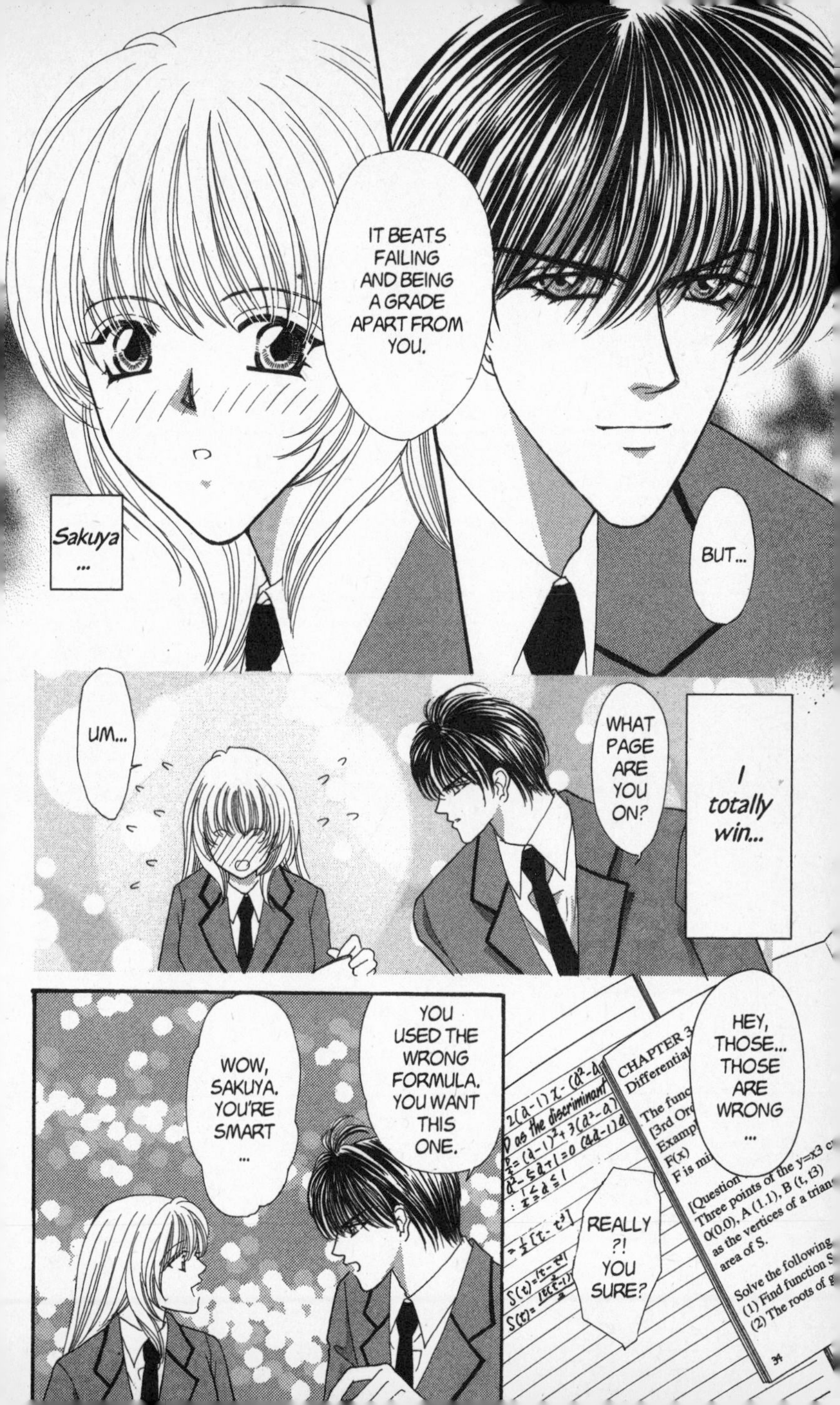
IT BEATS FAILING AND BEING A GRADE APART FROM YOU.
BUT...
Sakuya ...
I totally win...
WHAT PAGE ARE YOU ON?
UM...
HEY, THOSE... THOSE ARE WRONG ...
REALLY ?! YOU SURE?
YOU USED THE WRONG FORMULA. YOU WANT THIS ONE.
WOW, SAKUYA. YOU'RE SMART ...

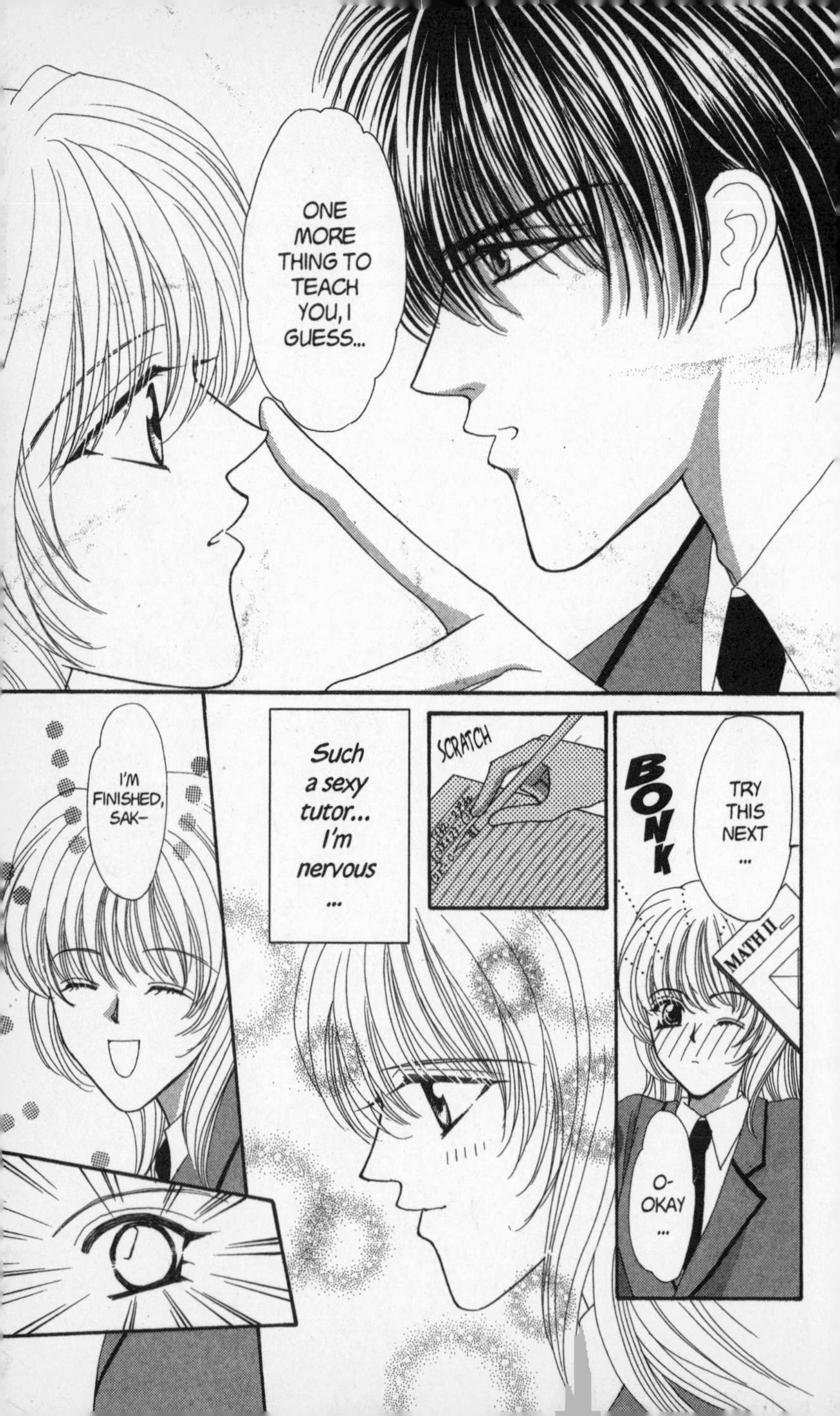
ONE MORE THING TO TEACH YOU, I GUESS...
TRY THIS NEXT ...
BONK
MATH II
O-OKAY ...
SCRATCH
Such a sexy tutor... I'm nervous ...
I'M FINISHED, SAK-

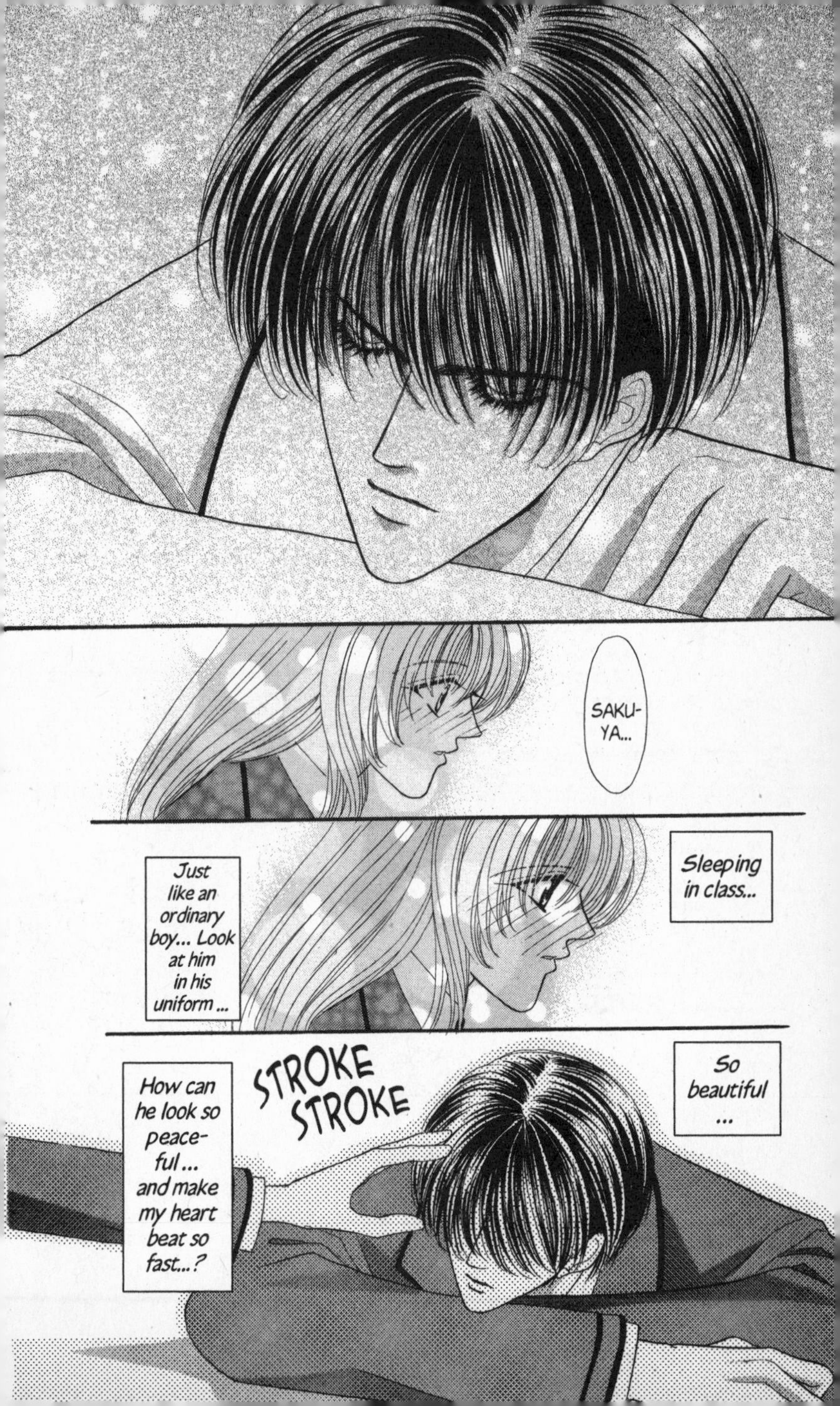
SAKU-YA...
Sleeping in class...
Just like an ordinary boy... Look at him in his uniform ...
So beautiful ...
STROKE STROKE
How can he look so peace-ful ... and make my heart beat so fast...?

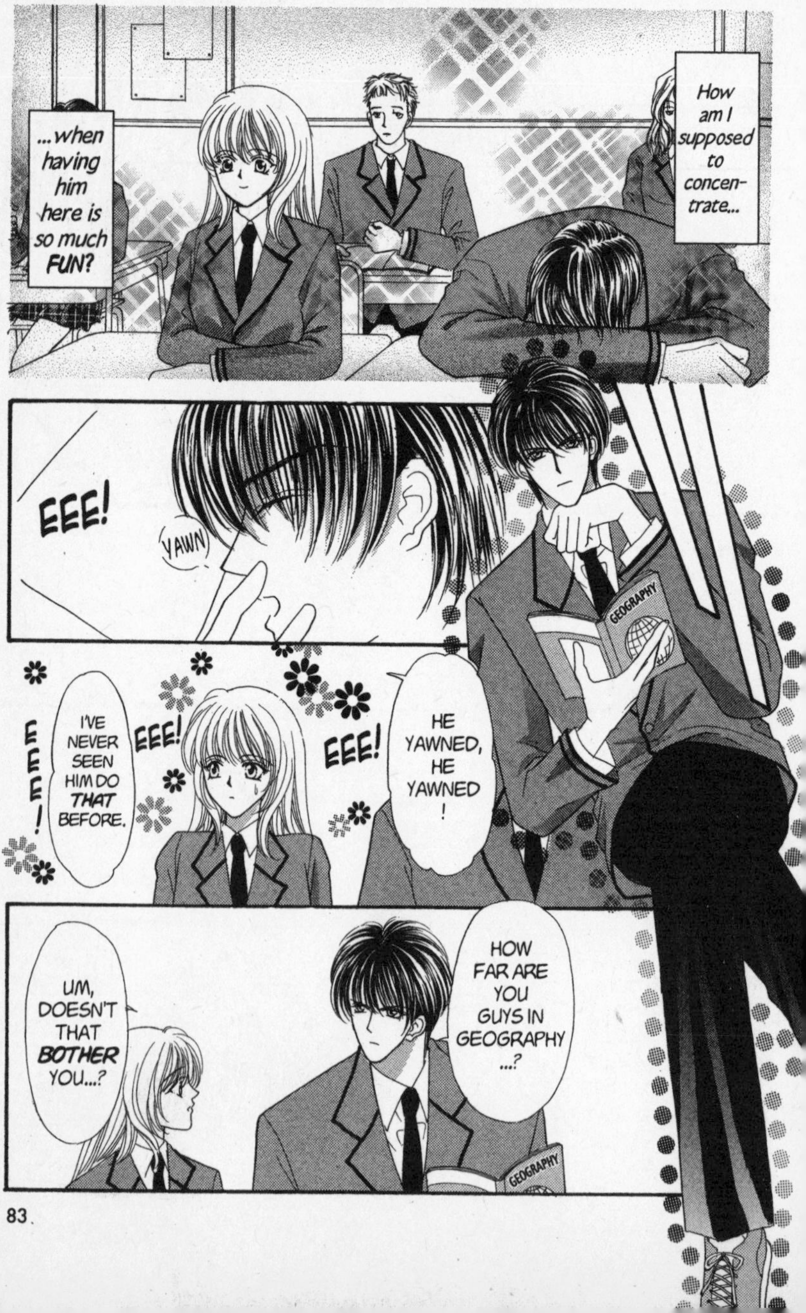
How am I supposed to concentrate...
...when having him here is so much FUN?
EEE!
YAWN
GEOGRAPHY
HE YAWNED, HE YAWNED!
EEE!
EEE!
I'VE NEVER SEEN HIM DO THAT BEFORE.
EEE!
HOW FAR ARE YOU GUYS IN GEOGRAPHY ...?
UM, DOESN'T THAT BOTHER YOU...?
GEOGRAPHY

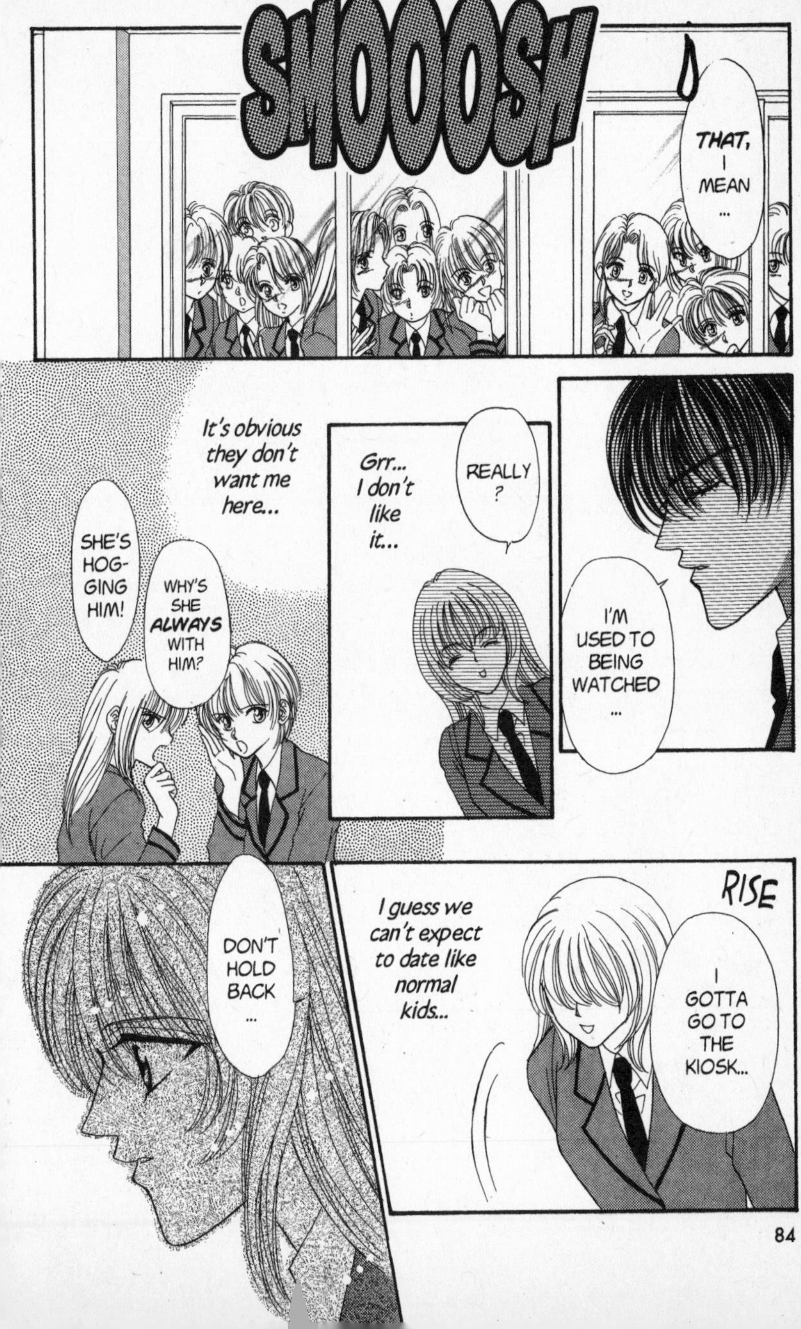

SHOOOSH
THAT, I MEAN ...
I'M USED TO BEING WATCHED ...
REALLY?
Grr... I don't like it...
It's obvious they don't want me here...
WHY'S SHE ALWAYS WITH HIM?
SHE'S HOGGING HIM!
RISE
I GOTTA GO TO THE KIOSK...
I guess we can't expect to date like normal kids...
DON'T HOLD BACK ...

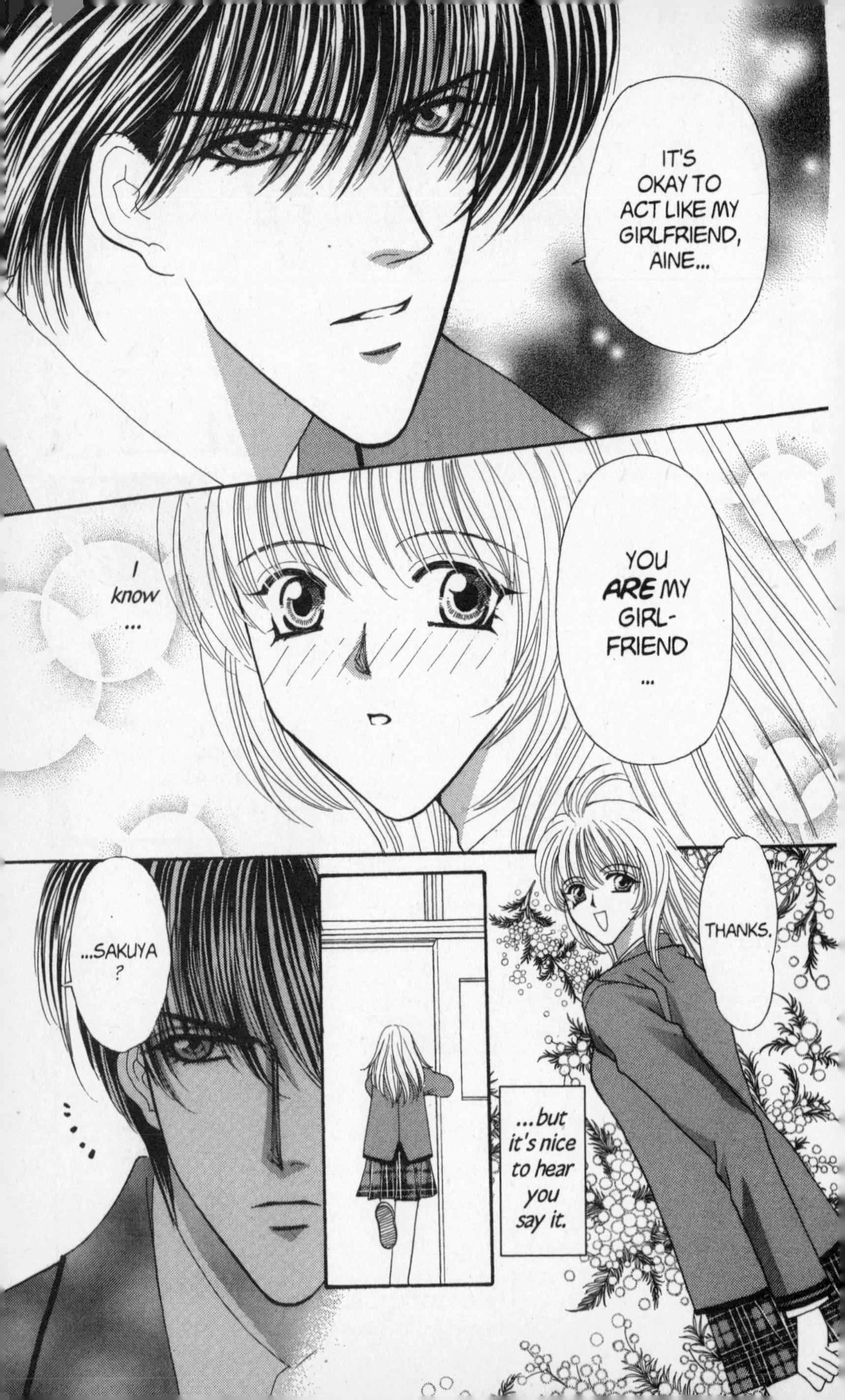
IT'S OKAY TO ACT LIKE MY GIRLFRIEND, AINE...
YOU **ARE** MY GIRLFRIEND ...
I know ...
THANKS.
...but it's nice to hear you say it.
...SAKUYA?
...

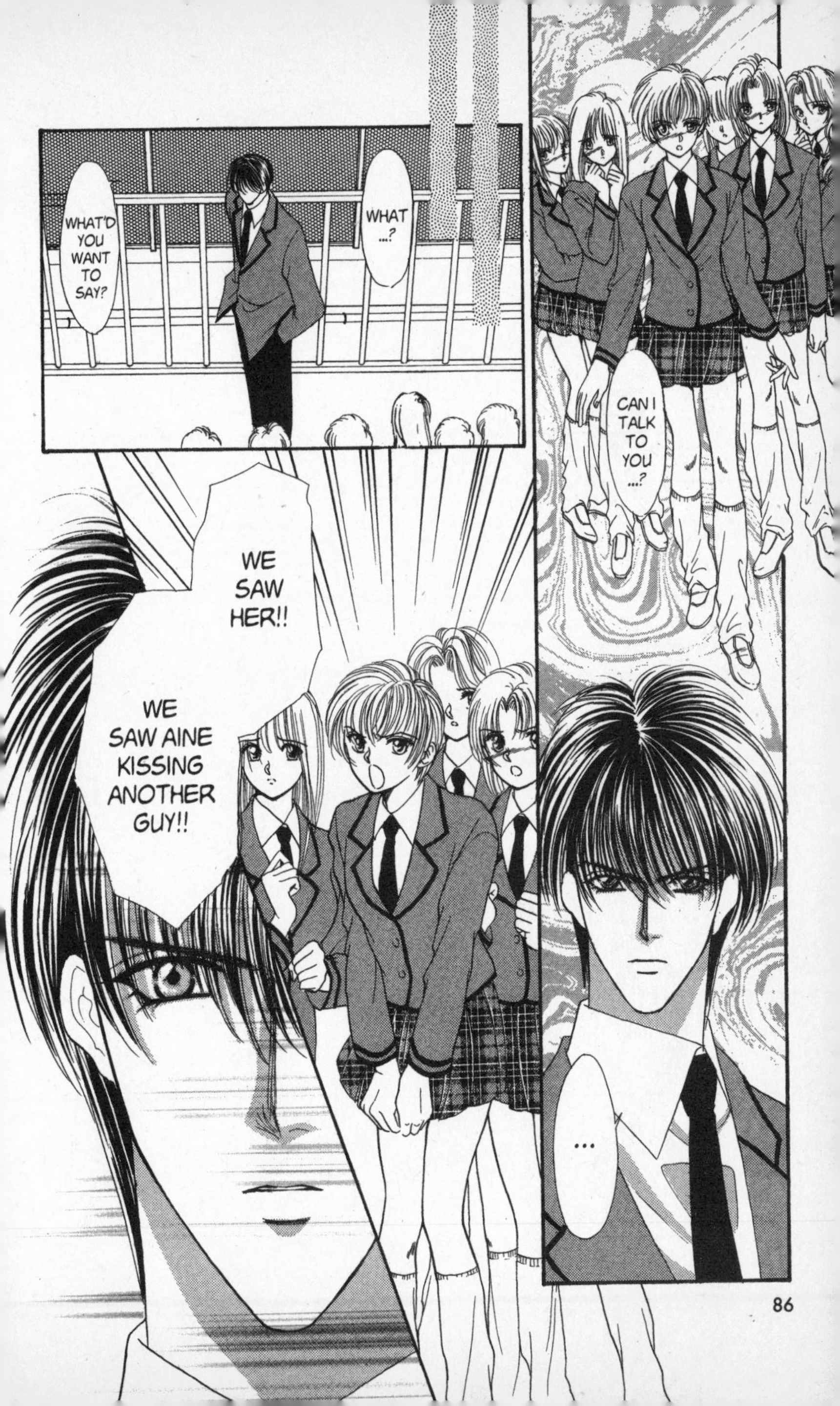

CAN I TALK TO YOU ...?
...
WHAT ...?
WHAT'D YOU WANT TO SAY?
WE SAW HER!!
WE SAW AINE KISSING ANOTHER GUY!!

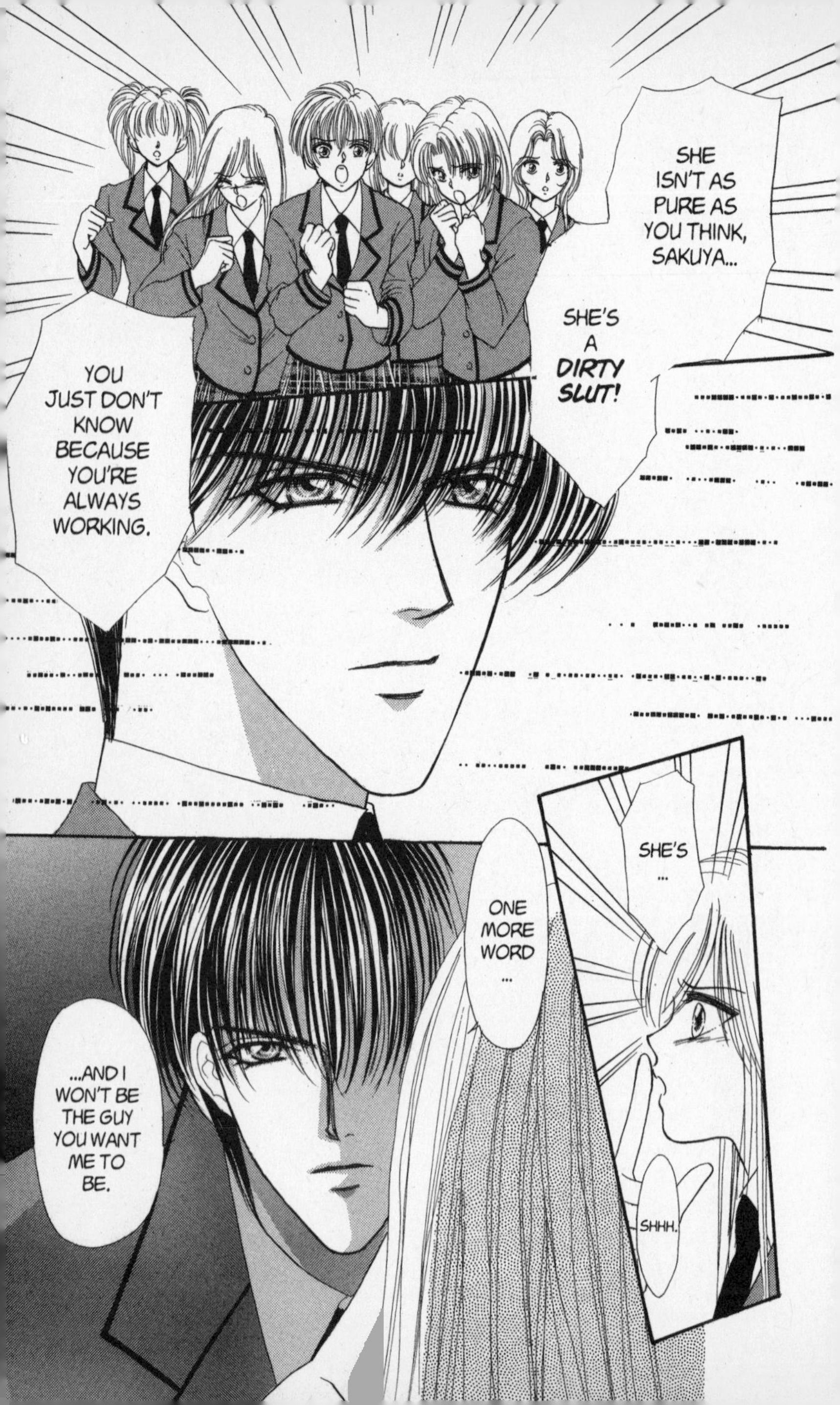
SHE ISN'T AS PURE AS YOU THINK, SAKUYA...
SHE'S A **DIRTY SLUT!**
YOU JUST DON'T KNOW BECAUSE YOU'RE ALWAYS WORKING.
SHE'S ...
SHHH.
ONE MORE WORD ...
...AND I WON'T BE THE GUY YOU WANT ME TO BE.

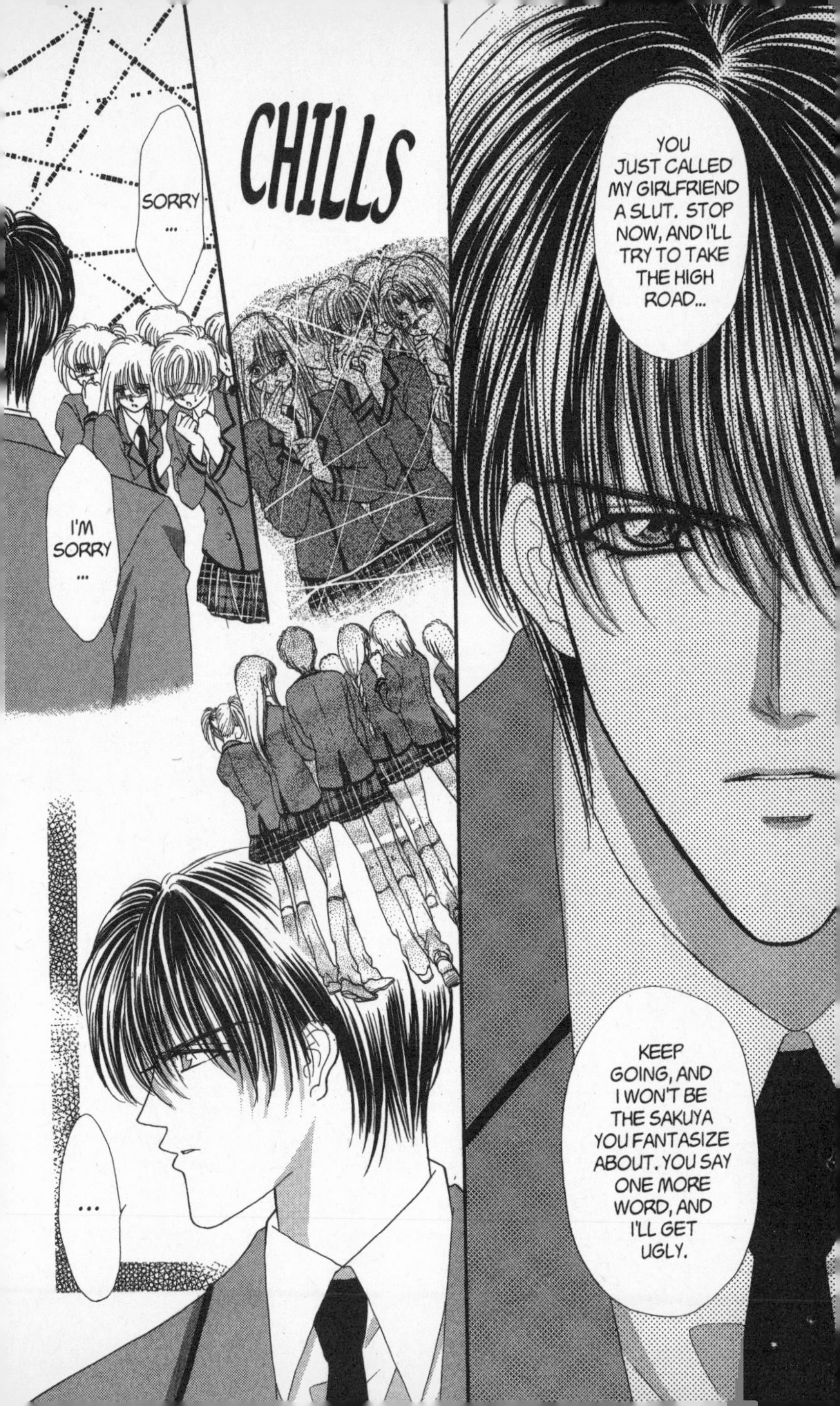
YOU JUST CALLED MY GIRLFRIEND A SLUT. STOP NOW, AND I'LL TRY TO TAKE THE HIGH ROAD...
KEEP GOING, AND I WON'T BE THE SAKUYA YOU FANTASIZE ABOUT. YOU SAY ONE MORE WORD, AND I'LL GET UGLY.
CHILLS
SORRY ...
I'M SORRY ...
...

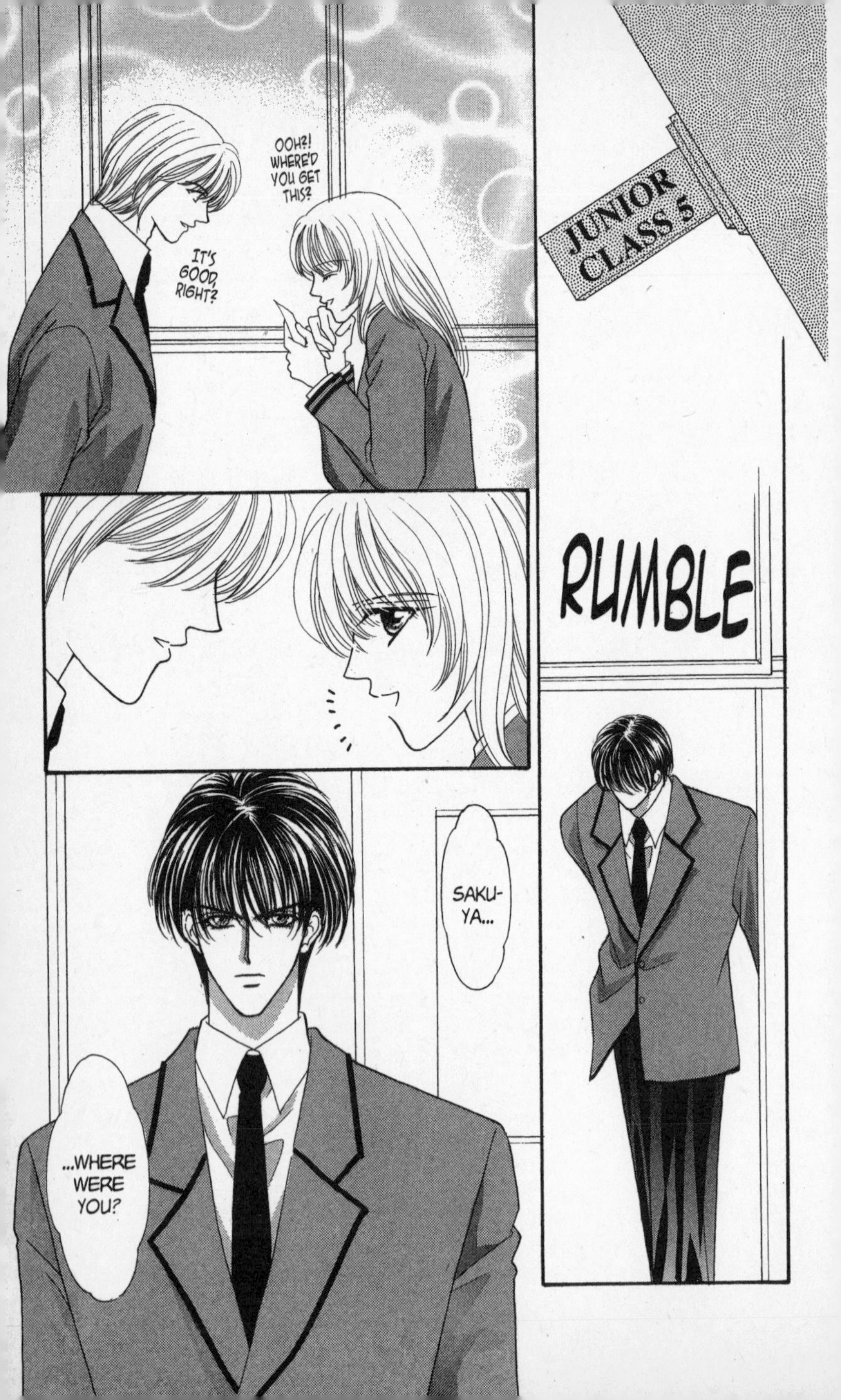
JUNIOR CLASS 5
OOH?! WHERE'D YOU GET THIS?
IT'S GOOD, RIGHT?
RUMBLE
SAKU-YA...
...WHERE WERE YOU?

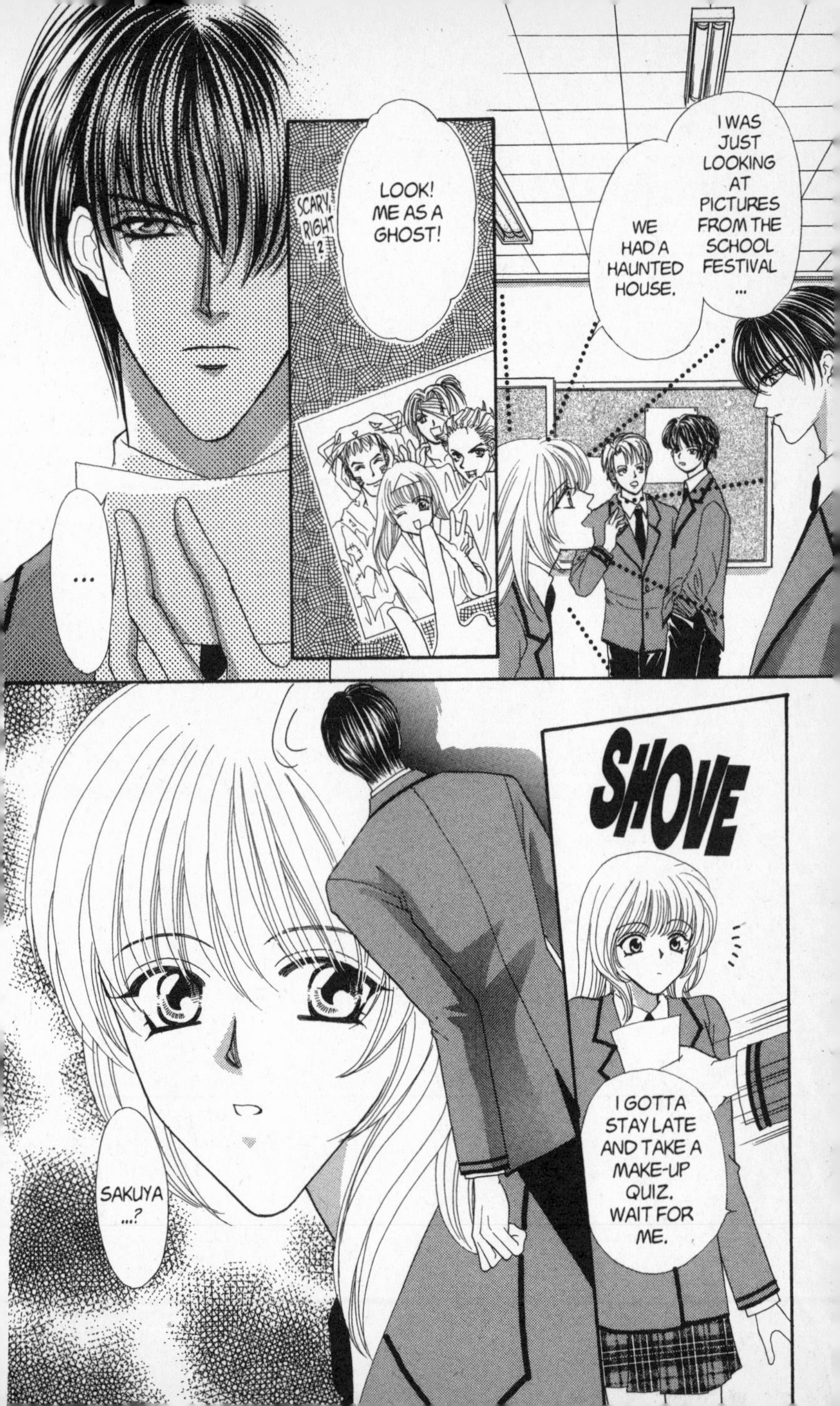
I WAS JUST LOOKING AT PICTURES FROM THE SCHOOL FESTIVAL ...
WE HAD A HAUNTED HOUSE.
LOOK! ME AS A GHOST!
SCARY, RIGHT?
...
SHOVE
I GOTTA STAY LATE AND TAKE A MAKE-UP QUIZ. WAIT FOR ME.
SAKUYA ...?

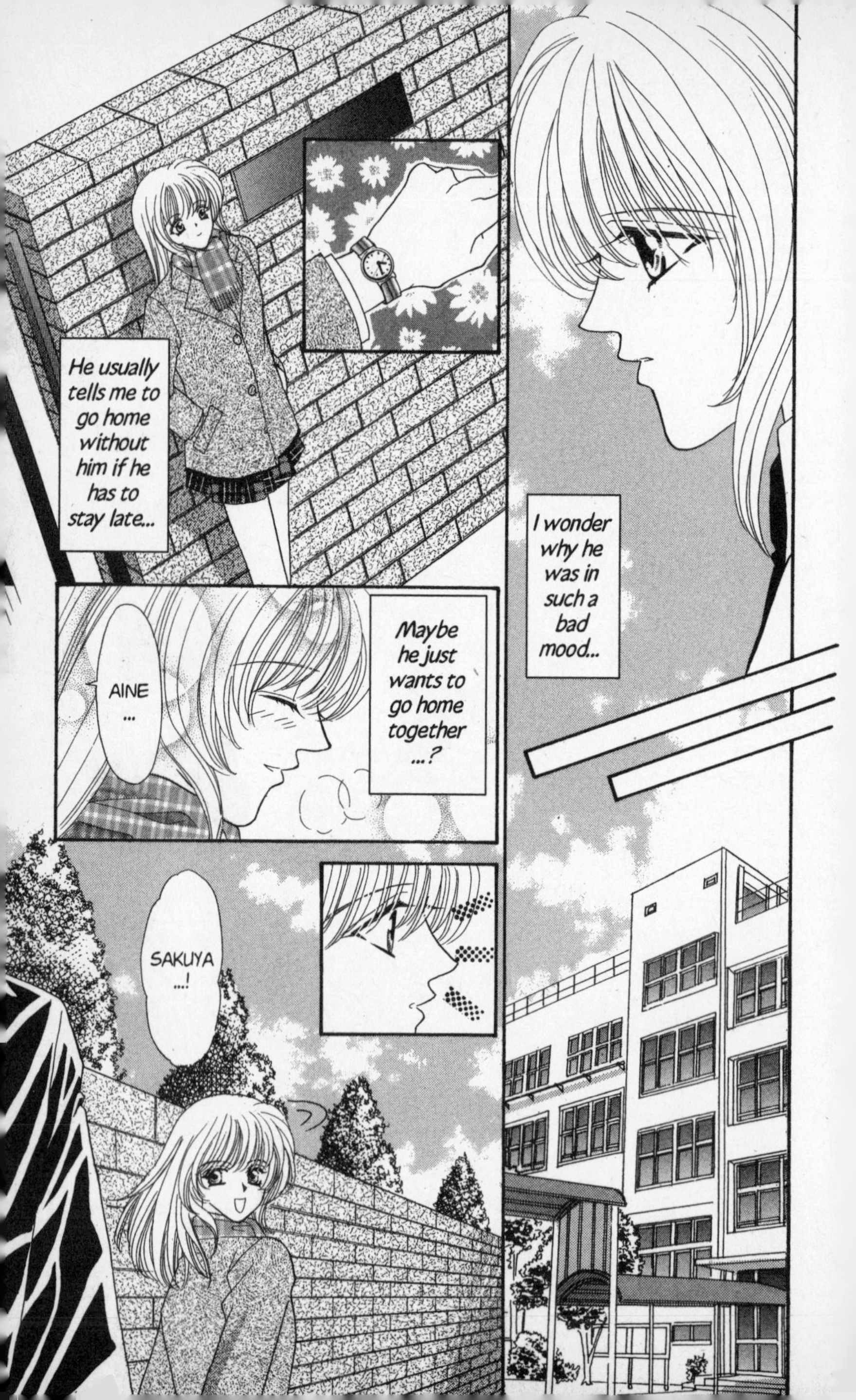
I wonder why he was in such a bad mood...
He usually tells me to go home without him if he has to stay late...
Maybe he just wants to go home together ...?
AINE ...
SAKUYA ...!

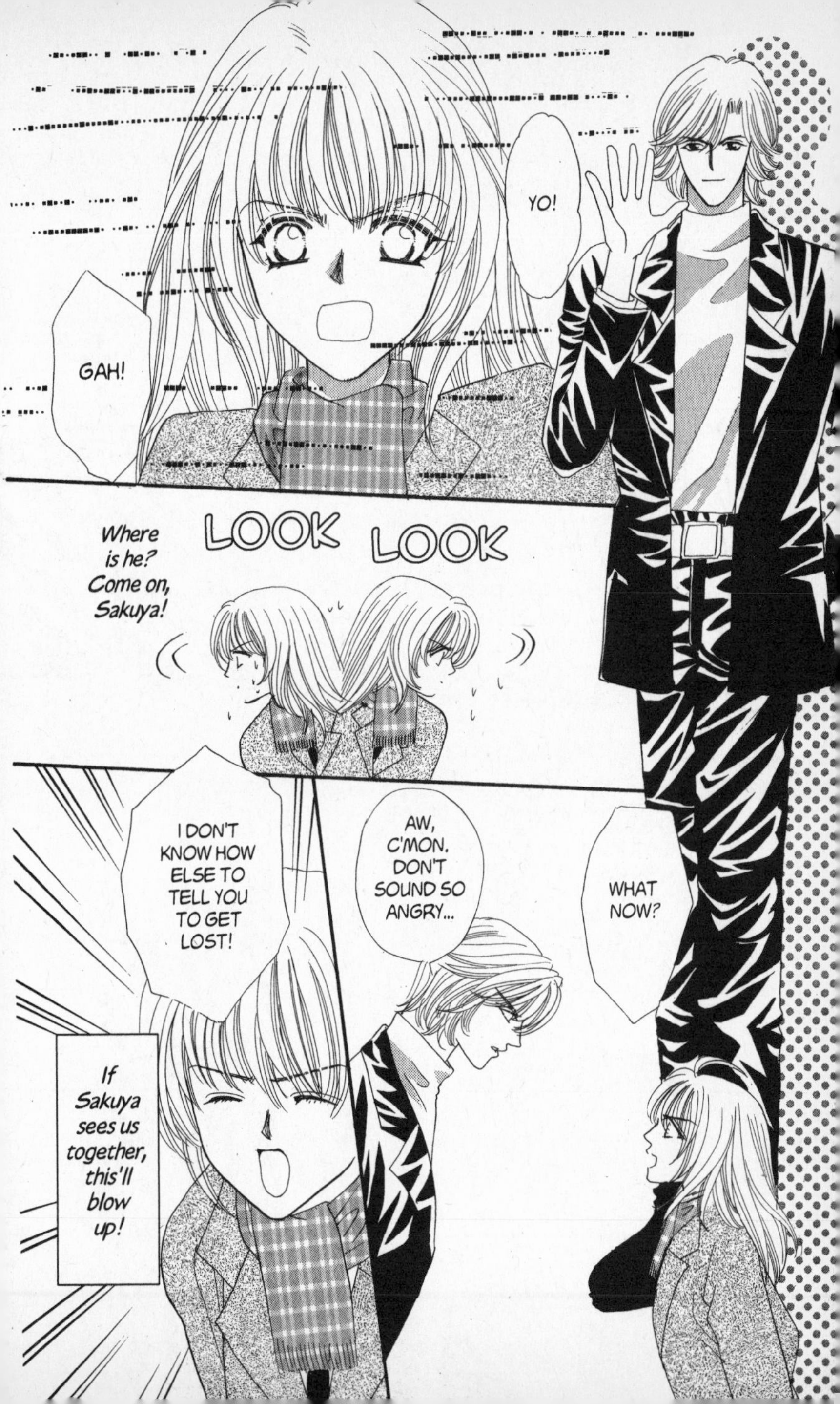
YO!
GAH!
LOOK LOOK
Where is he? Come on, Sakuya!
WHAT NOW?
AW, C'MON. DON'T SOUND SO ANGRY...
I DON'T KNOW HOW ELSE TO TELL YOU TO GET LOST!
If Sakuya sees us together, this'll blow up!

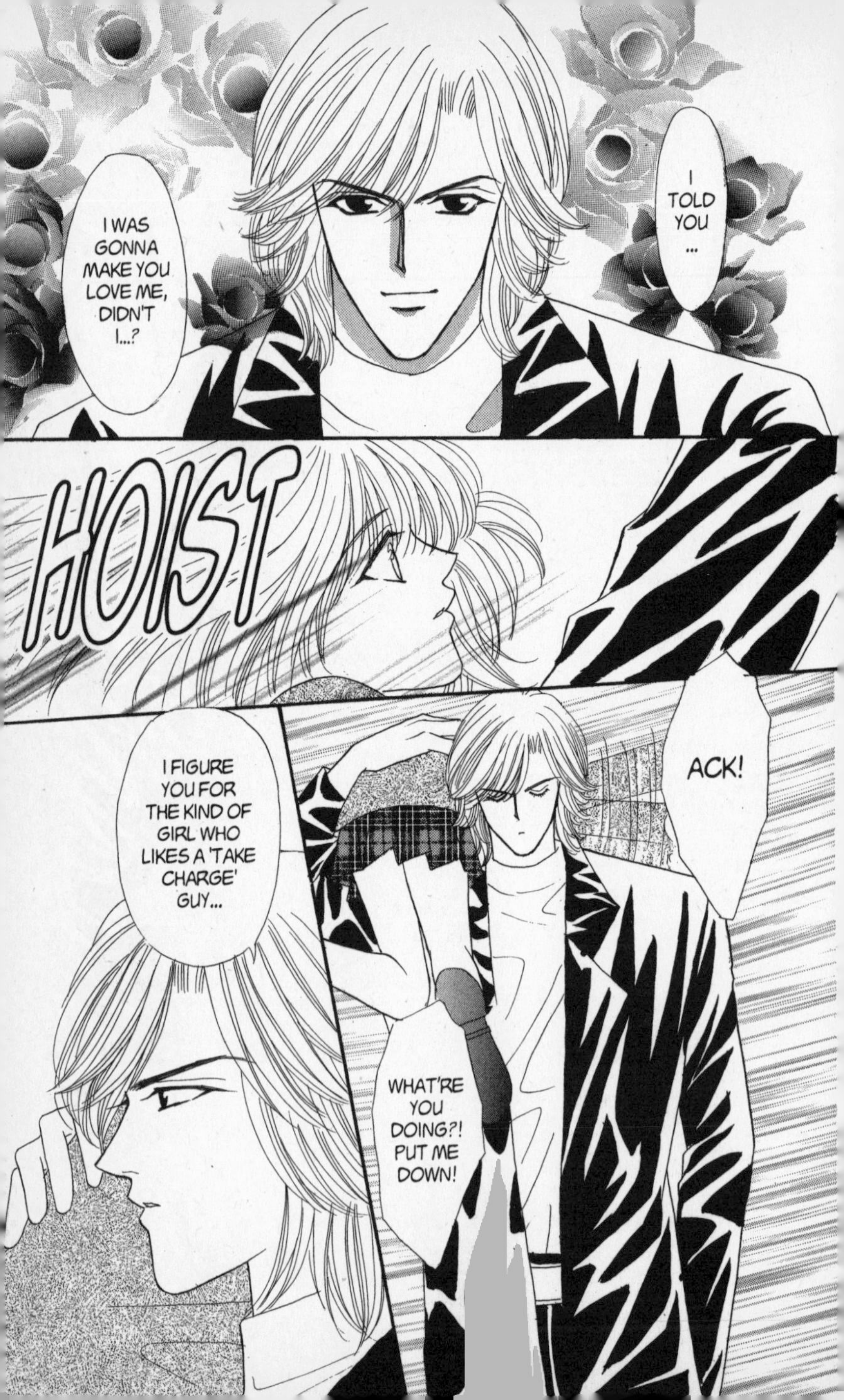
I TOLD YOU ...
I WAS GONNA MAKE YOU LOVE ME, DIDN'T I...?
HOIST
ACK!
WHAT'RE YOU DOING?! PUT ME DOWN!
I FIGURE YOU FOR THE KIND OF GIRL WHO LIKES A 'TAKE CHARGE' GUY...

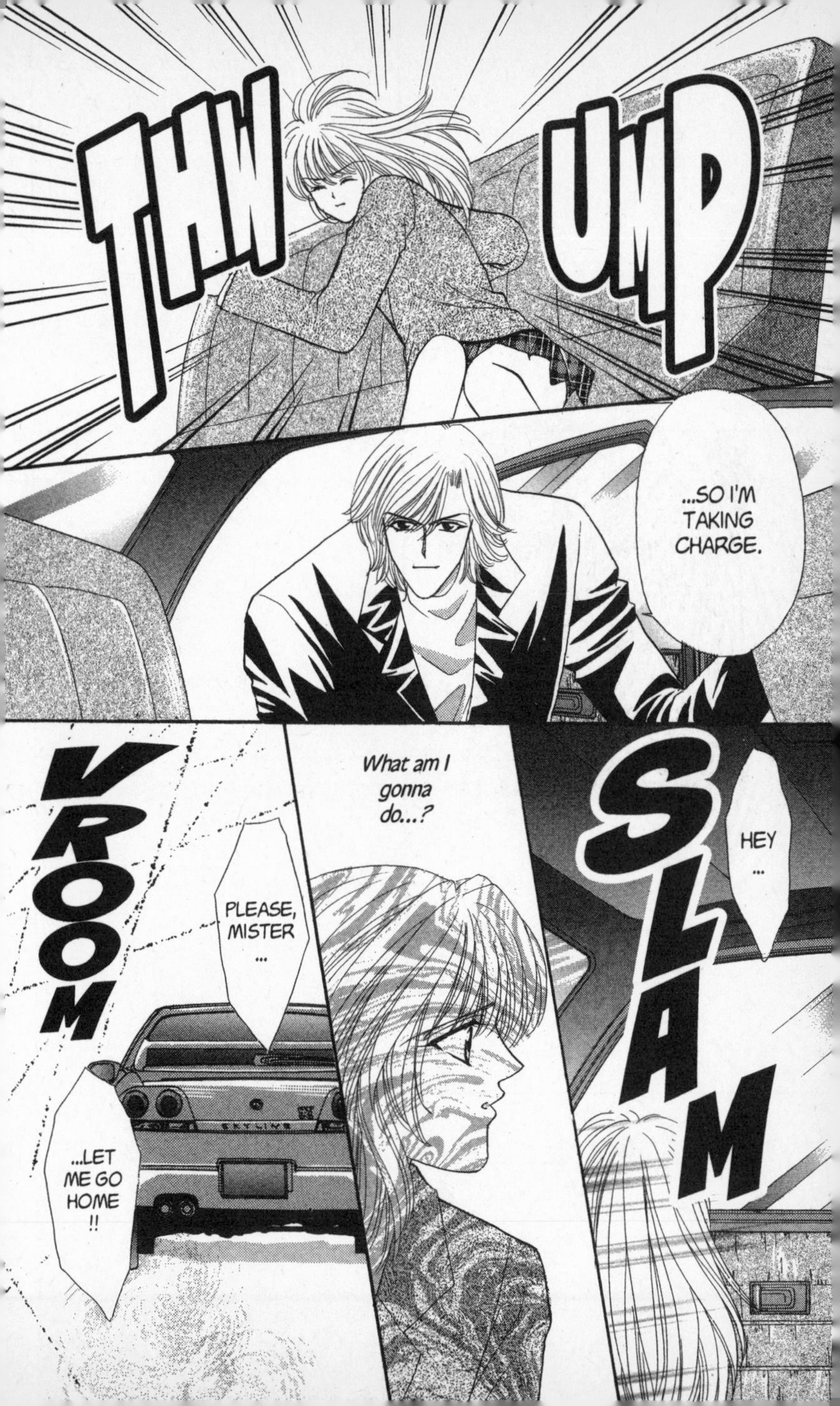
THWUMP
...SO I'M TAKING CHARGE.
SLAM
HEY ...
What am I gonna do...?
VROOM
PLEASE, MISTER ...
...LET ME GO HOME !!

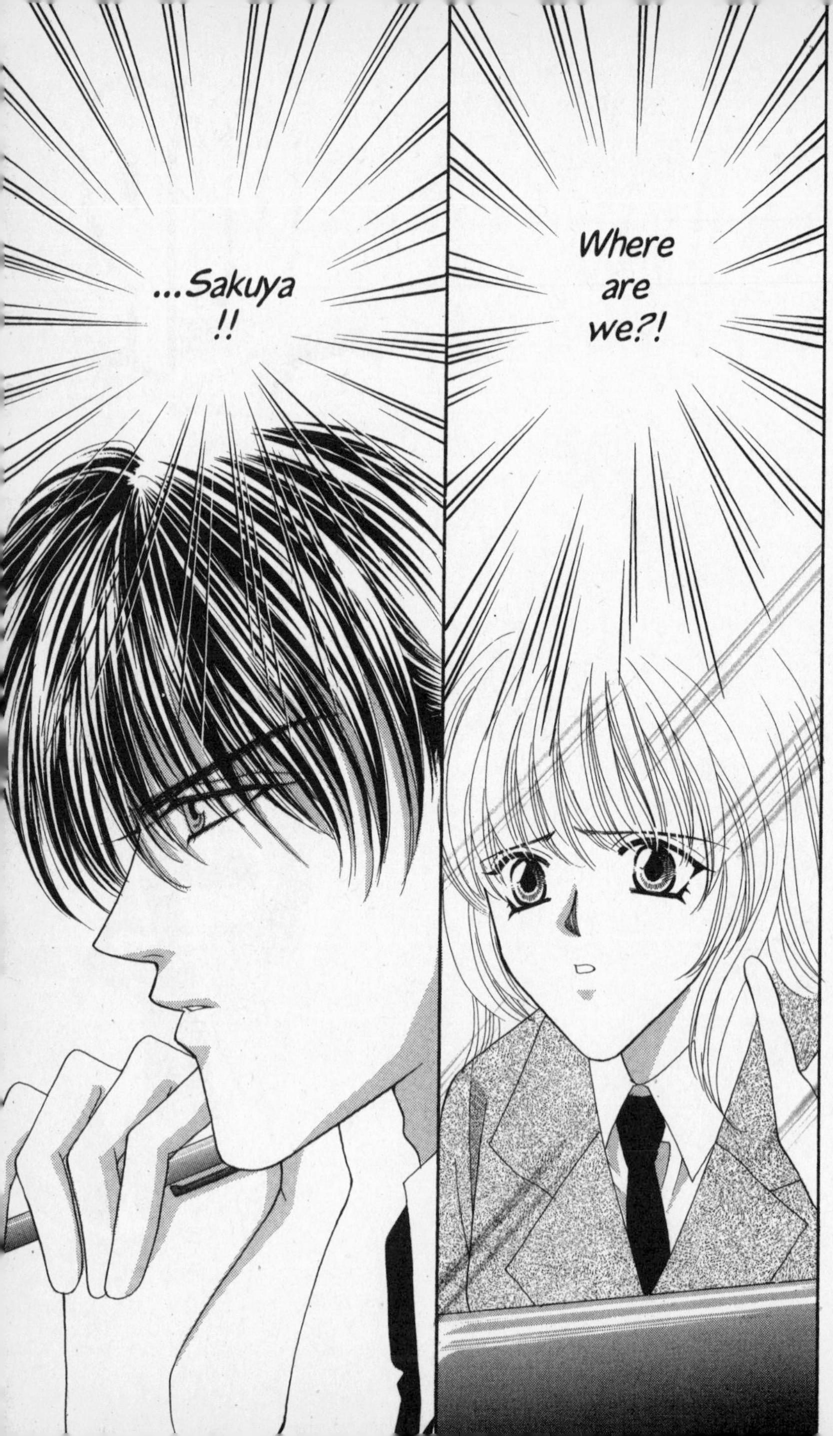
Where are we?!
...Sakuya !!

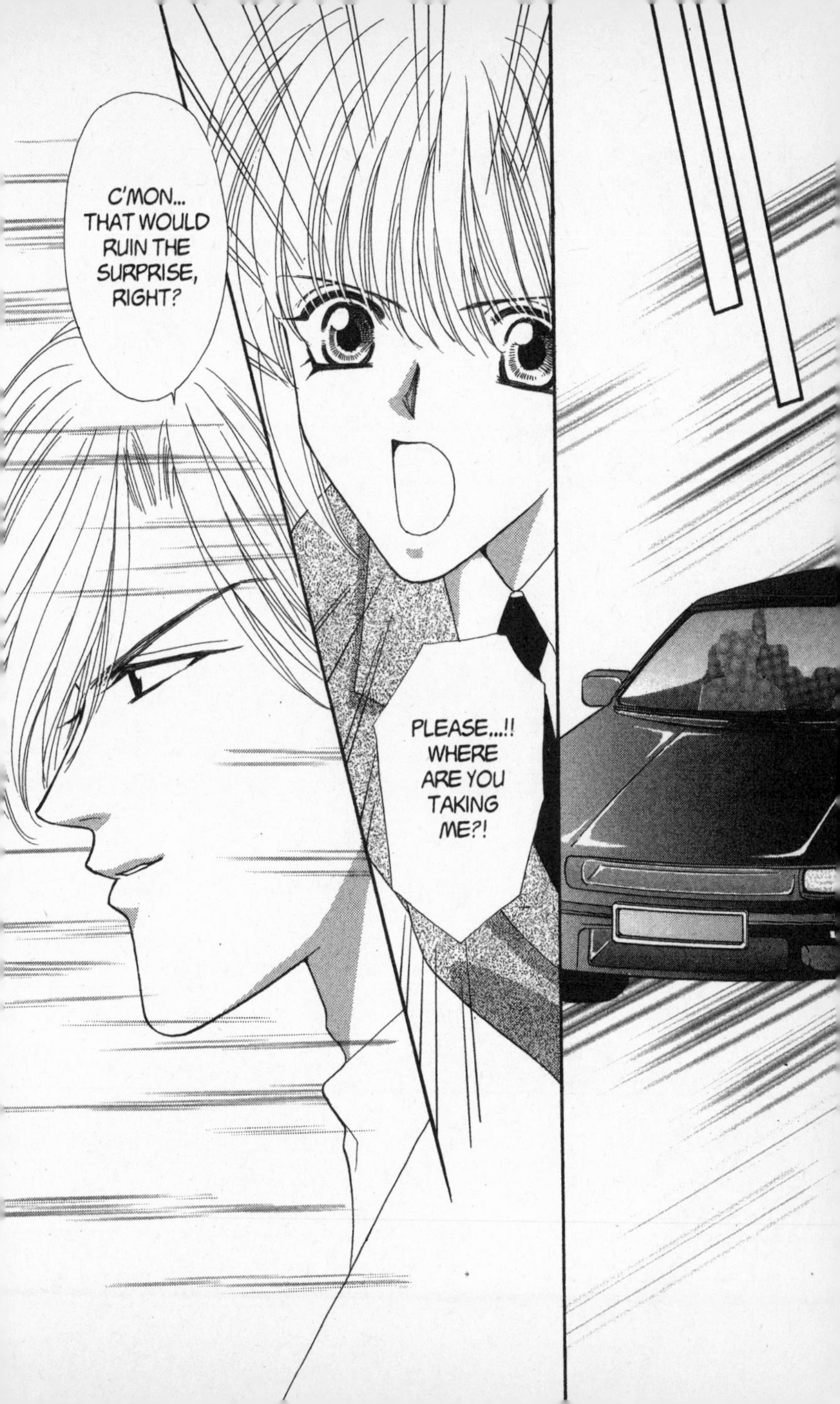
PLEASE...!! WHERE ARE YOU TAKING ME?!
C'MON... THAT WOULD RUIN THE SURPRISE, RIGHT?

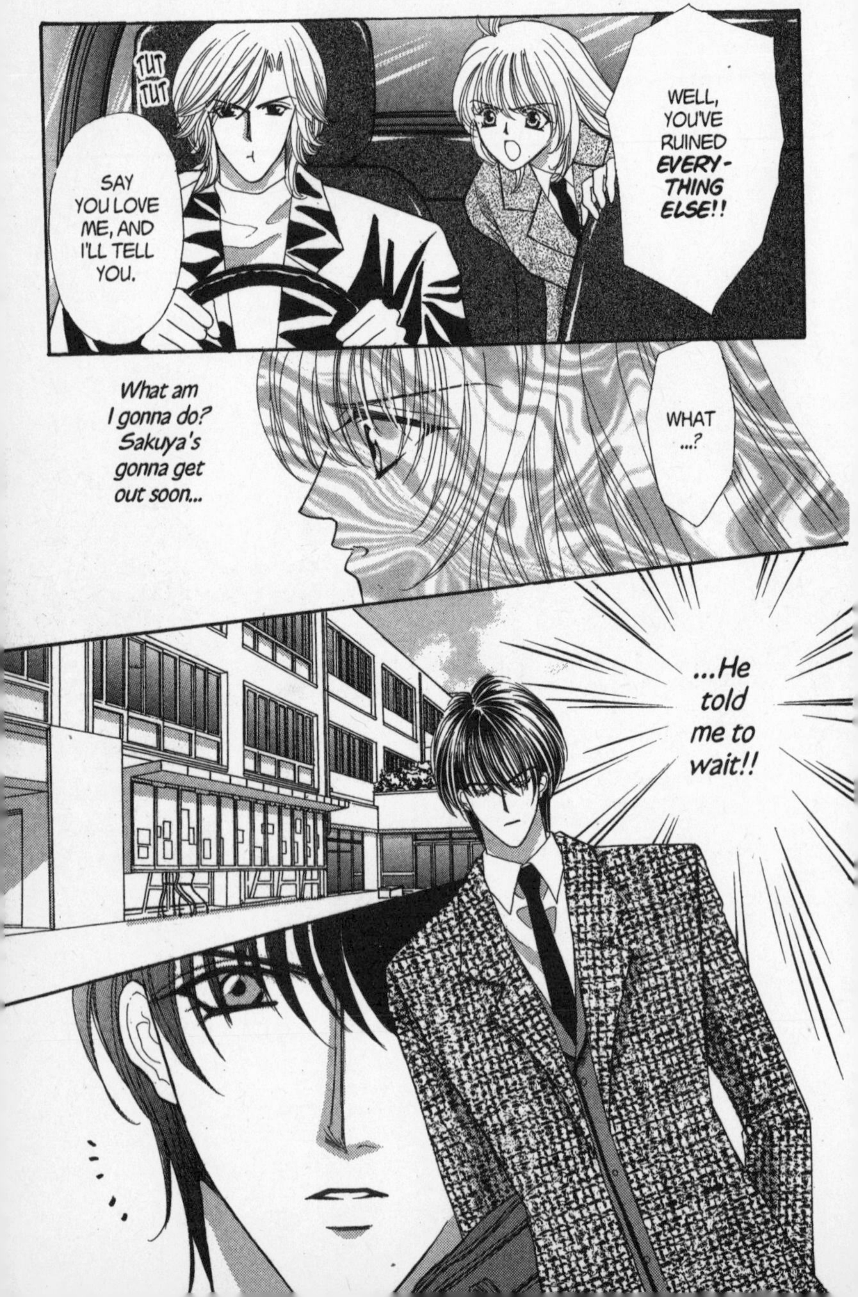

WELL, YOU'VE RUINED EVERY-THING ELSE!!
TUT TUT
SAY YOU LOVE ME, AND I'LL TELL YOU.
WHAT ...?
What am I gonna do? Sakuya's gonna get out soon...
...He told me to wait!!

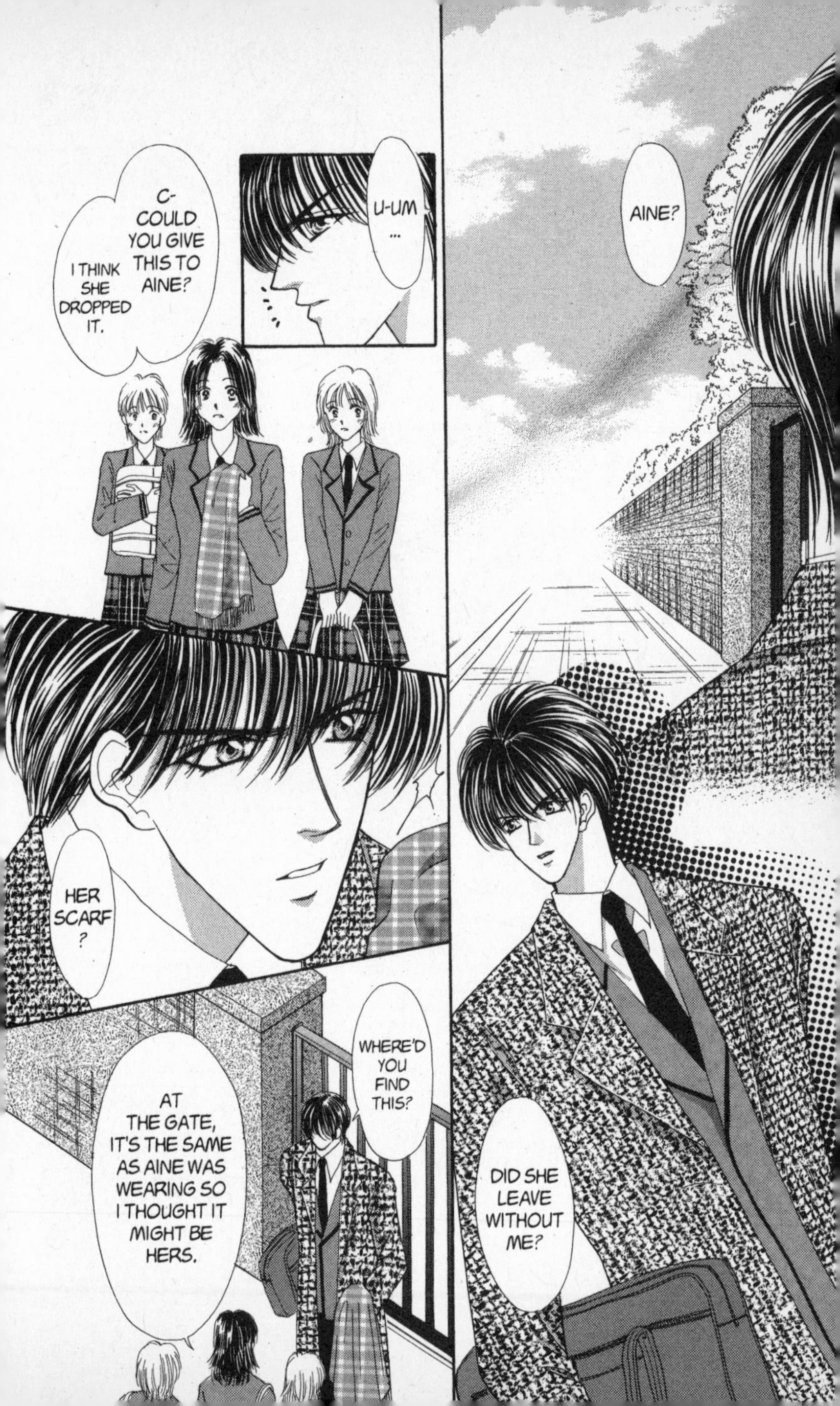
AINE?
DID SHE LEAVE WITHOUT ME?
U-UM ...
C- COULD YOU GIVE THIS TO AINE?
I THINK SHE DROPPED IT.
HER SCARF?
WHERE'D YOU FIND THIS?
AT THE GATE, IT'S THE SAME AS AINE WAS WEARING SO I THOUGHT IT MIGHT BE HERS.

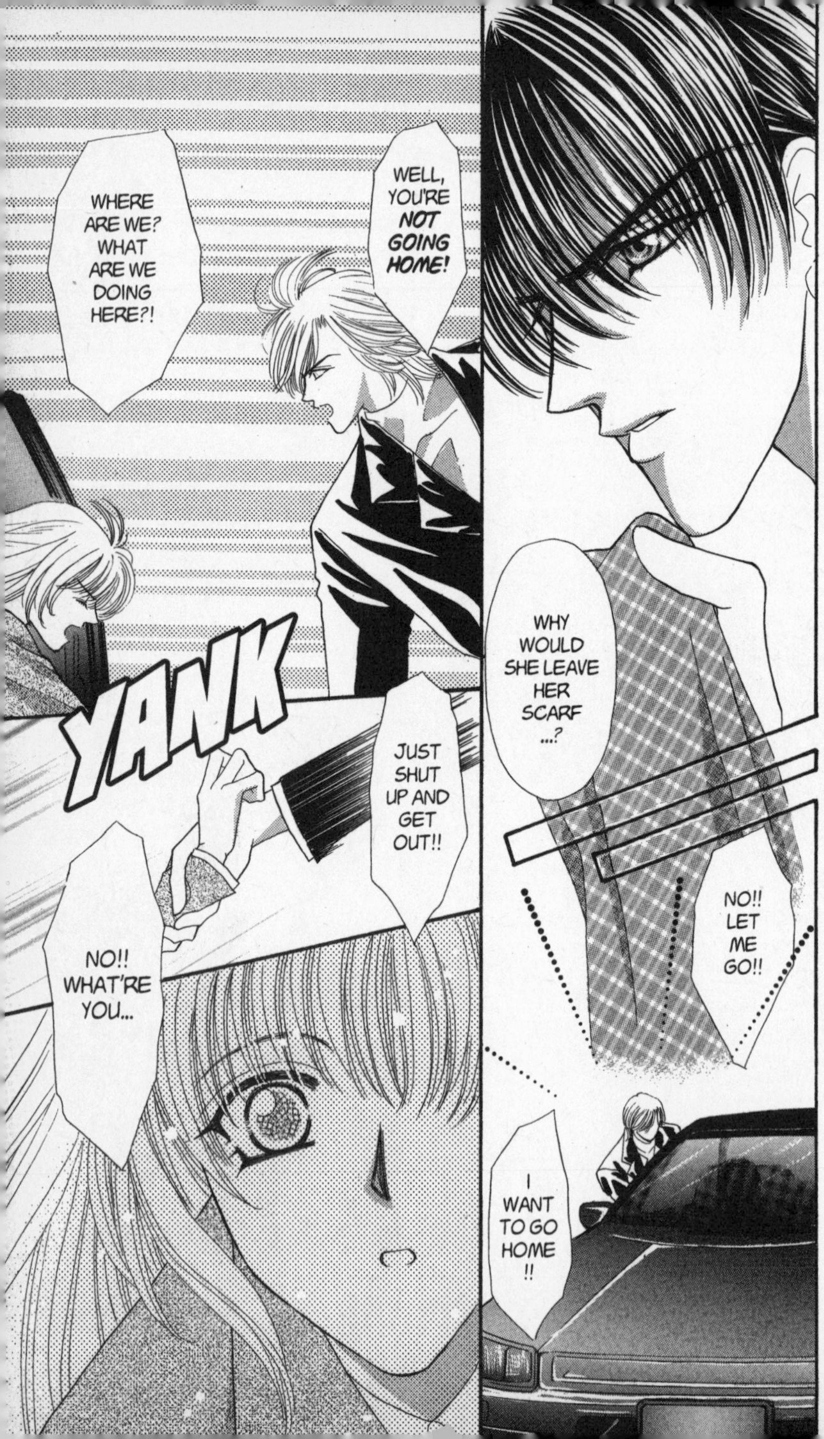
WHY WOULD SHE LEAVE HER SCARF ...?
NO!! LET ME GO!!
I WANT TO GO HOME !!
WELL, YOU'RE NOT GOING HOME!
WHERE ARE WE? WHAT ARE WE DOING HERE?!
YANK
JUST SHUT UP AND GET OUT!!
NO!! WHAT'RE YOU...

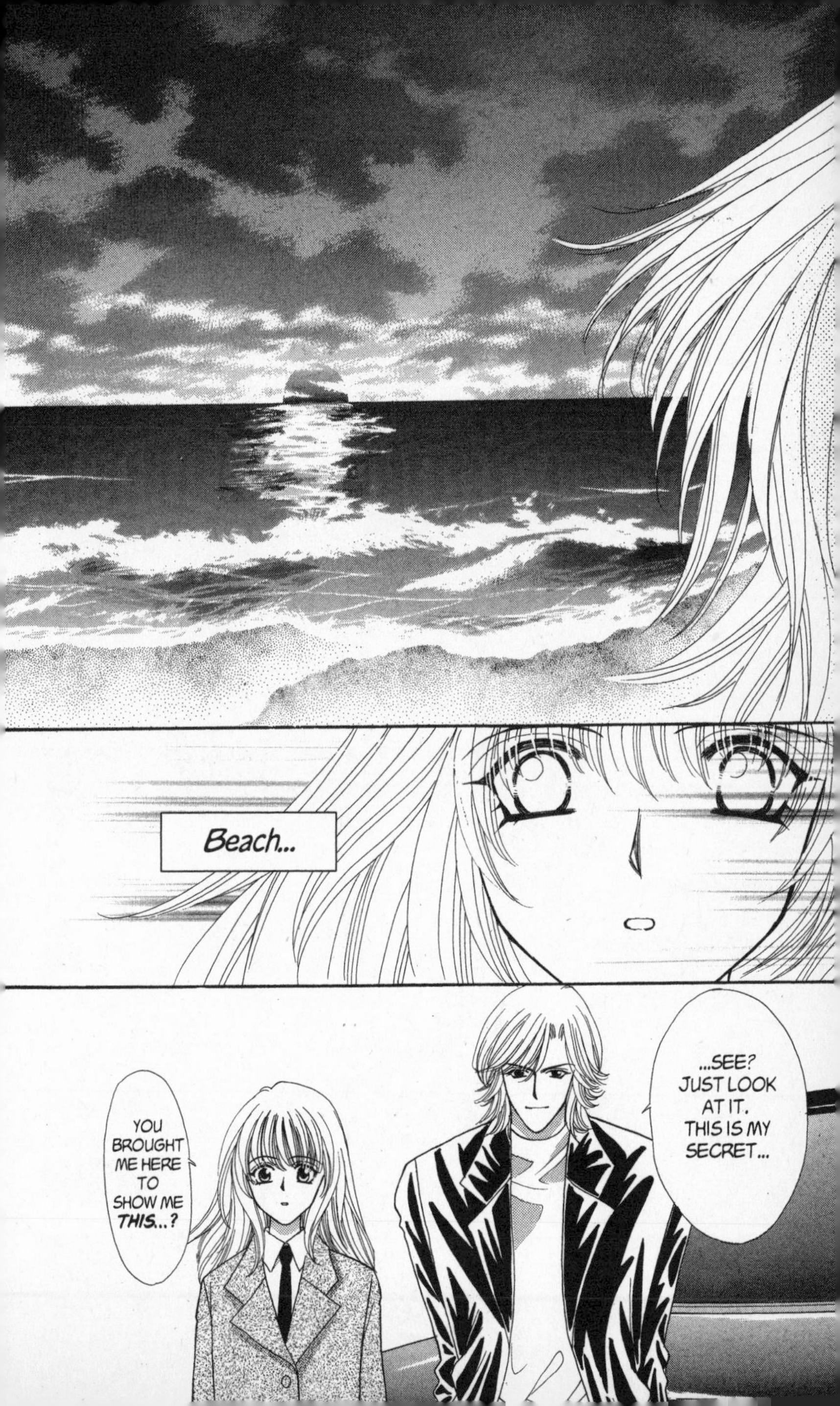
Beach...
...SEE? JUST LOOK AT IT. THIS IS MY SECRET...
YOU BROUGHT ME HERE TO SHOW ME *THIS*...?

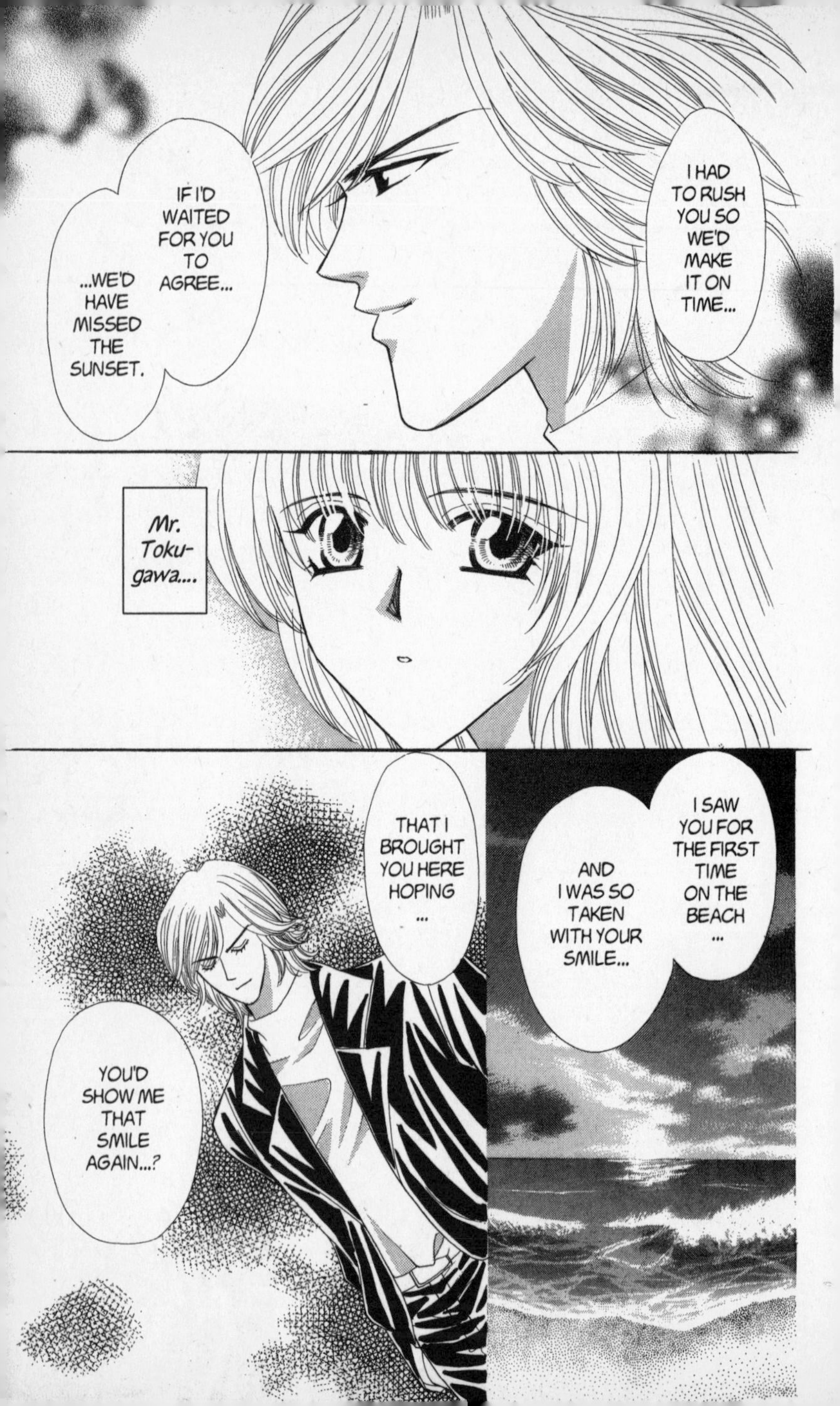
I HAD TO RUSH YOU SO WE'D MAKE IT ON TIME...
IF I'D WAITED FOR YOU TO AGREE...
...WE'D HAVE MISSED THE SUNSET.
Mr. Toku-gawa....
I SAW YOU FOR THE FIRST TIME ON THE BEACH ...
AND I WAS SO TAKEN WITH YOUR SMILE...
THAT I BROUGHT YOU HERE HOPING ...
YOU'D SHOW ME THAT SMILE AGAIN...?

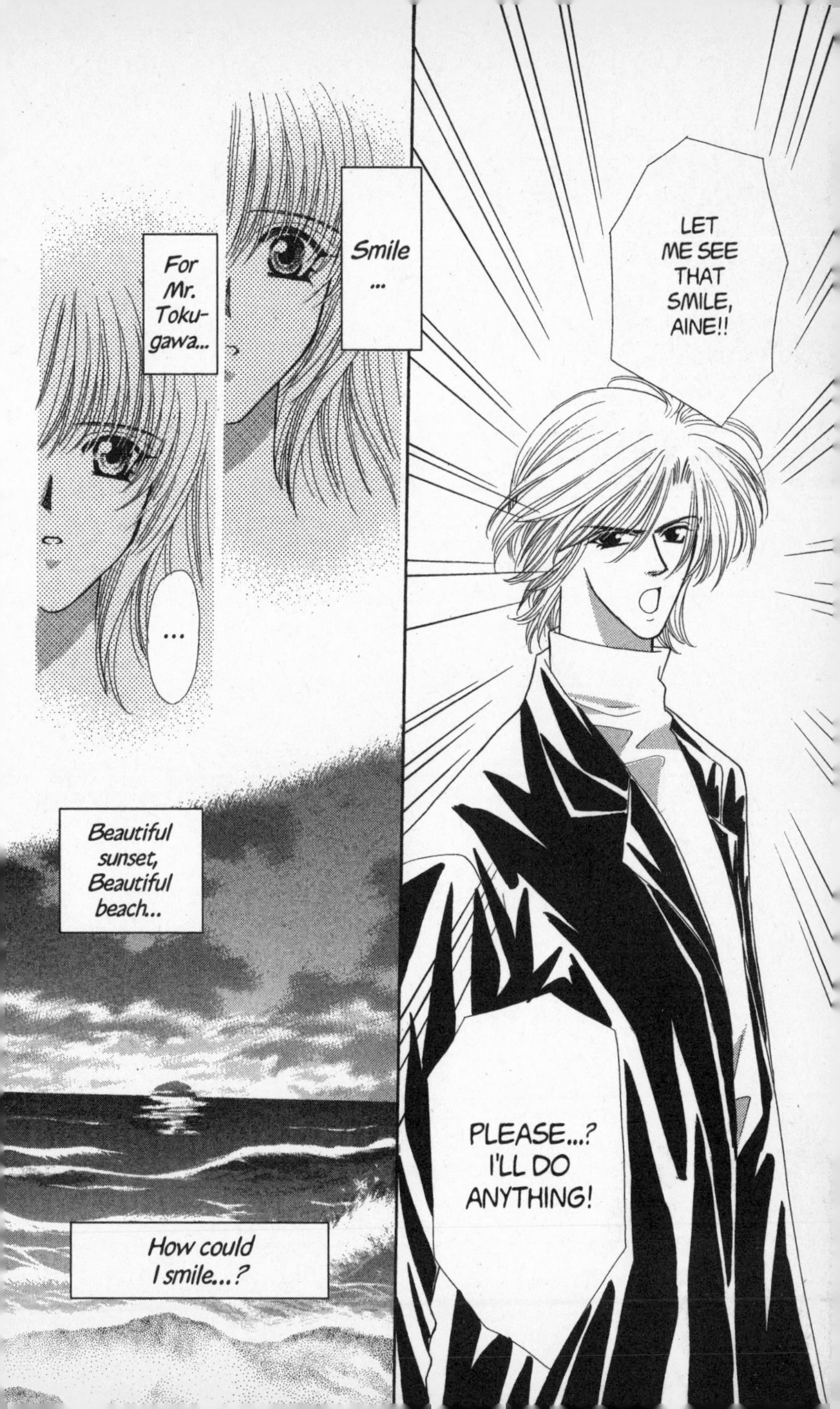
LET ME SEE THAT SMILE, AINE!!
PLEASE...? I'LL DO ANYTHING!
Smile ...
For Mr. Toku-gawa...
...
Beautiful sunset, Beautiful beach...
How could I smile...?

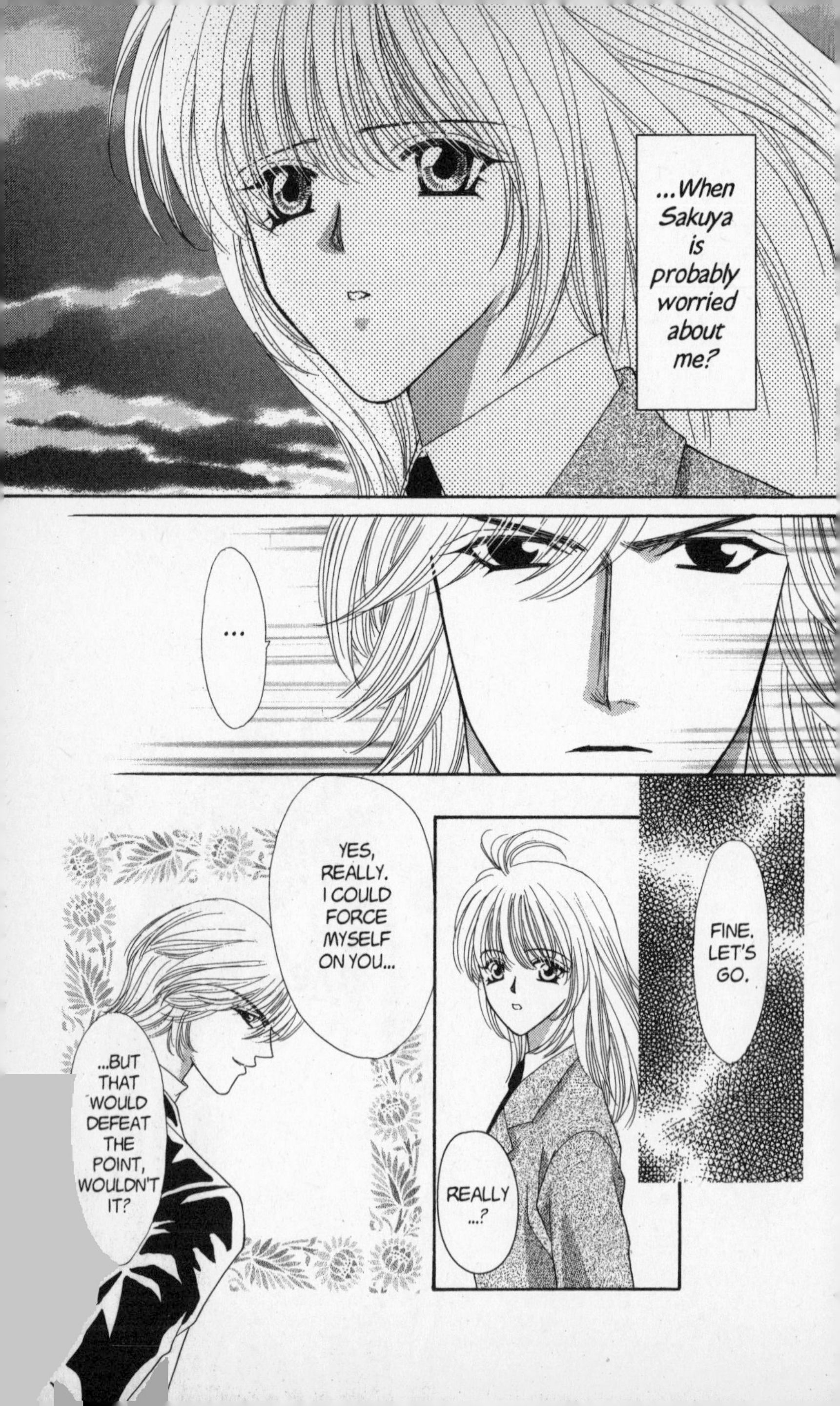
...When Sakuya is probably worried about me?
...
FINE. LET'S GO.
REALLY ...?
YES, REALLY. I COULD FORCE MYSELF ON YOU...
...BUT THAT WOULD DEFEAT THE POINT, WOULDN'T IT?

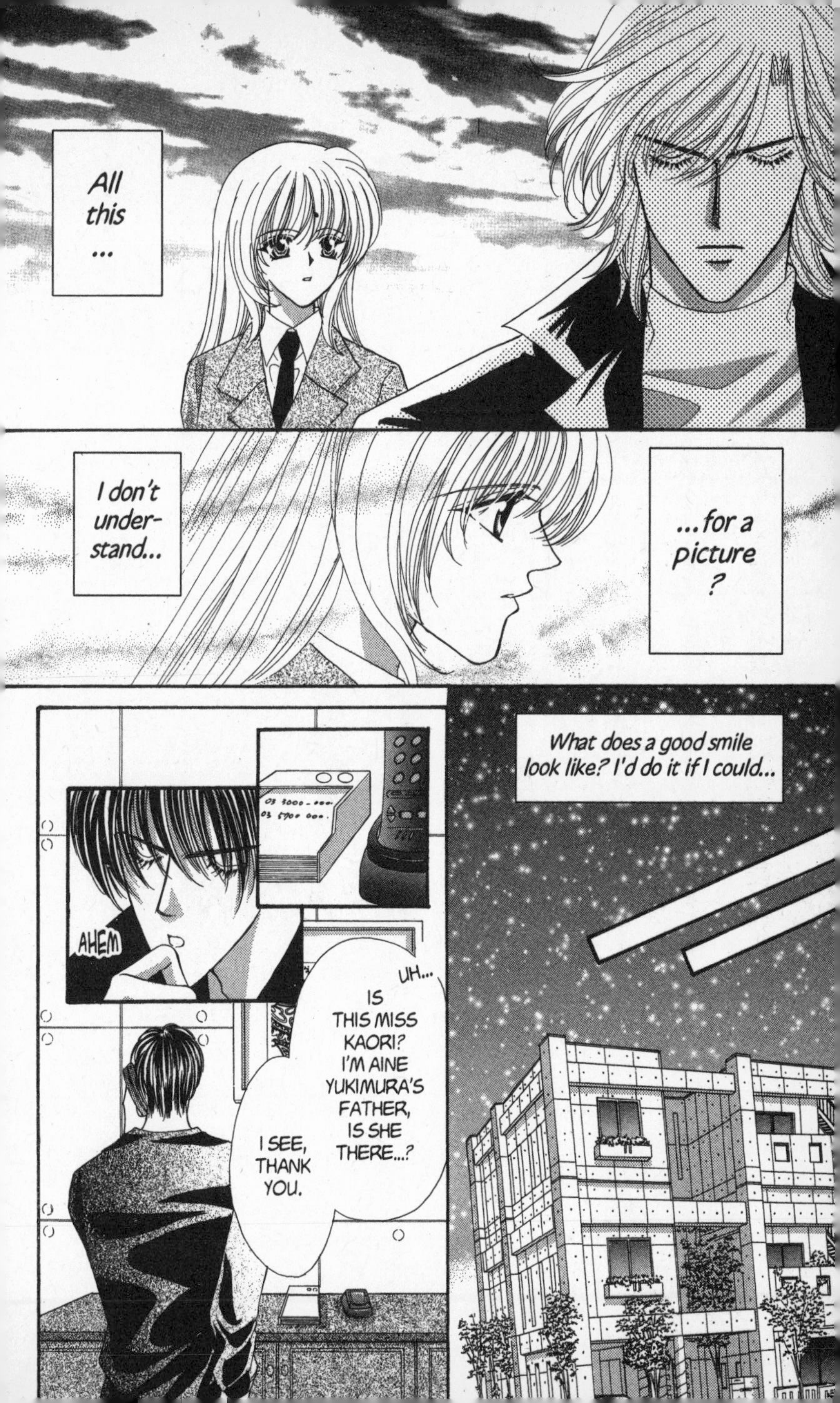
All this ...
...for a picture?
I don't understand...
What does a good smile look like? I'd do it if I could...
AHEM
UH...
IS THIS MISS KAORI? I'M AINE YUKIMURA'S FATHER, IS SHE THERE...?
I SEE, THANK YOU.

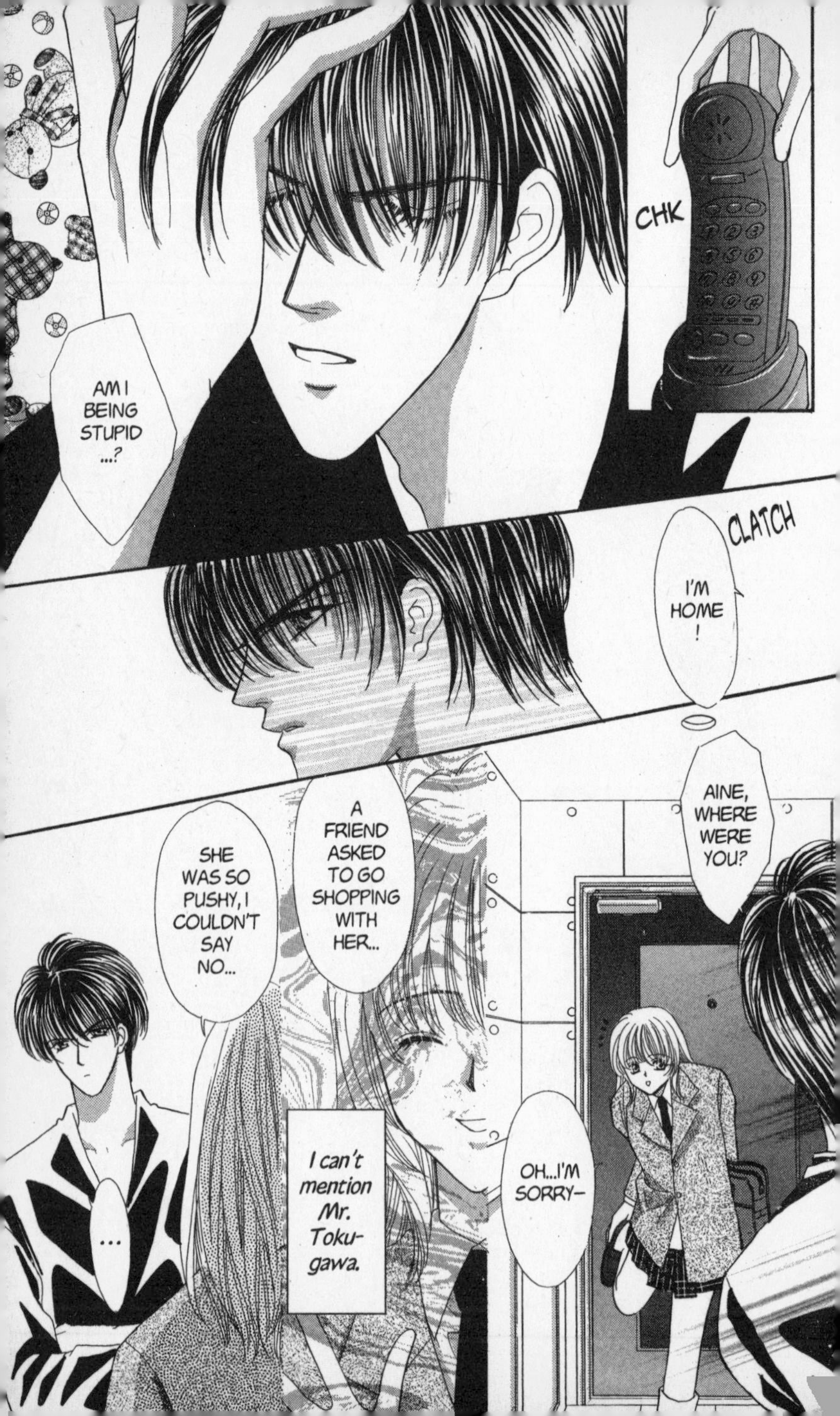
CHK
AM I BEING STUPID ...?
CLATCH
I'M HOME !
AINE, WHERE WERE YOU?
OH...I'M SORRY—
I can't mention Mr. Toku-gawa.
A FRIEND ASKED TO GO SHOPPING WITH HER...
SHE WAS SO PUSHY, I COULDN'T SAY NO...
...

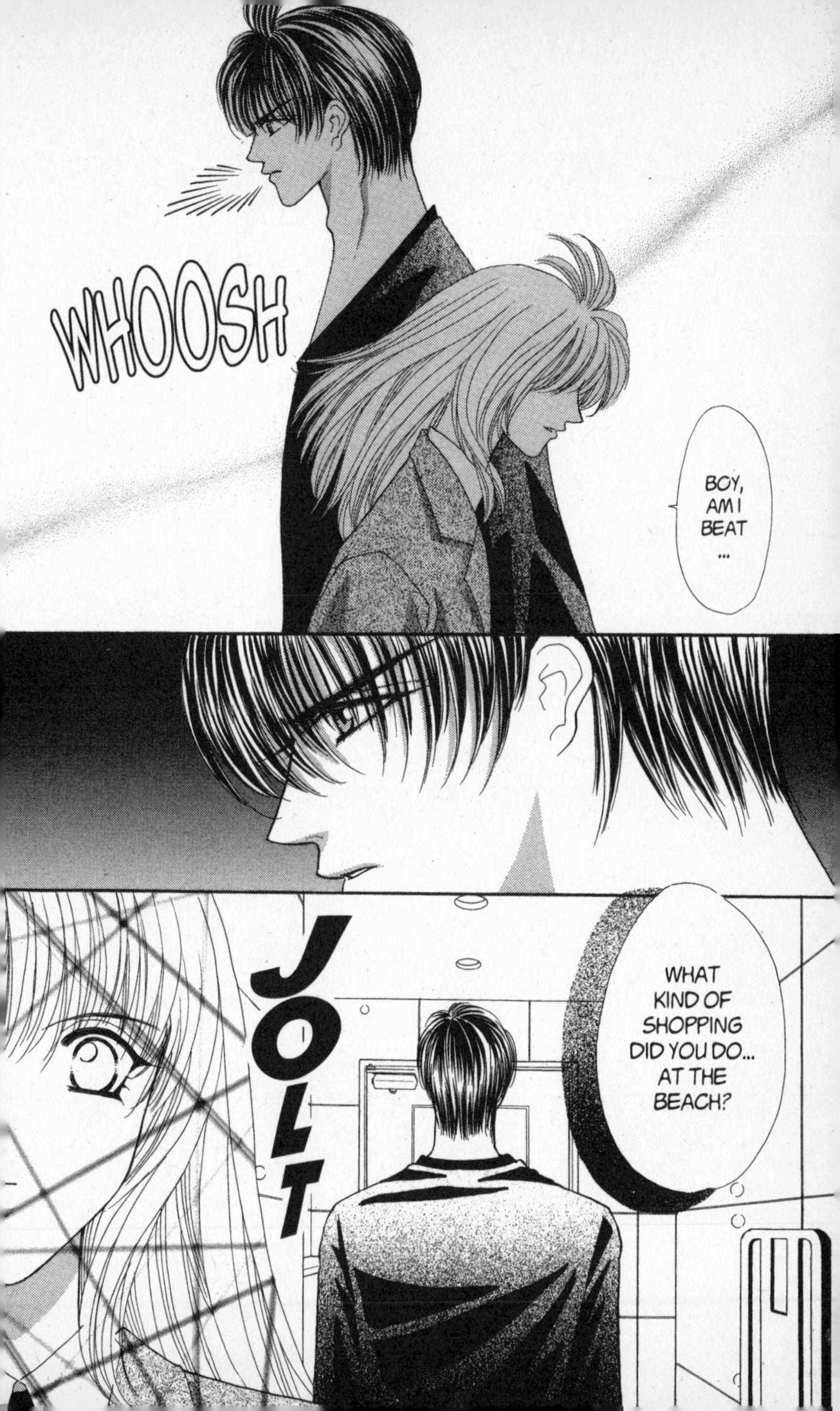
BOY, AM I BEAT ...
WHOOSH
JOLT
WHAT KIND OF SHOPPING DID YOU DO... AT THE BEACH?

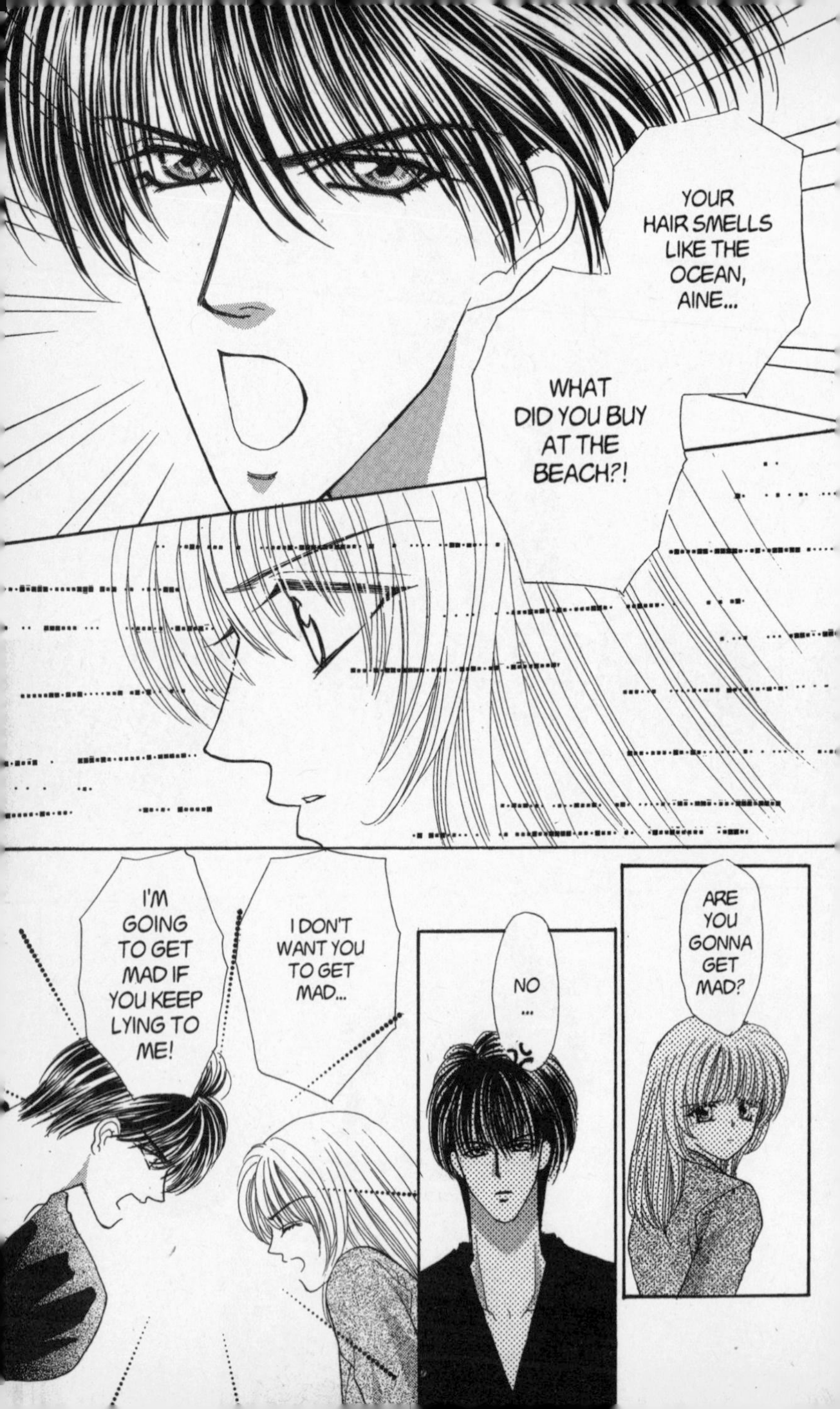
YOUR HAIR SMELLS LIKE THE OCEAN, AINE...
WHAT DID YOU BUY AT THE BEACH?!
ARE YOU GONNA GET MAD?
NO ...
I DON'T WANT YOU TO GET MAD...
I'M GOING TO GET MAD IF YOU KEEP LYING TO ME!

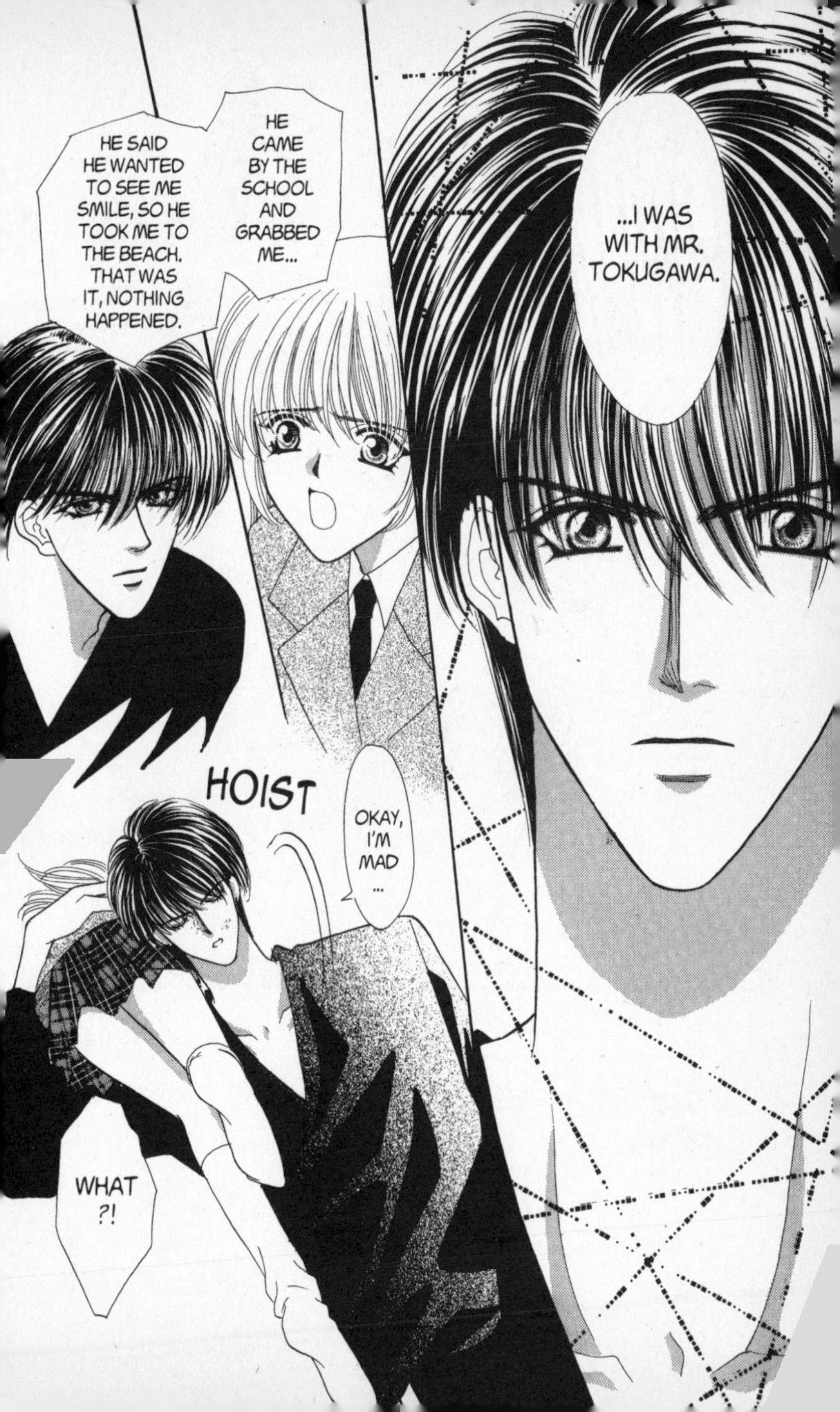
...I WAS WITH MR. TOKUGAWA.
HE CAME BY THE SCHOOL AND GRABBED ME...
HE SAID HE WANTED TO SEE ME SMILE, SO HE TOOK ME TO THE BEACH. THAT WAS IT, NOTHING HAPPENED.
OKAY, I'M MAD ...
HOIST
WHAT ?!

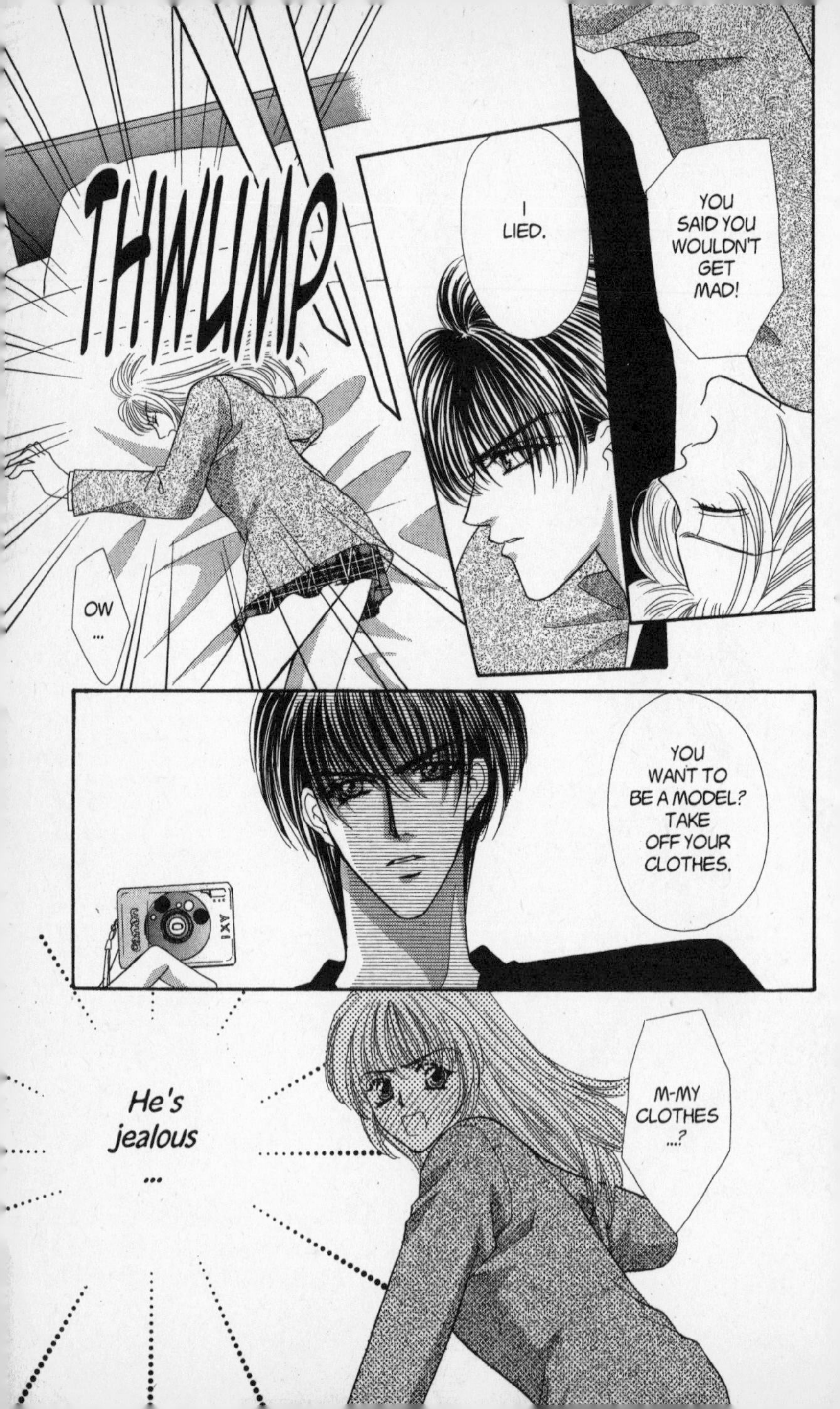
YOU SAID YOU WOULDN'T GET MAD!
I LIED.
THWUMP
OW ...
YOU WANT TO BE A MODEL? TAKE OFF YOUR CLOTHES.
M-MY CLOTHES ...?
He's jealous ...

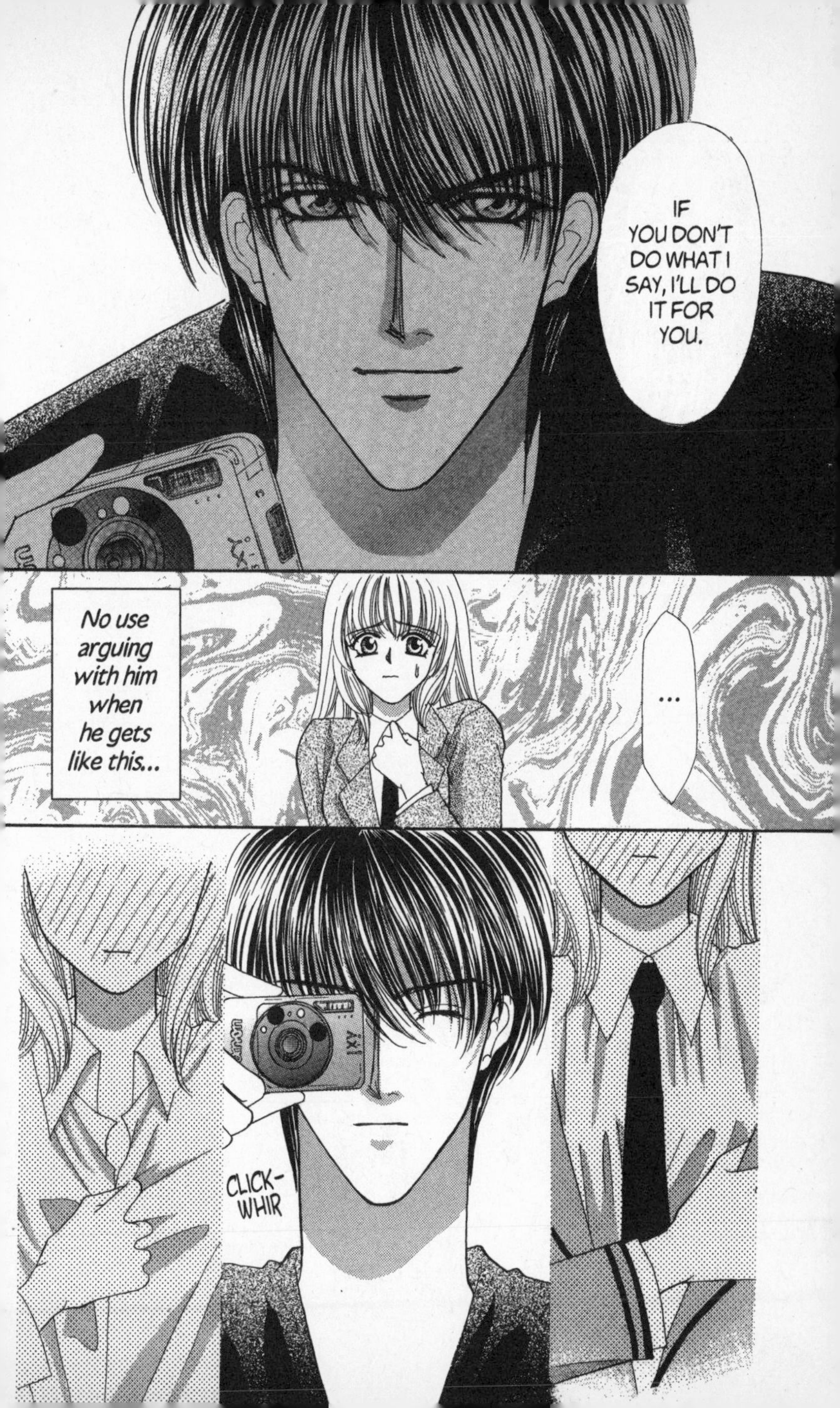
IF YOU DON'T DO WHAT I SAY, I'LL DO IT FOR YOU.
...
No use arguing with him when he gets like this...
CLICK-WHIR

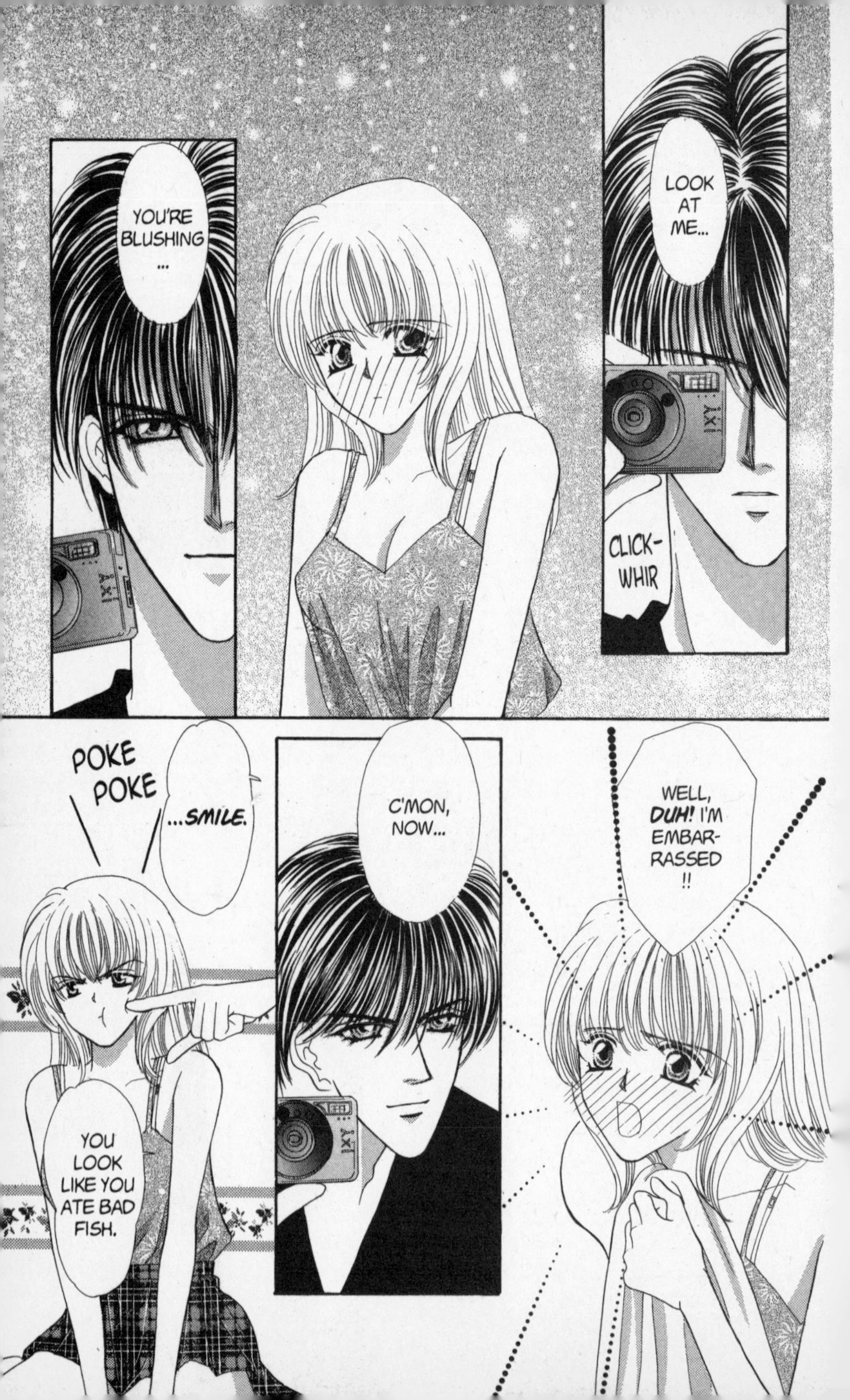
LOOK AT ME...
CLICK-WHIR
YOU'RE BLUSHING ...
WELL, **DUH!** I'M EMBARRASSED !!
C'MON, NOW...
POKE POKE
...*SMILE.*
YOU LOOK LIKE YOU ATE BAD FISH.

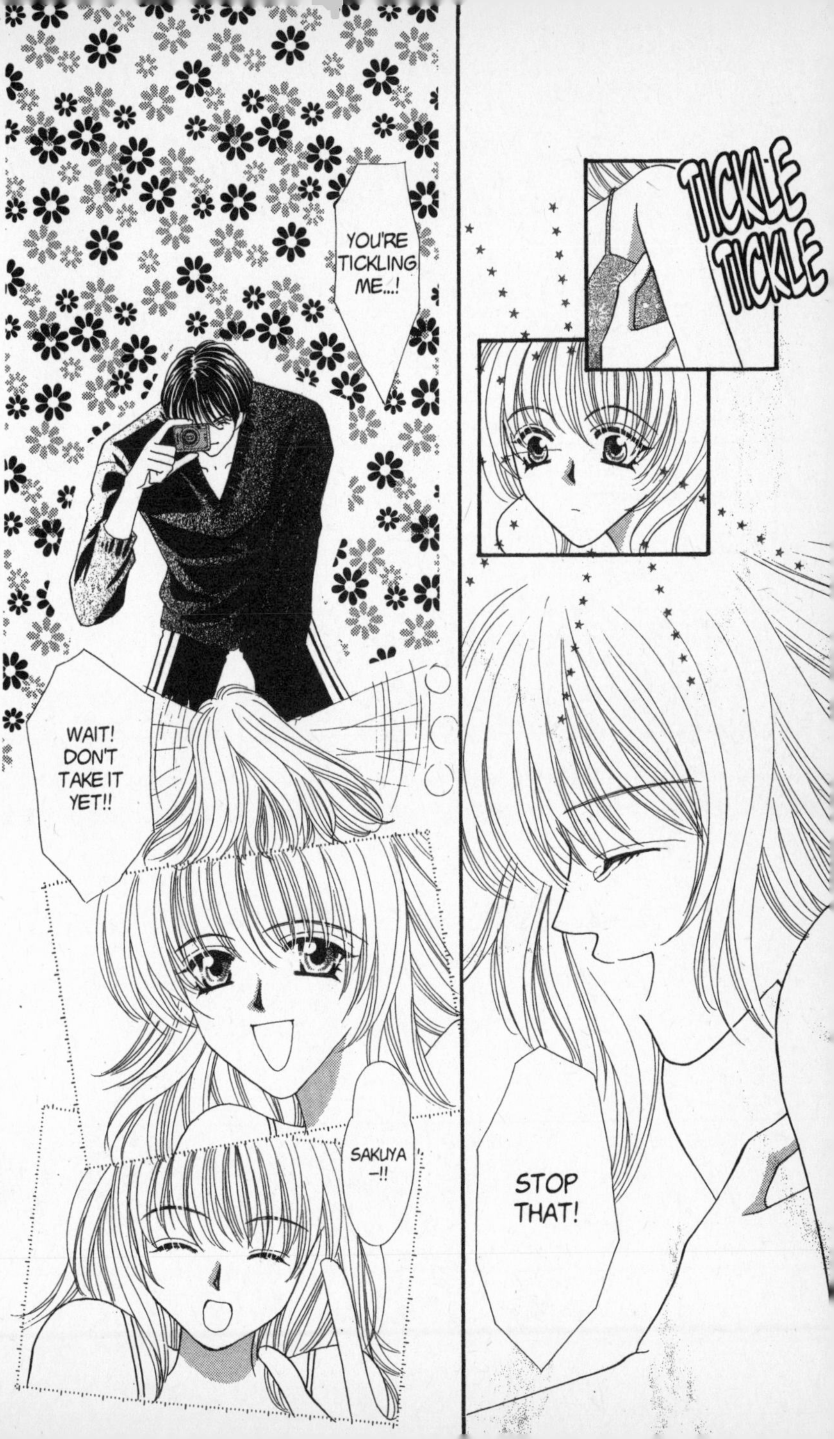
TICKLE TICKLE
STOP THAT!
YOU'RE TICKLING ME...!
WAIT! DON'T TAKE IT YET!!
SAKUYA—!!

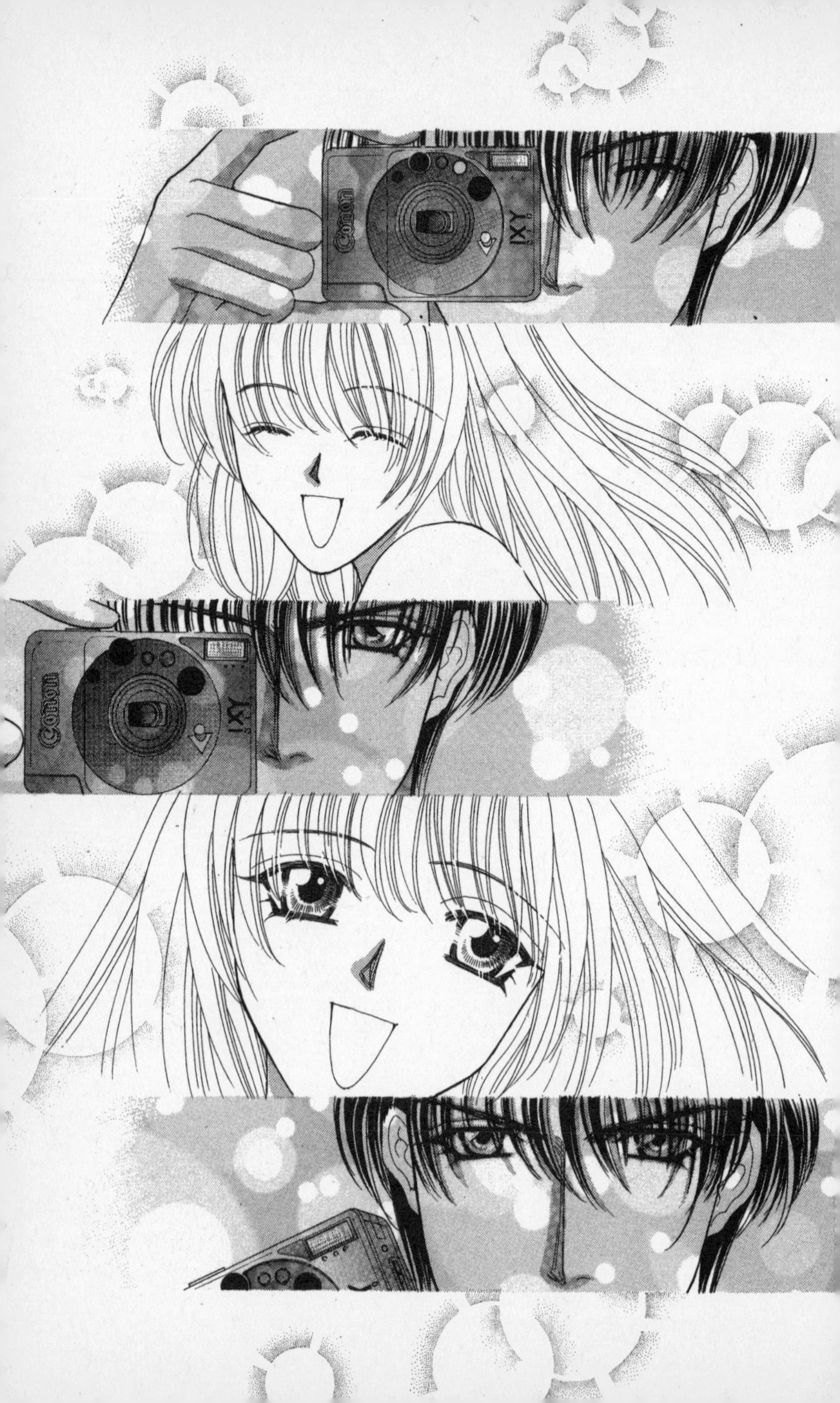
Canon
IXY
Canon
IXY

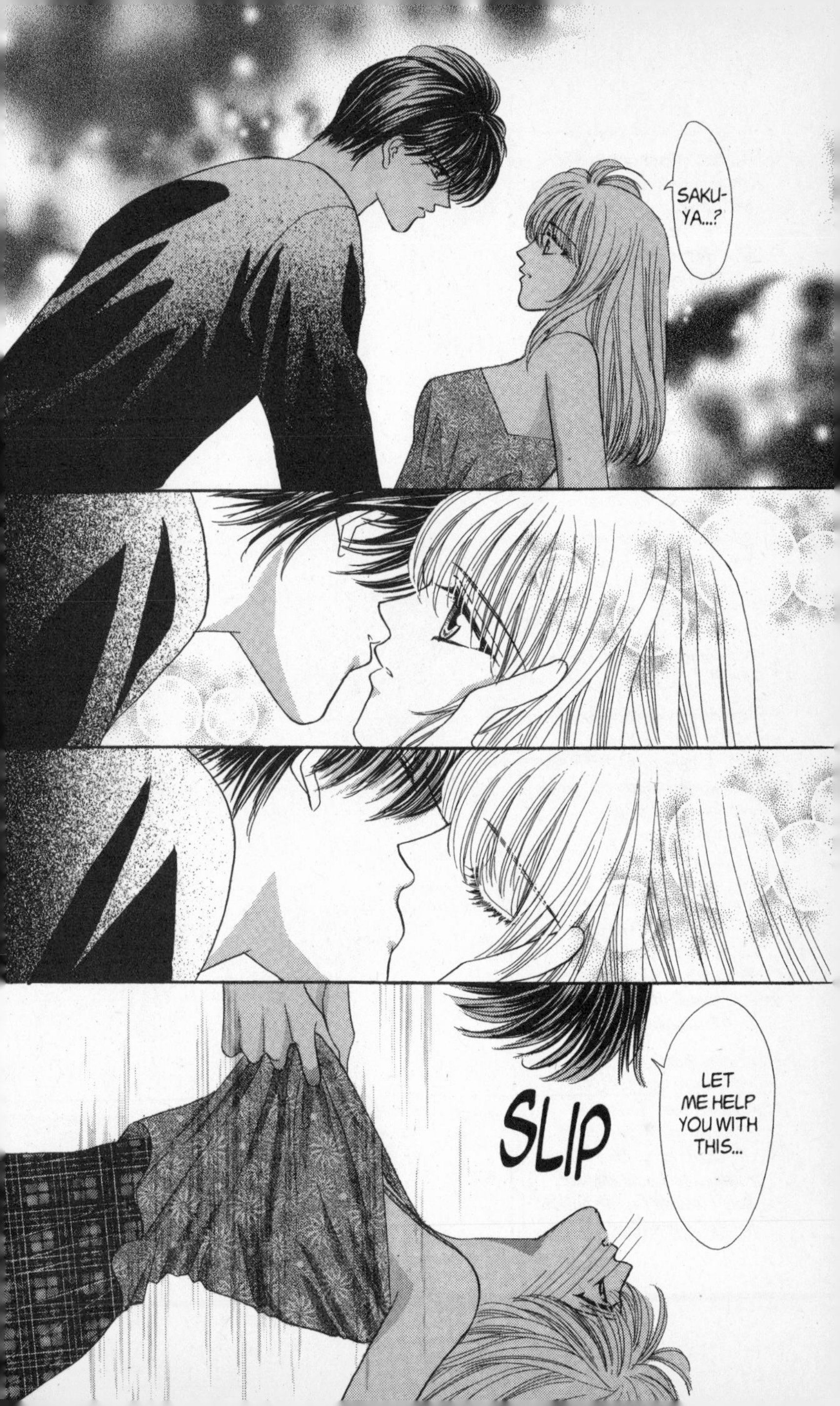
SAKU-YA...?
LET ME HELP YOU WITH THIS...
SLIP

So I hear there are actually fanzines on Sensual Phrase these days! I got an interview request from some pervy men's magazine, and they mentioned Sensual Phrase fanzines centered around Aine!! I was really surprised. I knew I'd picked up a few male readers recently, but that many...?

I was told there were fanzines on Lucifer, too–does anybody know for sure? Write and tell me, okay?

I really want to see what Sensual Phrase fanzines are like. I want to read one! If you've made one, I don't care what's written in it–just, please, please send me a copy!

Many of you mention your favorite lines and your favorite scenes in your letters and –surprisingly–everybody's favorite scene seems to be Sakuya's post-accident press conference. The favorite lines aren't as consistent. It's fascinating and all your feedback really makes me feel like my hard work was worthwhile. I'm hoping for more comments and opinions, so keep sending them in.

I'm sure some of you know this already, but I wrote a story all about Towa in a special issue. I guess the number of Towa fans is growing, so I said why not! I said I wouldn't write one but I'm weak against your pleas.

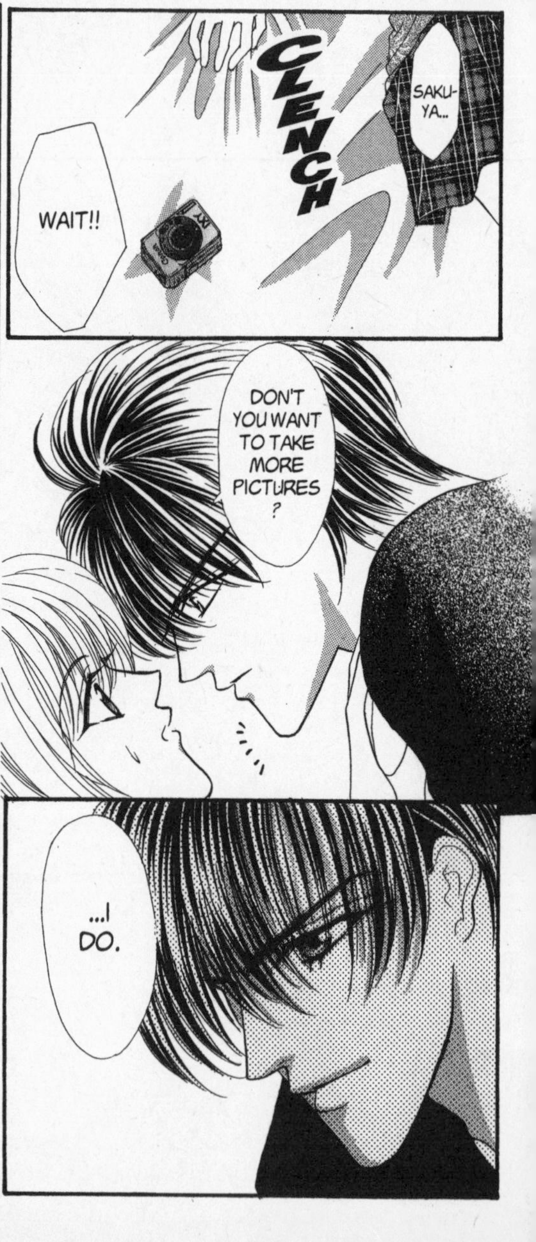
SAKU-YA...
CLENCH
WAIT!!
DON'T YOU WANT TO TAKE MORE PICTURES?
...I DO.

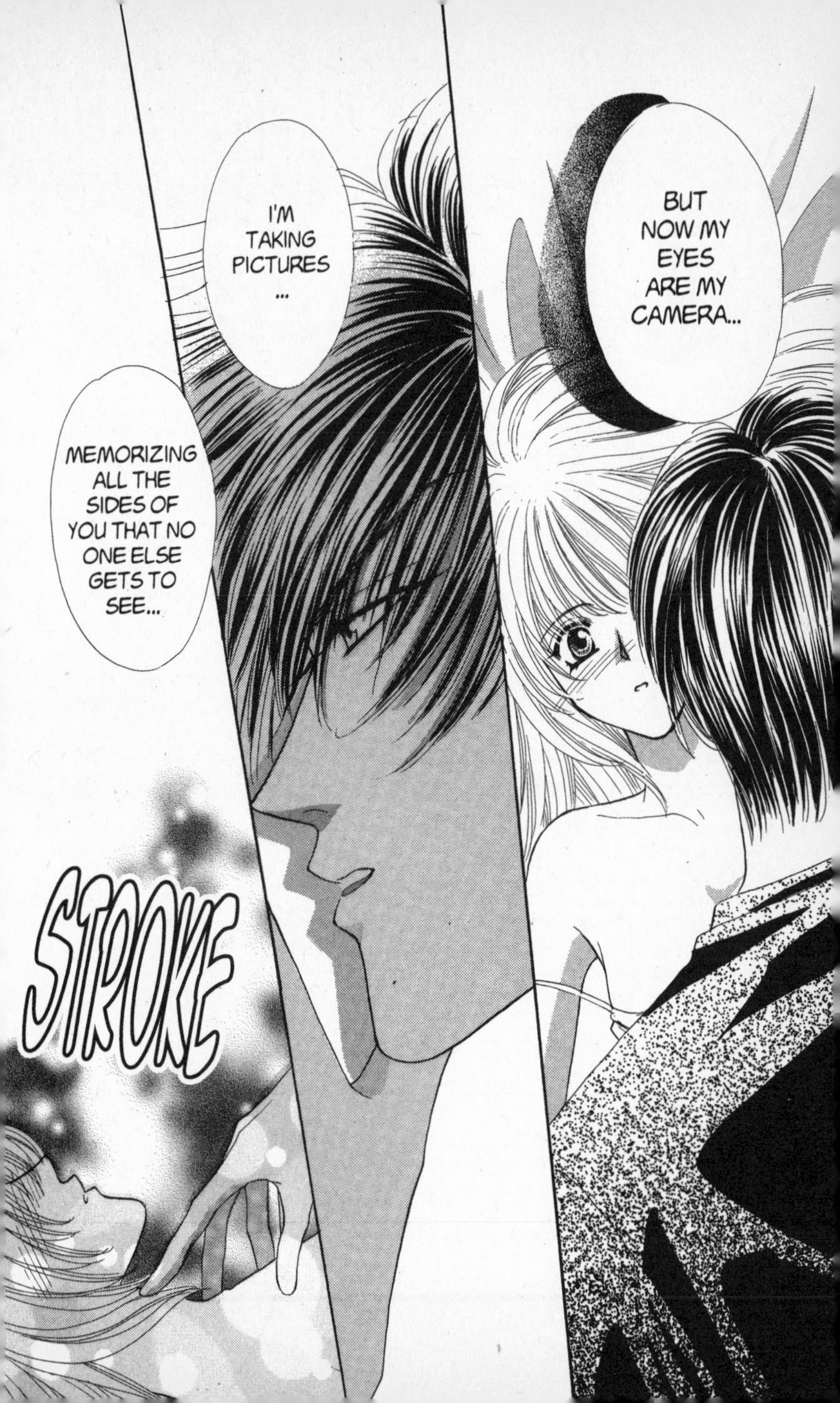
BUT NOW MY EYES ARE MY CAMERA...
I'M TAKING PICTURES ...
MEMORIZING ALL THE SIDES OF YOU THAT NO ONE ELSE GETS TO SEE...
STROKE

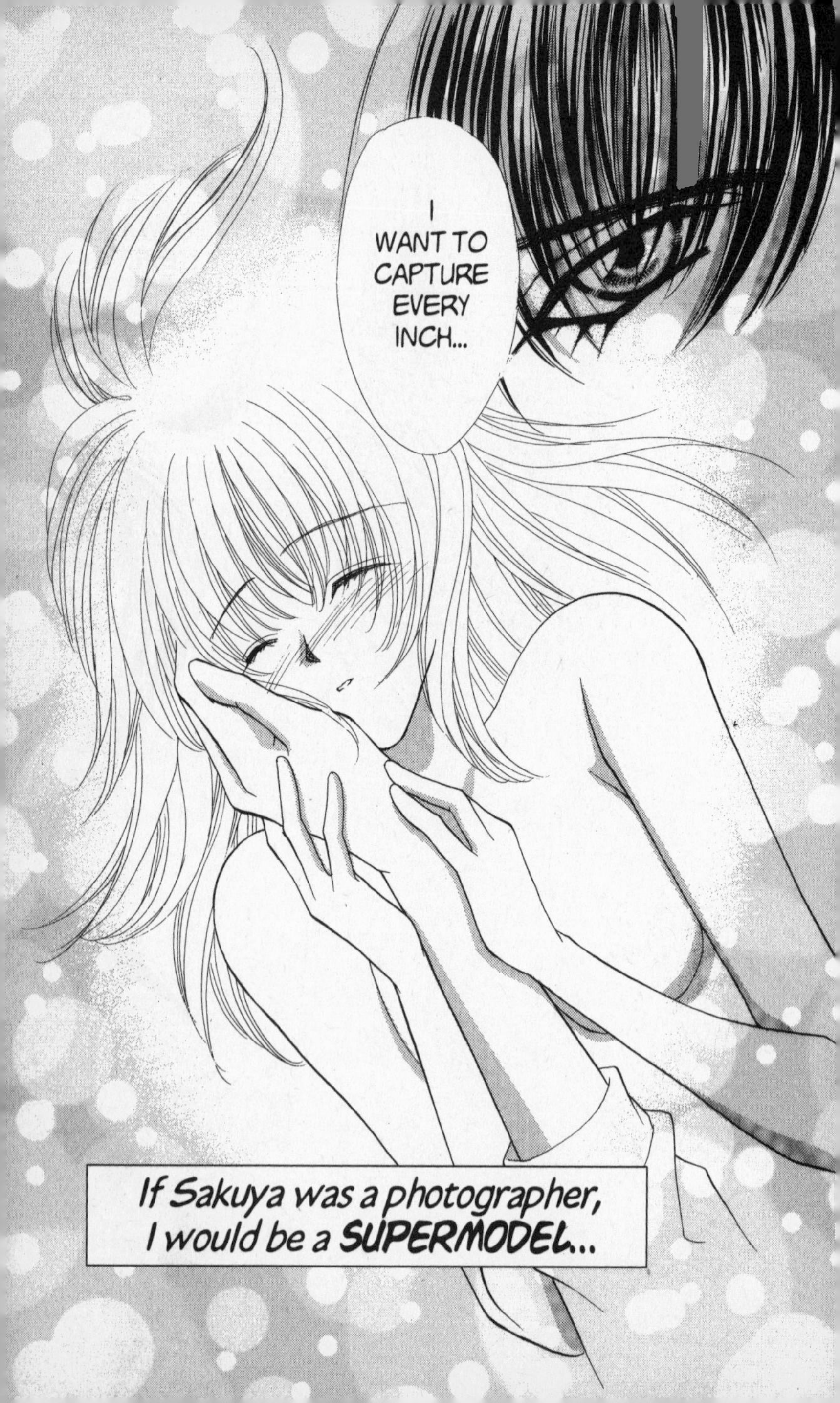
I WANT TO CAPTURE EVERY INCH...
If Sakuya was a photographer, I would be a SUPERMODEL...

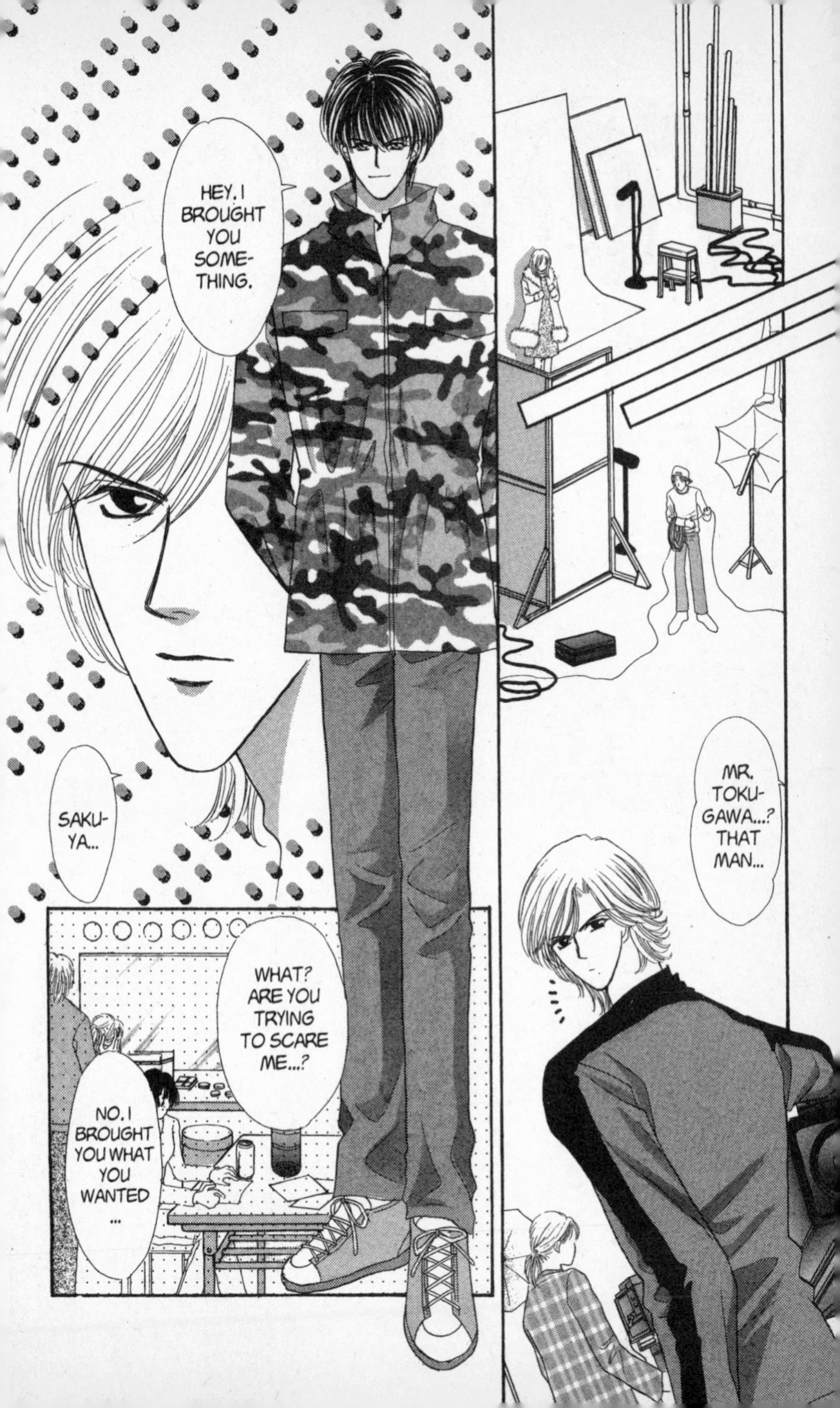
MR. TOKUGAWA...? THAT MAN...
HEY. I BROUGHT YOU SOMETHING.
SAKUYA...
WHAT? ARE YOU TRYING TO SCARE ME...?
NO. I BROUGHT YOU WHAT YOU WANTED ...

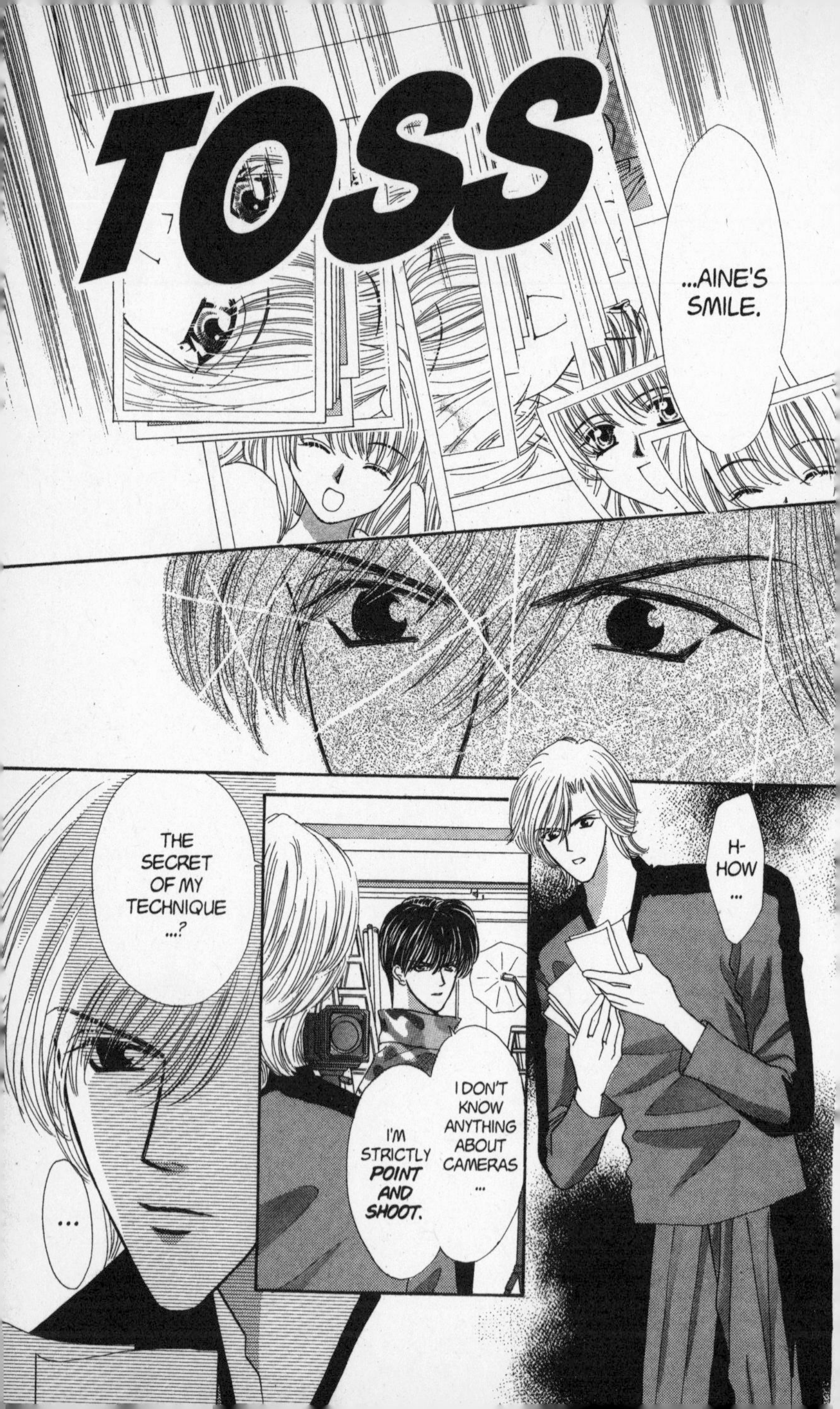
TOSS
...AINE'S SMILE.
H-HOW ...
I DON'T KNOW ANYTHING ABOUT CAMERAS ...
I'M STRICTLY *POINT AND SHOOT.*
THE SECRET OF MY TECHNIQUE ...?
...

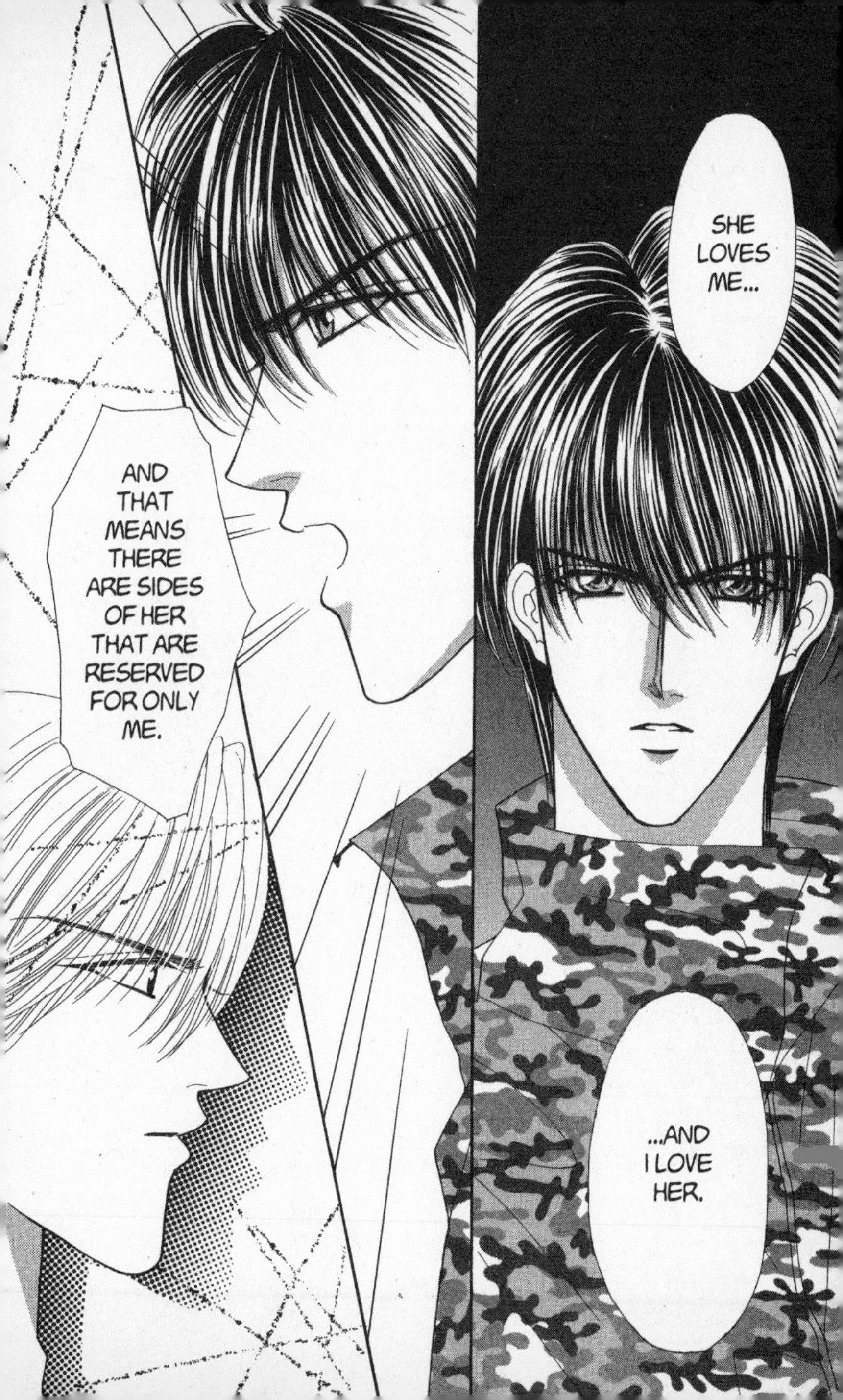
SHE LOVES ME...
...AND I LOVE HER.
AND THAT MEANS THERE ARE SIDES OF HER THAT ARE RESERVED FOR ONLY ME.

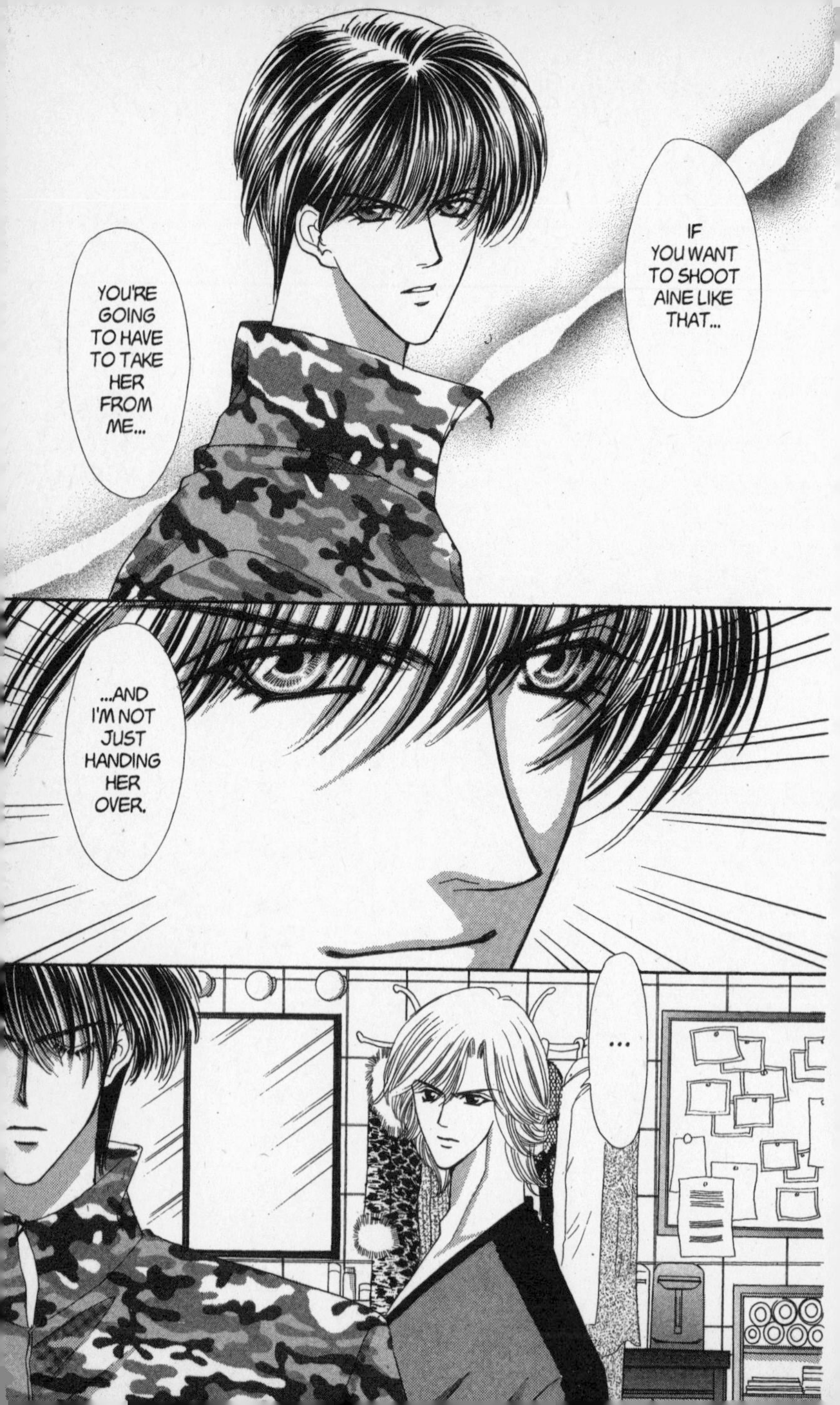
IF YOU WANT TO SHOOT AINE LIKE THAT...
YOU'RE GOING TO HAVE TO TAKE HER FROM ME...
...AND I'M NOT JUST HANDING HER OVER.
...

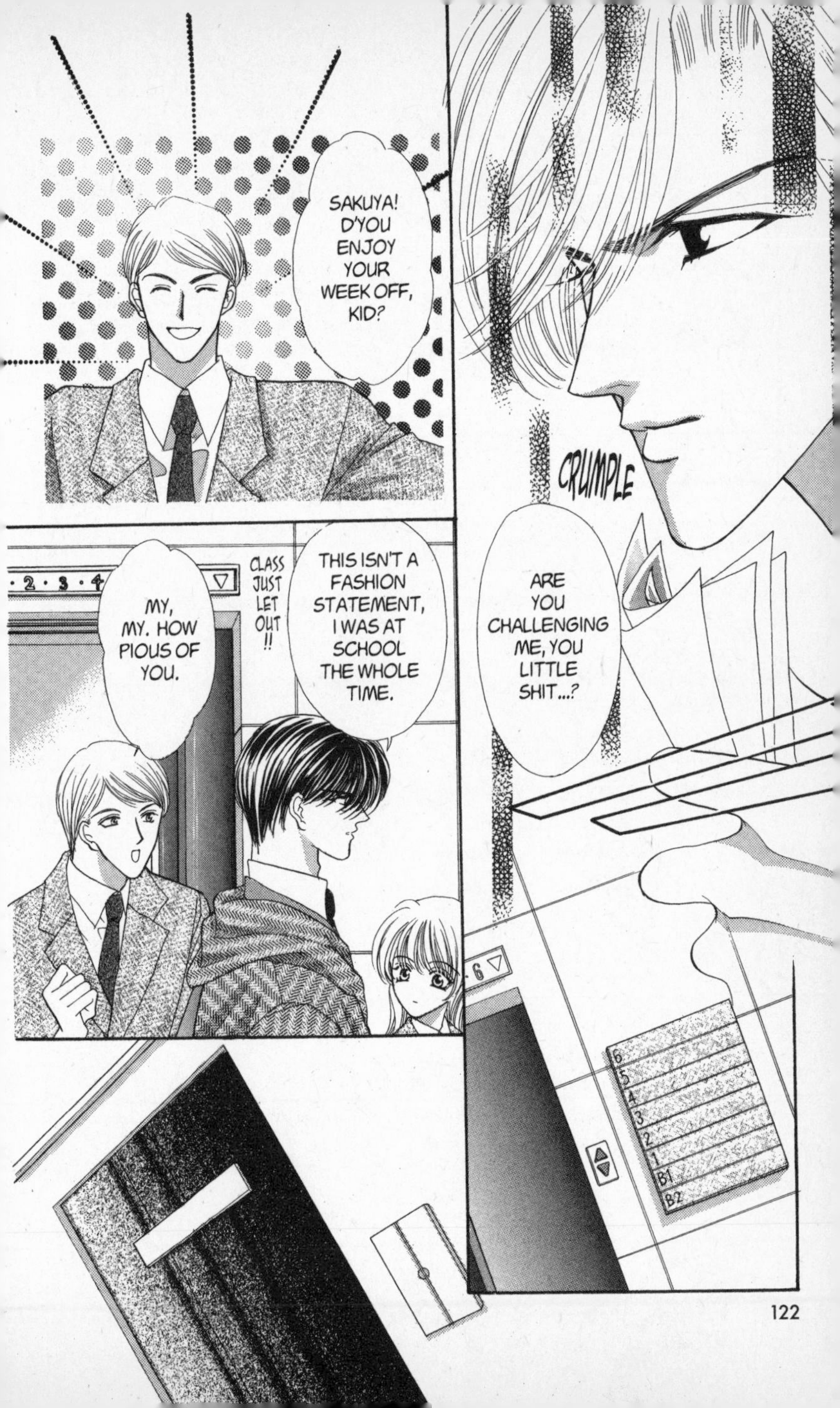
CRUMPLE
ARE YOU CHALLENGING ME, YOU LITTLE SHIT...?
SAKUYA! D'YOU ENJOY YOUR WEEK OFF, KID?
THIS ISN'T A FASHION STATEMENT, I WAS AT SCHOOL THE WHOLE TIME.
CLASS JUST LET OUT !!
MY, MY. HOW PIOUS OF YOU.

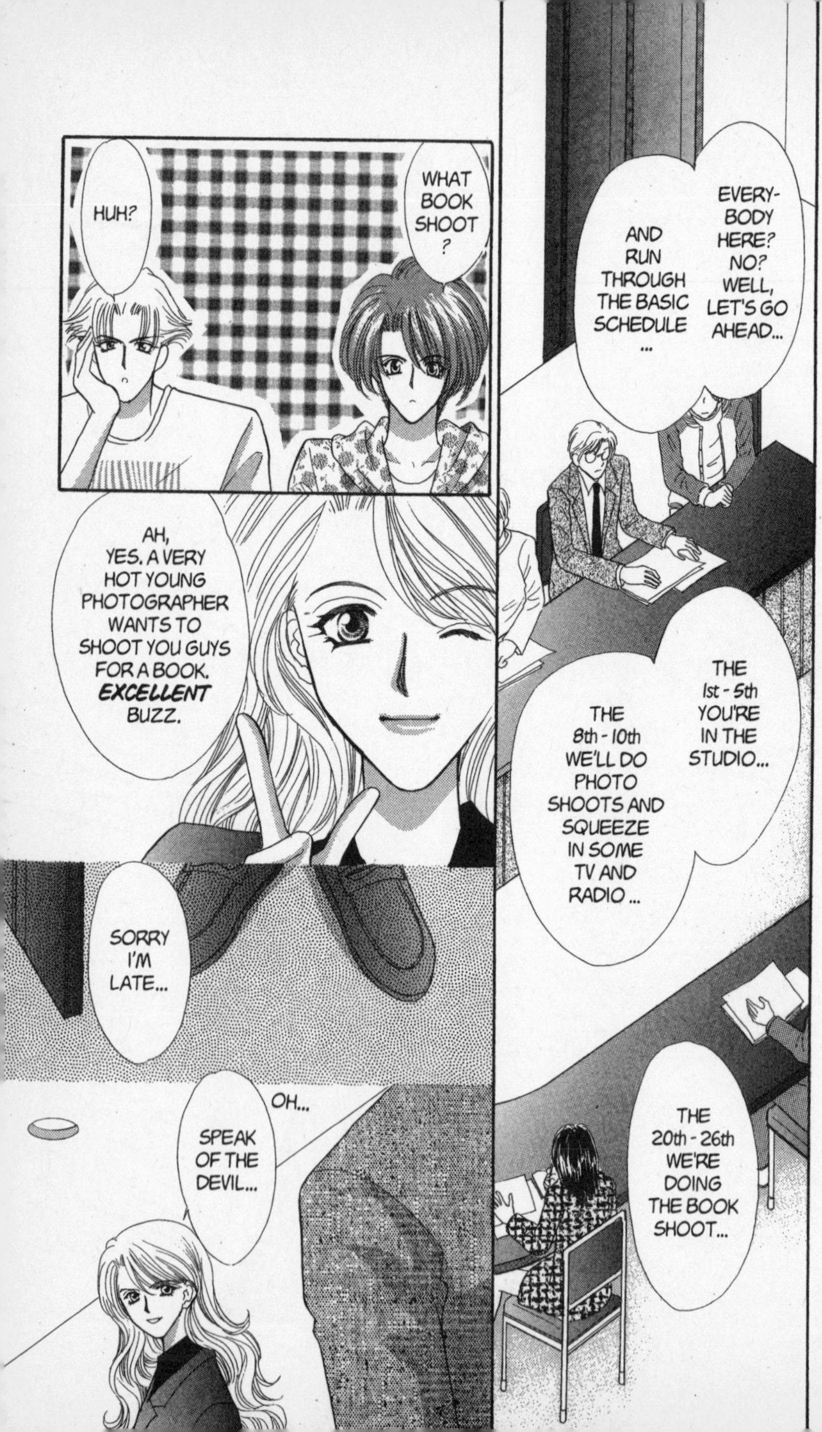
EVERY-BODY HERE? NO? WELL, LET'S GO AHEAD...
AND RUN THROUGH THE BASIC SCHEDULE ...
THE 1st - 5th YOU'RE IN THE STUDIO...
THE 8th - 10th WE'LL DO PHOTO SHOOTS AND SQUEEZE IN SOME TV AND RADIO ...
THE 20th - 26th WE'RE DOING THE BOOK SHOOT...
WHAT BOOK SHOOT?
HUH?
AH, YES. A VERY HOT YOUNG PHOTOGRAPHER WANTS TO SHOOT YOU GUYS FOR A BOOK. ***EXCELLENT*** BUZZ.
SORRY I'M LATE...
OH...
SPEAK OF THE DEVIL...

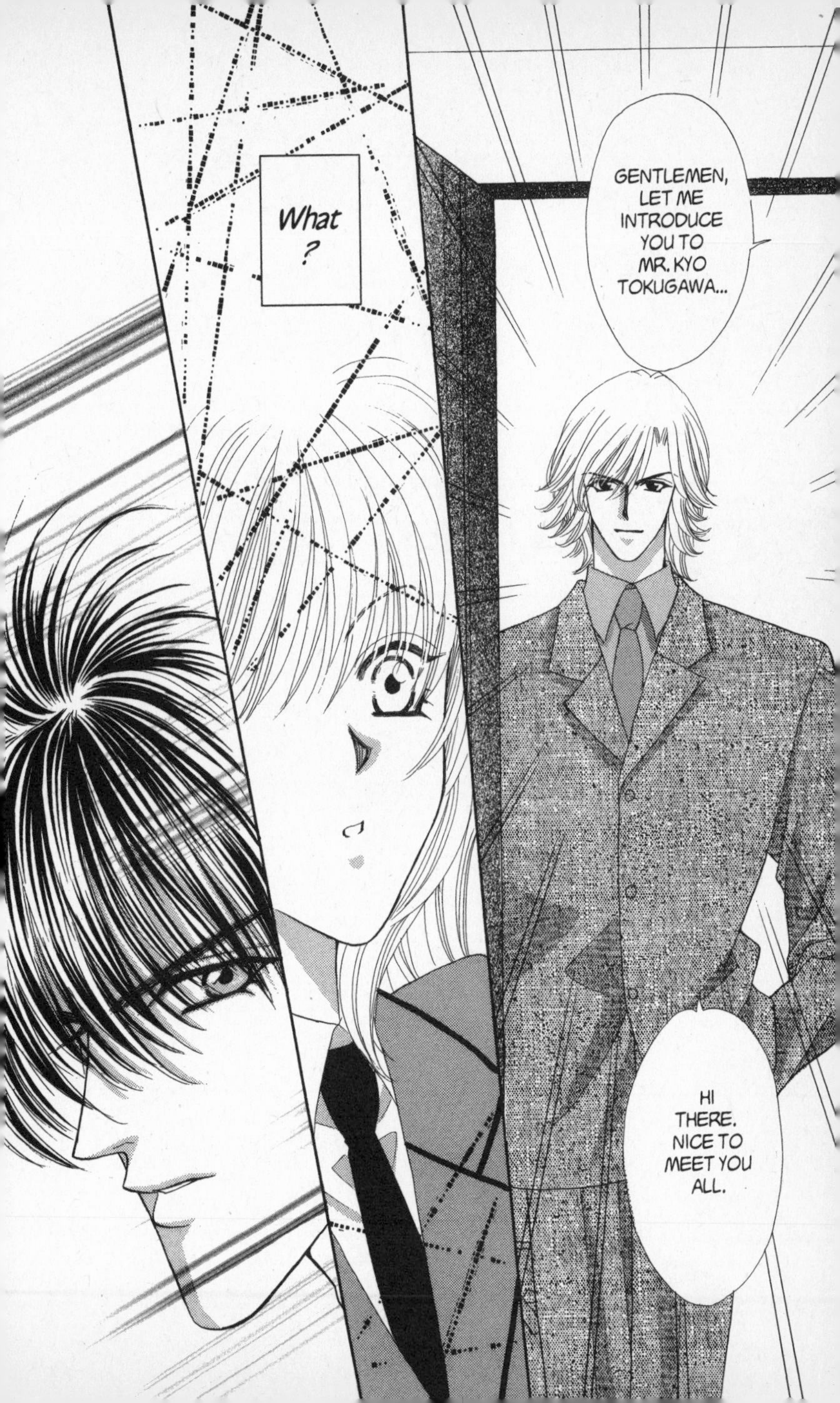
GENTLEMEN, LET ME INTRODUCE YOU TO MR. KYO TOKUGAWA...
HI THERE. NICE TO MEET YOU ALL.
What ?

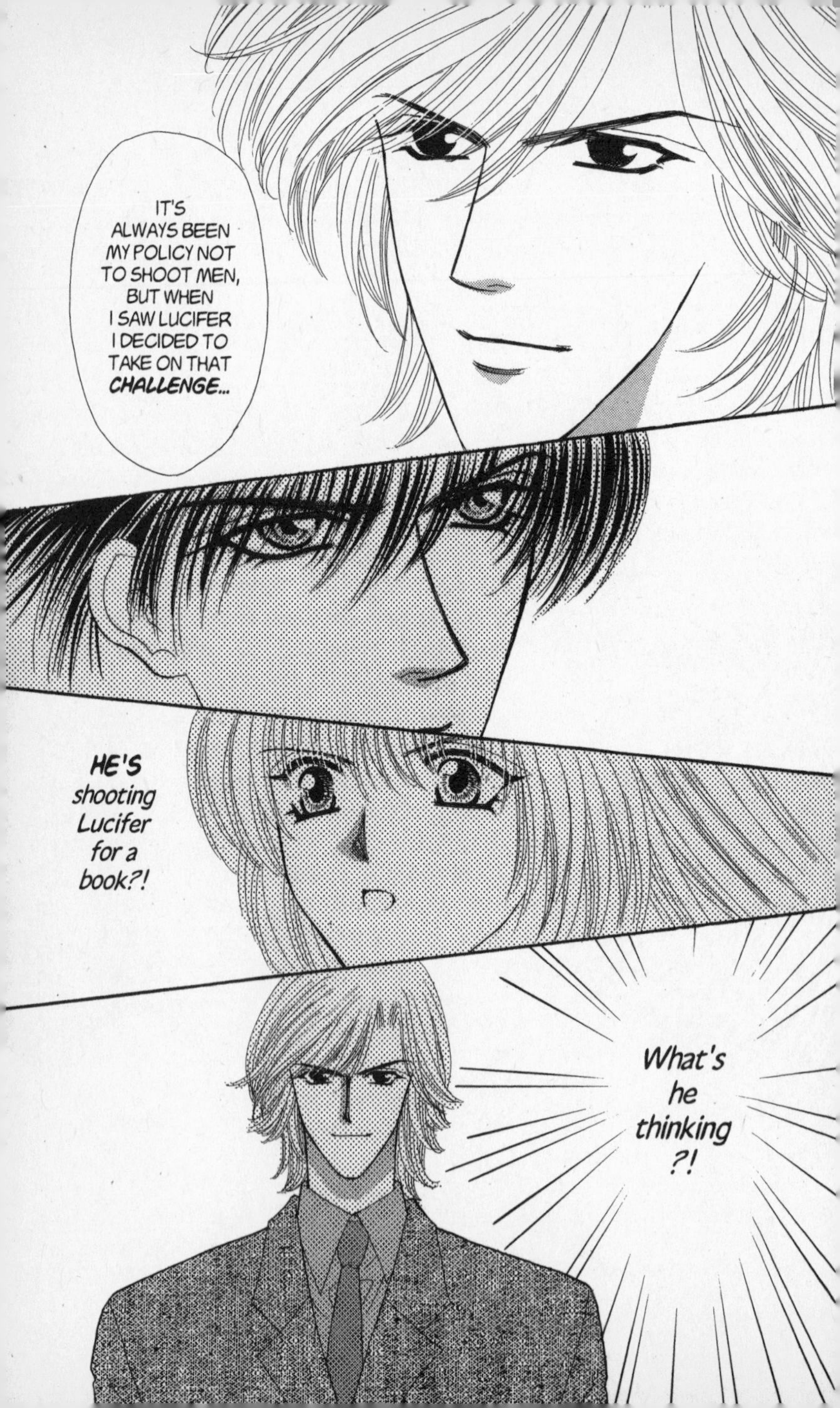
IT'S ALWAYS BEEN MY POLICY NOT TO SHOOT MEN, BUT WHEN I SAW LUCIFER I DECIDED TO TAKE ON THAT CHALLENGE...
HE'S shooting Lucifer for a book?!
What's he thinking ?!

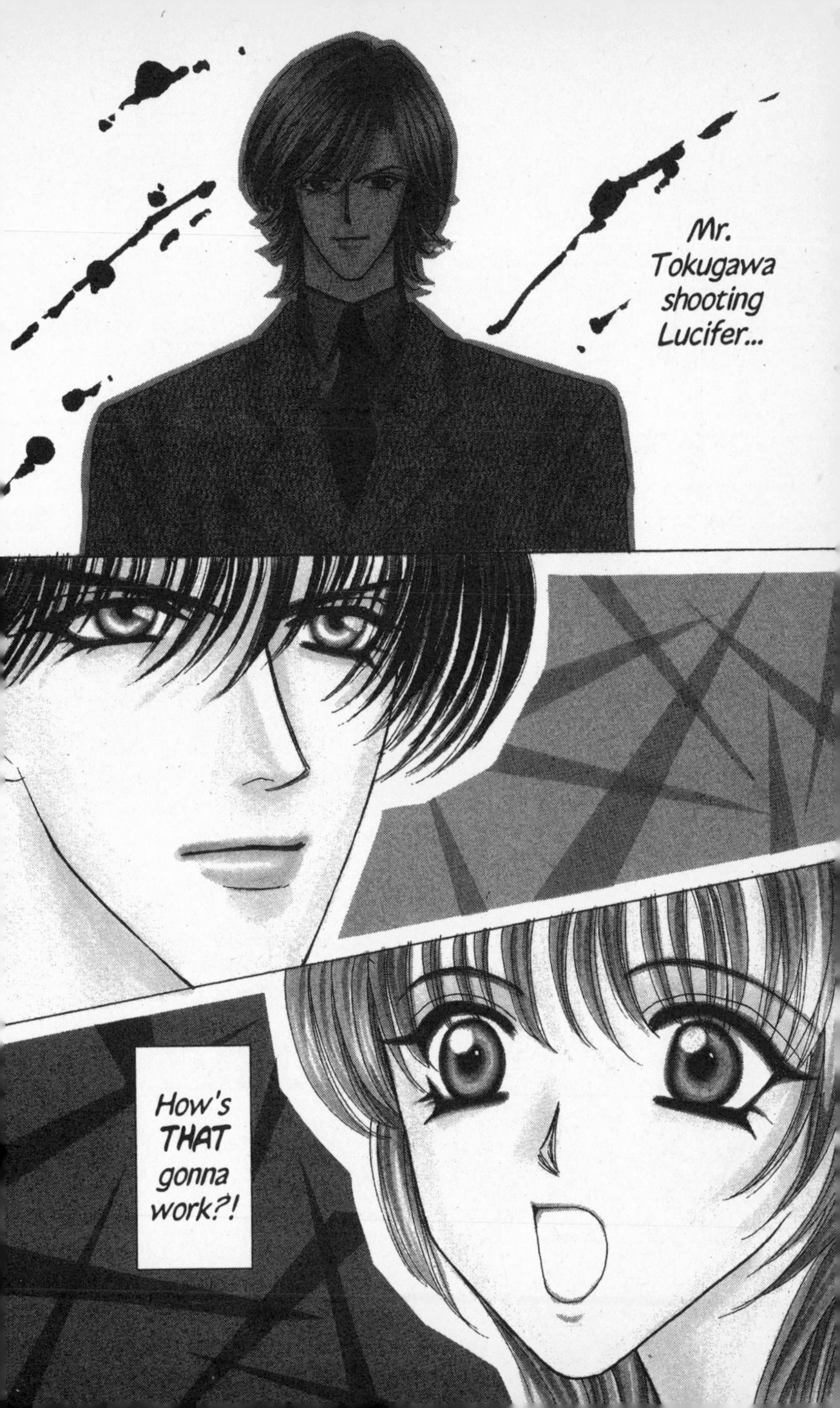
Mr. Tokugawa shooting Lucifer...
How's THAT gonna work?!

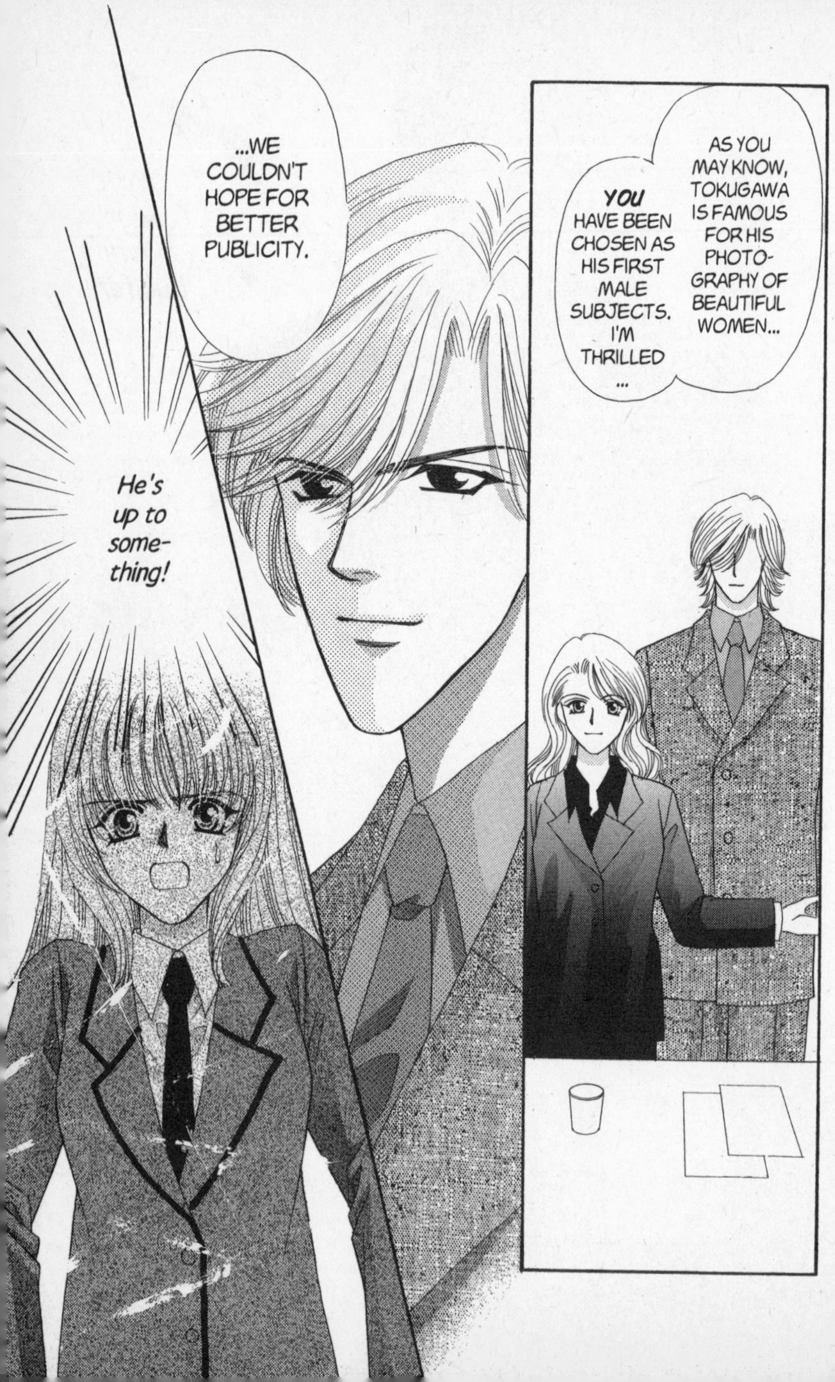
AS YOU MAY KNOW, TOKUGAWA IS FAMOUS FOR HIS PHOTOGRAPHY OF BEAUTIFUL WOMEN...
YOU HAVE BEEN CHOSEN AS HIS FIRST MALE SUBJECTS. I'M THRILLED ...
...WE COULDN'T HOPE FOR BETTER PUBLICITY.
He's up to something!

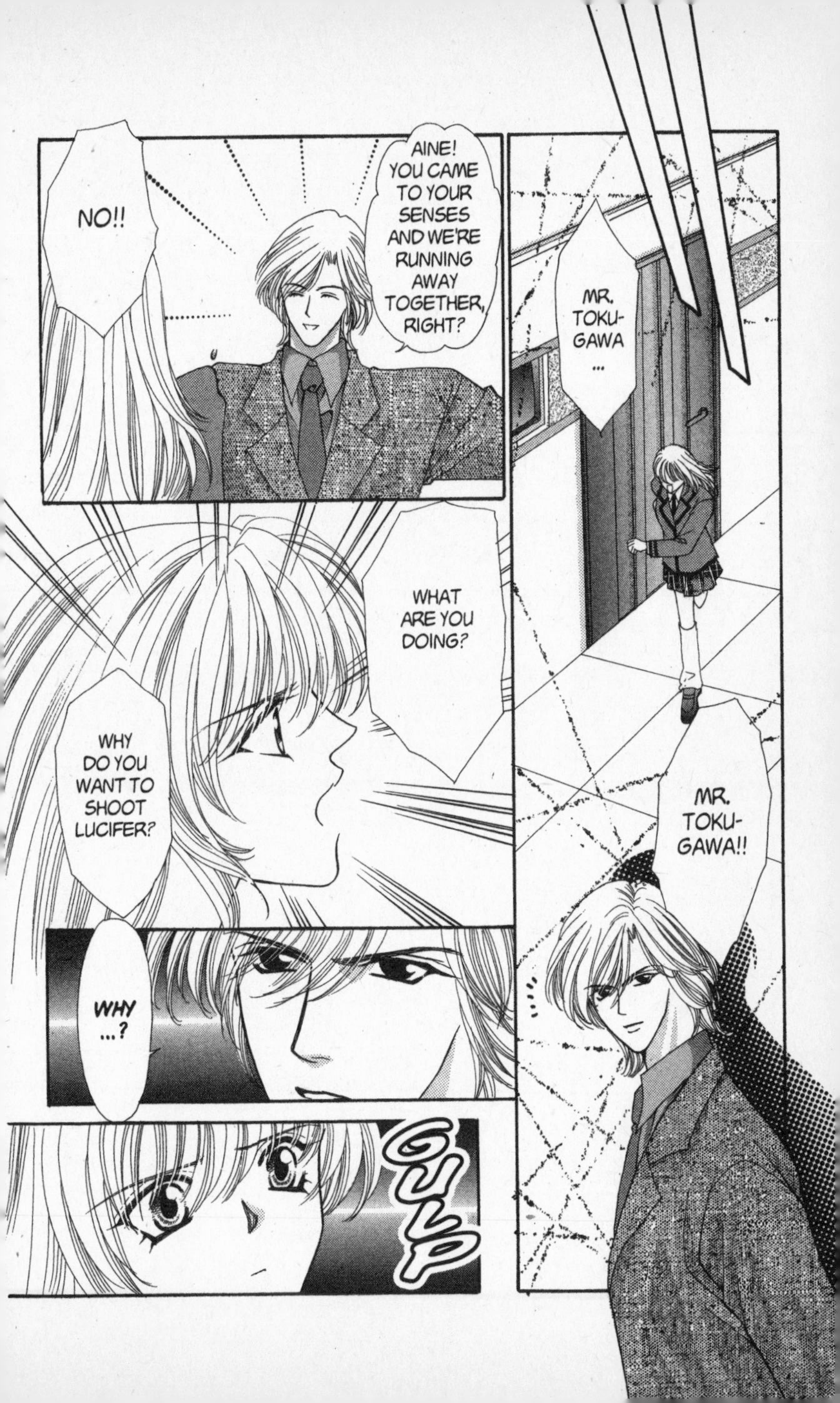
MR. TOKU-GAWA ...
MR. TOKU-GAWA!!
AINE! YOU CAME TO YOUR SENSES AND WE'RE RUNNING AWAY TOGETHER, RIGHT?
NO!!
WHAT ARE YOU DOING?
WHY DO YOU WANT TO SHOOT LUCIFER?
WHY ...?
GULP

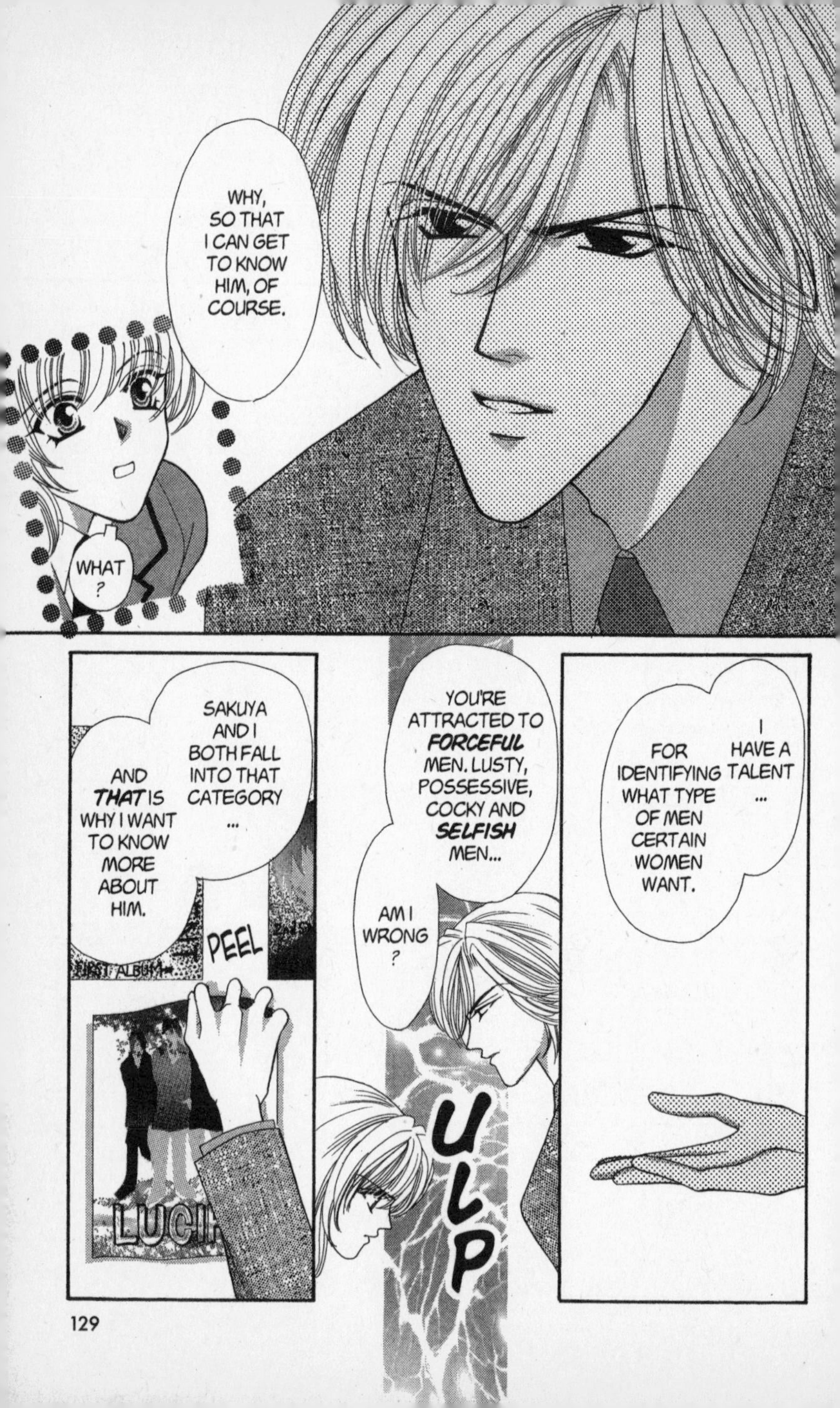
WHY, SO THAT I CAN GET TO KNOW HIM, OF COURSE.
WHAT?
I HAVE A TALENT...
FOR IDENTIFYING WHAT TYPE OF MEN CERTAIN WOMEN WANT.
YOU'RE ATTRACTED TO **FORCEFUL** MEN. LUSTY, POSSESSIVE, COCKY AND **SELFISH** MEN...
AM I WRONG?
ULP
SAKUYA AND I BOTH FALL INTO THAT CATEGORY...
AND **THAT** IS WHY I WANT TO KNOW MORE ABOUT HIM.
PEEL
FIRST ALBUM

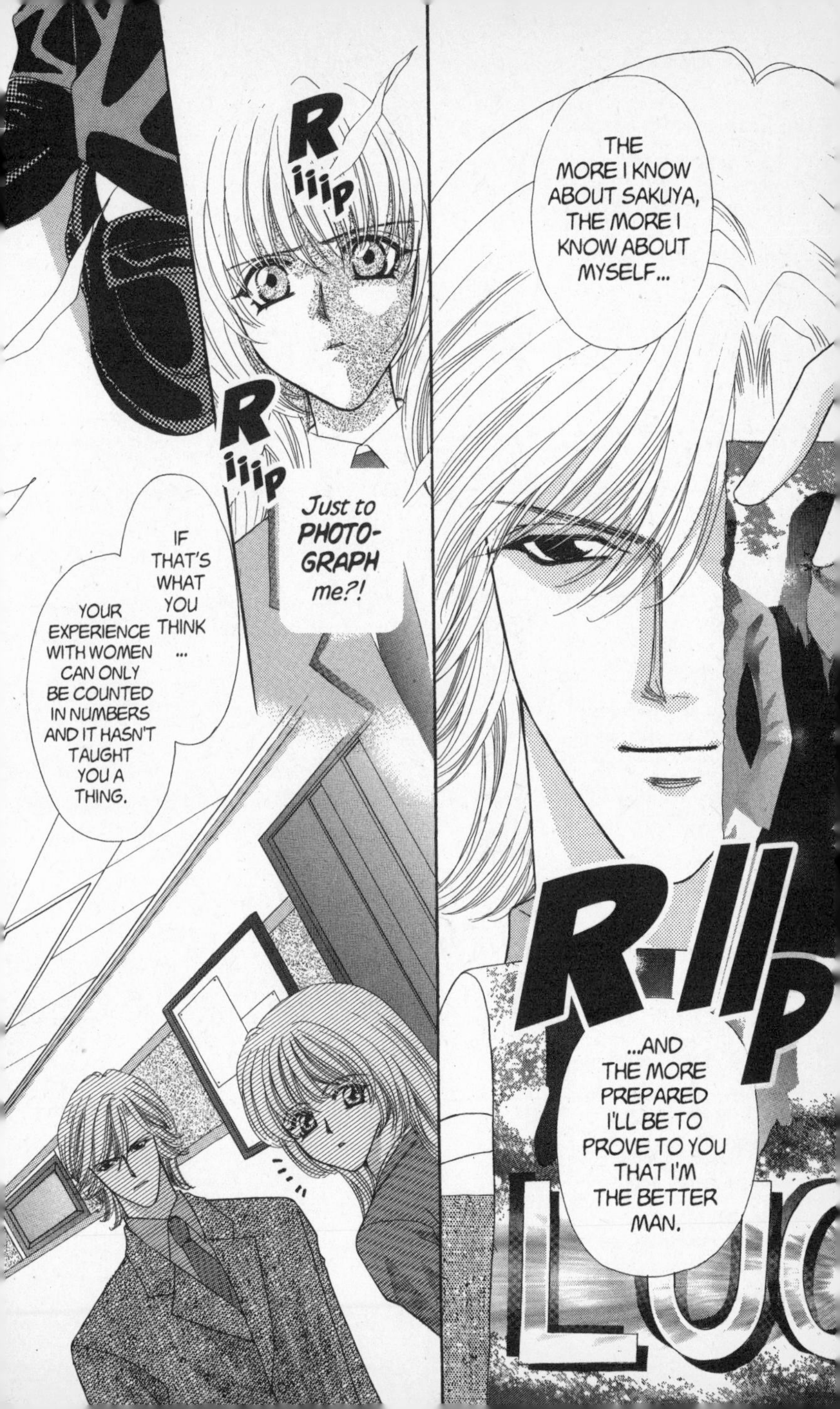
THE MORE I KNOW ABOUT SAKUYA, THE MORE I KNOW ABOUT MYSELF...
RIIP
...AND THE MORE PREPARED I'LL BE TO PROVE TO YOU THAT I'M THE BETTER MAN.
Riiip
Riiip
Just to PHOTOGRAPH me?!
IF THAT'S WHAT YOU THINK...
YOUR EXPERIENCE WITH WOMEN CAN ONLY BE COUNTED IN NUMBERS AND IT HASN'T TAUGHT YOU A THING.

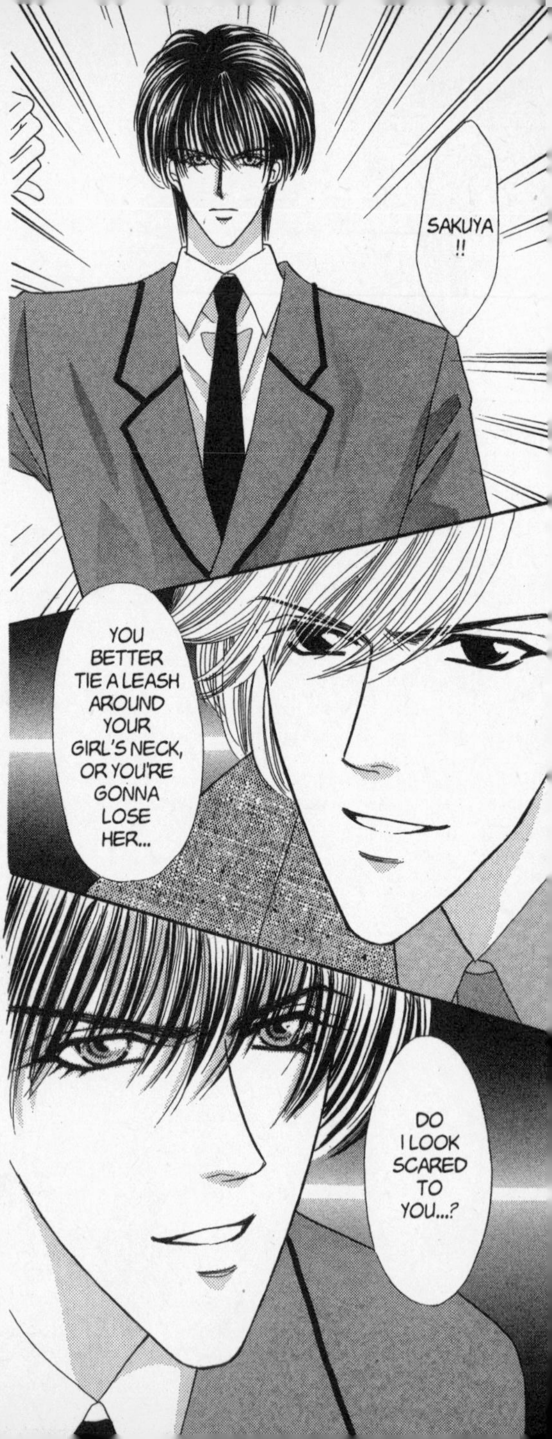
SAKUYA !!
YOU BETTER TIE A LEASH AROUND YOUR GIRL'S NECK, OR YOU'RE GONNA LOSE HER...
DO I LOOK SCARED TO YOU...?

The only person left is... yes, Santa!! Right now, I don't plan on doing one for him—he doesn't even have a girlfriend...! But I can tell from your letters that his fan base is growing, so we'll see...

When I wrote the story for Towa, it was only 31 pages. My editor just wanted something funny with a romantic angle, so I thought I'd write a story with a boy as the protagonist. (Confidentially: I am a tomboy at heart. All my early submissions were centered around boys. It wasn't until someone explained to me that shōjo had to be about girls, that I made a girl the main character.) So, I grabbed a pen thinking: I'm gonna write a Towa story, and... I-I couldn't write!! I couldn't write a story about a boy after I'd been wanting to so badly...

By that time I was so accustomed to writing about girls that my pen didn't move. Where did my inner tomboy go?!

I don't know when that arduous piece will appear in a book, but I do hope it'll create more fans of Towa.

Oh yeah, the Lucifer Legend hasn't made it into a book yet either has it? Soon, soon...

Sensual Phrase will continue for a while so please keep reading!

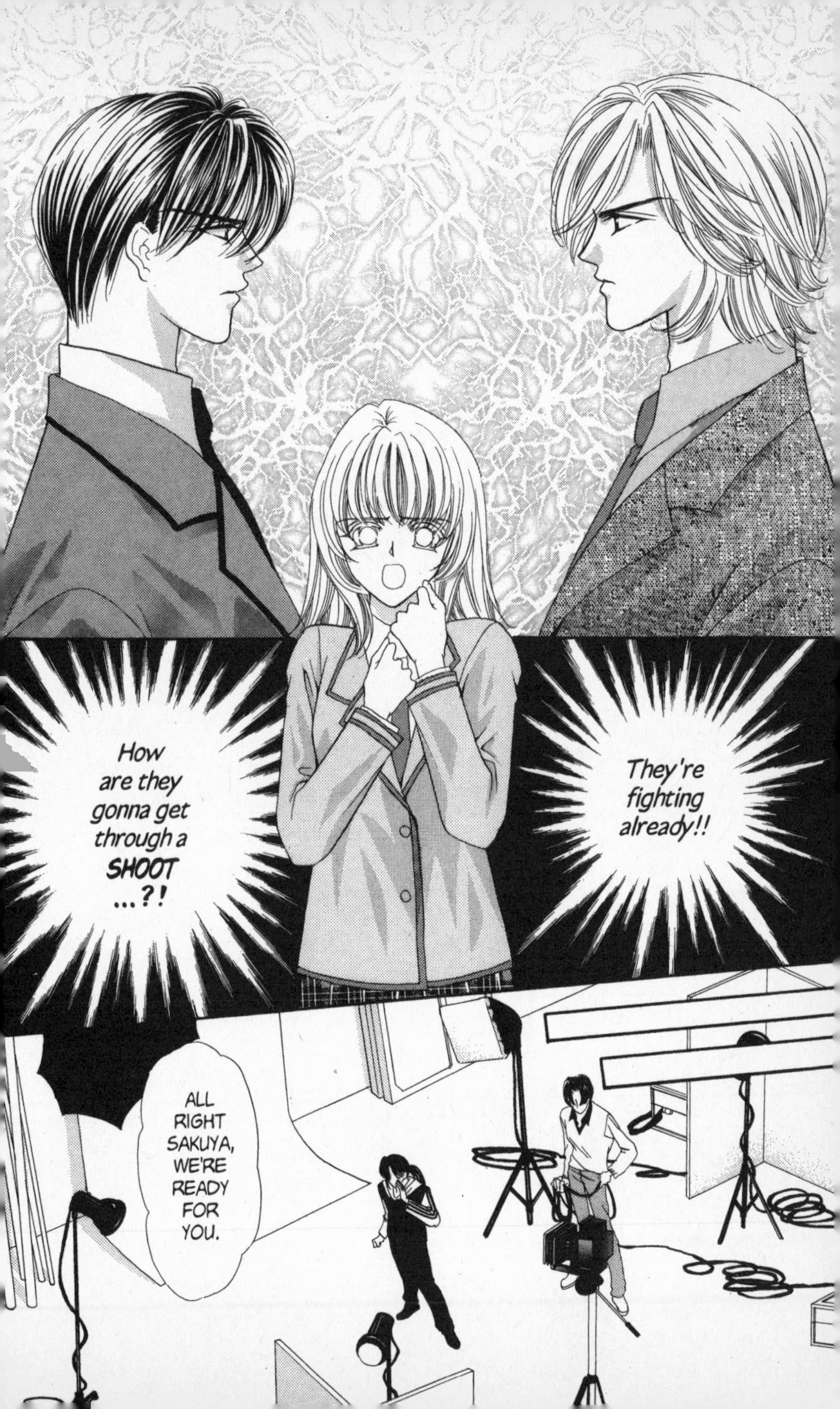
They're fighting already!!
How are they gonna get through a **SHOOT** ...?!
ALL RIGHT SAKUYA, WE'RE READY FOR YOU.

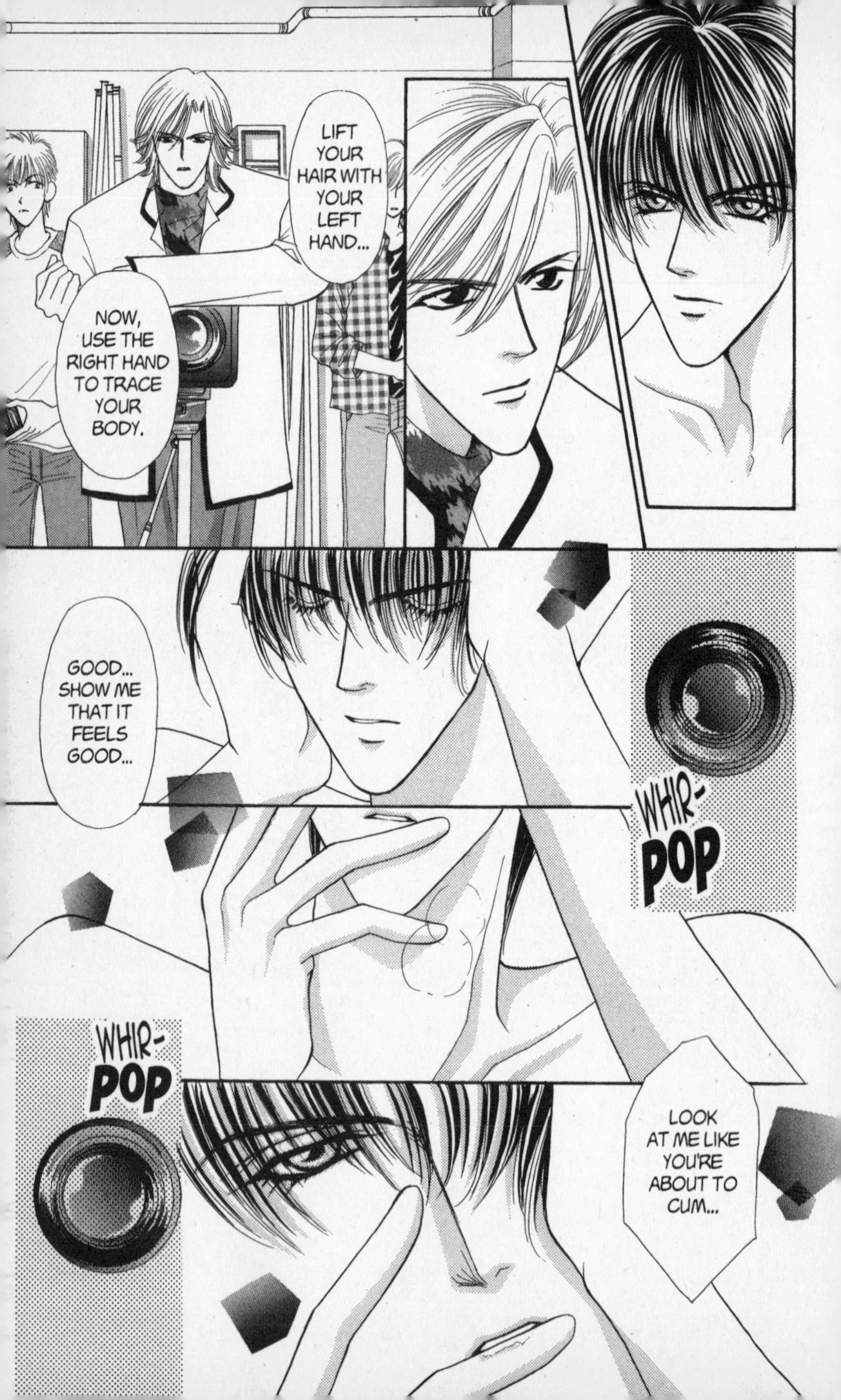
LIFT YOUR HAIR WITH YOUR LEFT HAND...
NOW, USE THE RIGHT HAND TO TRACE YOUR BODY.
WHIR-POP
GOOD... SHOW ME THAT IT FEELS GOOD...
LOOK AT ME LIKE YOU'RE ABOUT TO CUM...
WHIR-POP

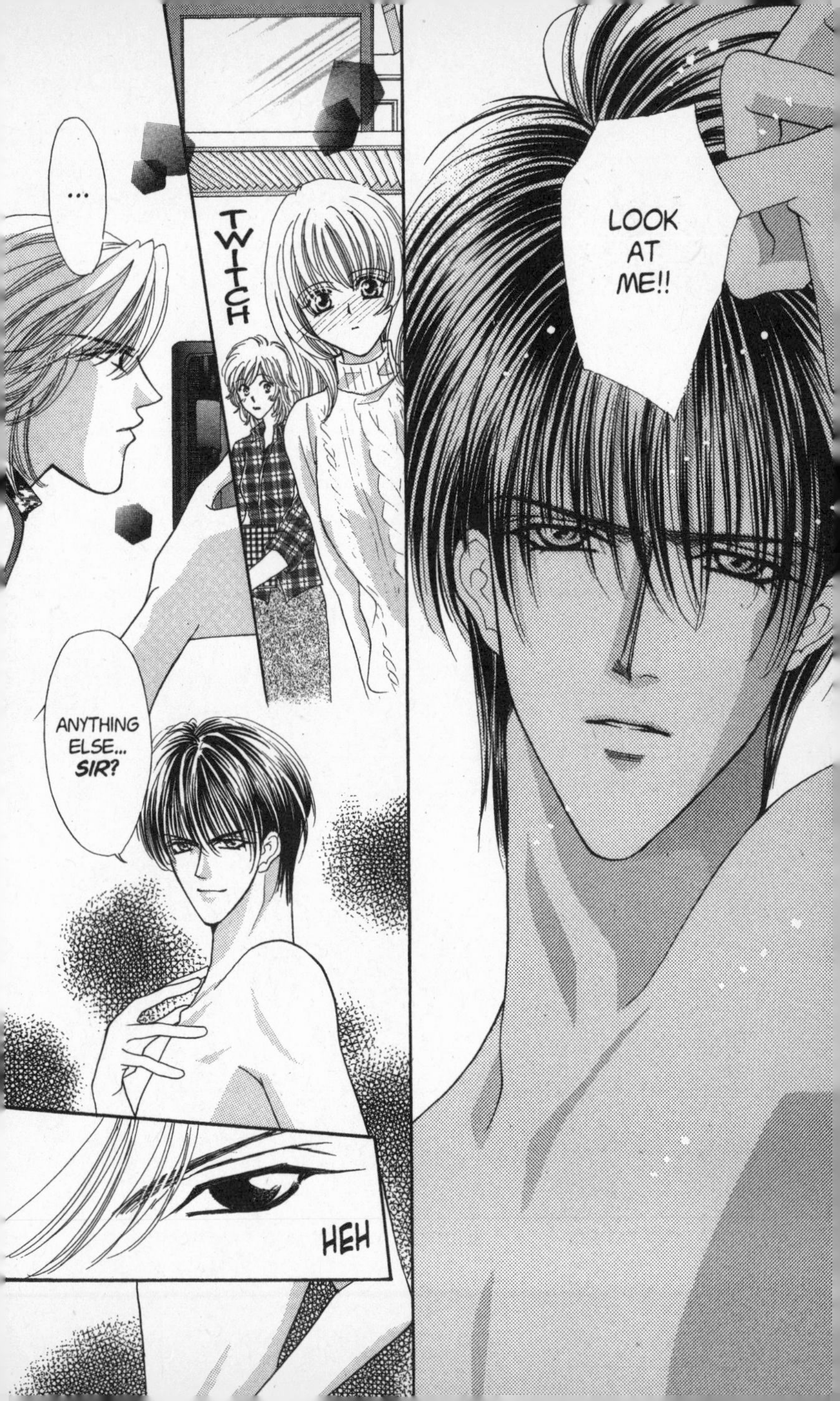

LOOK AT ME!!
TWITCH
...
ANYTHING ELSE... SIR?
HEH

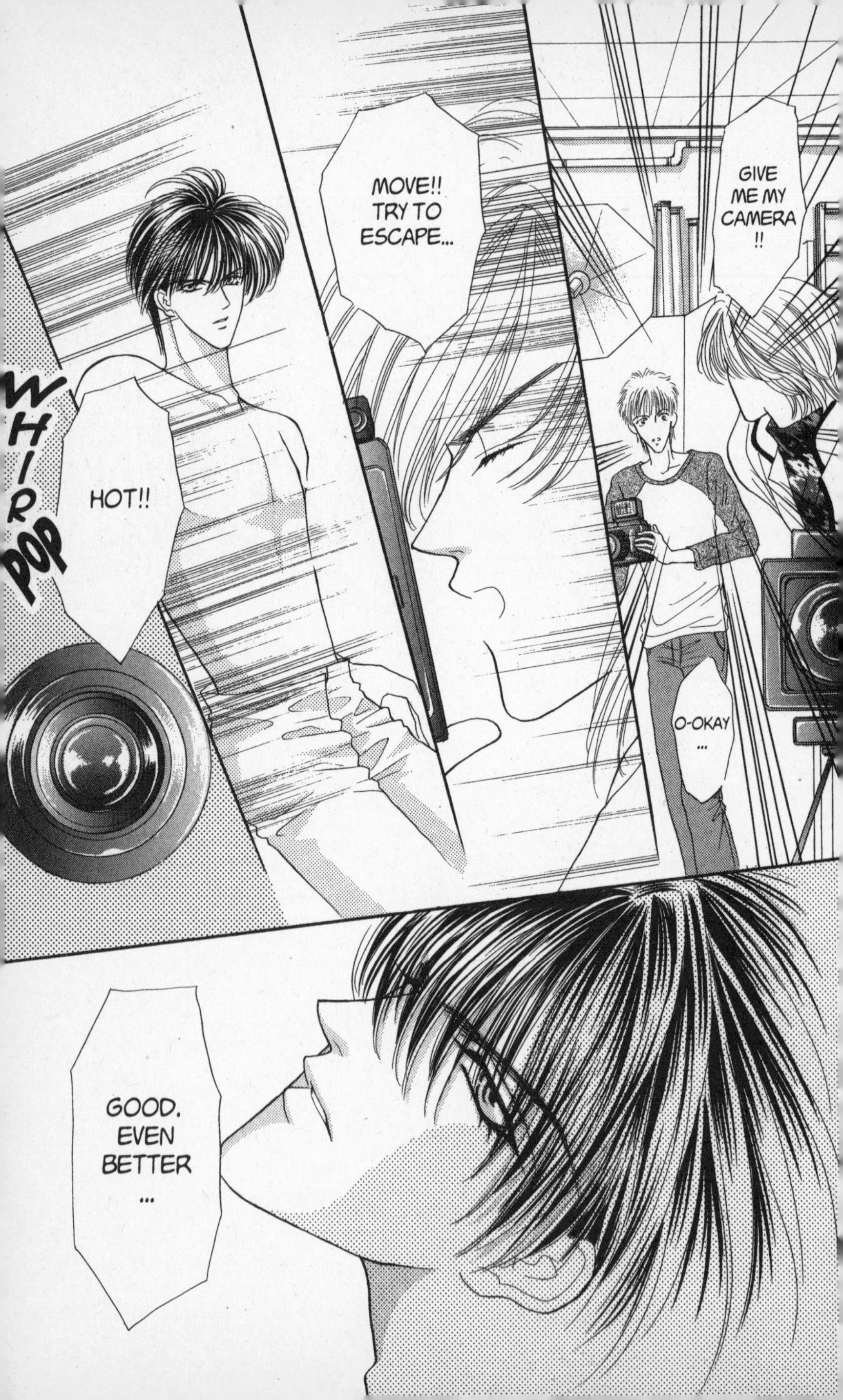
GIVE ME MY CAMERA !!
O-OKAY ...
MOVE!! TRY TO ESCAPE...
WHIR
POP
HOT!!
GOOD. EVEN BETTER ...

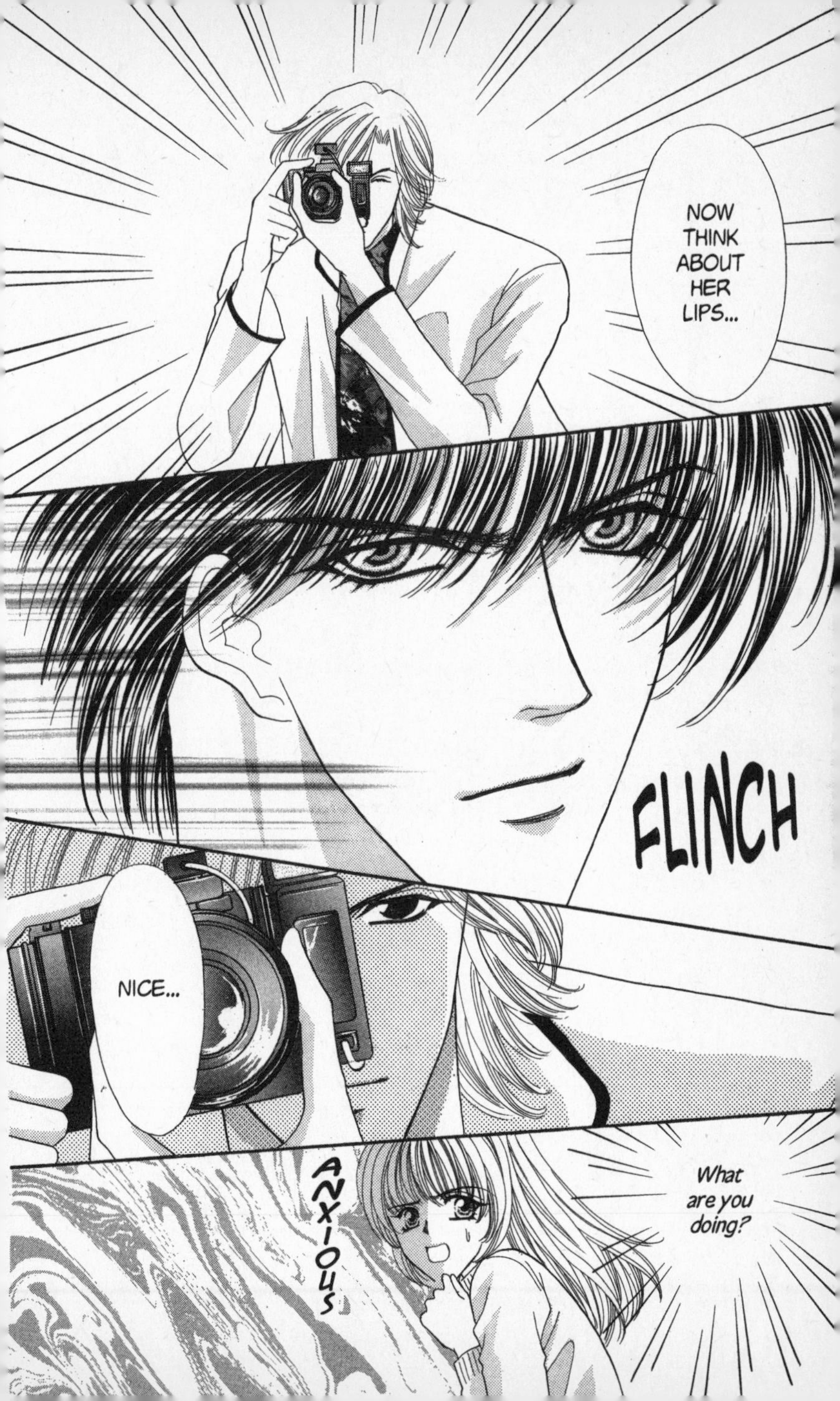
NOW THINK ABOUT HER LIPS...
FLINCH
NICE...
What are you doing?
ANXIOUS

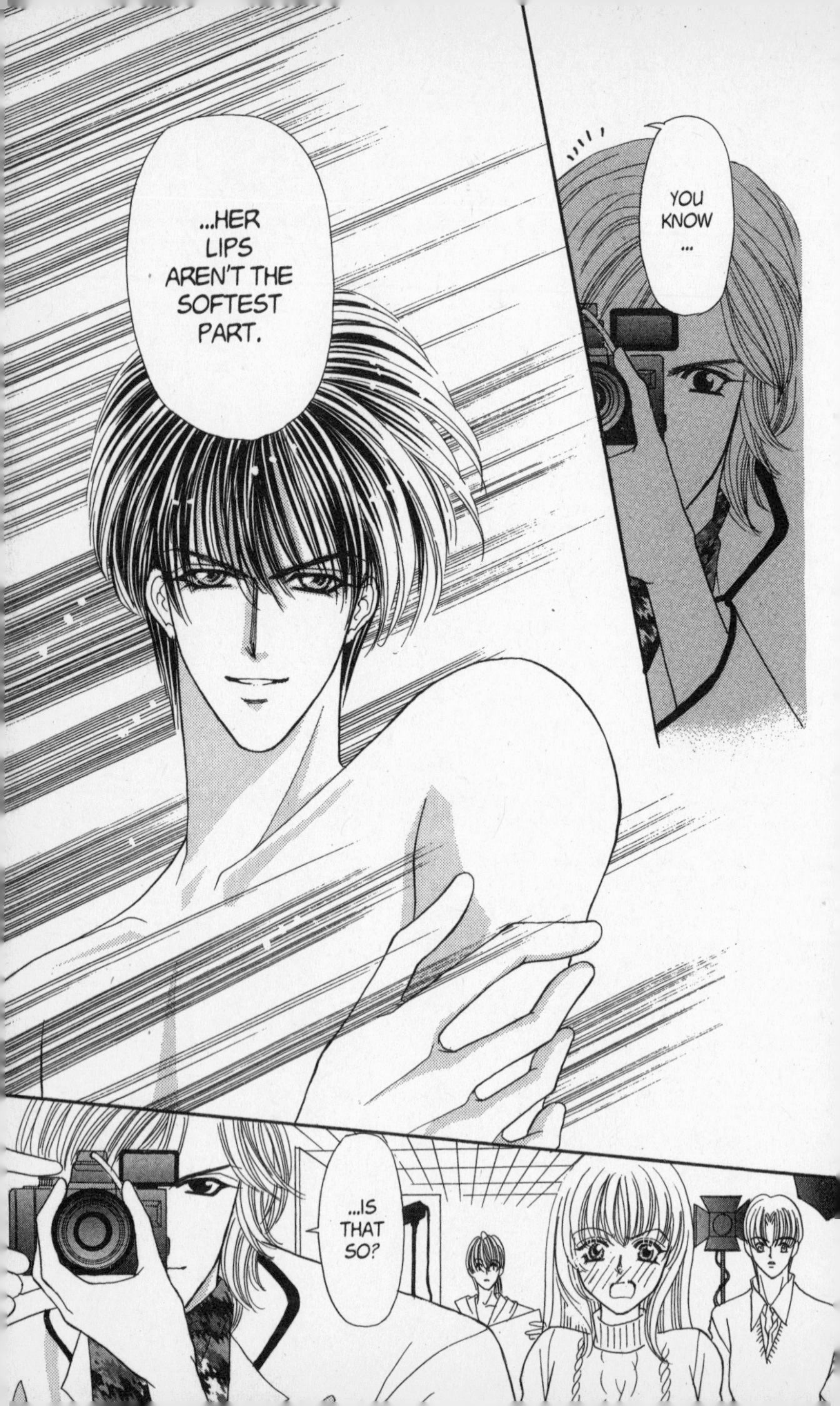
YOU KNOW ...
...HER LIPS AREN'T THE SOFTEST PART.
...IS THAT SO?

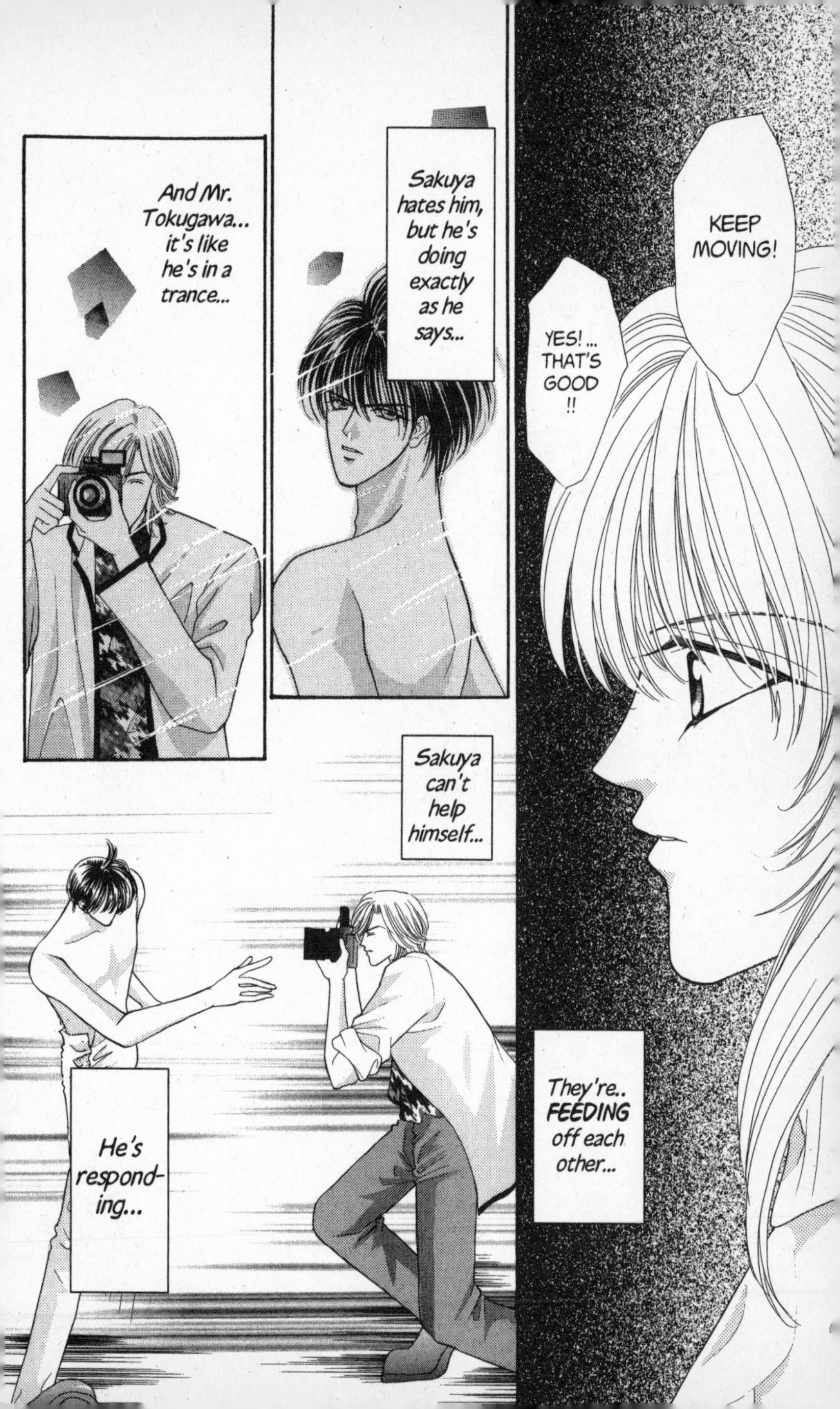
KEEP MOVING!
YES! ... THAT'S GOOD !!
They're.. **FEEDING** off each other...
Sakuya hates him, but he's doing exactly as he says...
And Mr. Tokugawa... it's like he's in a trance...
Sakuya can't help himself...
He's respond-ing...

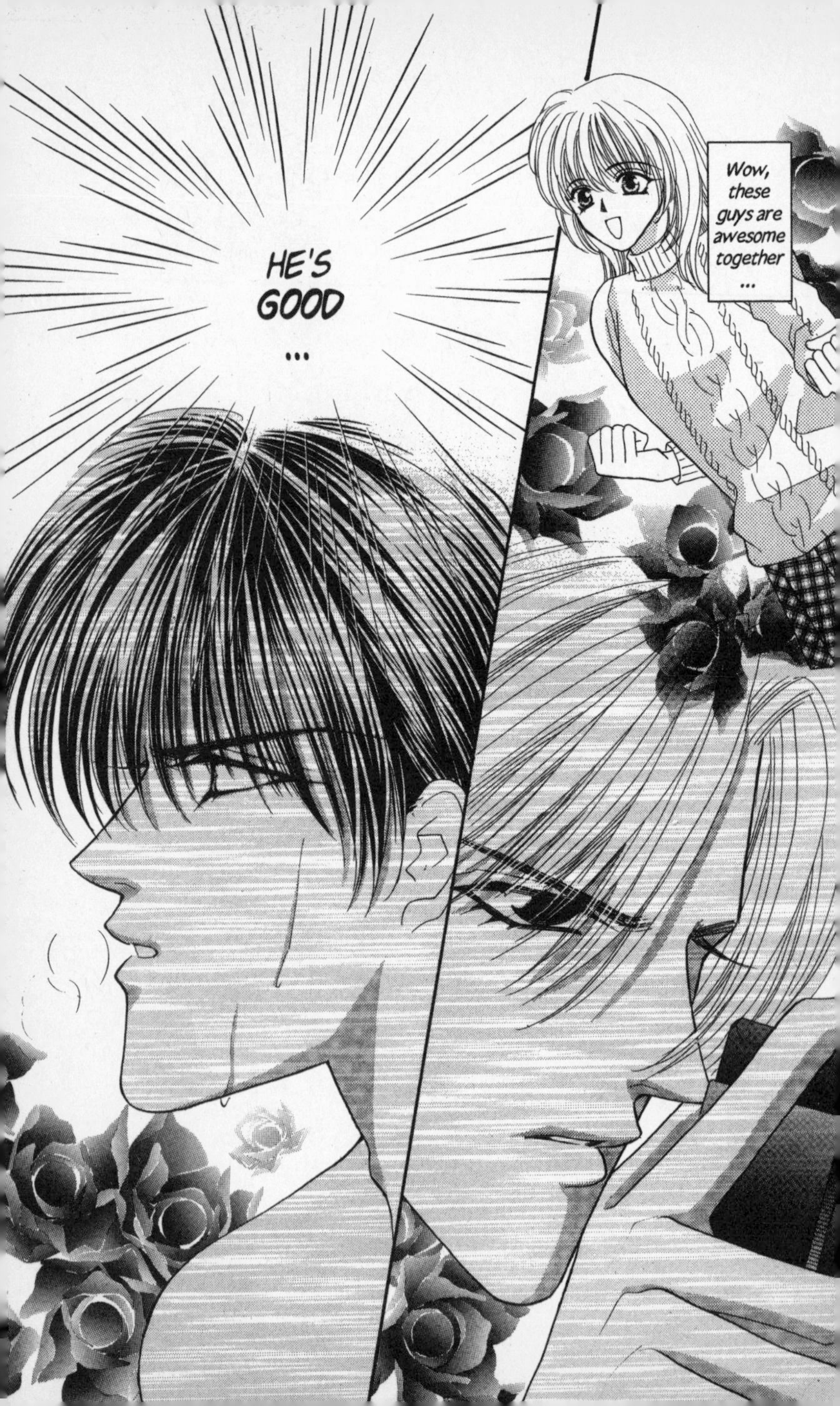
Wow, these guys are awesome together ...
HE'S GOOD ...

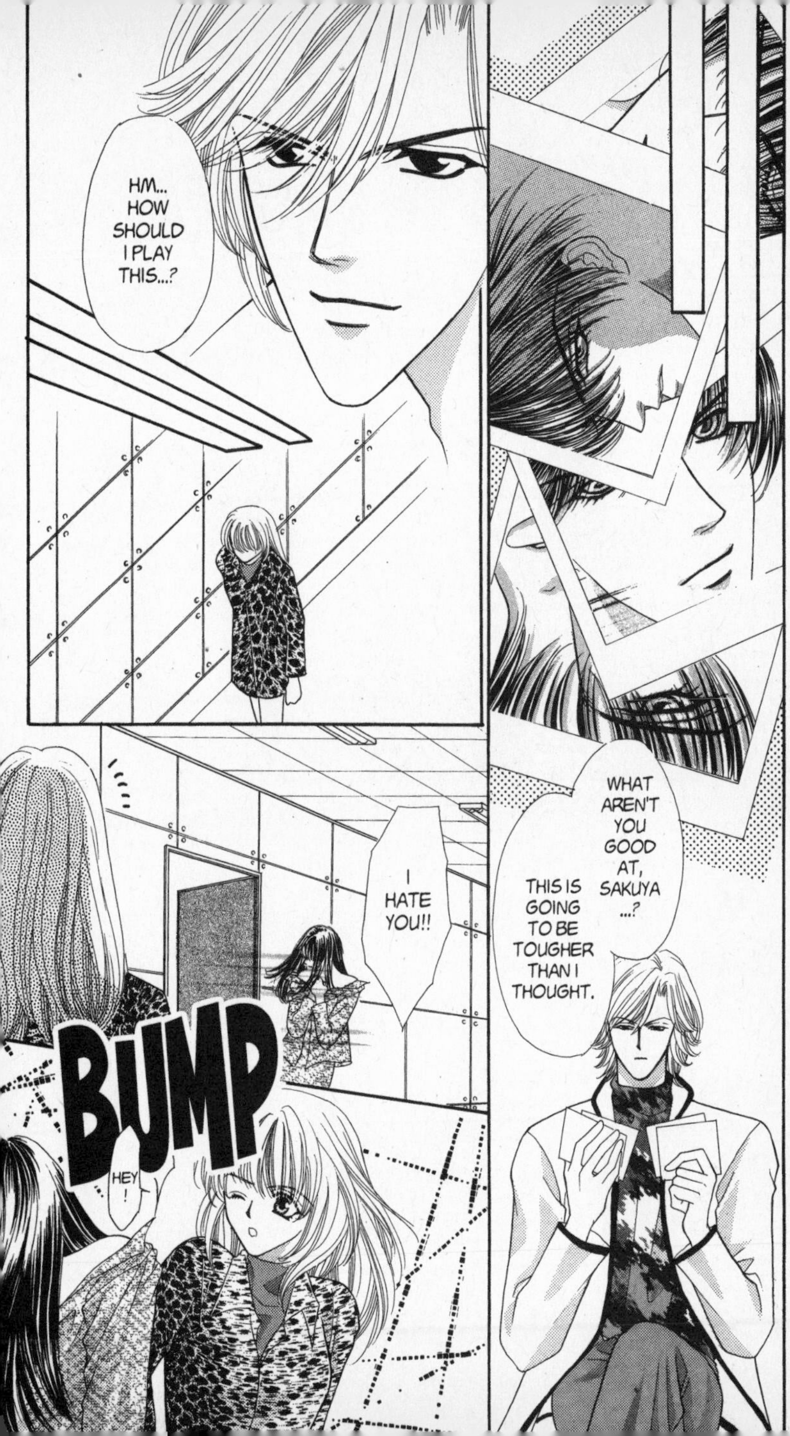
WHAT AREN'T YOU GOOD AT, SAKUYA ...?
THIS IS GOING TO BE TOUGHER THAN I THOUGHT.
HM... HOW SHOULD I PLAY THIS...?
I HATE YOU!!
BUMP
HEY!

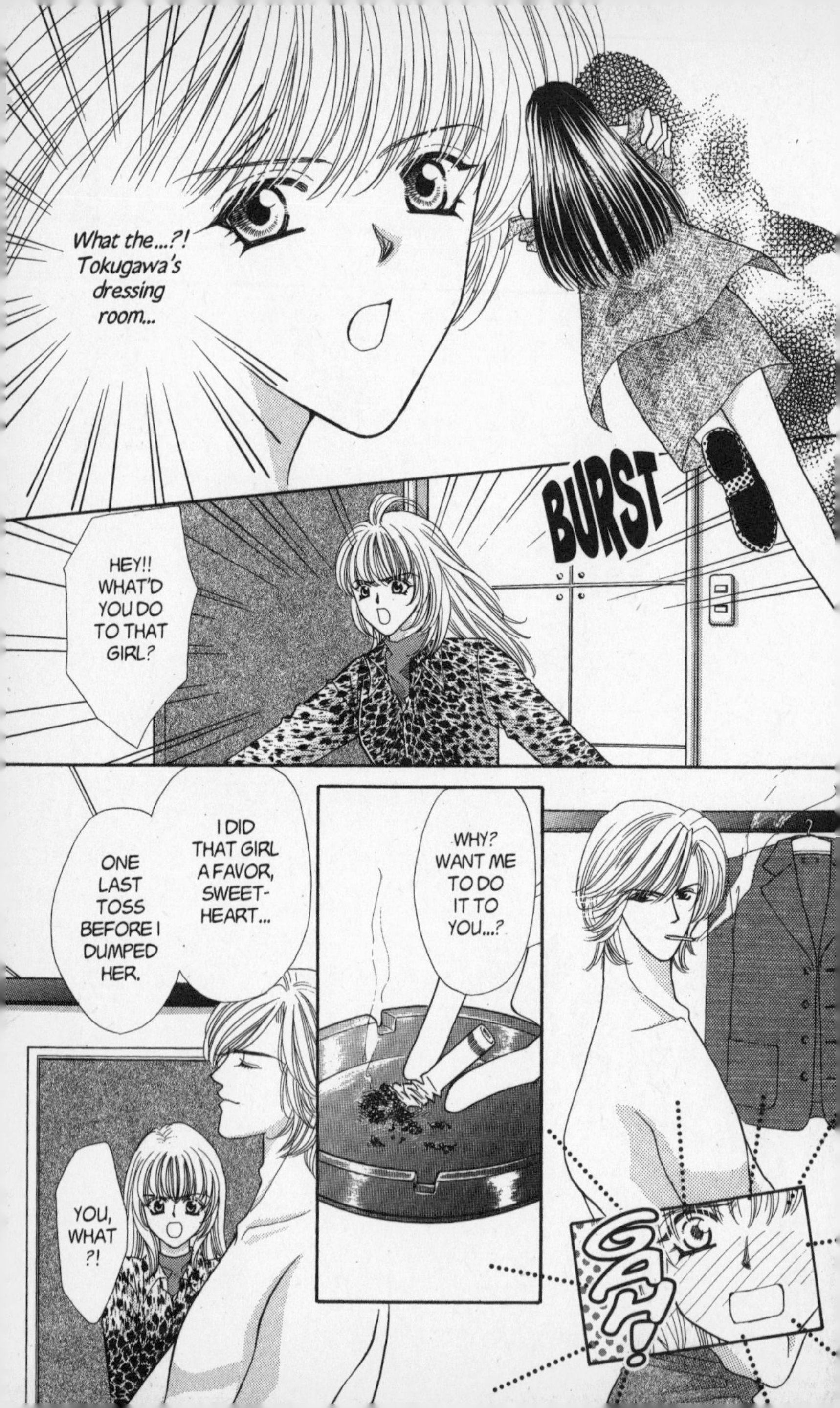

What the...?! Tokugawa's dressing room...
BURST
HEY!! WHAT'D YOU DO TO THAT GIRL?
I DID THAT GIRL A FAVOR, SWEETHEART...
ONE LAST TOSS BEFORE I DUMPED HER.
YOU, WHAT ?!
WHY? WANT ME TO DO IT TO YOU...?
GAH!

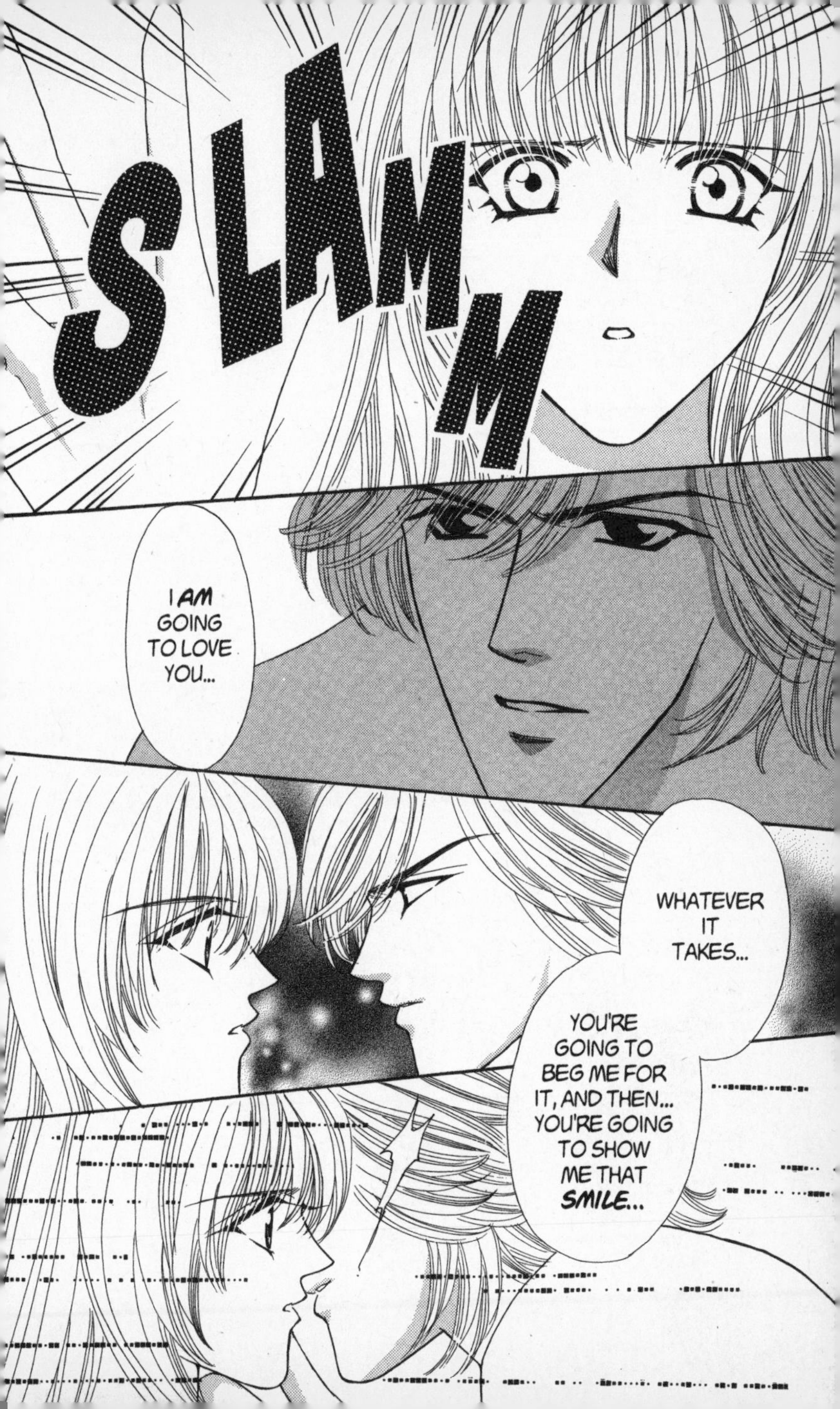
SLAMM
I AM GOING TO LOVE YOU...
WHATEVER IT TAKES...
YOU'RE GOING TO BEG ME FOR IT, AND THEN... YOU'RE GOING TO SHOW ME THAT SMILE...

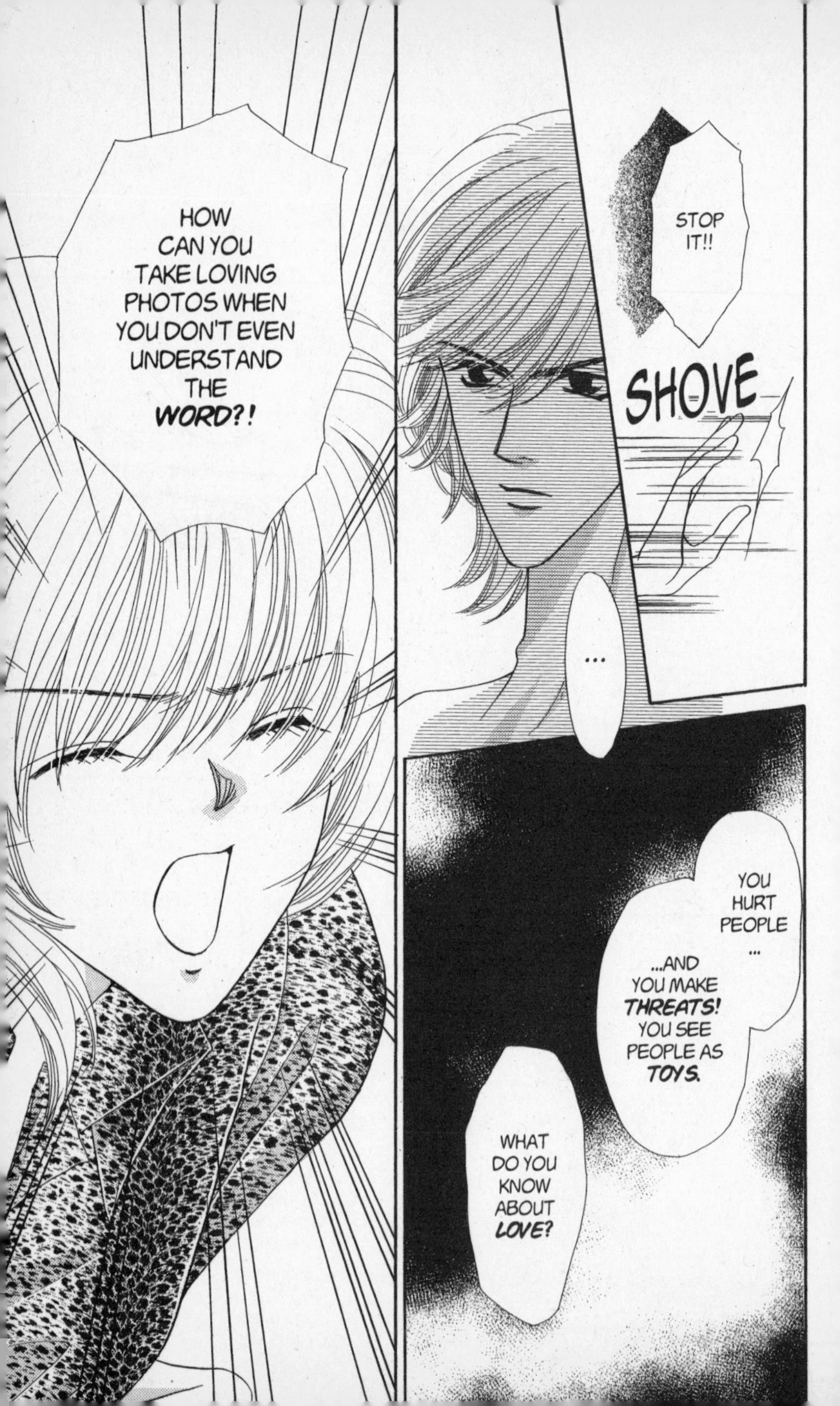
STOP IT!!
SHOVE
...
YOU HURT PEOPLE ...
...AND YOU MAKE **THREATS!** YOU SEE PEOPLE AS **TOYS.**
WHAT DO YOU KNOW ABOUT **LOVE?**
HOW CAN YOU TAKE LOVING PHOTOS WHEN YOU DON'T EVEN UNDERSTAND THE **WORD?!**

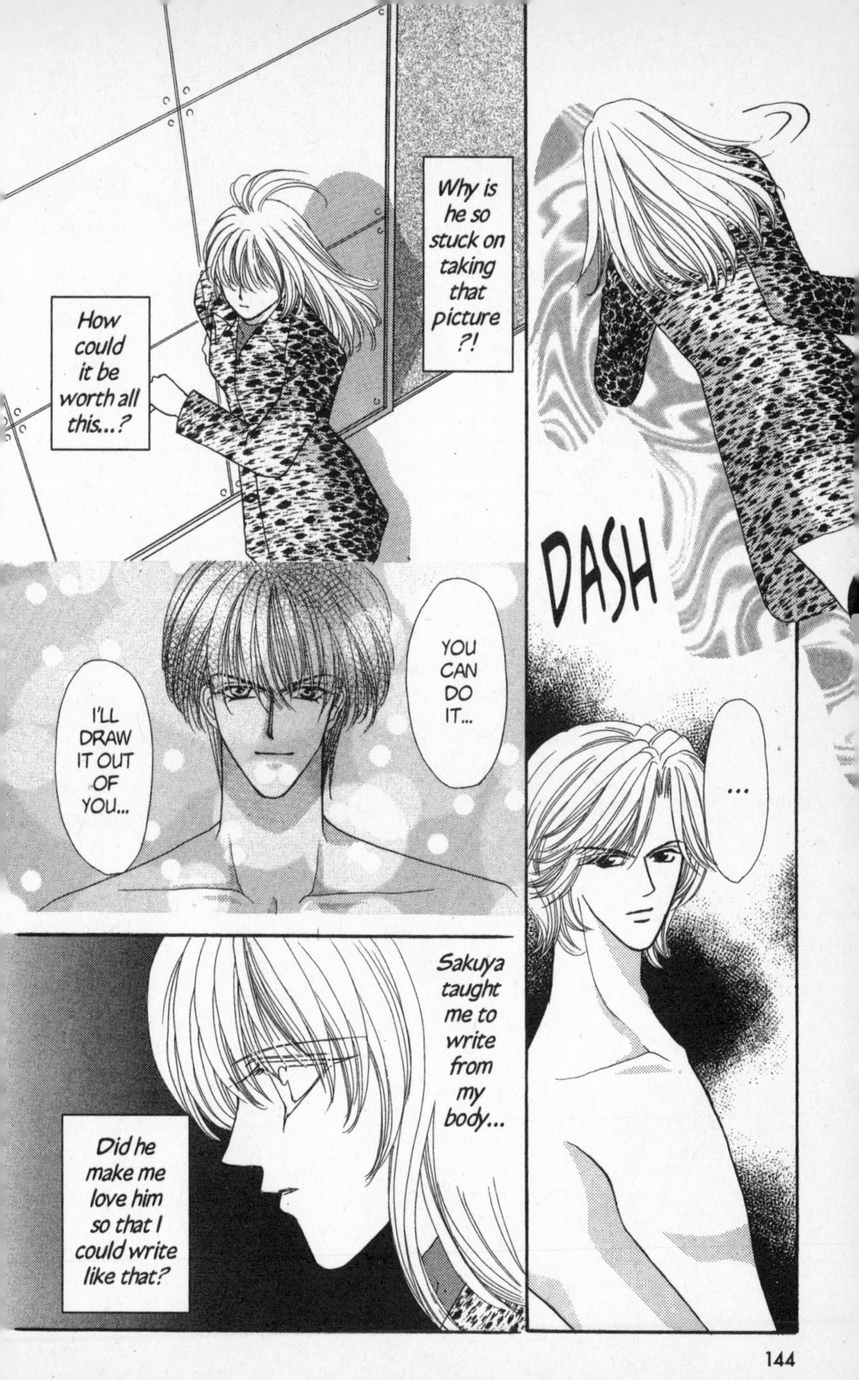
DASH
...
Why is he so stuck on taking that picture?!
How could it be worth all this...?
YOU CAN DO IT...
I'LL DRAW IT OUT OF YOU...
Sakuya taught me to write from my body...
Did he make me love him so that I could write like that?

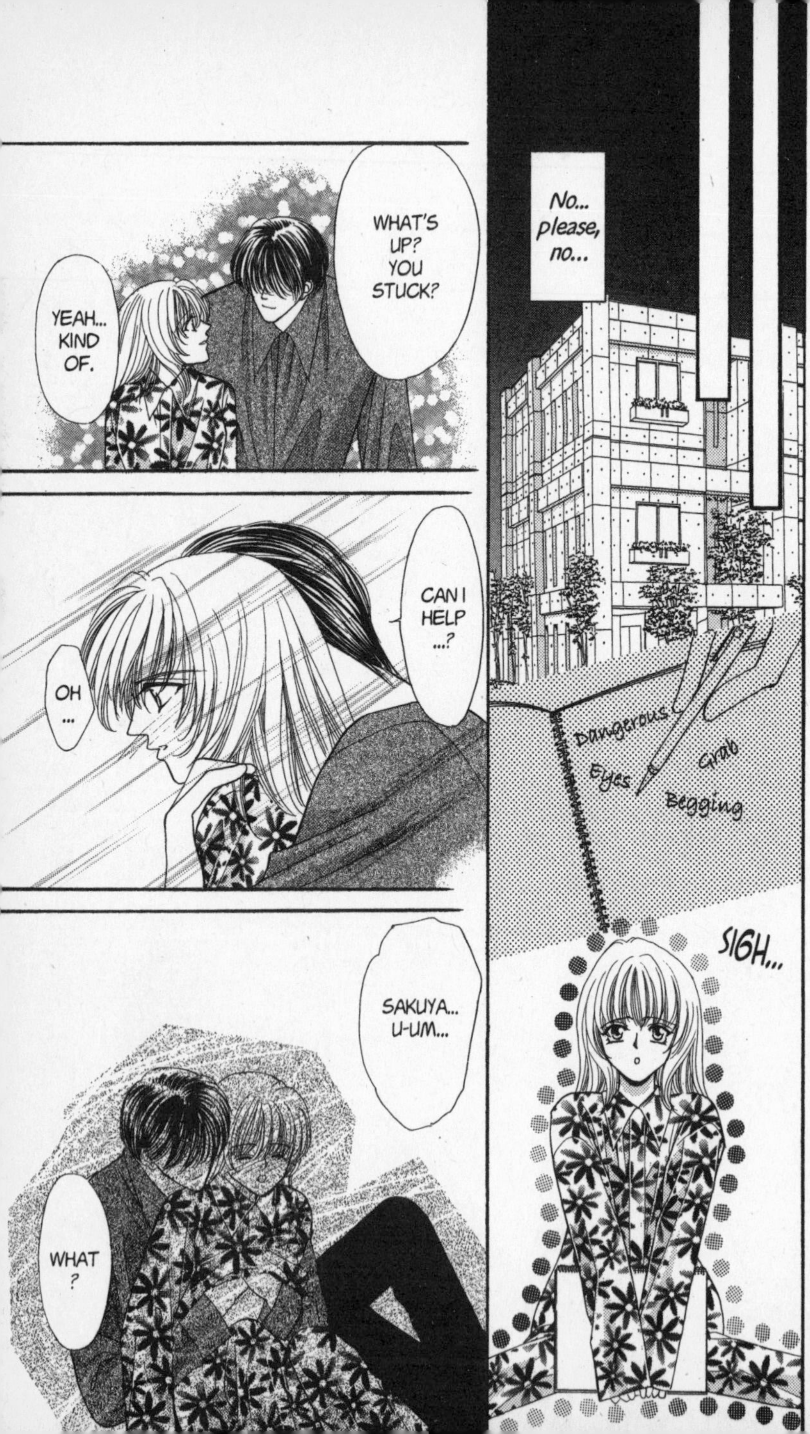
No... please, no...
Dangerous
Eyes
Grab
Begging
SIGH...
WHAT'S UP? YOU STUCK?
YEAH... KIND OF.
CAN I HELP ...?
OH ...
SAKUYA... U-UM...
WHAT ?

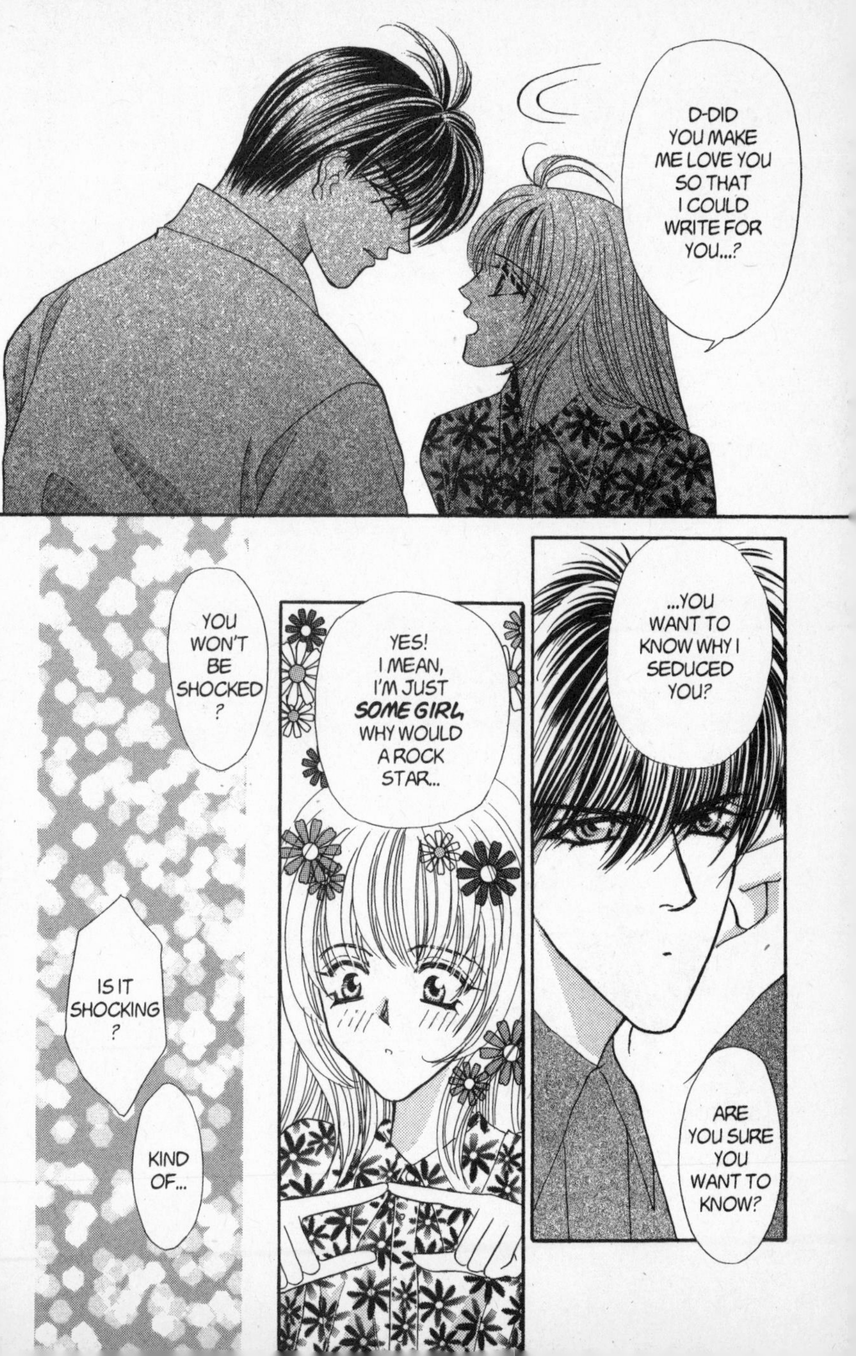
D-DID YOU MAKE ME LOVE YOU SO THAT I COULD WRITE FOR YOU...?
...YOU WANT TO KNOW WHY I SEDUCED YOU?
ARE YOU SURE YOU WANT TO KNOW?
YES! I MEAN, I'M JUST **SOME GIRL,** WHY WOULD A ROCK STAR...
YOU WON'T BE SHOCKED?
IS IT SHOCKING?
KIND OF...

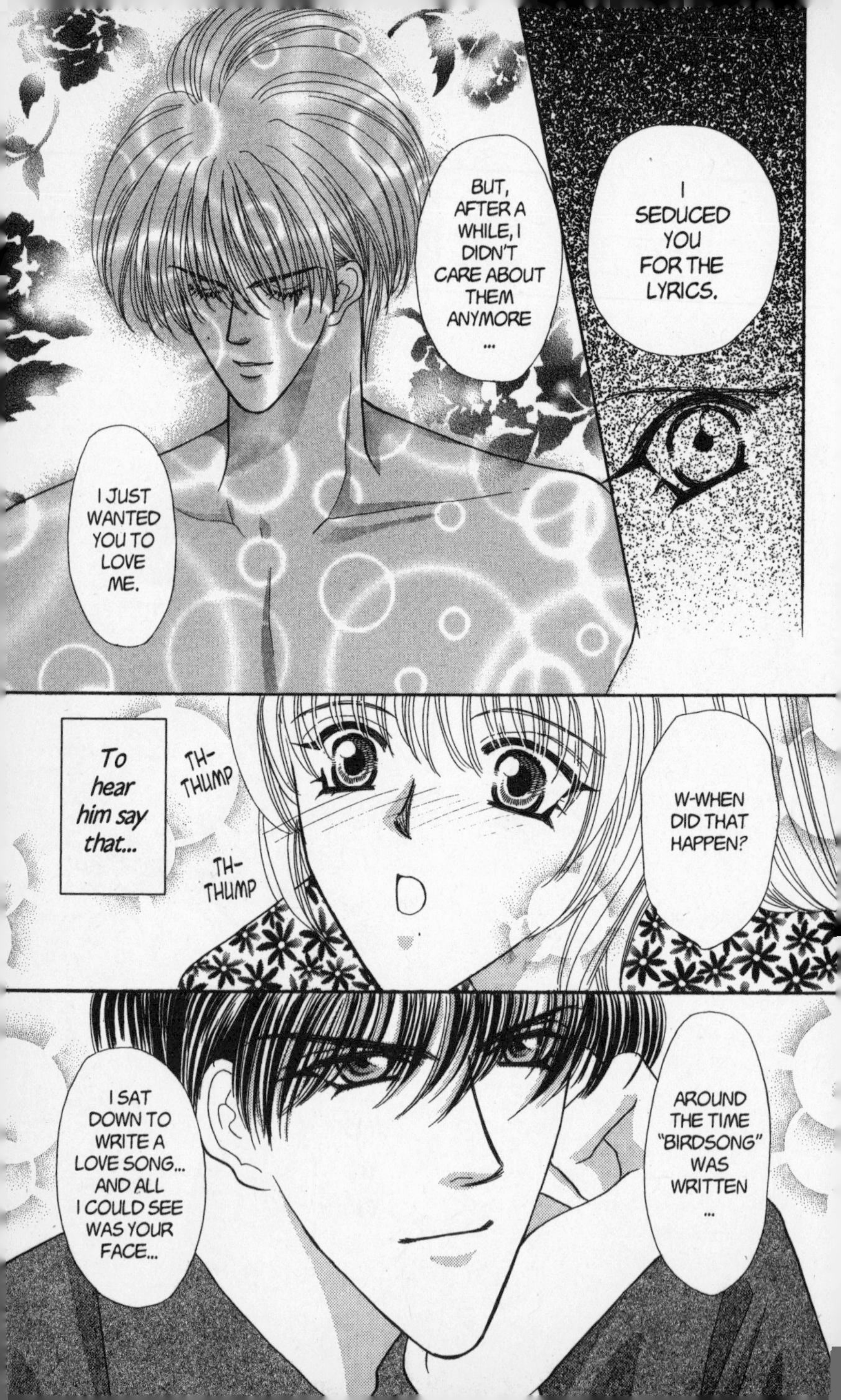
I SEDUCED YOU FOR THE LYRICS.
BUT, AFTER A WHILE, I DIDN'T CARE ABOUT THEM ANYMORE ...
I JUST WANTED YOU TO LOVE ME.
W-WHEN DID THAT HAPPEN?
TH-THUMP
TH-THUMP
To hear him say that...
AROUND THE TIME "BIRDSONG" WAS WRITTEN ...
I SAT DOWN TO WRITE A LOVE SONG... AND ALL I COULD SEE WAS YOUR FACE...

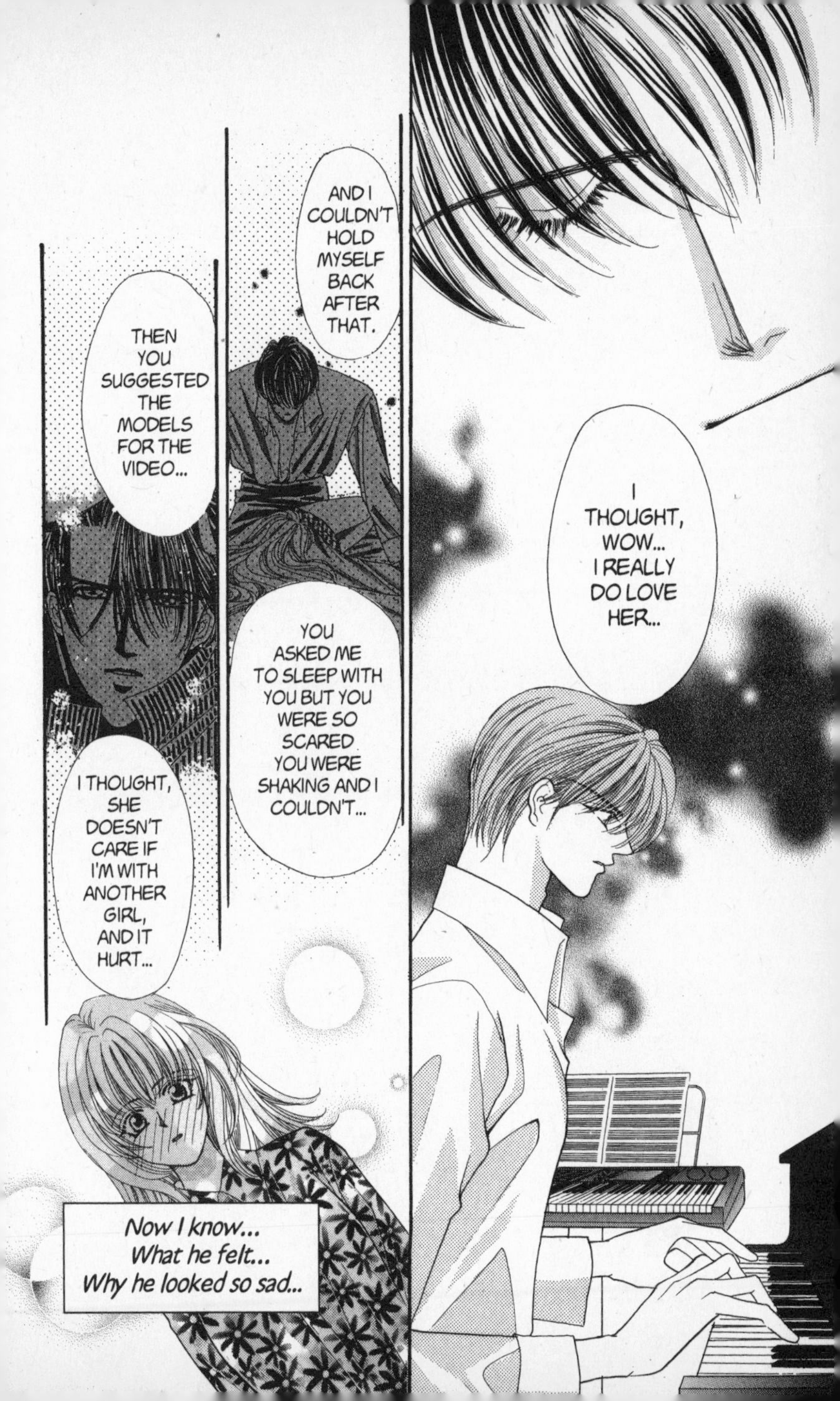
I THOUGHT, WOW... I REALLY DO LOVE HER...
AND I COULDN'T HOLD MYSELF BACK AFTER THAT.
YOU ASKED ME TO SLEEP WITH YOU BUT YOU WERE SO SCARED YOU WERE SHAKING AND I COULDN'T...
THEN YOU SUGGESTED THE MODELS FOR THE VIDEO...
I THOUGHT, SHE DOESN'T CARE IF I'M WITH ANOTHER GIRL, AND IT HURT...
Now I know... What he felt... Why he looked so sad...

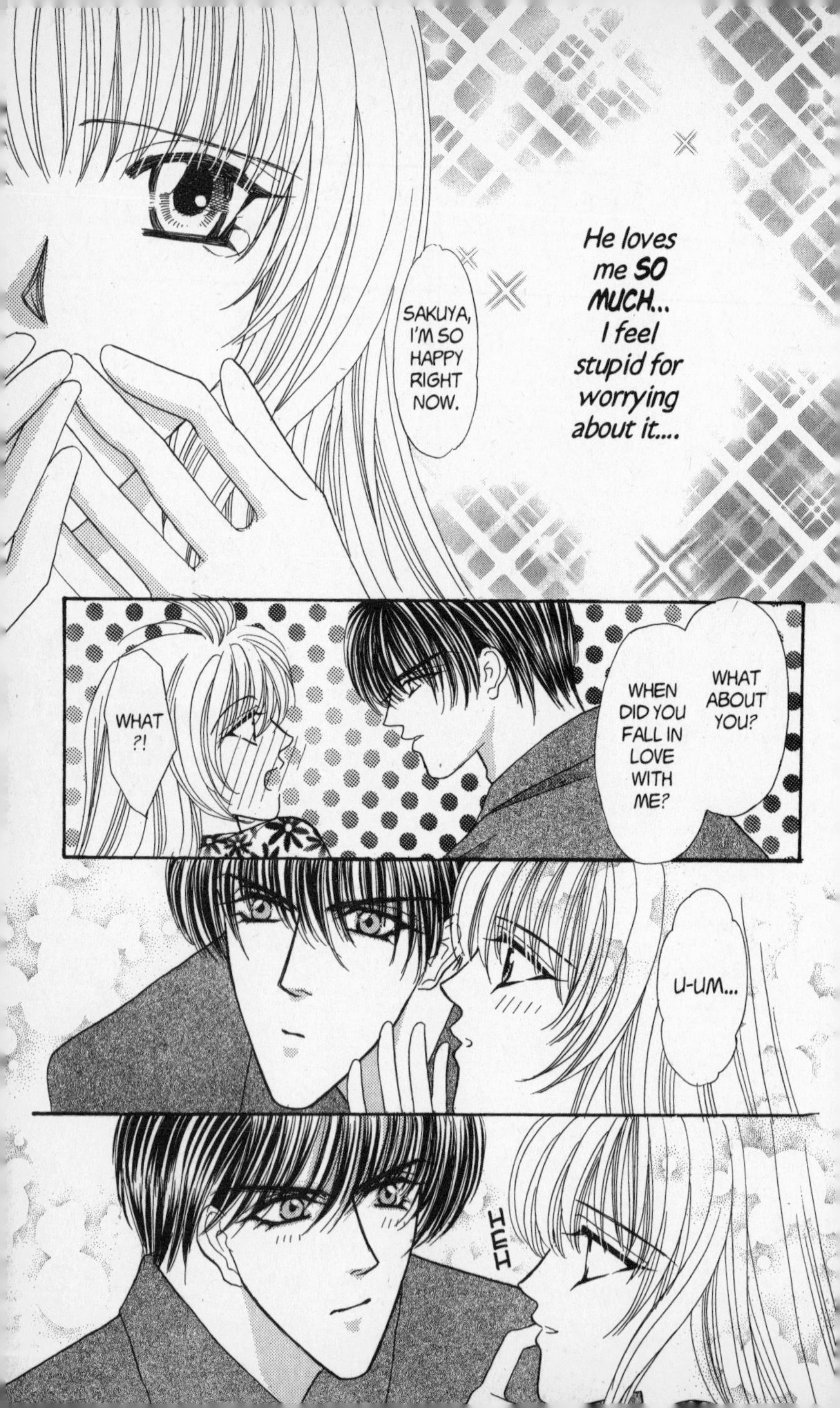
He loves me SO MUCH... I feel stupid for worrying about it....
SAKUYA, I'M SO HAPPY RIGHT NOW.
WHAT ABOUT YOU?
WHEN DID YOU FALL IN LOVE WITH ME?
WHAT ?!
U-UM...
HEH

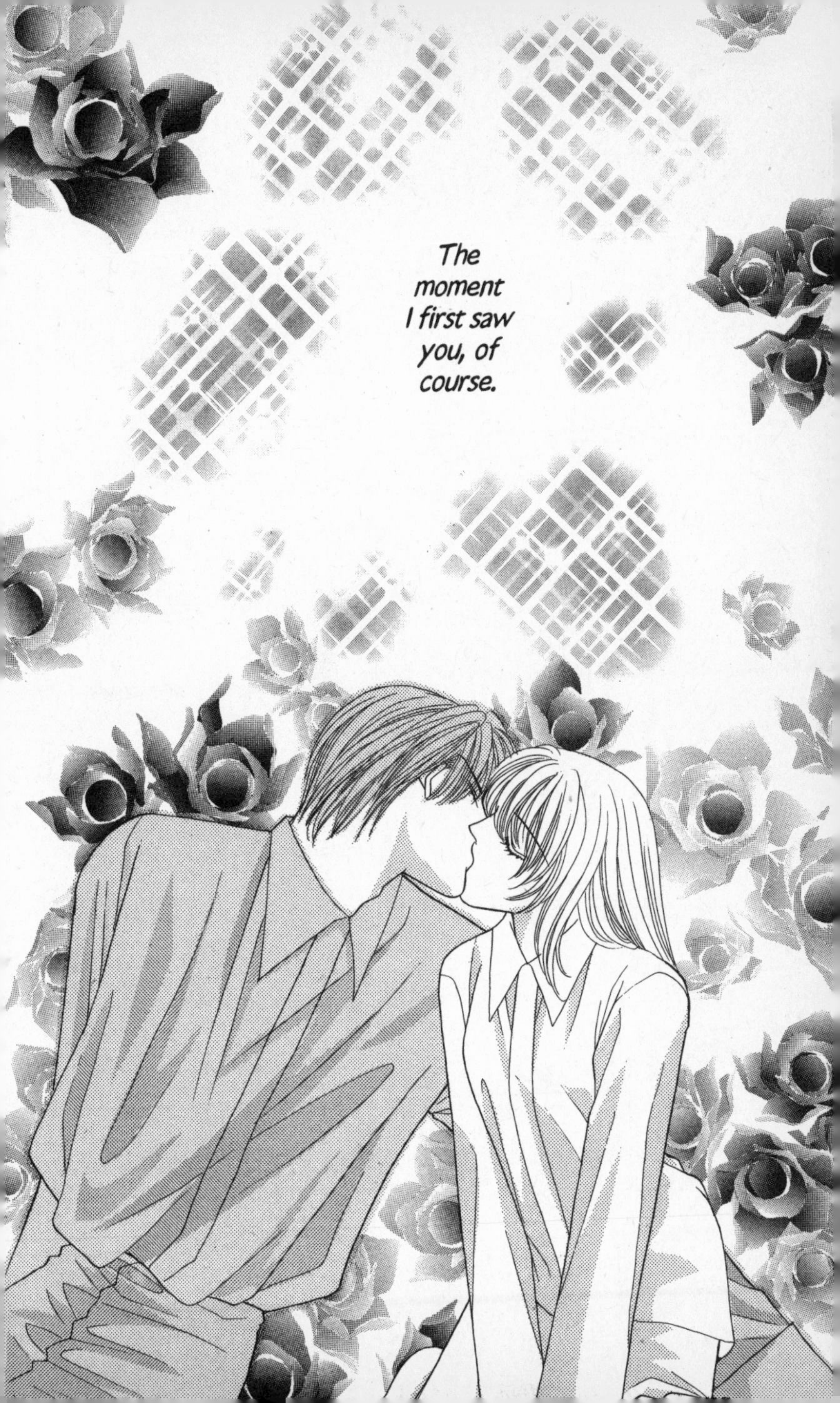
The moment I first saw you, of course.

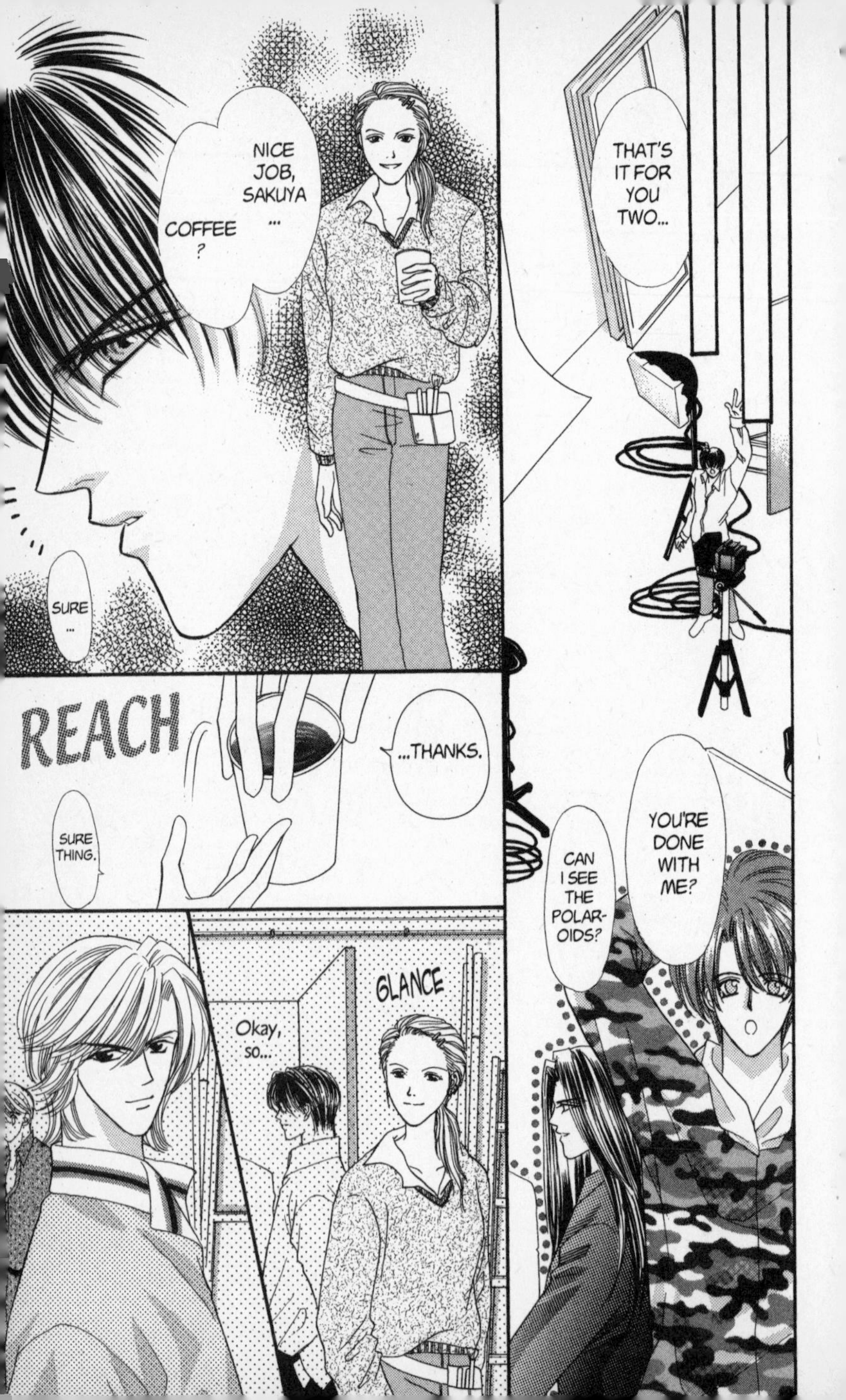
THAT'S IT FOR YOU TWO...
NICE JOB, SAKUYA ...
COFFEE ?
SURE ...
REACH
...THANKS.
SURE THING.
YOU'RE DONE WITH ME?
CAN I SEE THE POLAR-OIDS?
GLANCE
Okay, so...

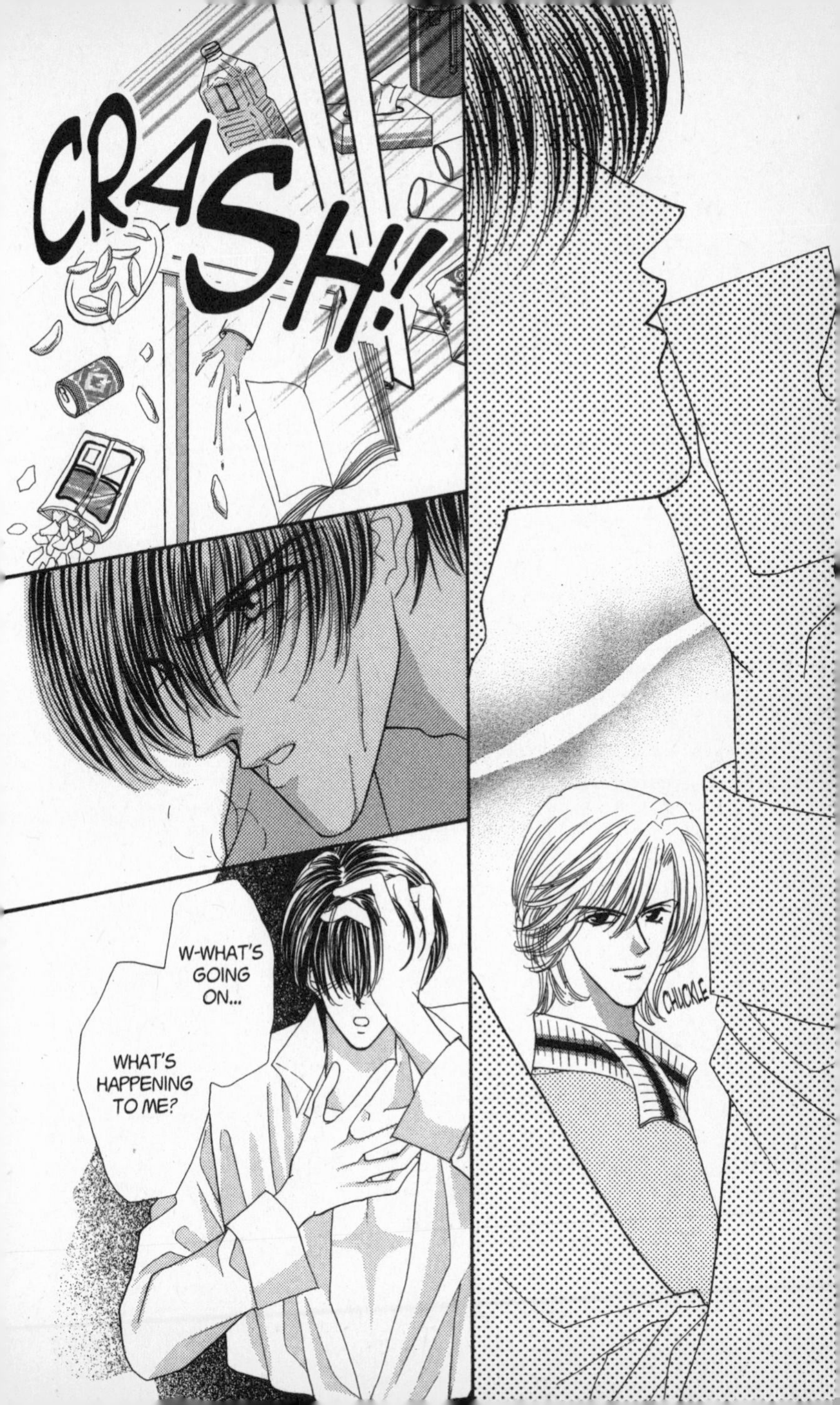
CHUCKLE
CRASH!!
W-WHAT'S GOING ON...
WHAT'S HAPPENING TO ME?

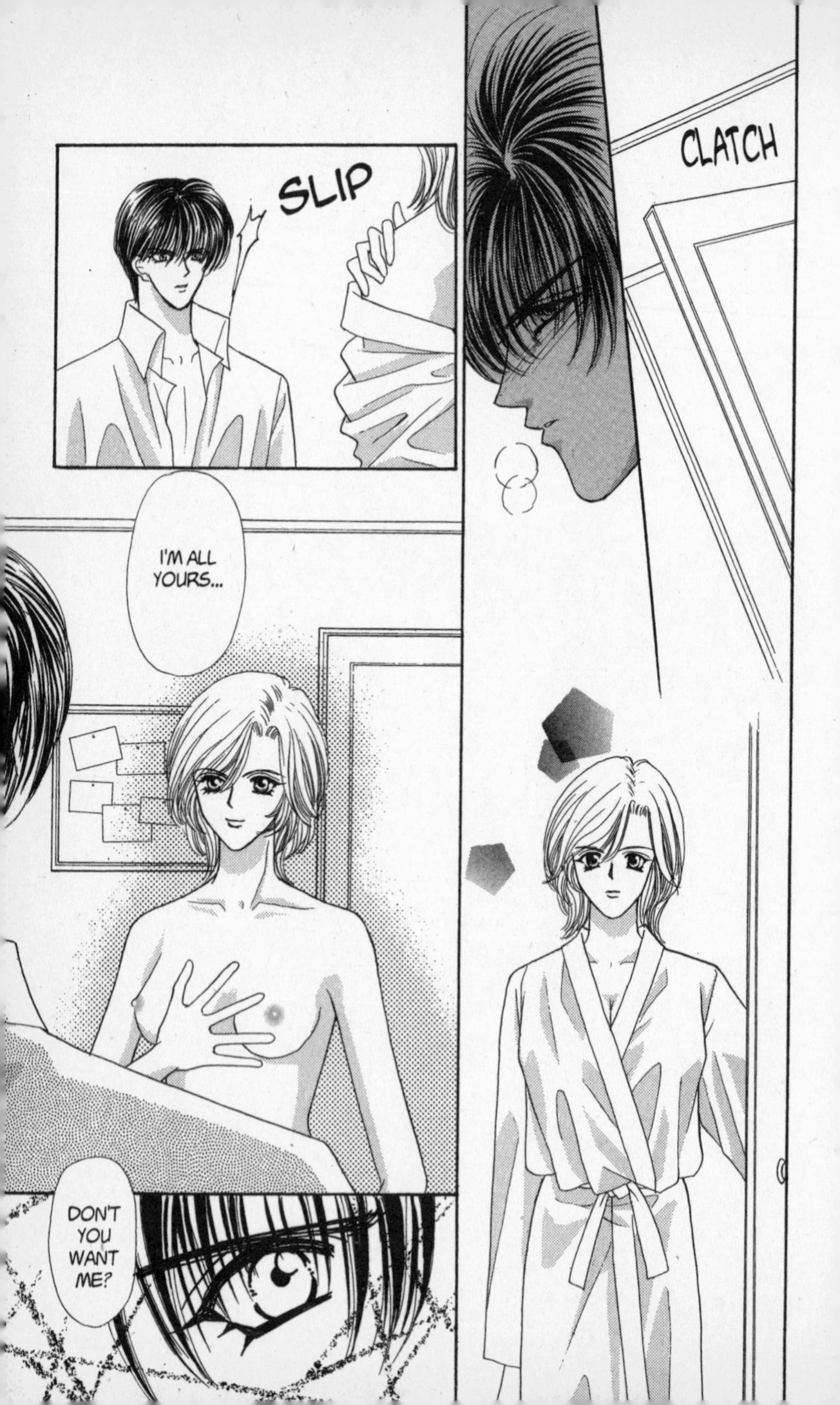
CLATCH
SLIP
I'M ALL YOURS...
DON'T YOU WANT ME?

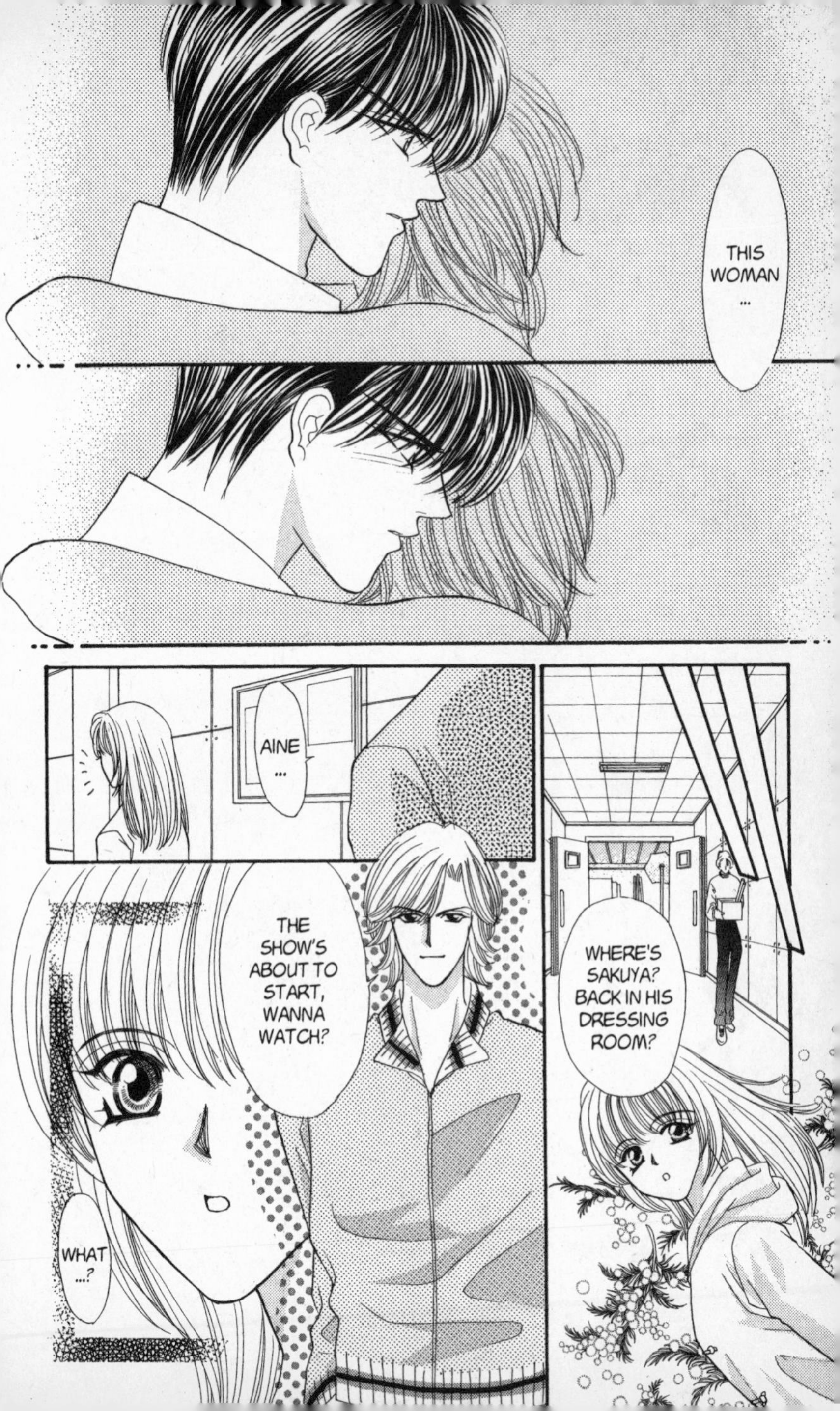
THIS WOMAN ...
WHERE'S SAKUYA? BACK IN HIS DRESSING ROOM?
AINE ...
THE SHOW'S ABOUT TO START, WANNA WATCH?
WHAT ...?

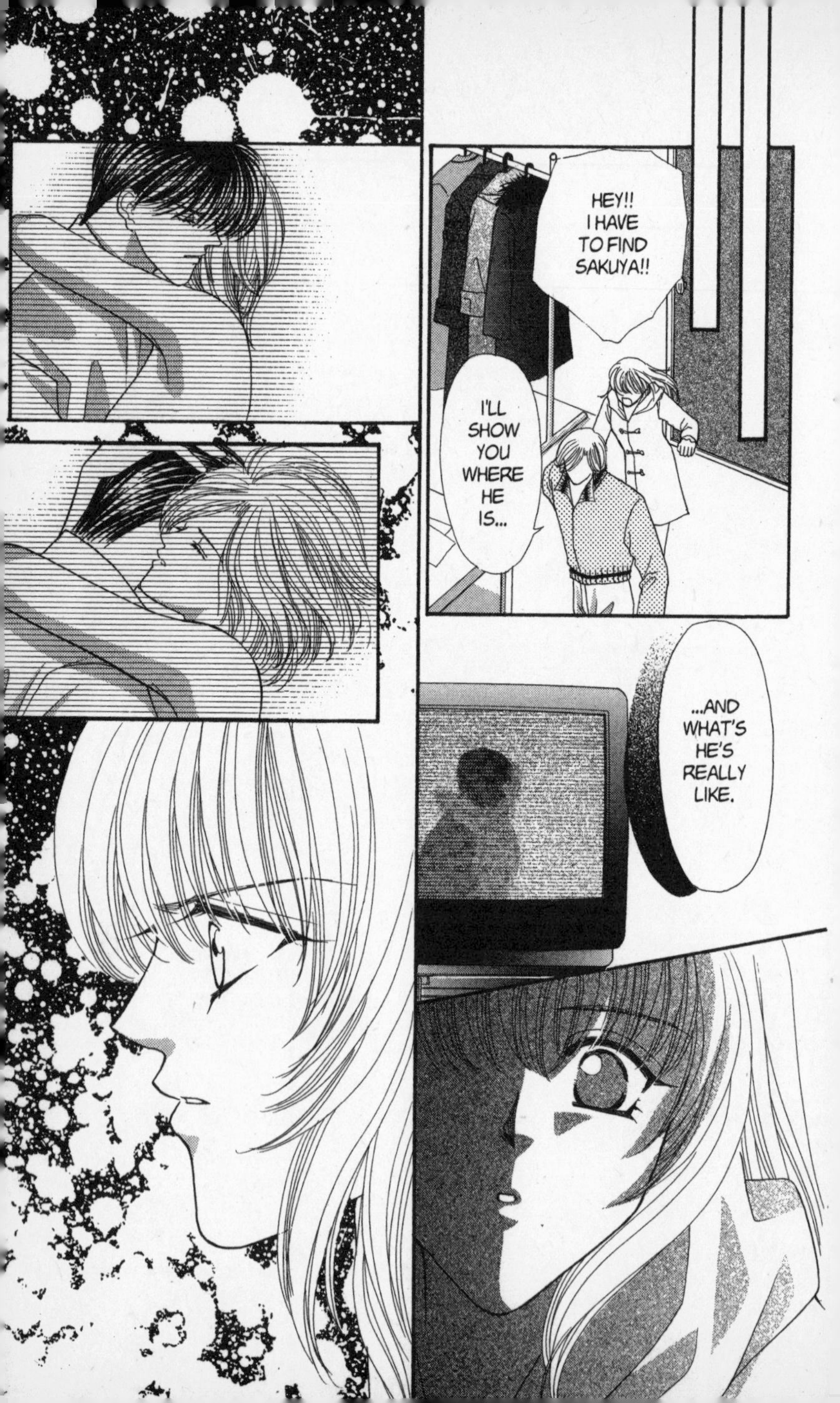
HEY!! I HAVE TO FIND SAKUYA!!
I'LL SHOW YOU WHERE HE IS...
...AND WHAT'S HE'S REALLY LIKE.

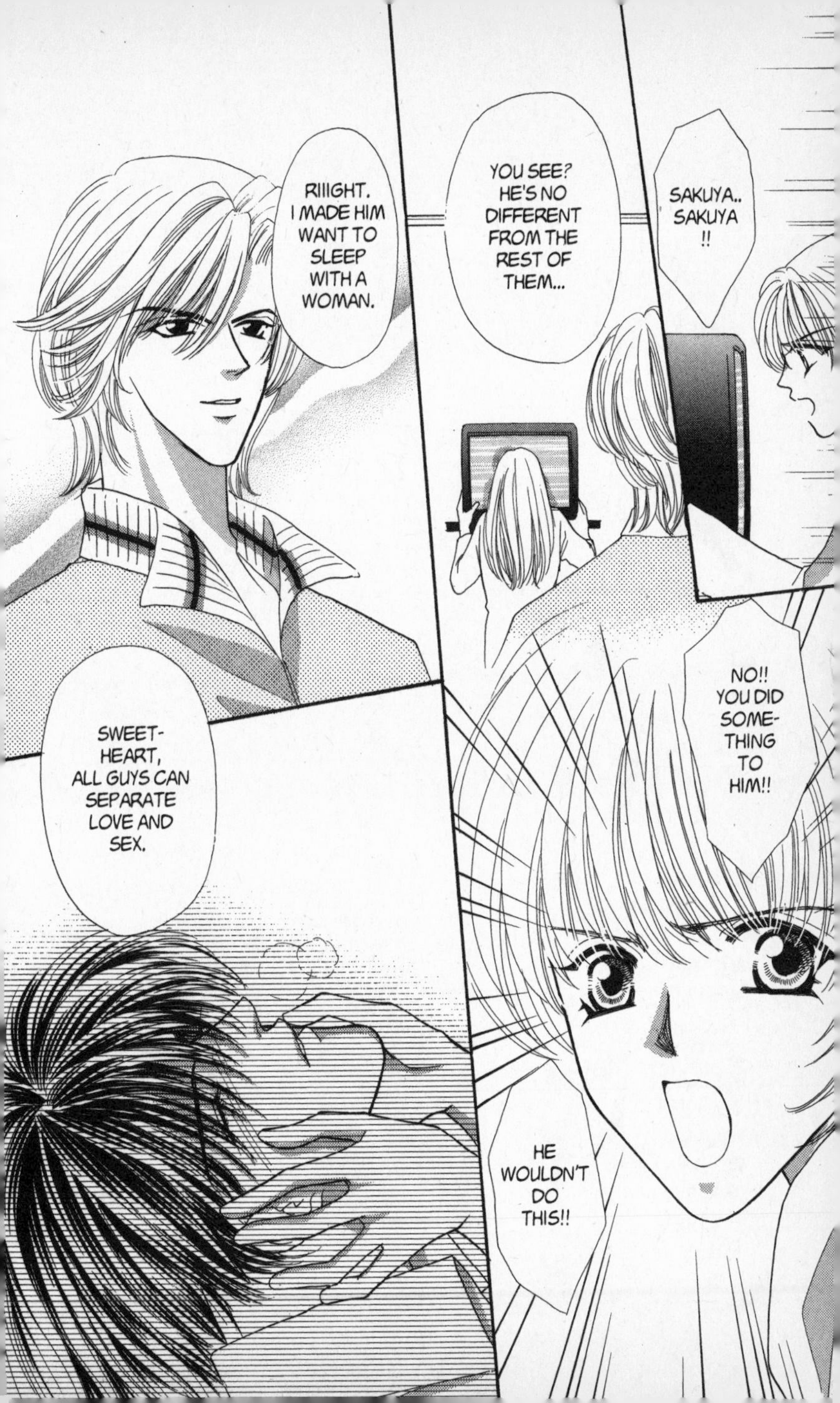
SAKUYA.. SAKUYA !!
YOU SEE? HE'S NO DIFFERENT FROM THE REST OF THEM...
RIIIGHT. I MADE HIM WANT TO SLEEP WITH A WOMAN.
NO!! YOU DID SOME-THING TO HIM!!
HE WOULDN'T DO THIS!!
SWEET-HEART, ALL GUYS CAN SEPARATE LOVE AND SEX.

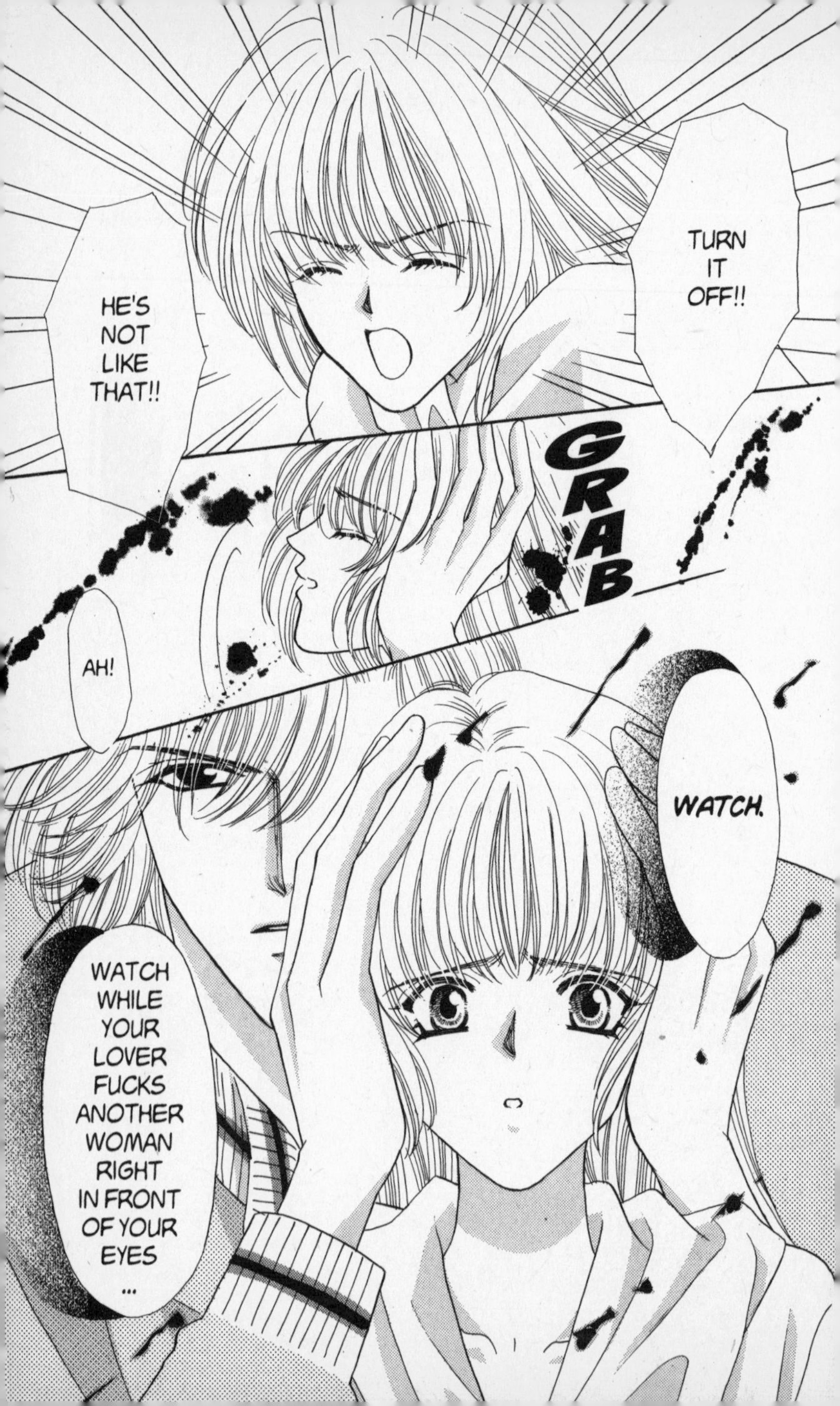
TURN IT OFF!!
HE'S NOT LIKE THAT!!
GRAB
AH!
WATCH.
WATCH WHILE YOUR LOVER FUCKS ANOTHER WOMAN RIGHT IN FRONT OF YOUR EYES ...

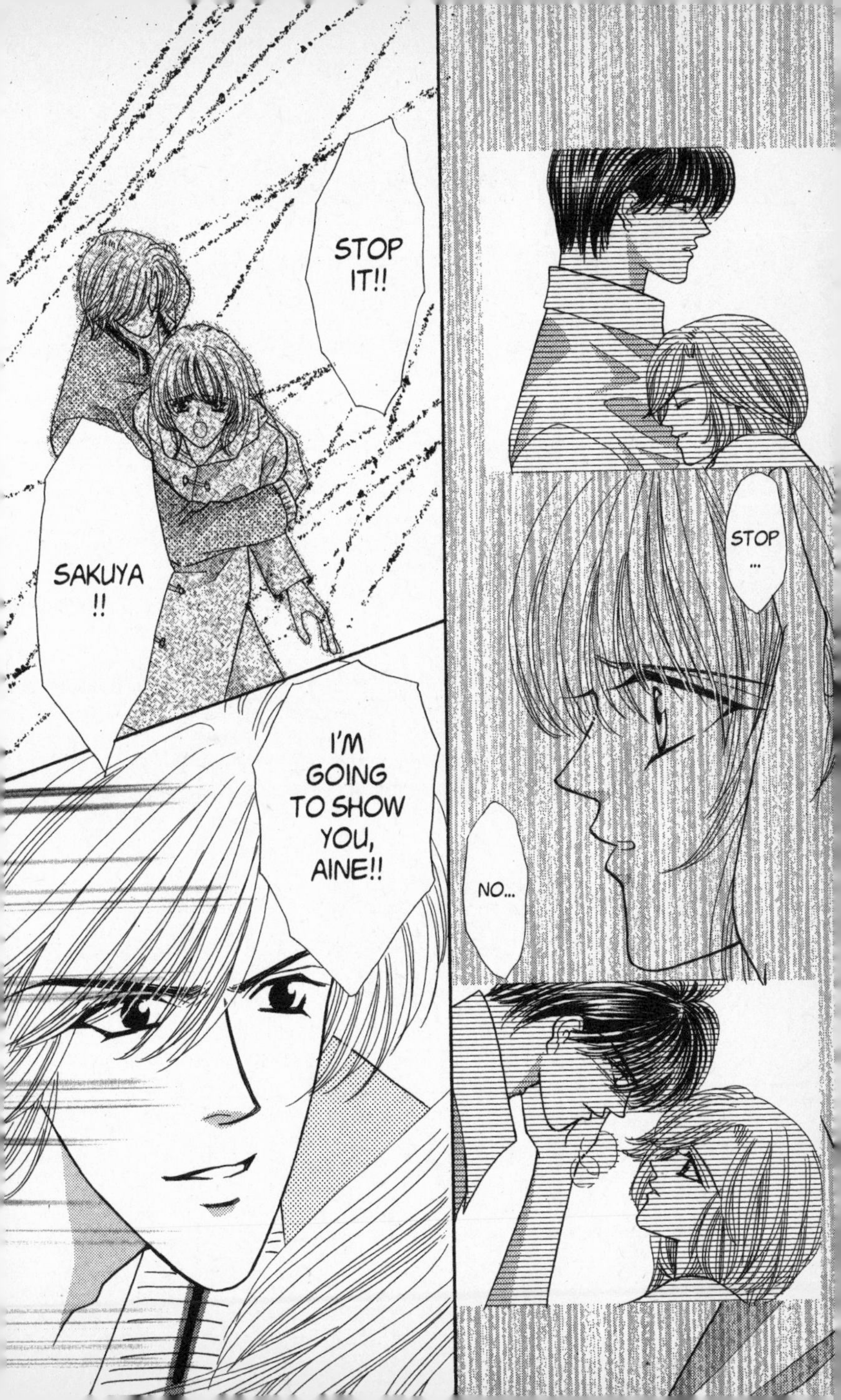
STOP ...
NO...
STOP IT!!
SAKUYA !!
I'M GOING TO SHOW YOU, AINE!!

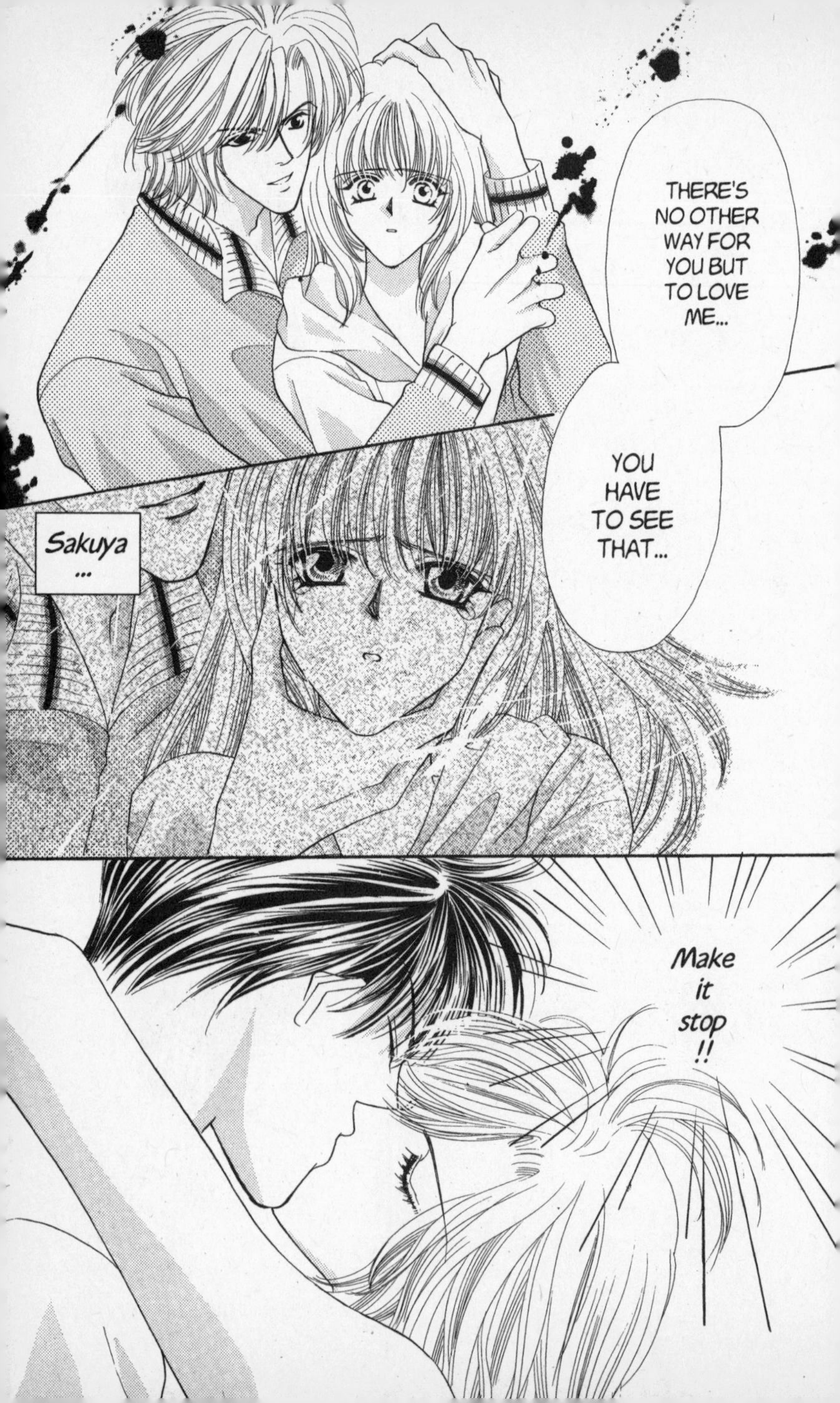
THERE'S NO OTHER WAY FOR YOU BUT TO LOVE ME...
YOU HAVE TO SEE THAT...
Sakuya ...
Make it stop !!

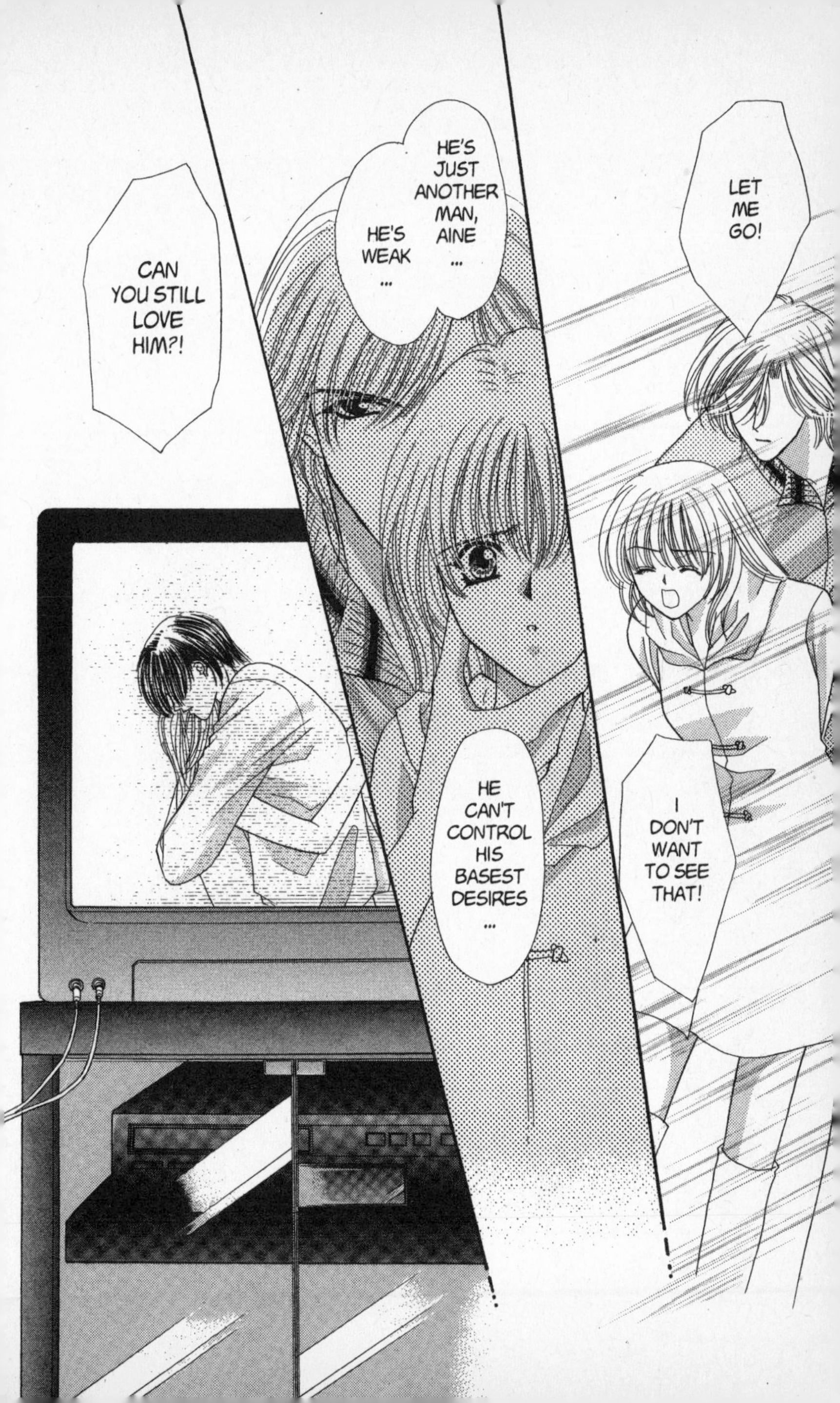
LET ME GO!
I DON'T WANT TO SEE THAT!
HE'S JUST ANOTHER MAN, AINE ...
HE'S WEAK ...
HE CAN'T CONTROL HIS BASEST DESIRES ...
CAN YOU STILL LOVE HIM?!

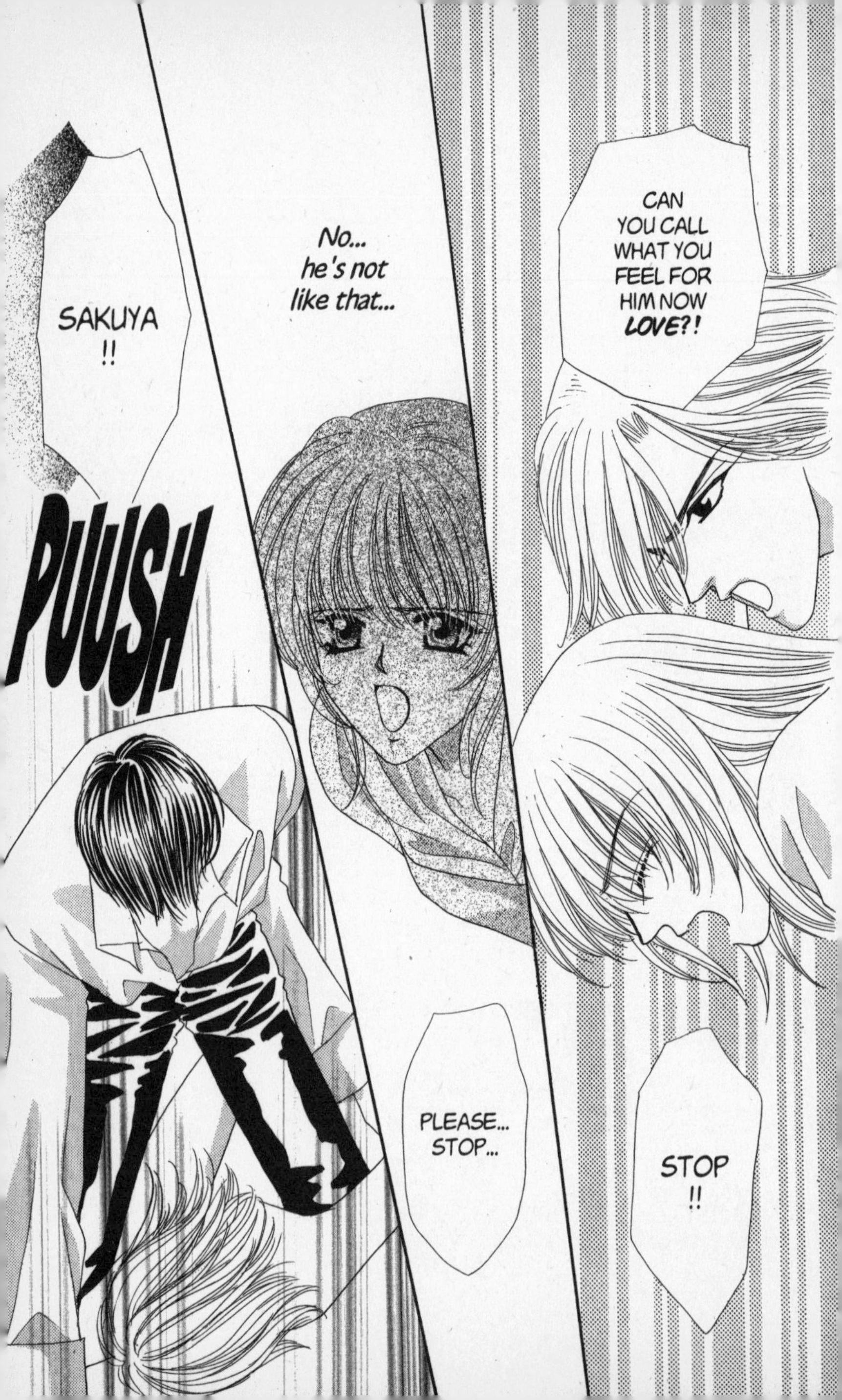
CAN YOU CALL WHAT YOU FEEL FOR HIM NOW ***LOVE***?!
STOP !!
No... he's not like that...
PLEASE... STOP...
SAKUYA !!
PUUSH

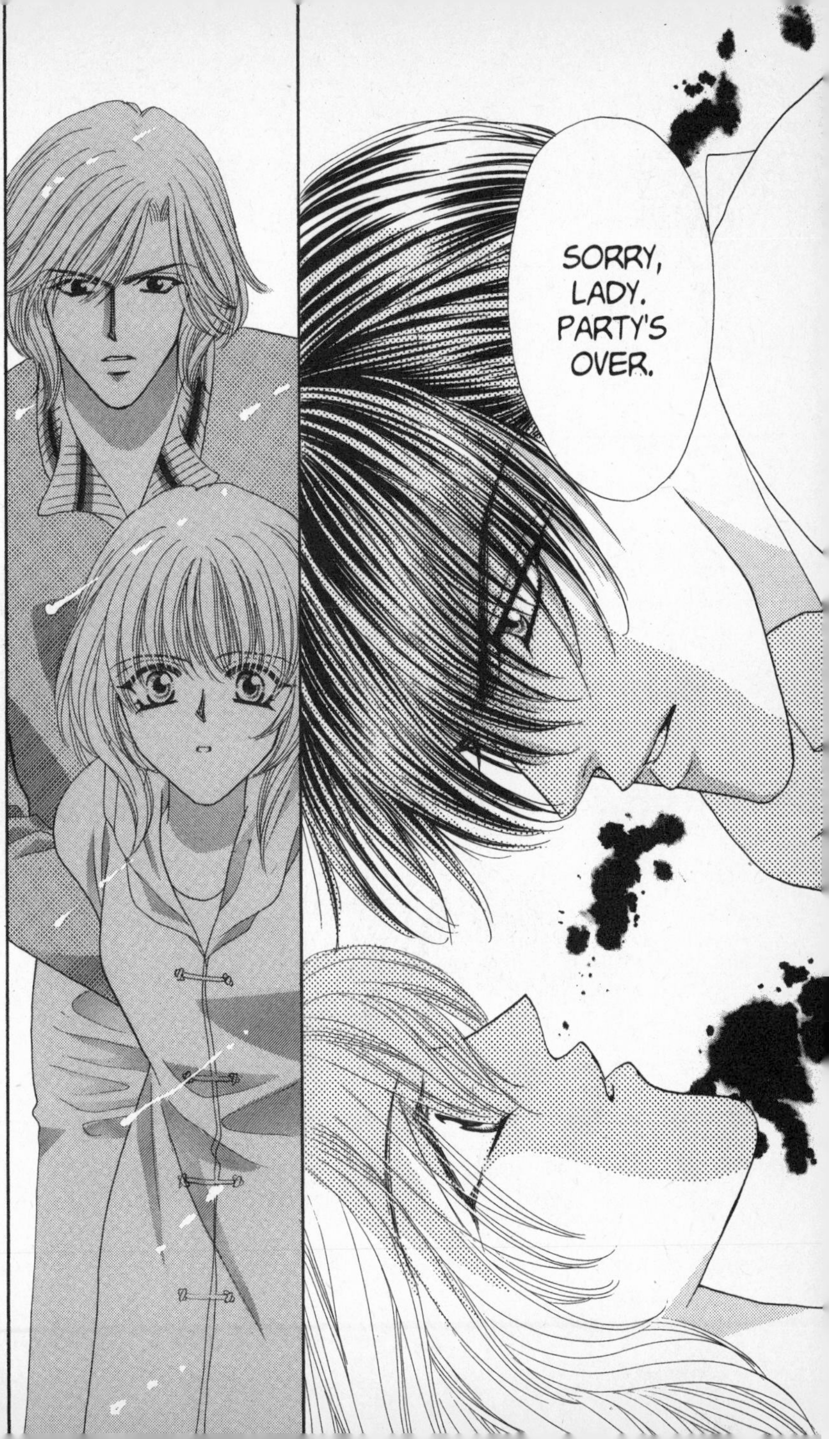
SORRY, LADY. PARTY'S OVER.

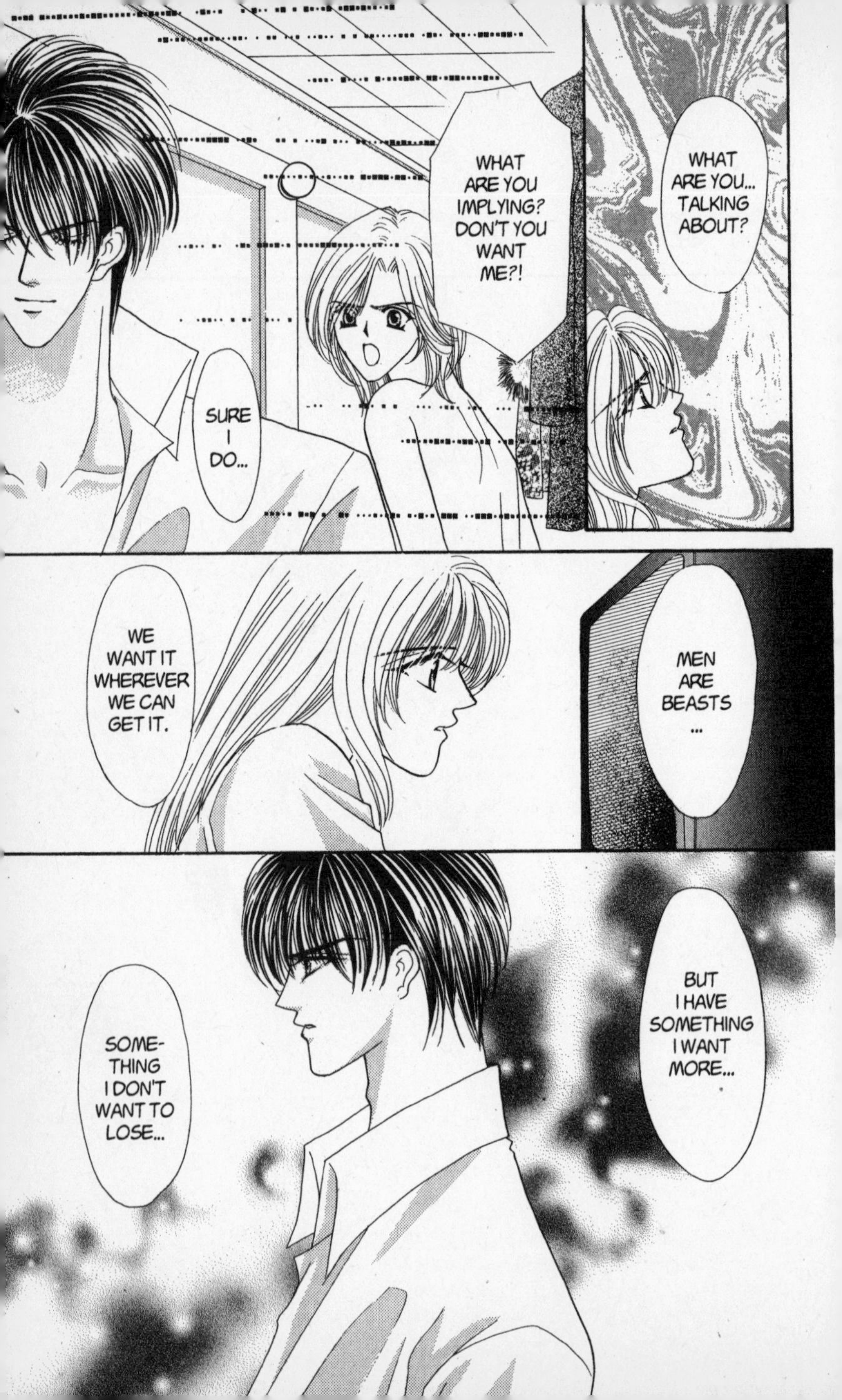
WHAT ARE YOU... TALKING ABOUT?
WHAT ARE YOU IMPLYING? DON'T YOU WANT ME?!
SURE I DO...
MEN ARE BEASTS ...
WE WANT IT WHEREVER WE CAN GET IT.
BUT I HAVE SOMETHING I WANT MORE...
SOME-THING I DON'T WANT TO LOSE...

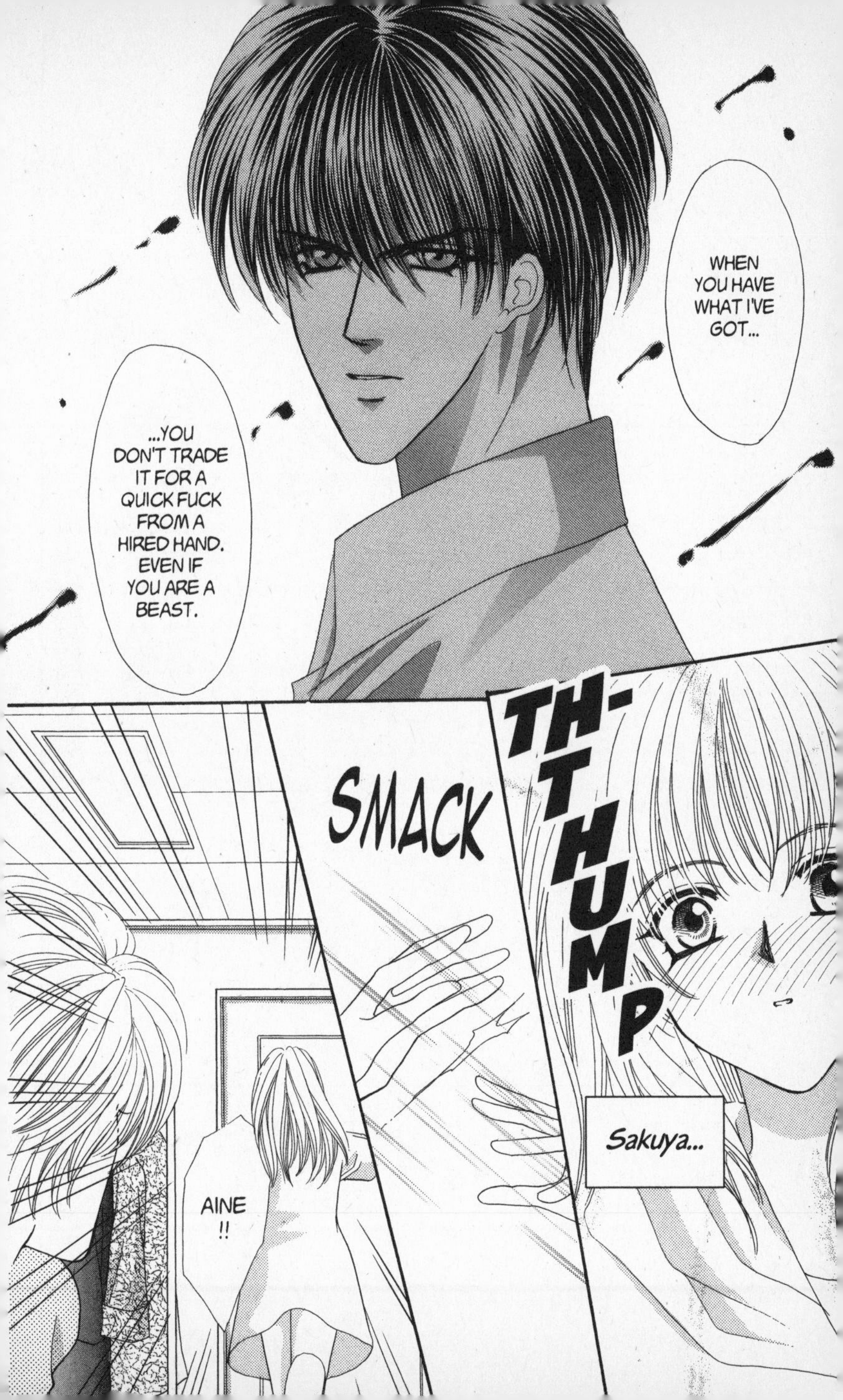
WHEN YOU HAVE WHAT I'VE GOT...
...YOU DON'T TRADE IT FOR A QUICK FUCK FROM A HIRED HAND. EVEN IF YOU ARE A BEAST.
TH-THUMP
Sakuya...
SMACK
AINE !!

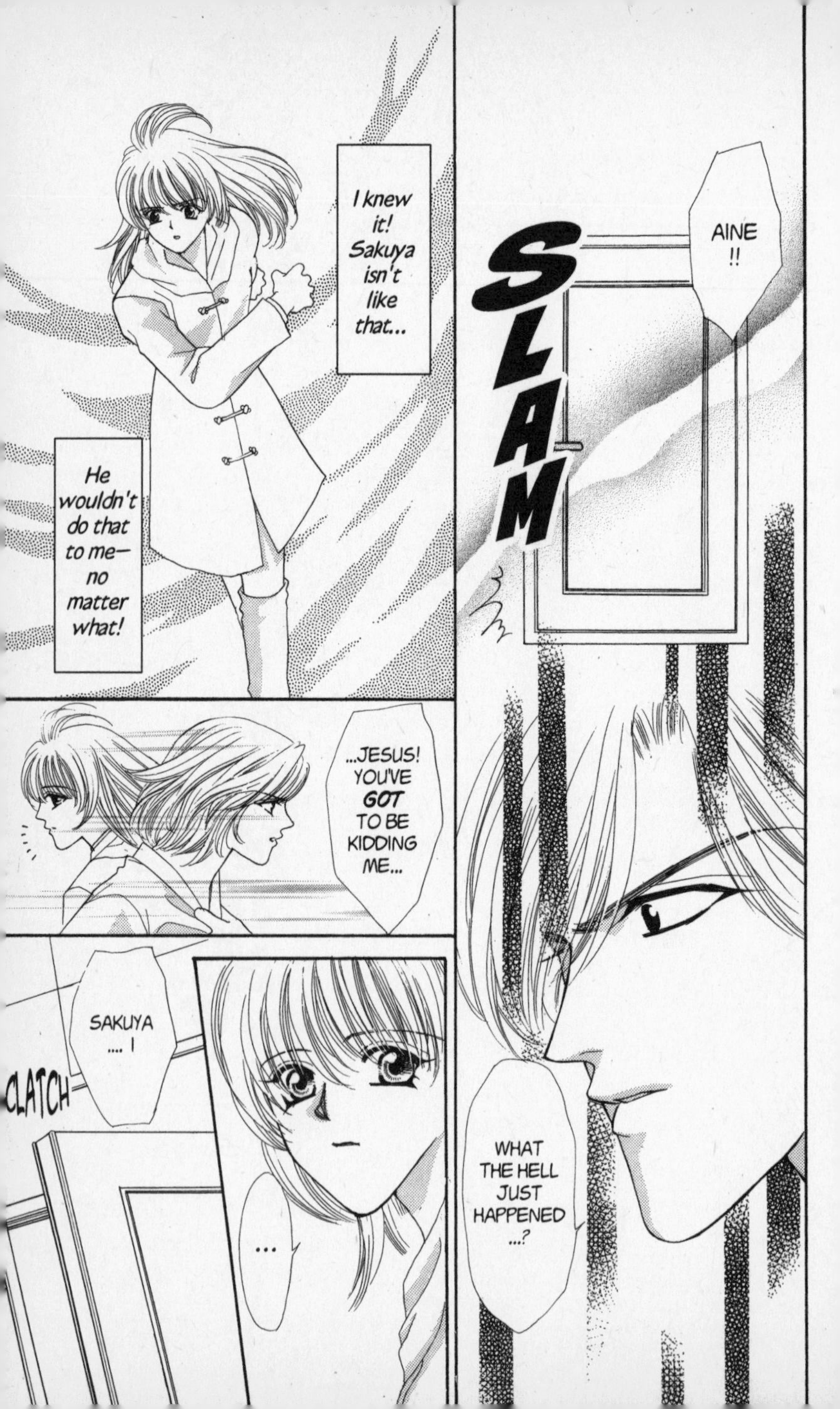
AINE !!
SLAM
WHAT THE HELL JUST HAPPENED ...?
I knew it! Sakuya isn't like that...
He wouldn't do that to me—no matter what!
...JESUS! YOU'VE GOT TO BE KIDDING ME...
...
SAKUYA I
CLATCH

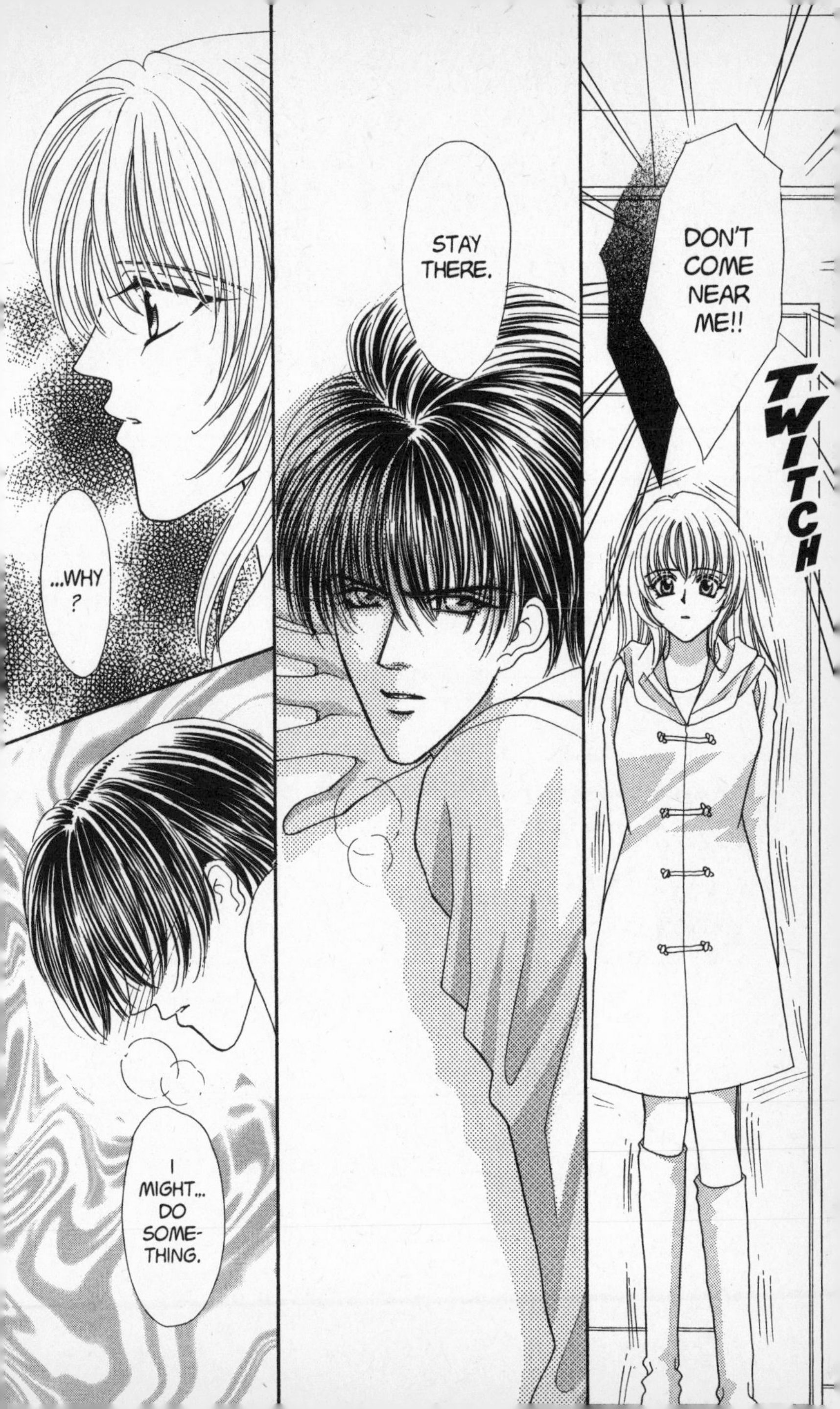

DON'T COME NEAR ME!!
TWITCH
STAY THERE.
...WHY ?
I MIGHT... DO SOME-THING.

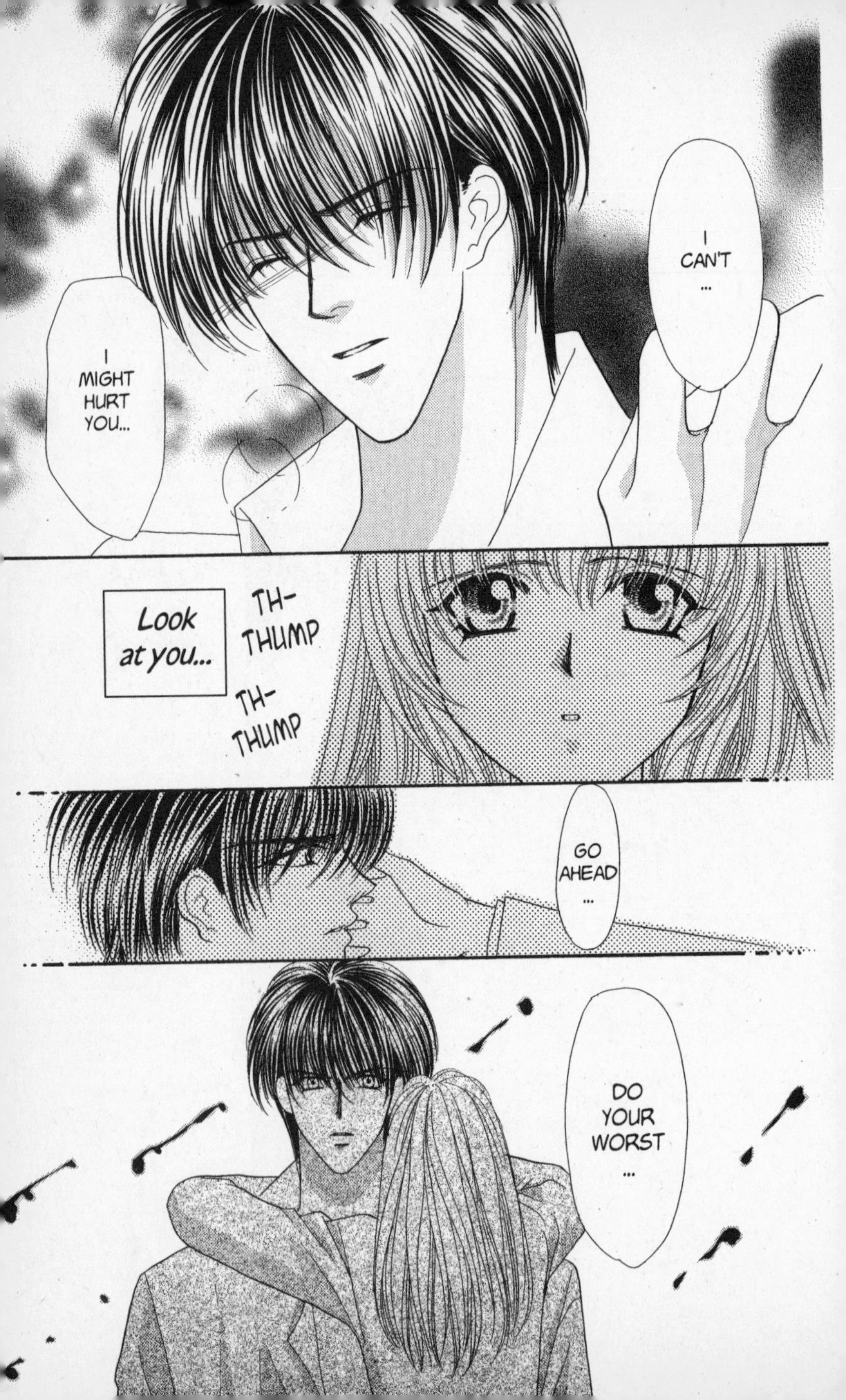
I CAN'T ...
I MIGHT HURT YOU...
TH-THUMP
Look at you...
TH-THUMP
GO AHEAD ...
DO YOUR WORST ...

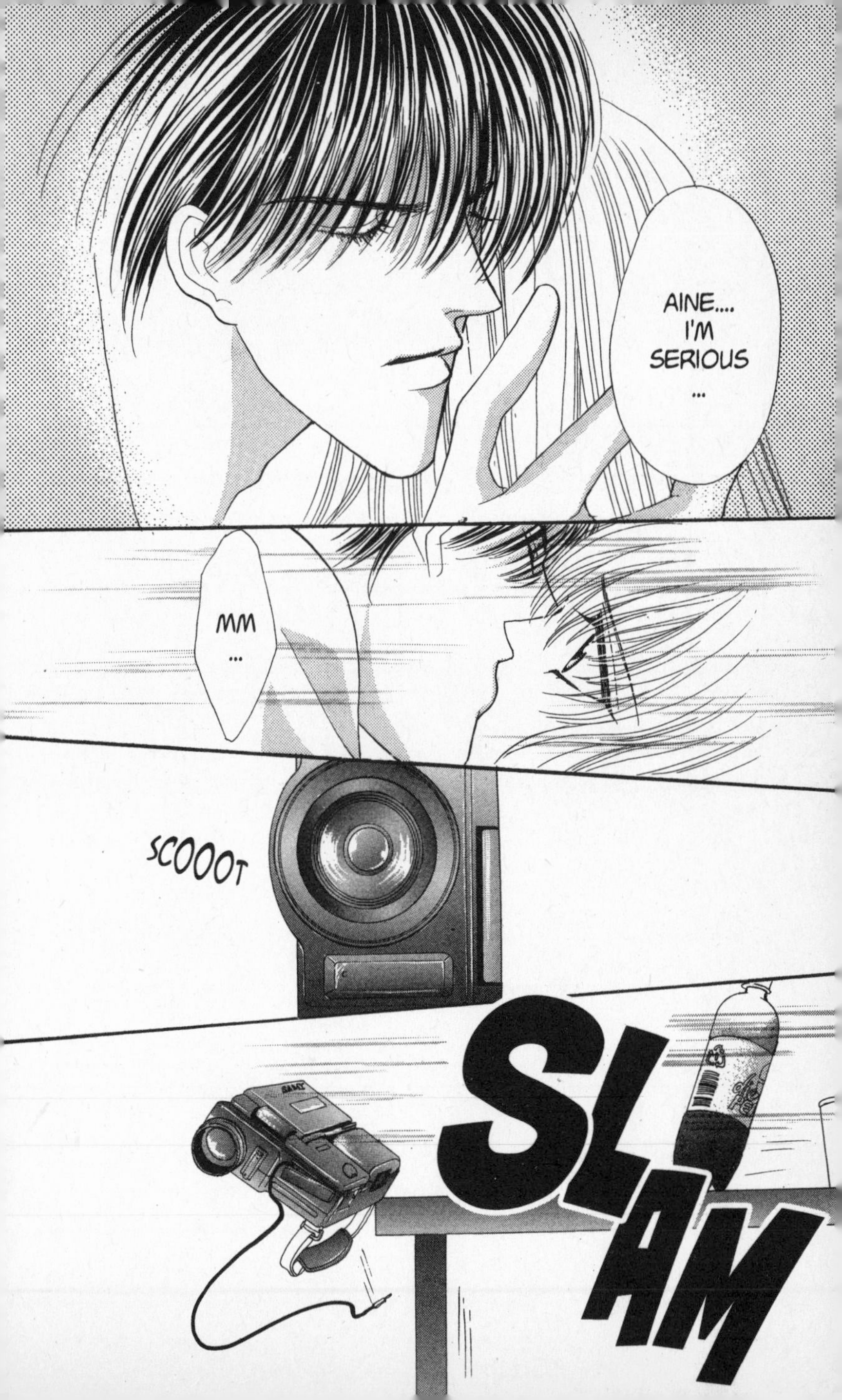
AINE.... I'M SERIOUS ...
MM ...
SCOOOT
SLAM

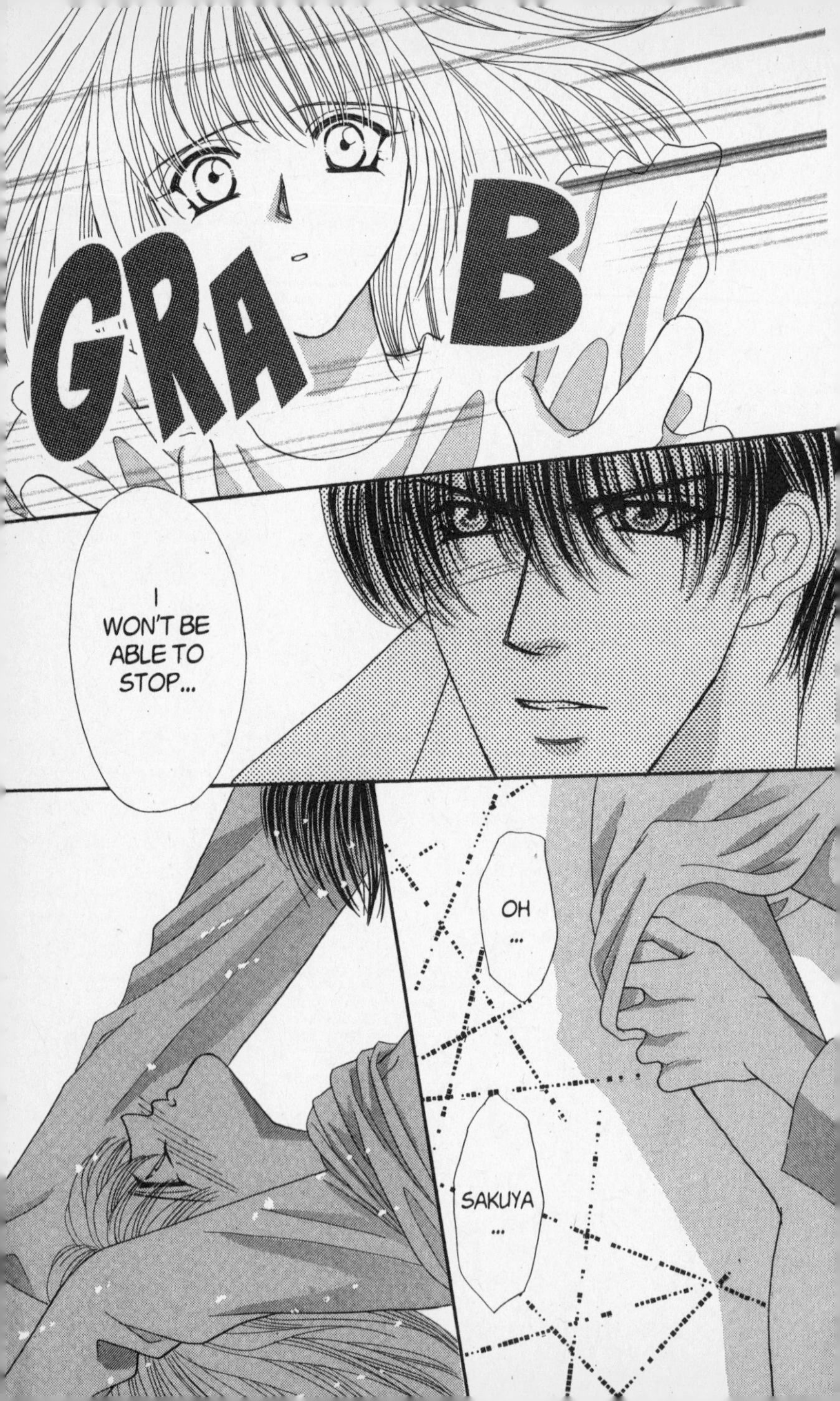
GRAB
I WON'T BE ABLE TO STOP...
OH ...
SAKUYA ...

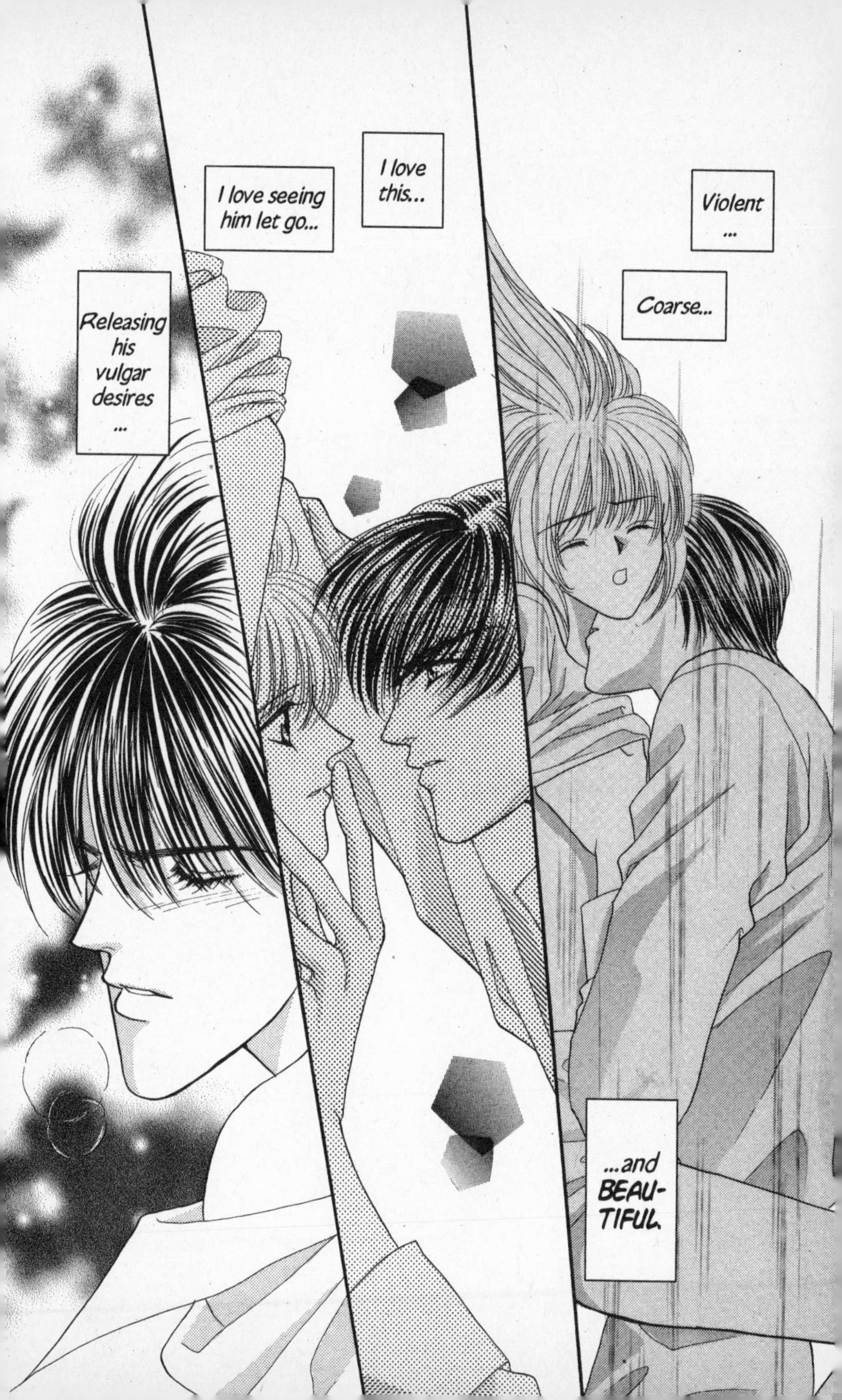
Violent ...
Coarse...
...and BEAU-TIFUL.
I love this...
I love seeing him let go...
Releasing his vulgar desires ...

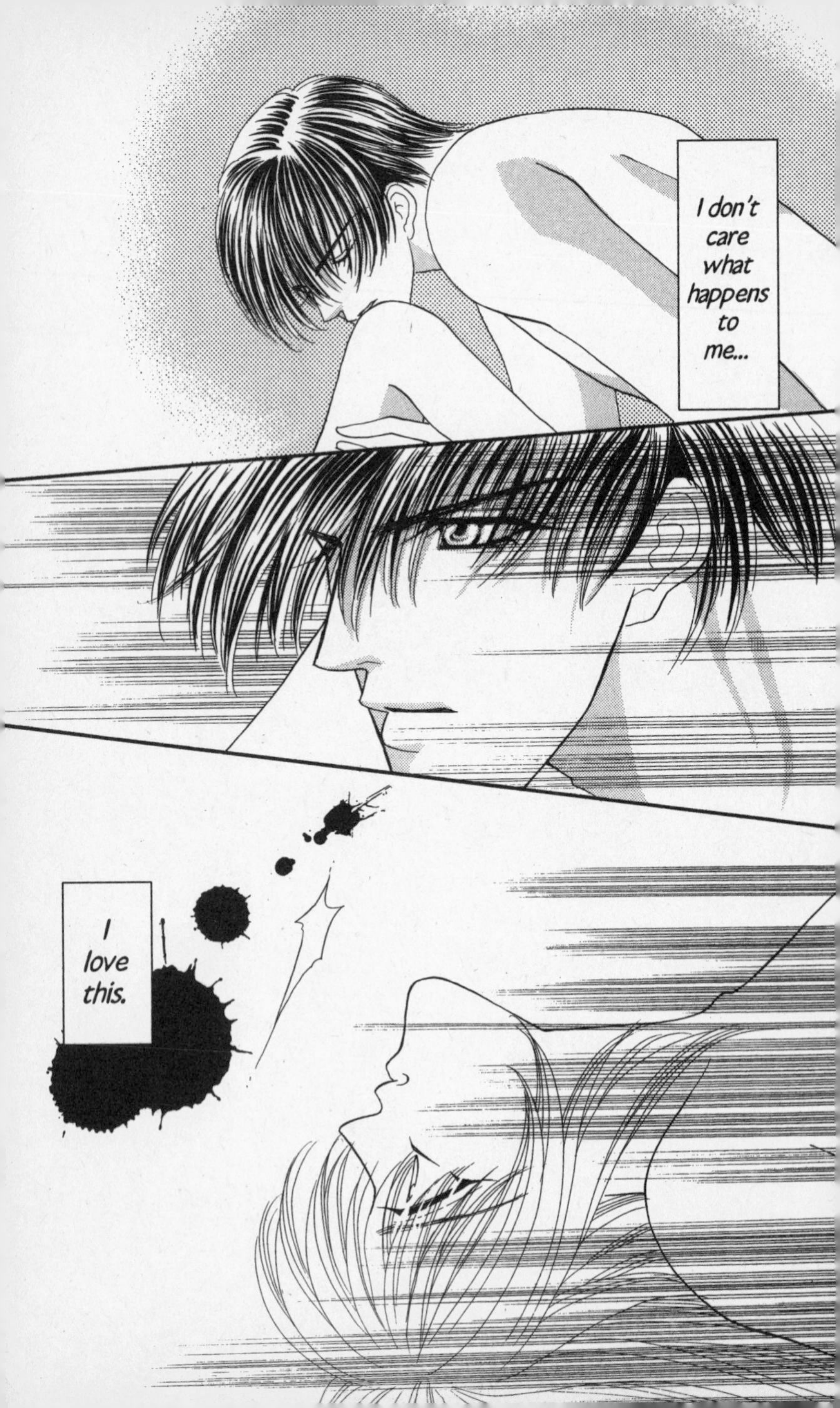
I don't care what happens to me...
I love this.

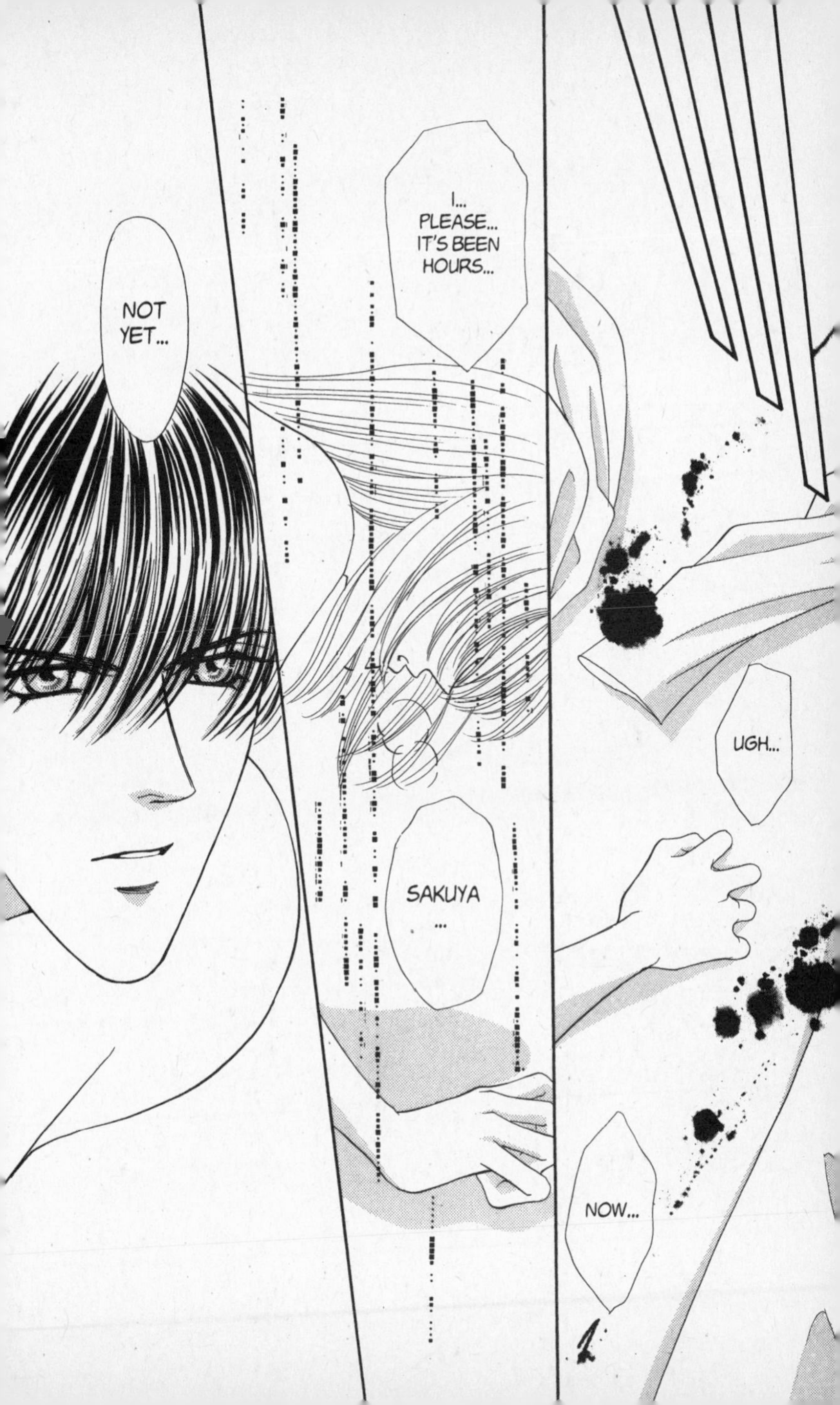
UGH...
NOW...
I... PLEASE... IT'S BEEN HOURS...
SAKUYA...
NOT YET...

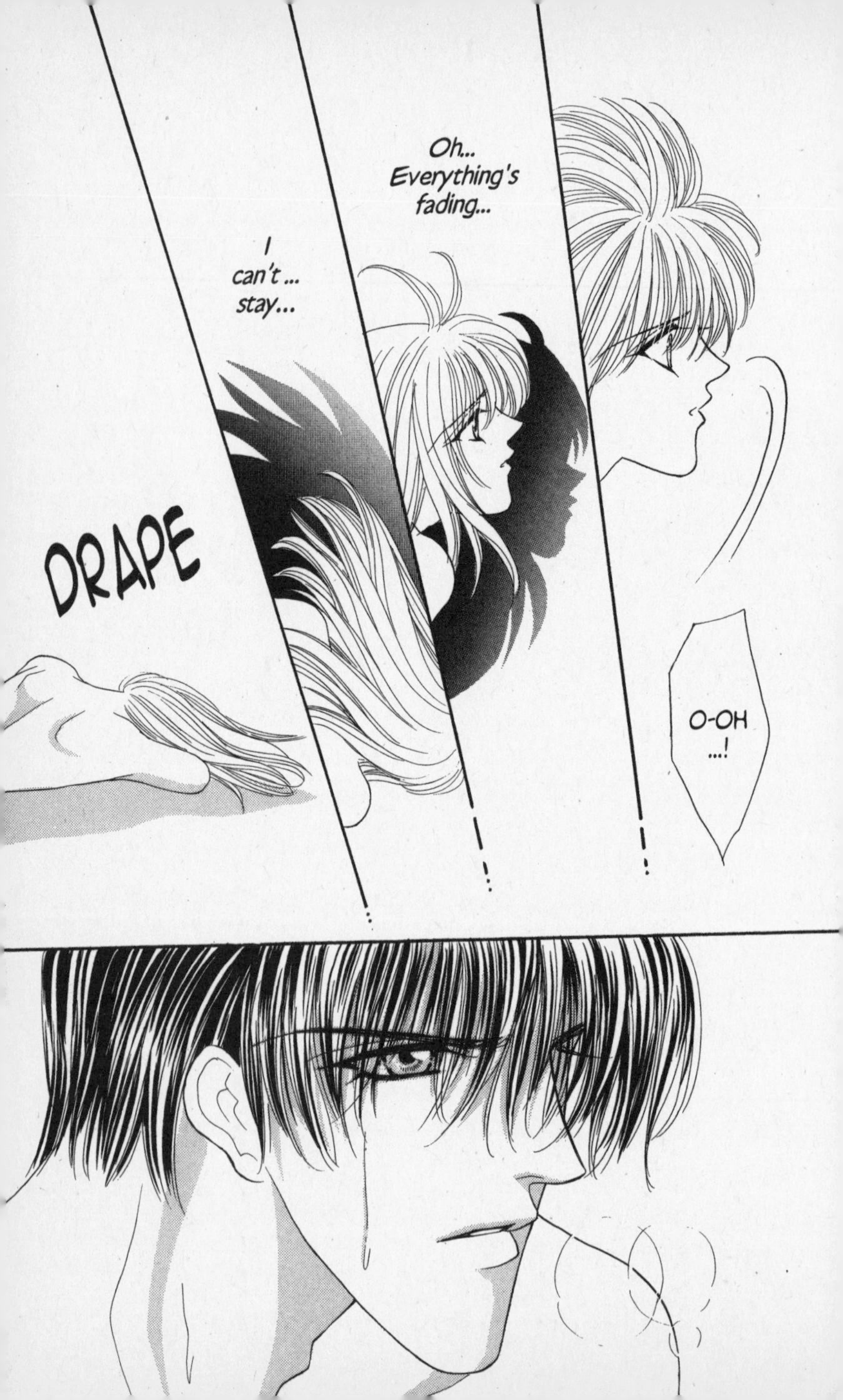
O-OH ...!
Oh... Everything's fading...
I can't ... stay...
DRAPE

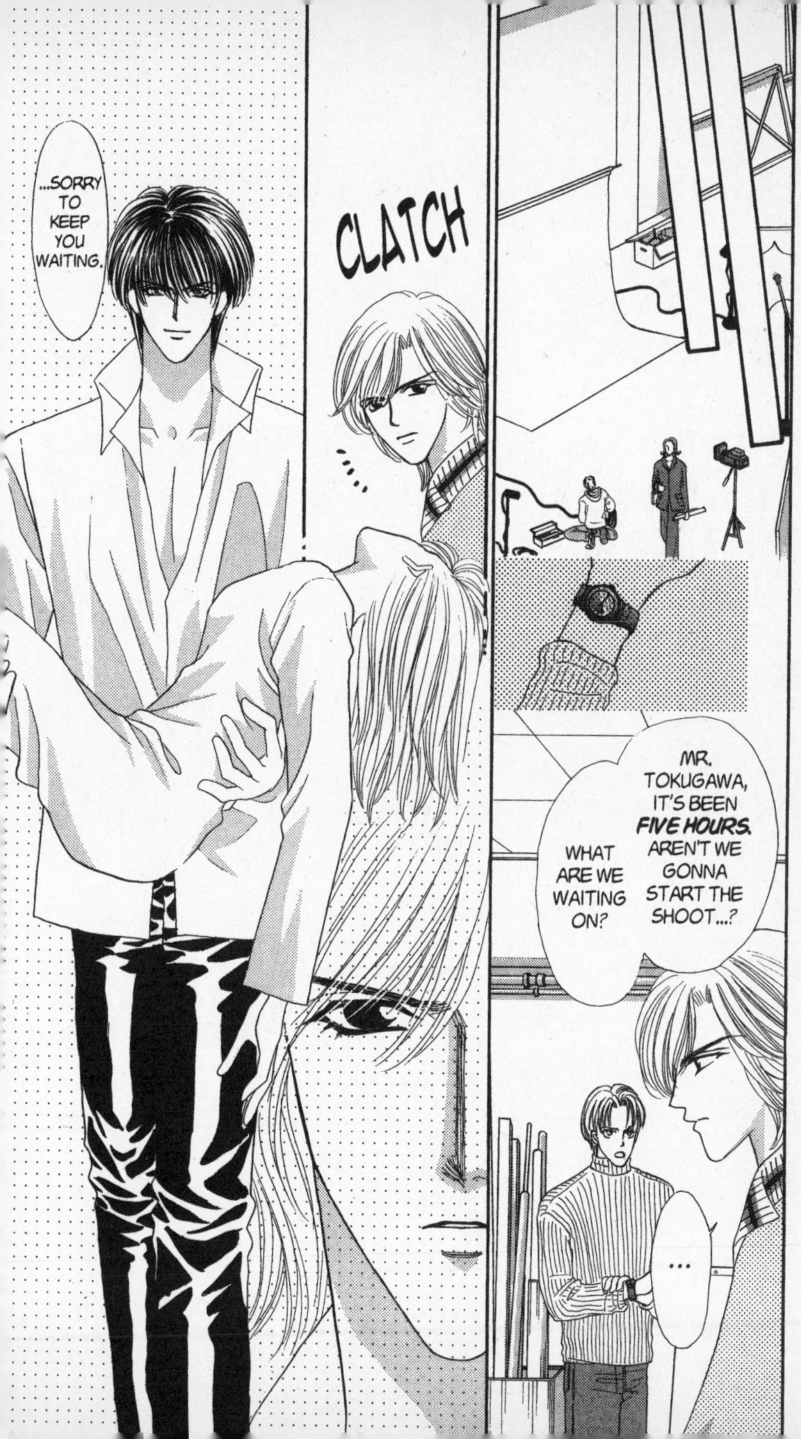
MR. TOKUGAWA, IT'S BEEN **FIVE HOURS.** AREN'T WE GONNA START THE SHOOT...?
WHAT ARE WE WAITING ON?
...
CLATCH
...
...SORRY TO KEEP YOU WAITING.

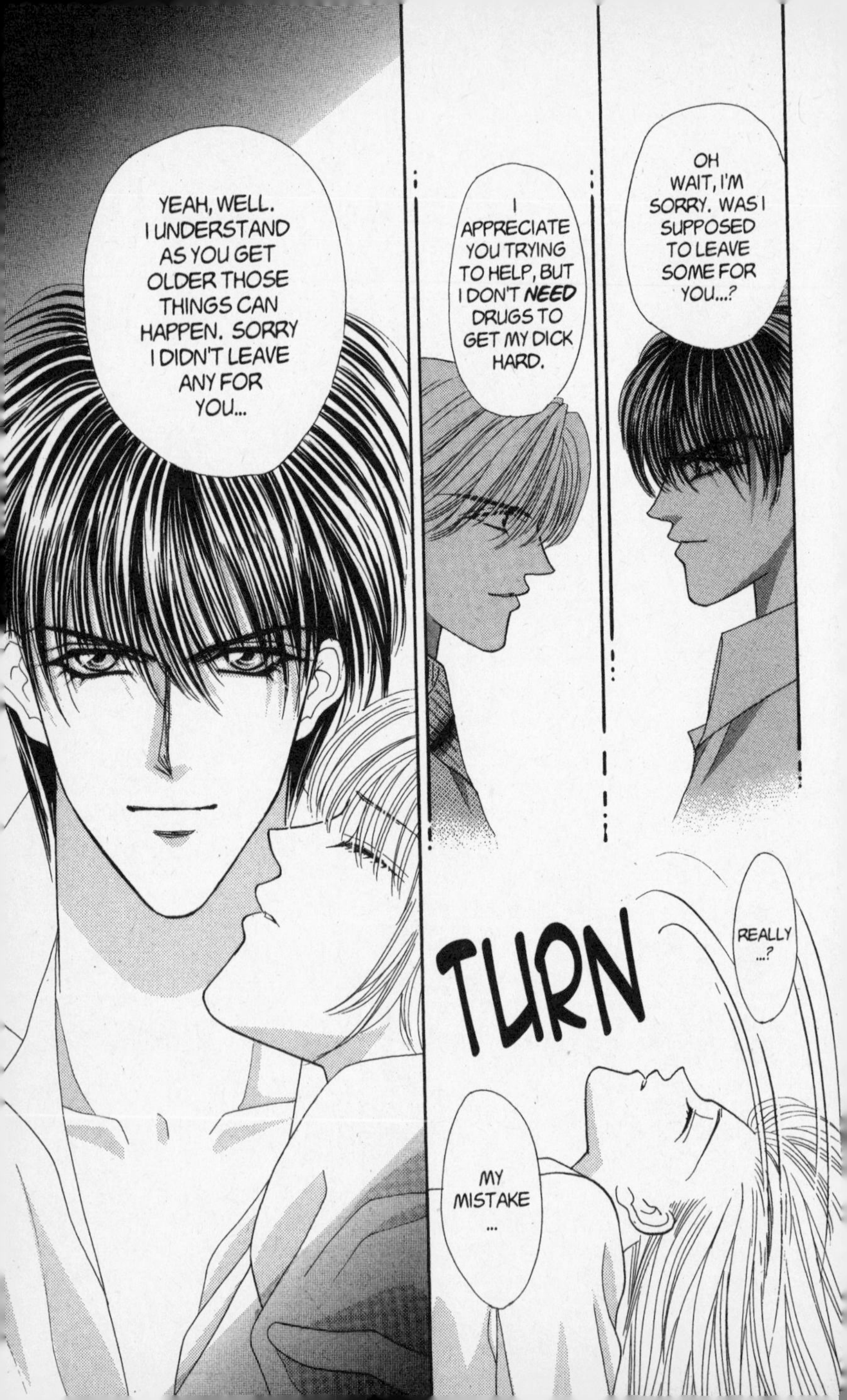
OH WAIT, I'M SORRY. WAS I SUPPOSED TO LEAVE SOME FOR YOU...?
I APPRECIATE YOU TRYING TO HELP, BUT I DON'T **NEED** DRUGS TO GET MY DICK HARD.
REALLY ...?
TURN
MY MISTAKE ...
YEAH, WELL. I UNDERSTAND AS YOU GET OLDER THOSE THINGS CAN HAPPEN. SORRY I DIDN'T LEAVE ANY FOR YOU...

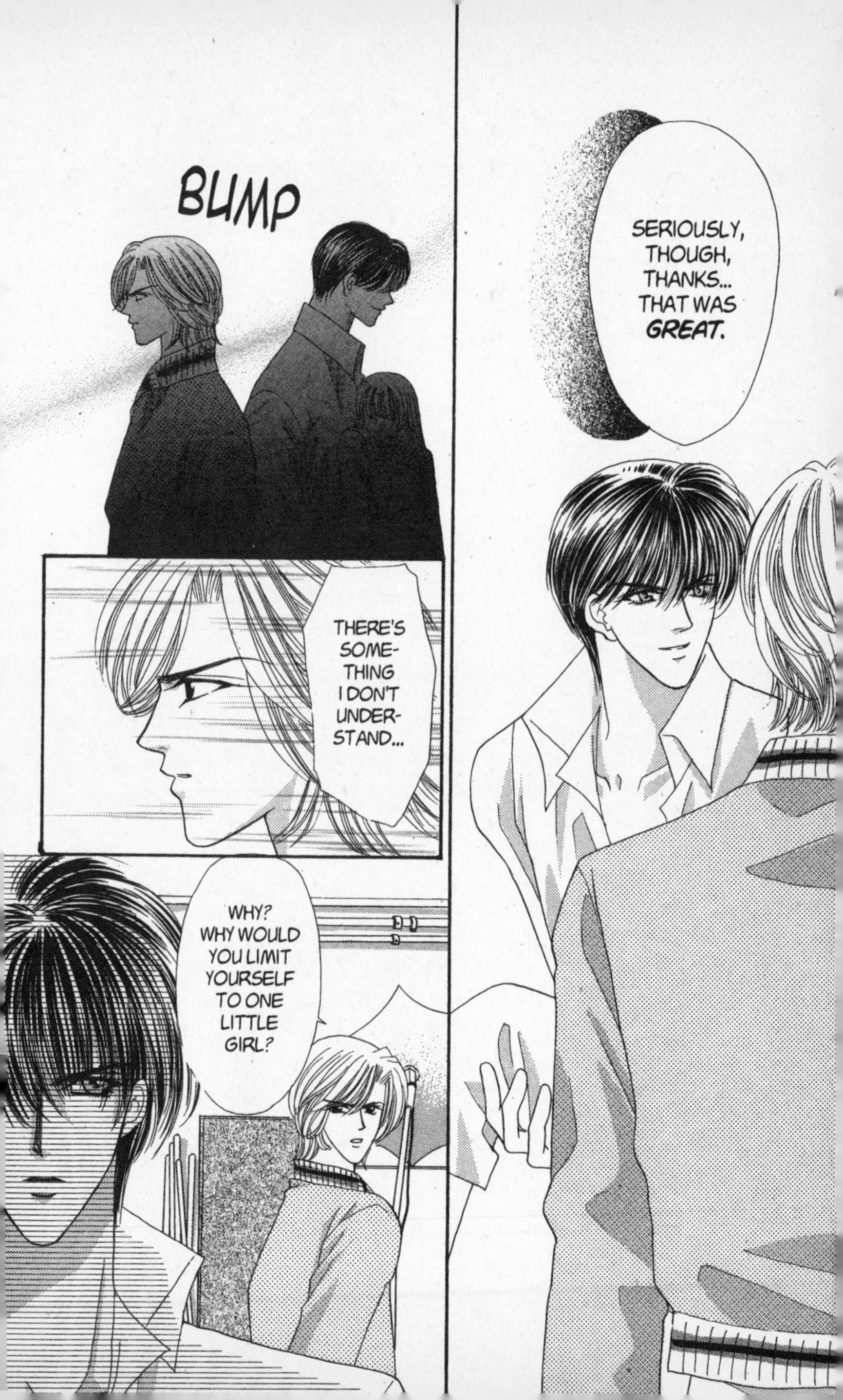
SERIOUSLY, THOUGH, THANKS... THAT WAS GREAT.
BUMP
THERE'S SOMETHING I DON'T UNDERSTAND...
WHY? WHY WOULD YOU LIMIT YOURSELF TO ONE LITTLE GIRL?

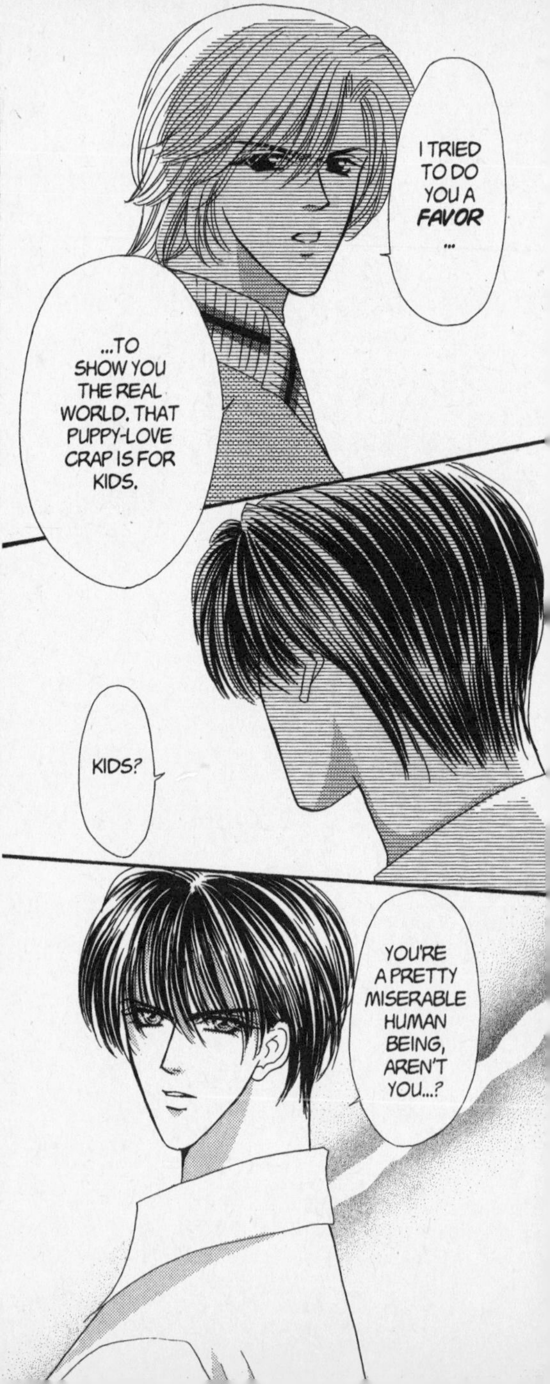
I TRIED TO DO YOU A **FAVOR** ...
...TO SHOW YOU THE REAL WORLD. THAT PUPPY-LOVE CRAP IS FOR KIDS.
KIDS?
YOU'RE A PRETTY MISERABLE HUMAN BEING, AREN'T YOU...?

Here we are in the final third again...

I meant to write about the anime, but it won't be on air for a while, so I'll save that for Volume 10. (I have the dirt, but I don't know how much of it I can dish...)

Anyway, it's an anime with a lot of twists and turns, so please tune in every week!

Send your comments to the address below as usual...

Mayu Shinjo
c/o VIZ, LLC
PO Box 77010
San Francisco, CA 94107

I'm especially looking for comments on the anime. We're accepting questions, too.

I was thinking of announcing an e-mail address specifically for readers, but I don't know how to set that up... Sniff... I should be able to tell you guys that by Volume 10, too. I hope to build a website too, but I can't do it on my own. Maybe somebody from the anime will help out...

Well then, see you in Volume 10!!

Special Thanks:
Mashin Osakabe, Migiwa Nakahara, Satomi Naruke, Ikuko Abe, Yuki Ikegami, Sawako Aitori

Thanks for all your help!! And I also want to thank anime-related staff, editors and people from the entertainment/record companies—thank you very much.

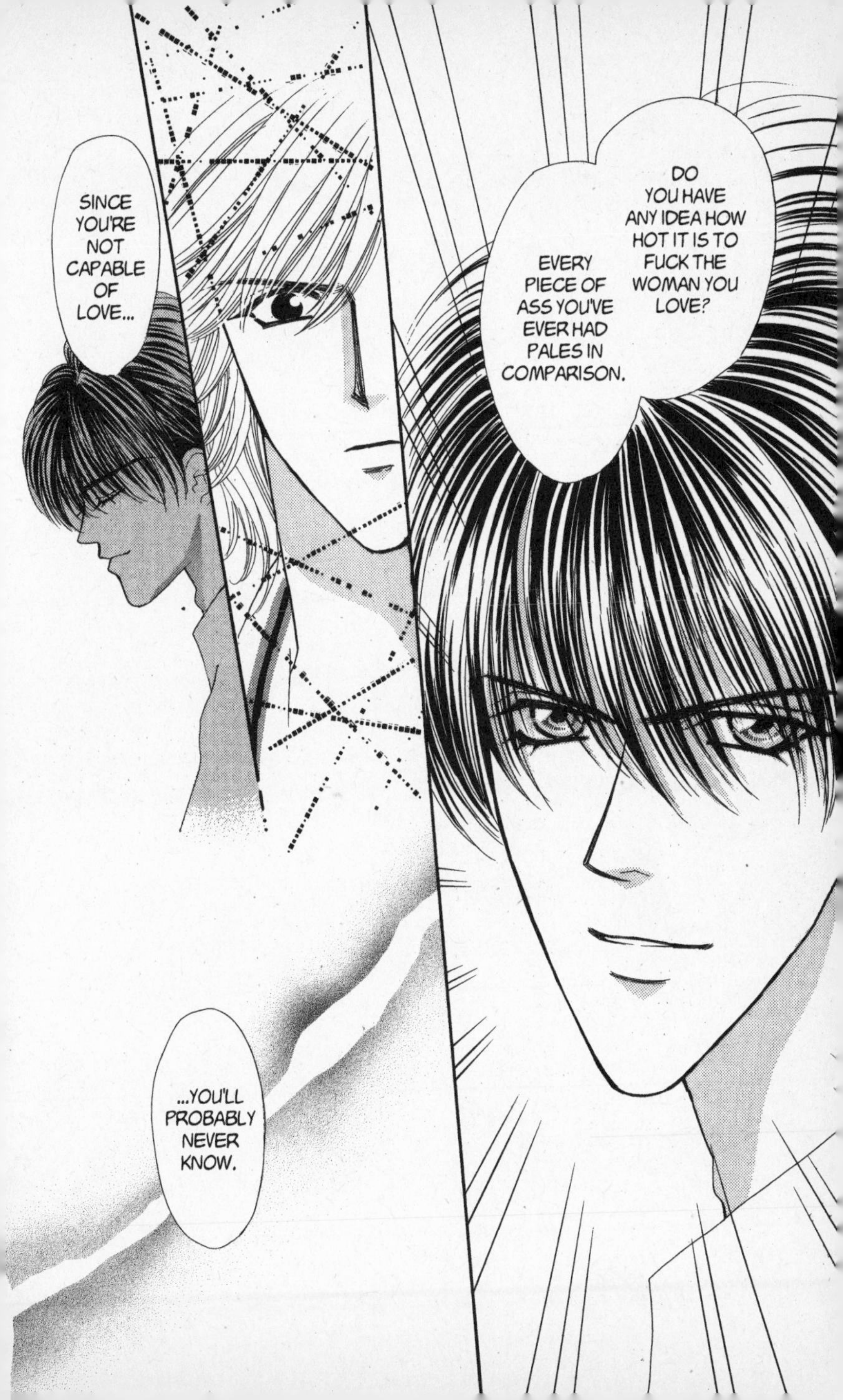
DO YOU HAVE ANY IDEA HOW HOT IT IS TO FUCK THE WOMAN YOU LOVE?
EVERY PIECE OF ASS YOU'VE EVER HAD PALES IN COMPARISON.
SINCE YOU'RE NOT CAPABLE OF LOVE...
...YOU'LL PROBABLY NEVER KNOW.

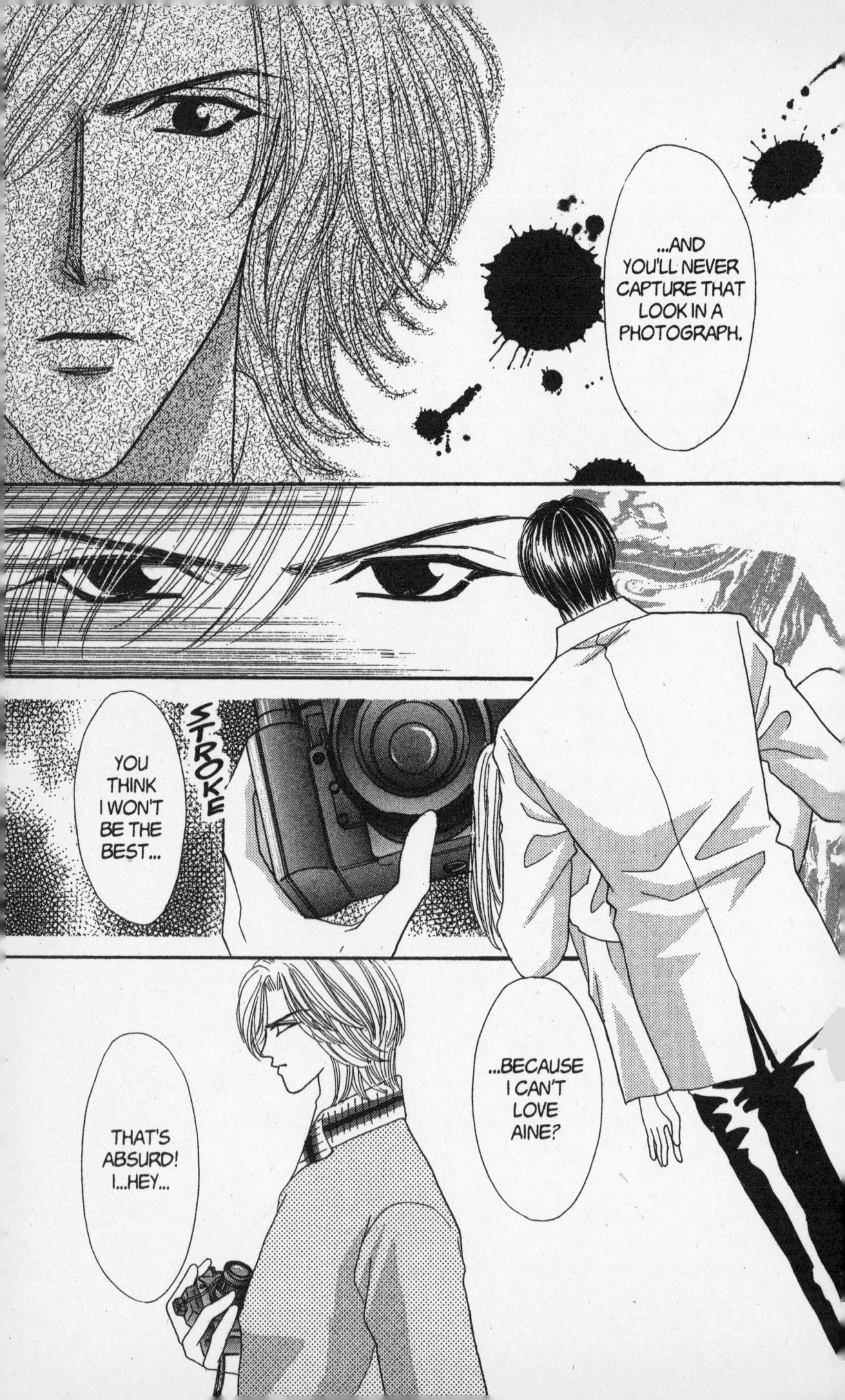
...AND YOU'LL NEVER CAPTURE THAT LOOK IN A PHOTOGRAPH.
STROKE
YOU THINK I WON'T BE THE BEST...
...BECAUSE I CAN'T LOVE AINE?
THAT'S ABSURD! I...HEY...

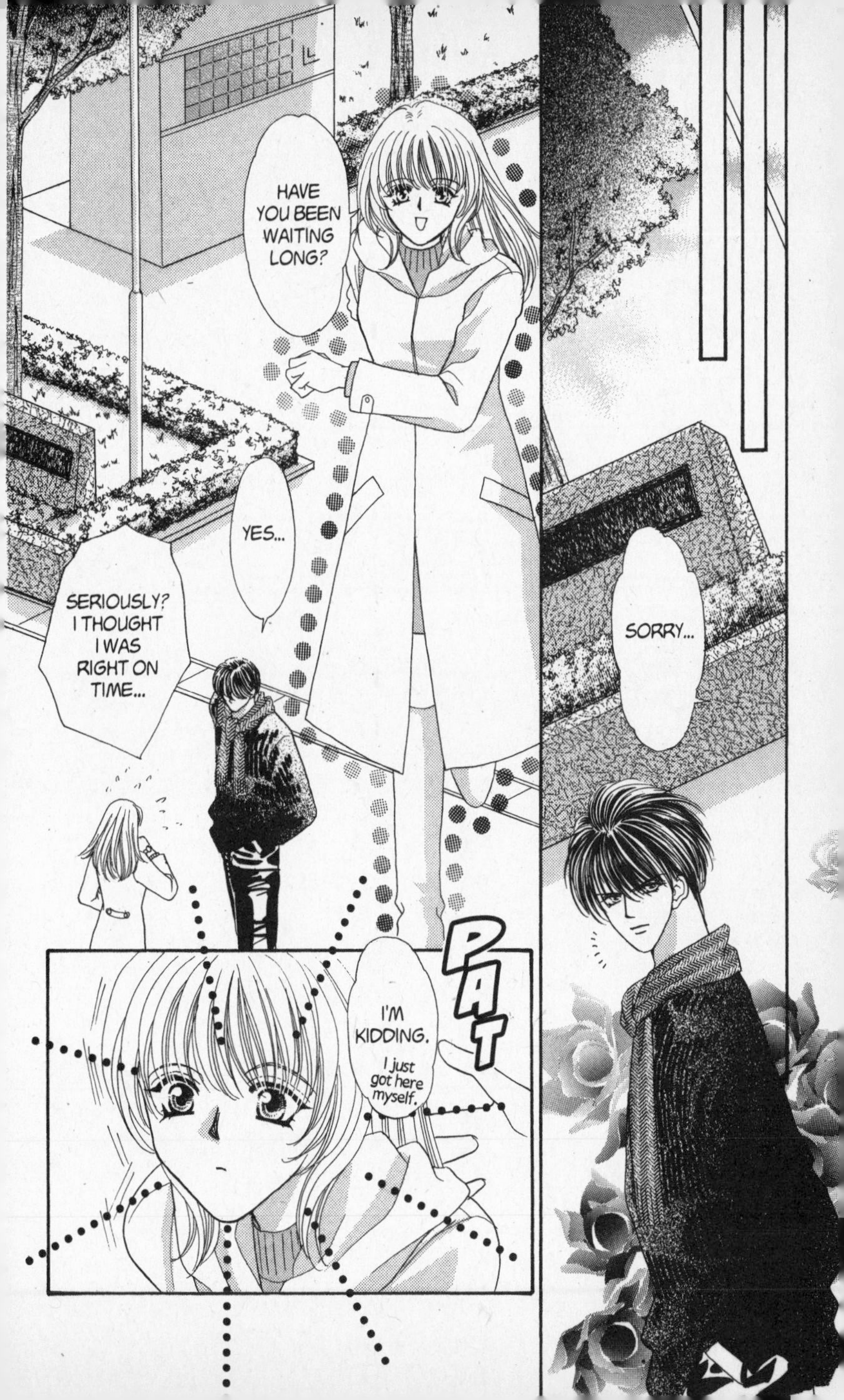
SORRY...
HAVE YOU BEEN WAITING LONG?
YES...
SERIOUSLY? I THOUGHT I WAS RIGHT ON TIME...
PAT
I'M KIDDING.
I just got here myself.

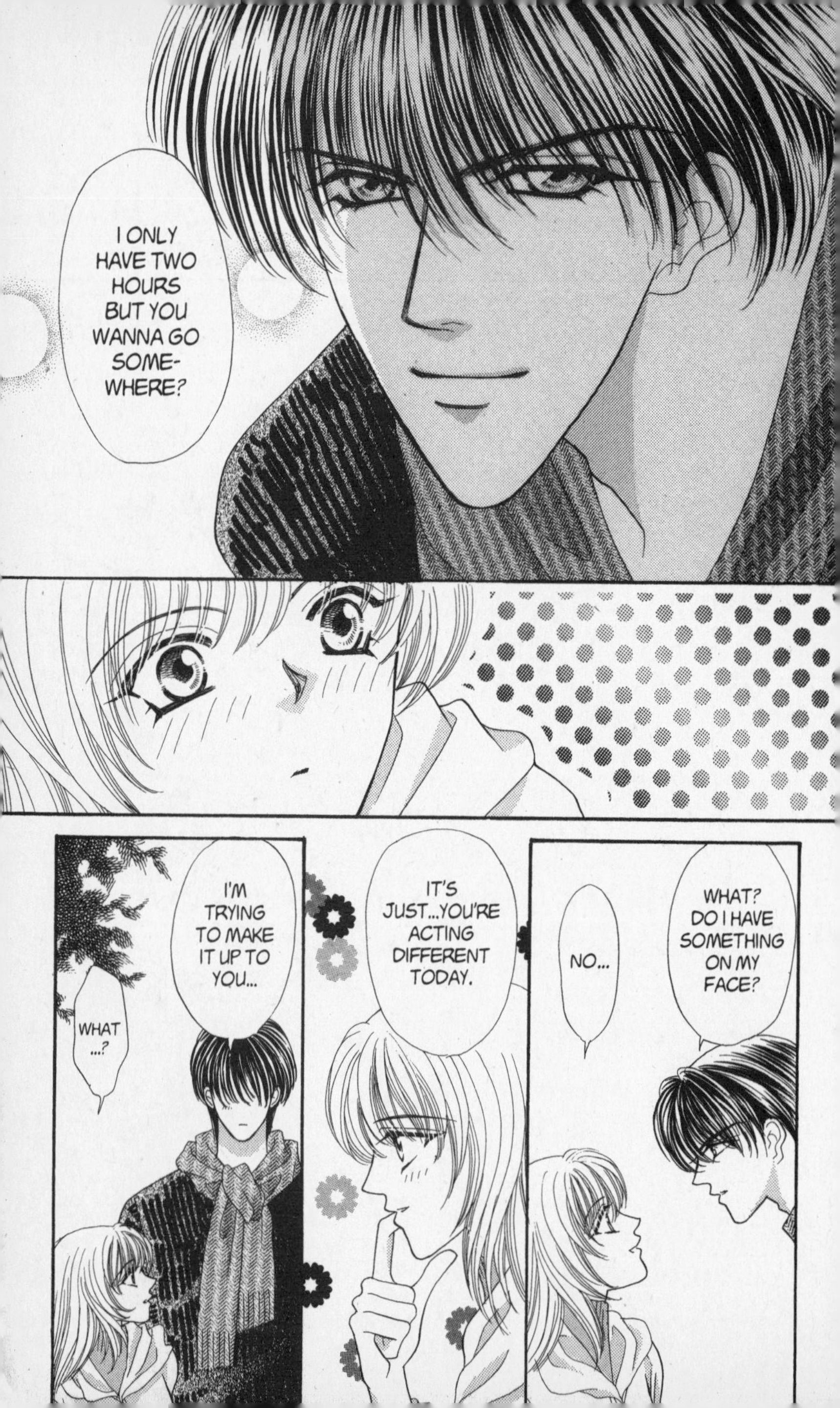
I ONLY HAVE TWO HOURS BUT YOU WANNA GO SOME-WHERE?
WHAT? DO I HAVE SOMETHING ON MY FACE?
NO...
IT'S JUST...YOU'RE ACTING DIFFERENT TODAY.
I'M TRYING TO MAKE IT UP TO YOU...
WHAT ...?

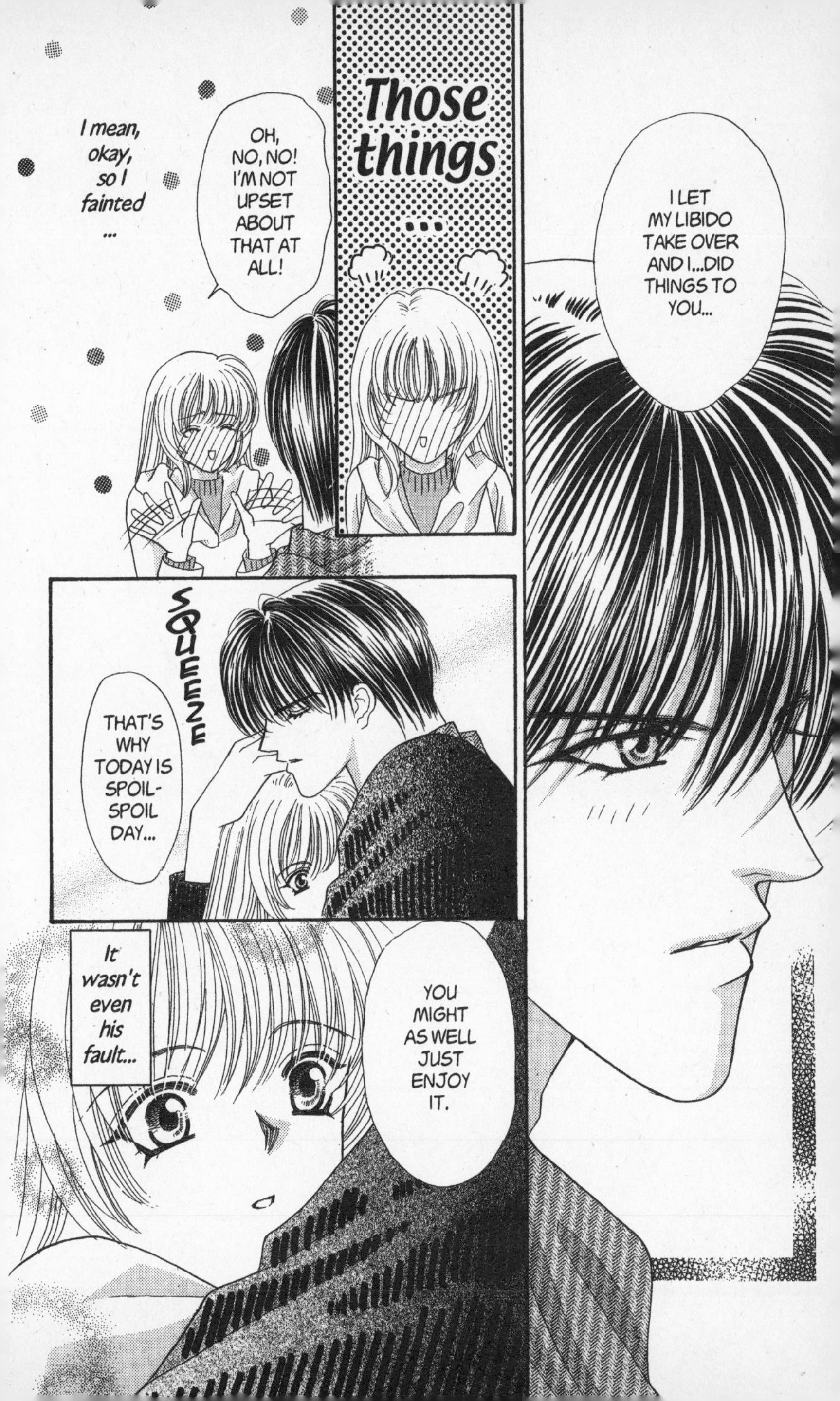
I LET MY LIBIDO TAKE OVER AND I...DID THINGS TO YOU...
Those things...
OH, NO, NO! I'M NOT UPSET ABOUT THAT AT ALL!
I mean, okay, so I fainted...
SQUEEZE
THAT'S WHY TODAY IS SPOIL-SPOIL DAY...
YOU MIGHT AS WELL JUST ENJOY IT.
It wasn't even his fault...

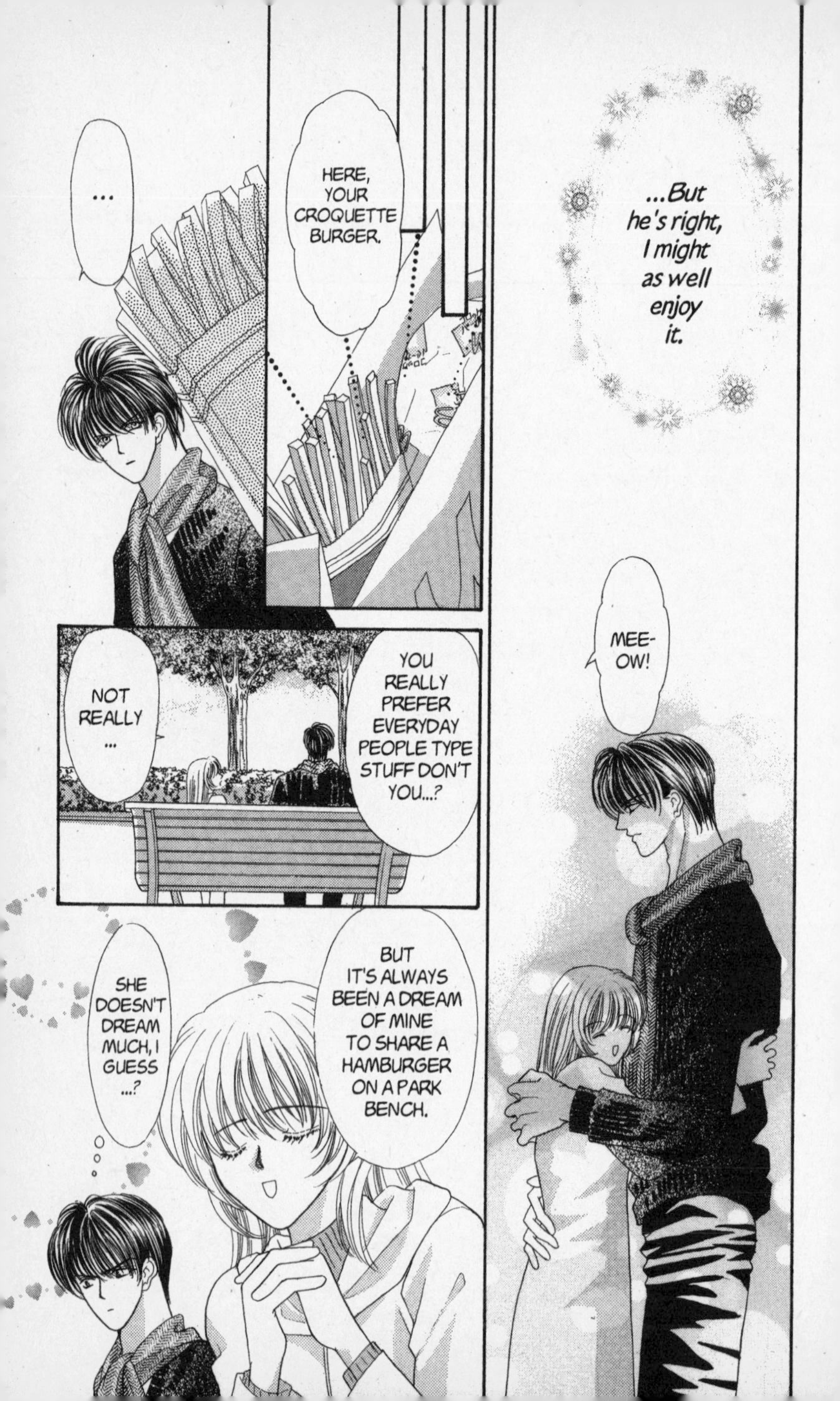
...But he's right, I might as well enjoy it.
MEE-OW!
HERE, YOUR CROQUETTE BURGER.
...
YOU REALLY PREFER EVERYDAY PEOPLE TYPE STUFF DON'T YOU...?
NOT REALLY ...
BUT IT'S ALWAYS BEEN A DREAM OF MINE TO SHARE A HAMBURGER ON A PARK BENCH.
SHE DOESN'T DREAM MUCH, I GUESS ...?

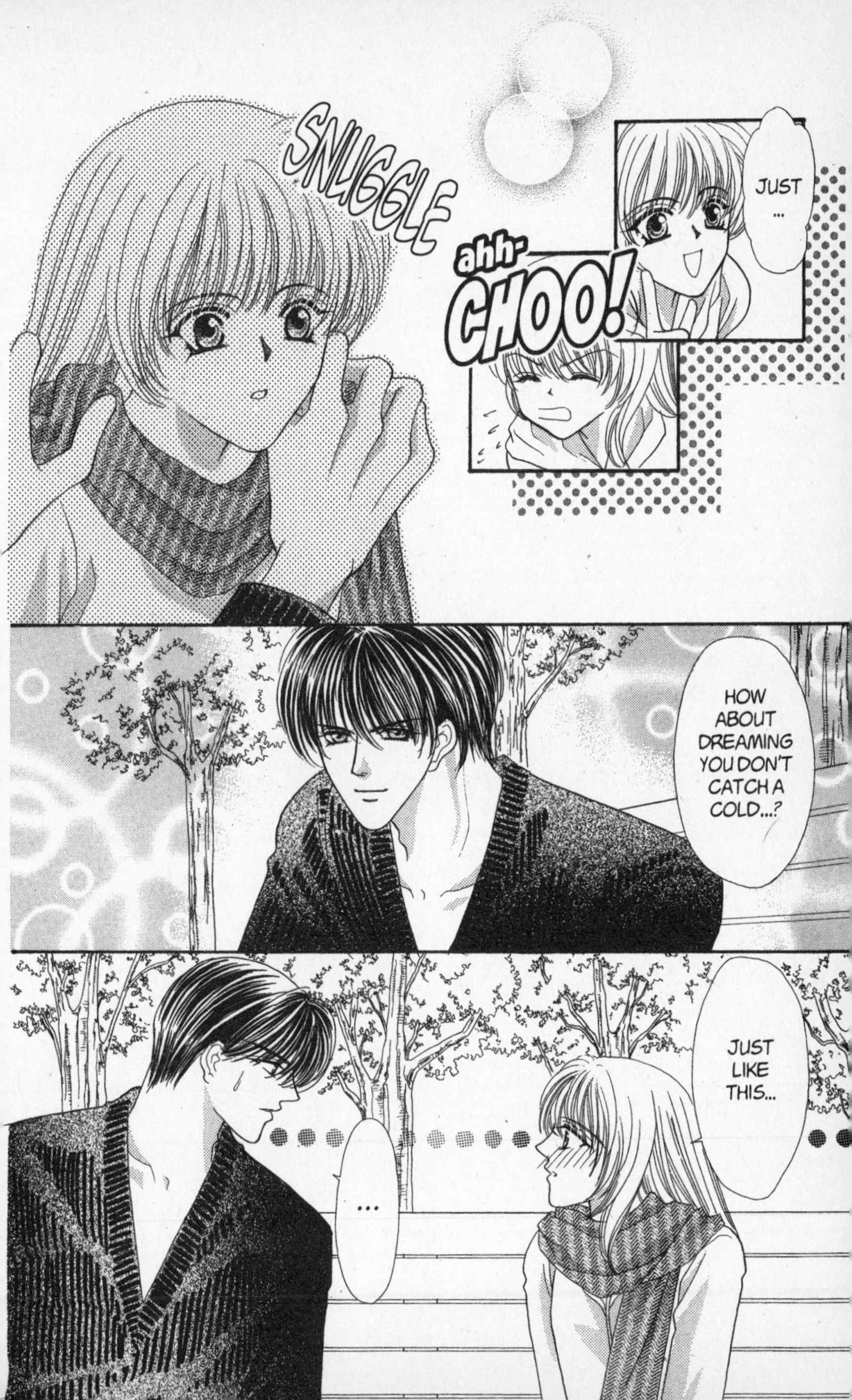
JUST ...
ahh-CHOO!
SNUGGLE
HOW ABOUT DREAMING YOU DON'T CATCH A COLD...?
JUST LIKE THIS...
...

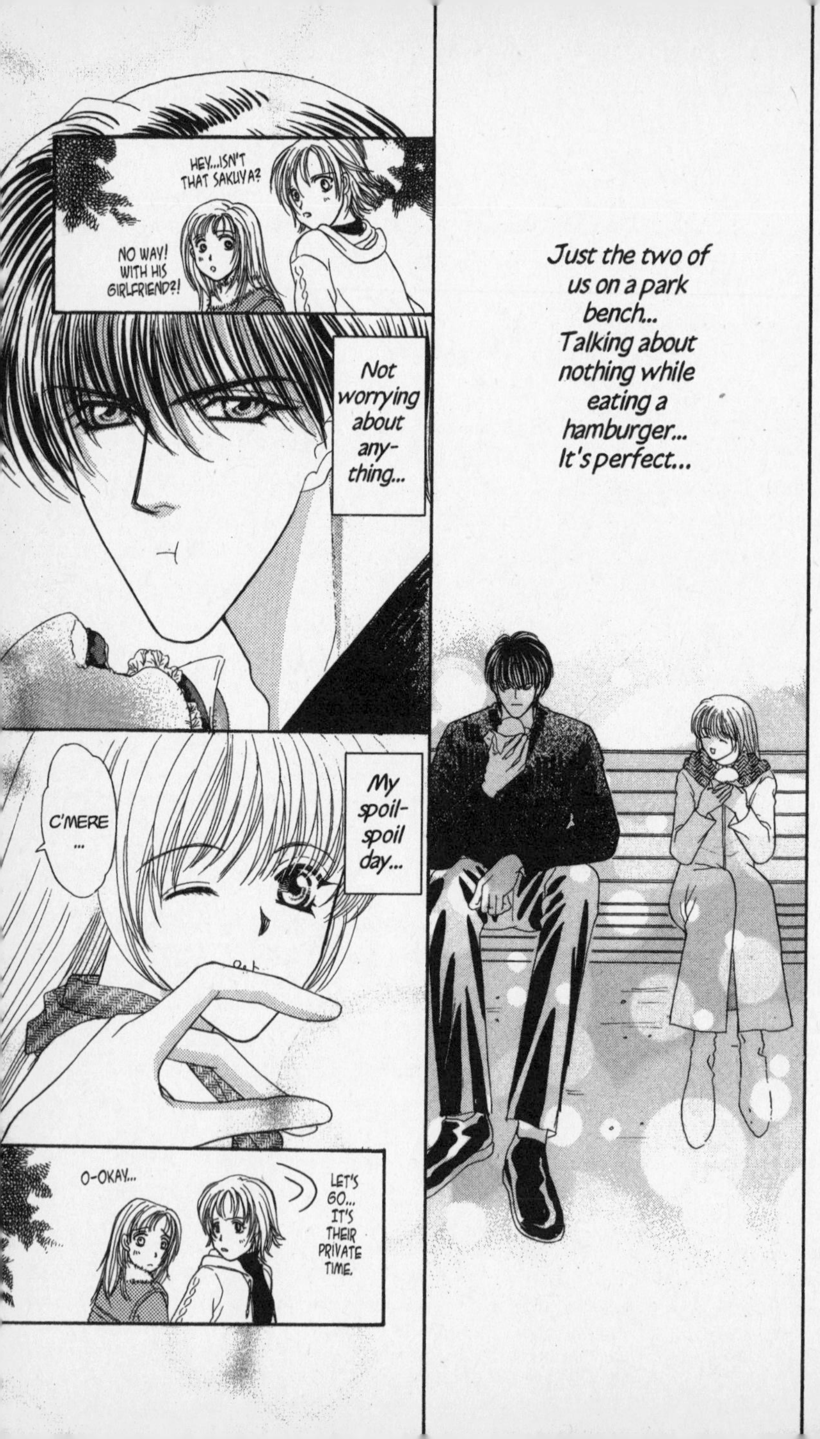
Just the two of us on a park bench... Talking about nothing while eating a hamburger... It's perfect...
HEY...ISN'T THAT SAKUYA?
NO WAY! WITH HIS GIRLFRIEND?!
Not worrying about any-thing...
My spoil-spoil day...
C'MERE ...
LET'S GO... IT'S THEIR PRIVATE TIME.
O-OKAY...

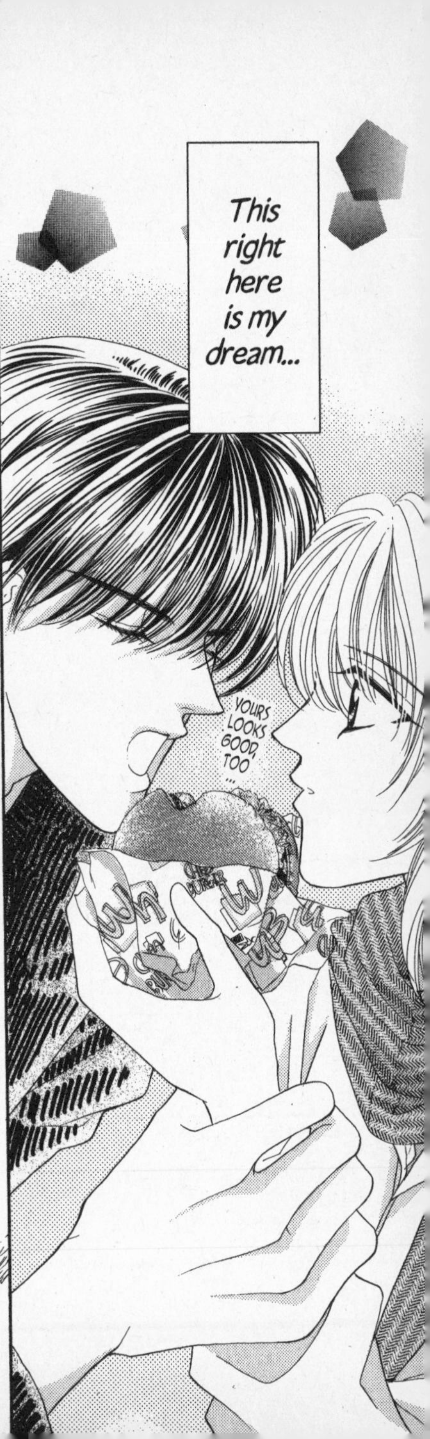
This right here is my dream...
YOURS LOOKS GOOD, TOO ...
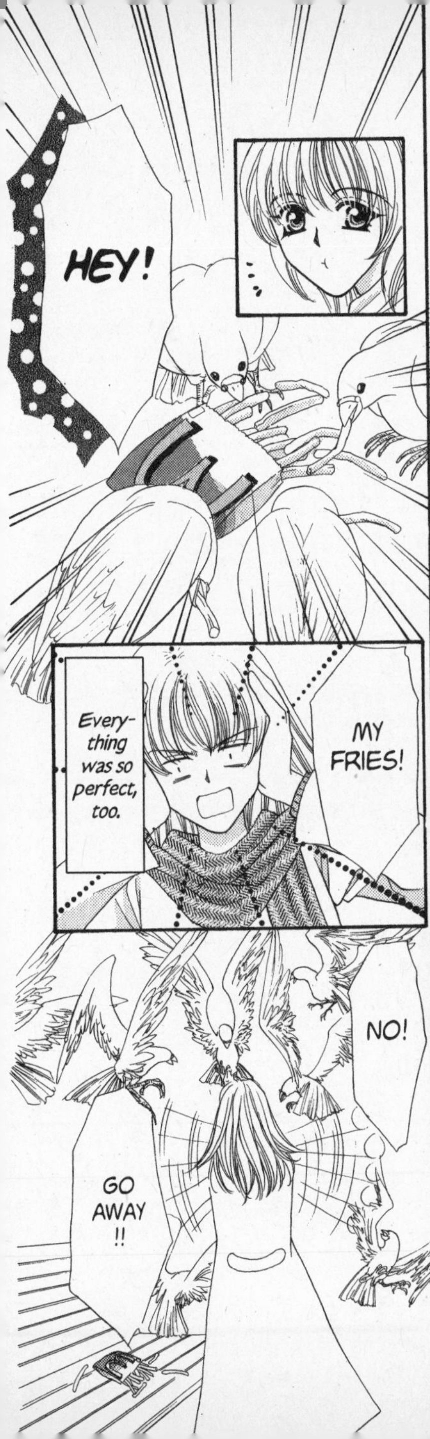
HEY!
MY FRIES!
Every-thing was so perfect, too.
NO!
GO AWAY !!

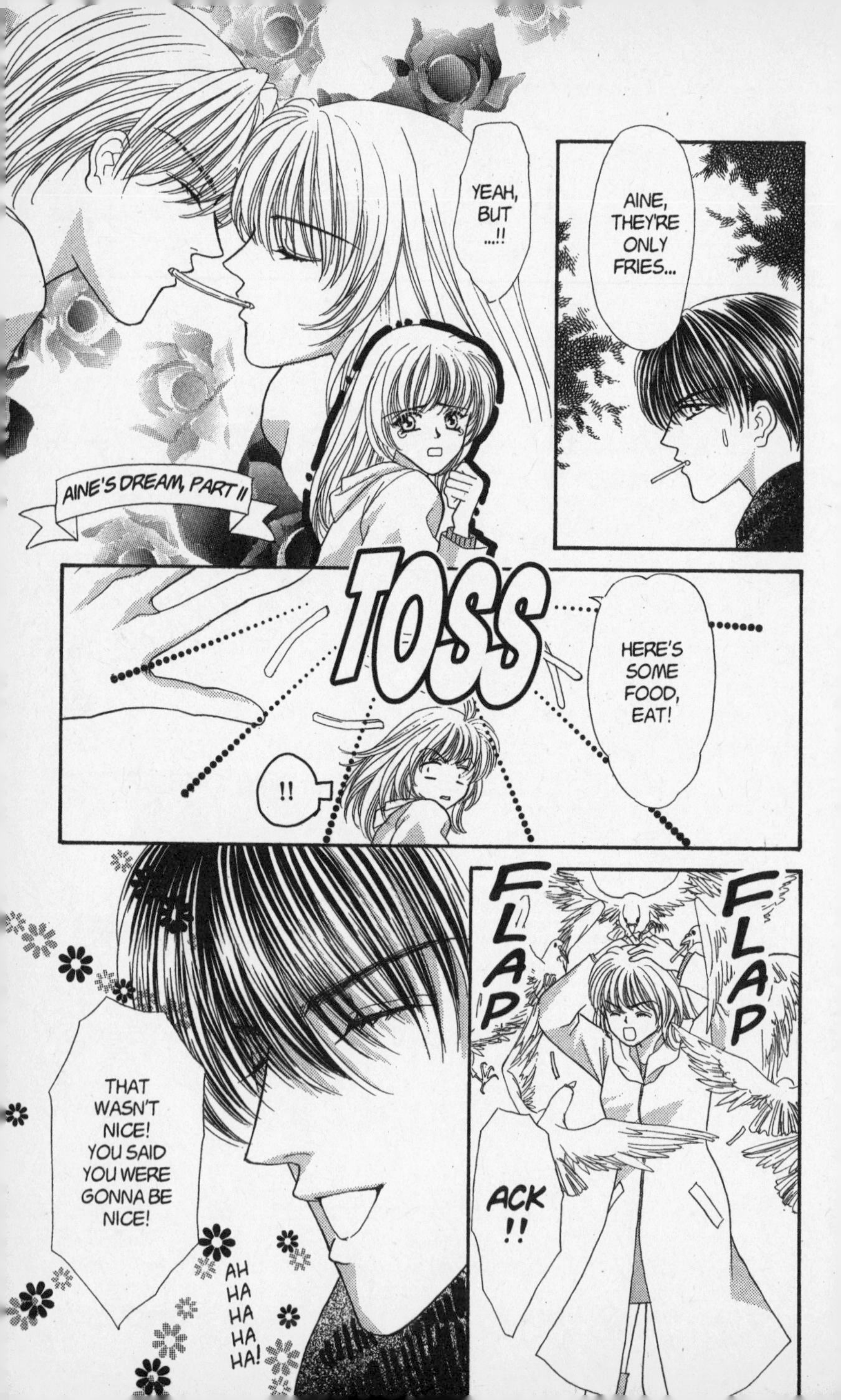
AINE, THEY'RE ONLY FRIES...
YEAH, BUT ...!!
AINE'S DREAM, PART II
HERE'S SOME FOOD, EAT!
TOSS
!!
FLAP
FLAP
ACK !!
THAT WASN'T NICE! YOU SAID YOU WERE GONNA BE NICE!
AH HA HA HA HA!

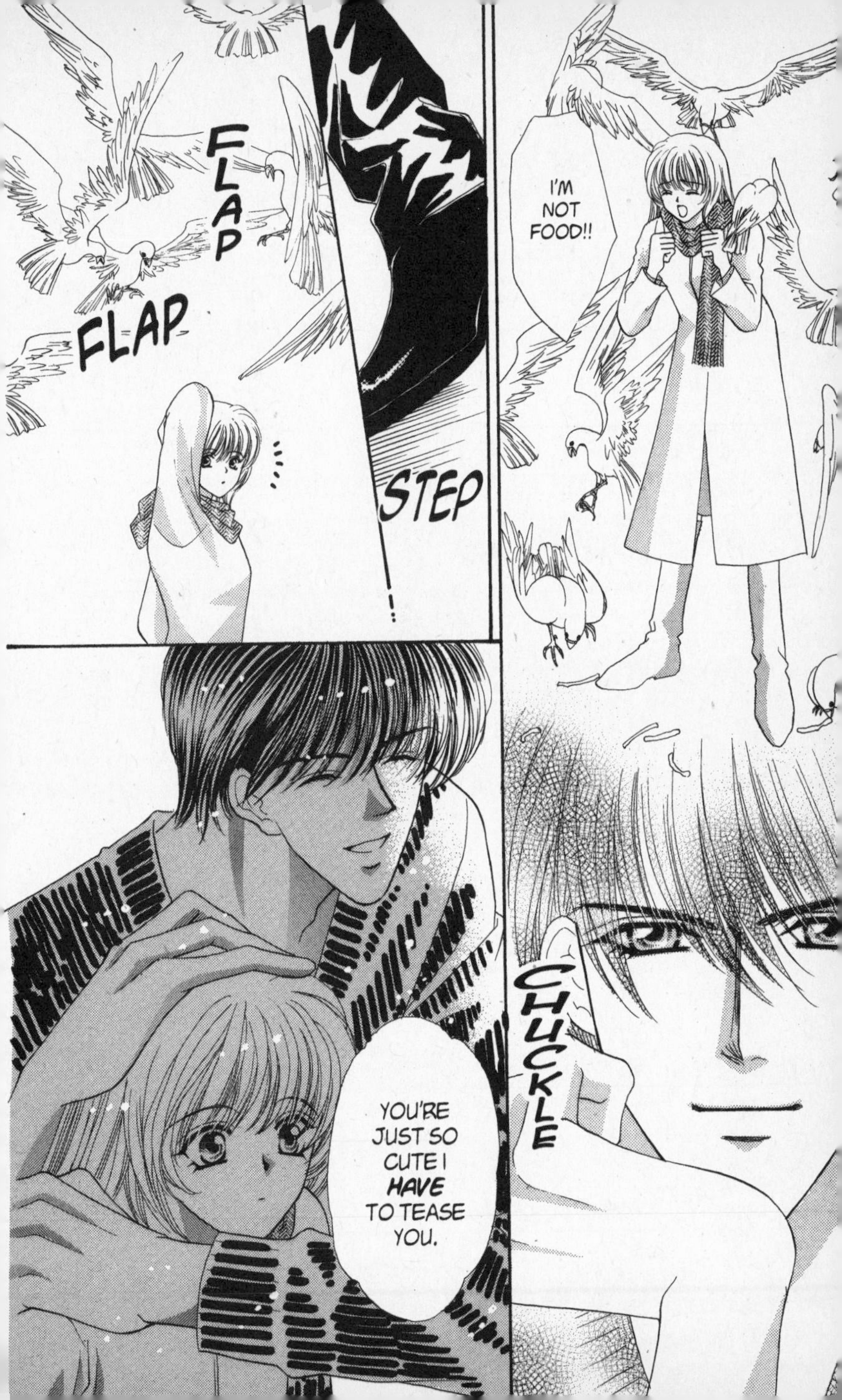
I'M NOT FOOD!!
STEP
!!
FLAP
FLAP
...
CHUCKLE
YOU'RE JUST SO CUTE I *HAVE* TO TEASE YOU.

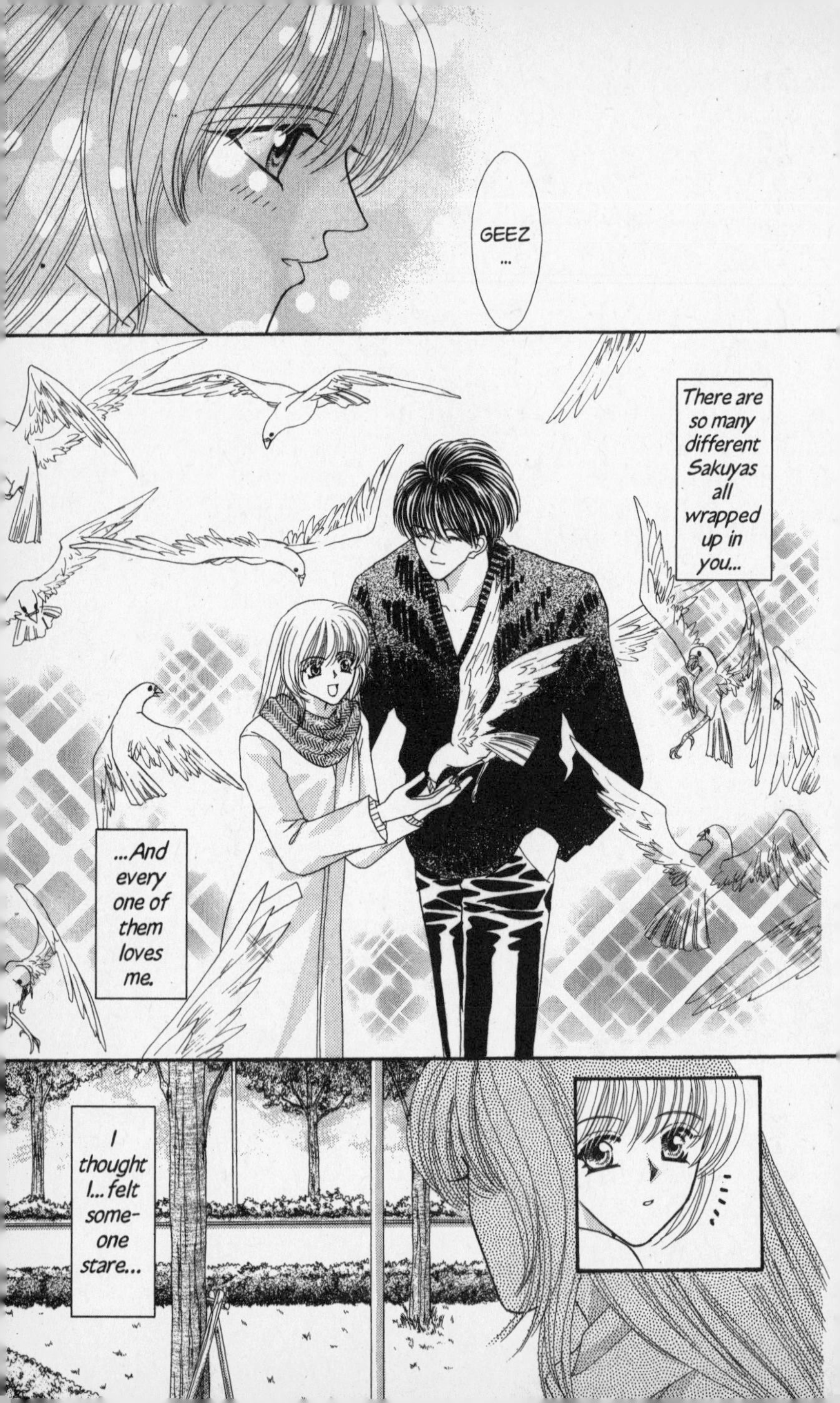
GEEZ
...
There are so many different Sakuyas all wrapped up in you...
...And every one of them loves me.
......
I thought I...felt some-one stare...

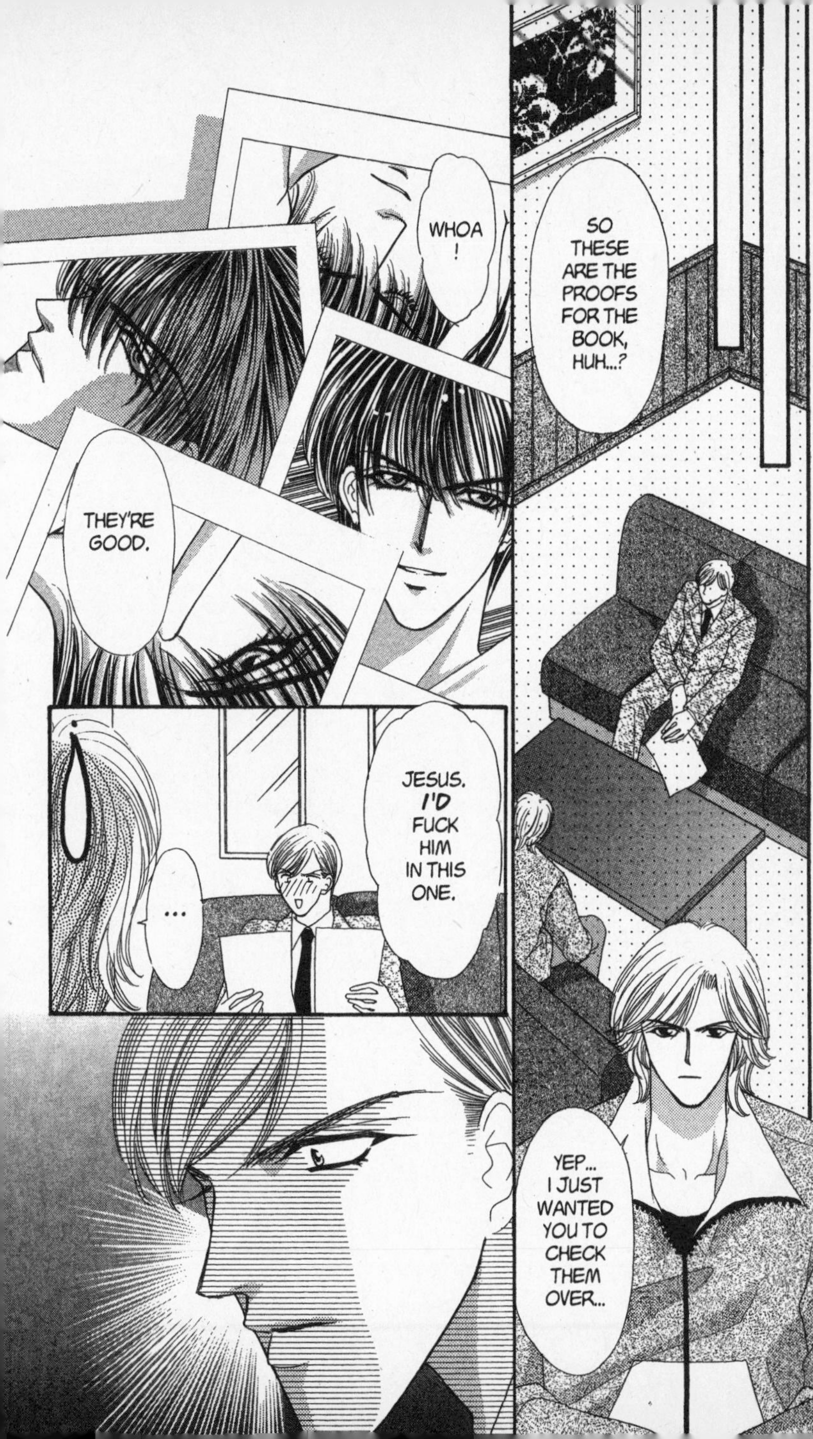
SO THESE ARE THE PROOFS FOR THE BOOK, HUH...?
YEP... I JUST WANTED YOU TO CHECK THEM OVER...
WHOA!
THEY'RE GOOD.
JESUS. **I'D** FUCK HIM IN THIS ONE.
...

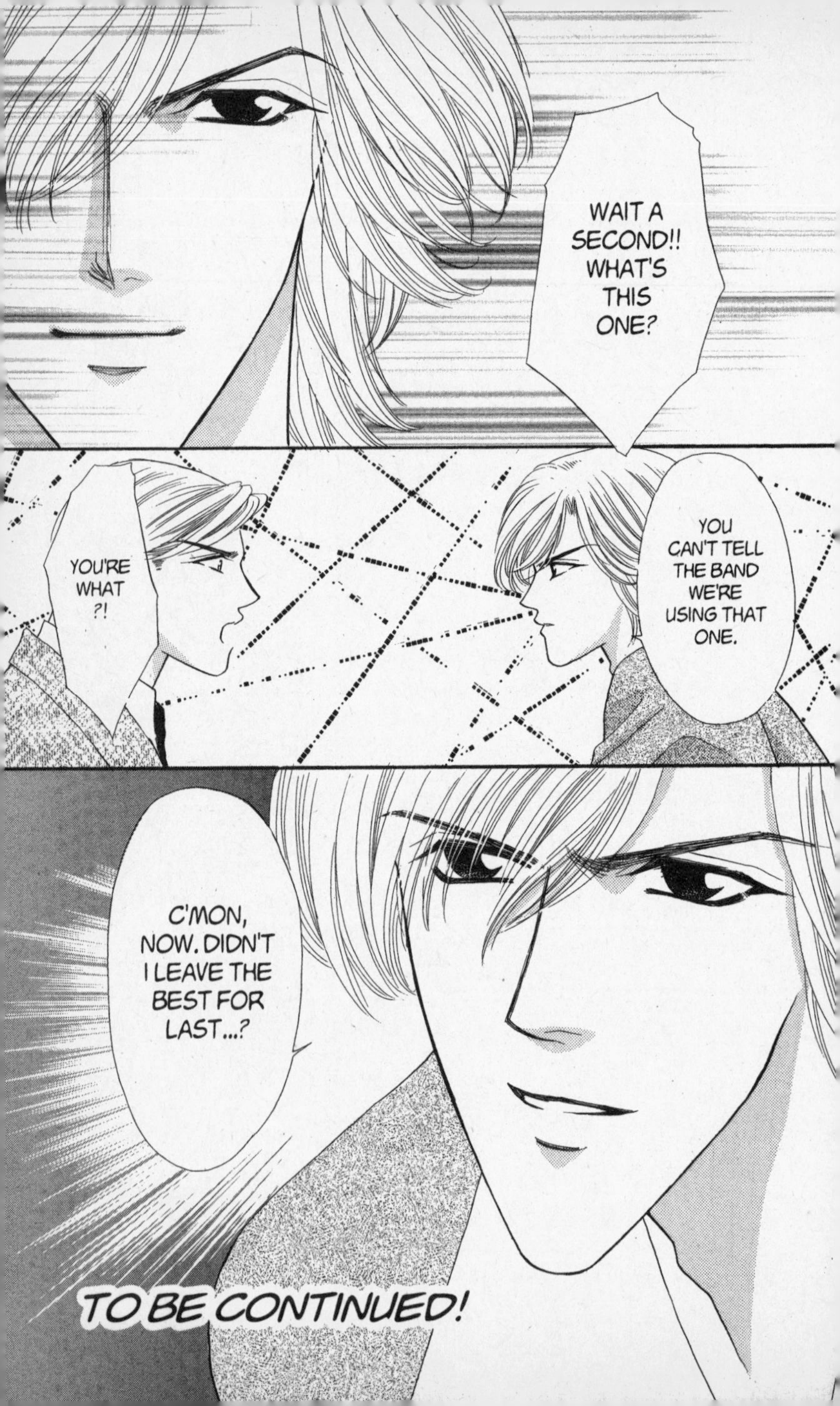
WAIT A SECOND!! WHAT'S THIS ONE?
YOU CAN'T TELL THE BAND WE'RE USING THAT ONE.
YOU'RE WHAT ?!
C'MON, NOW. DIDN'T I LEAVE THE BEST FOR LAST...?
TO BE CONTINUED!

Satanic Verses
Kelly Sue DeConnick

"Dress You Up in My Love," Part One

Fashion is made to become unfashionable.- Coco Chanel (1883–1971)

No change in musical style will survive unless it is accompanied by a change in clothing style. Rock is to dress up to.- Frank Zappa (1940–1994)

I beg of you, Kittens: let's not make a practice of comparing "Manga" and "American Comics" in broad strokes. Both categories are far too broad and any declaration outside "one reads left to right and the other, right to left" is well met with a staggering list of exceptions.

Let's not *make a practice of it*...let's just do it every once in a while on the down low. Real quiet like. Just between you and me, Kittens, okay? Okay.

So here's the thing: manga series are—generally speaking—more fashion-conscious than American comics. I could speculate as to *why*, but that conversation would be fairly academic, and I don't have the space to do it here anyway. (If you're dying to talk about it, you can write me c/o VIZ or e-mail me at kellysue@kellysue.com.) I opt instead to celebrate the trend with a super-fast drive-by Sakuya-centric two-part retrospective of Fashion hits and misses as demonstrated in our series so far. Ready? Superfast! Let's go:

Volume 1
HIT: The black button down (pages 106 and 152). First, I love that he wears the same shirt twice. Second, black button downs just *work*. Ask Johnny Cash, Elvis or Interpol.
MISS: The black pleather half-shirt (page 25)! Egads. No half-shirts on men, please. I don't care how ripped your abs are...a half-shirt screams, "Hi. I am a hesher. Want to see my squirrel gun? It's in my brown Camaro!"
TOO CLOSE TO CALL: The leopard-print long coat. On the one hand, it's very David Bowie. On the other hand, there are looks that only David Bowie can pull off. This might be one of them.

Volume 2
HIT: Tough choice, but I have to go with the grey pin-striped suit (page 93). What's more rock'n'roll than playing dress up?
TOO CLOSE TO CALL: The accessory bonanza that is page 11. Two bracelets *and* a necklace. It's more *Goodfellas* than good-looking, but it reminds me of a guy named Vinny I once knew. Ah, Vinny. Vinny, Vinny, Vinny. Sigh.

Volume 3
HIT: The sunglasses on page 58 and the shoes on page 167. Those are the accessories of a man who gives a damn and has the money to prove it. The man who wears those shoes has never owned a Velcro wallet. I knew a guy with a Velcro wallet and his nickname was, well, Velcro Wallet. Actually, it was more than a nickname because we didn't know his real name. Just sayin'.
MISS: That Horrible Coat (page 88). Hello, *Ilsa: She-Wolf of the SS*.
TOO CLOSE TO CALL: Page 182. The tweed's nice, but the tweed-turtleneck combo suggests that he might have a toy poodle in his Louis Vuitton Weekender.

Volume 4
HIT: The black, ribbed turtleneck sweater. Manly *and* snuggly. Meow.
MISS: Oh, look at page 132! Look! Look! Sakuya owns not one, but TWO long animal-print coats. This one appears to be ocelot. I think he borrowed it from Elton John. Miss!

Volume 5
MISS: The extra-pleated baggy pants (page 44). Um. Problem: We can't see his ass.
TOO CLOSE TO CALL: On the one hand, the rose-appliqué shirt (page 50) looks kind of kitschy, like something for The Grand Ole Opry. On the other hand, I think my mom has that shirt...

With http://www.japanesestreets.com bookmarked in my browser and my copy of *FRUiTS* clutched tight to my breast, I remain,

Yours,

Kelly Sue DeConnick
January 2005

Kelly Sue DeConnick is responsible for the English adaptation of *Sensual Phrase*. She also works (or has worked) on the titles *Descendants of Darkness*, *Kare First Love*, *Sexy Voice and Robo*, *Doubt!!* and *Blue Spring*. She lives in Kansas City and can be contacted c/o VIZ.

EDITOR'S RECOMMENDATIONS

More manga!

If you like

Sensual Phrase ™

here are three more books the editor thinks you'll enjoy:

© 2002, 2003 Iou
Kuroda/Shogakukan, Inc.

Sexy Voice and Robo
Today, Nico is a 14-year-old telephone-dating call girl. But tomorrow, who knows? She might be a fortuneteller or a spy. Don't miss this award-winning effort from Iou Kuroda.

vol.1   story and art by Kaori Yuki
Tenshi Kinryou Ku © Kaori
Yuki 1994/HAKUSENSHA,
Inc.

Angel Sanctuary
In a war between Heaven and Hell, there's only one thing forbidden: the love between a brother and sister!

© 2000 Kaneyoshi
Izumi/Shogakukan, Inc.

Doubt!!
With a little bit of this and a little bit of that, Ai transforms herself into a cute and popular teenager. What she needs most, however, is a dash of confidence. A story of self-identity by creator Kaneyoshi Izumi.

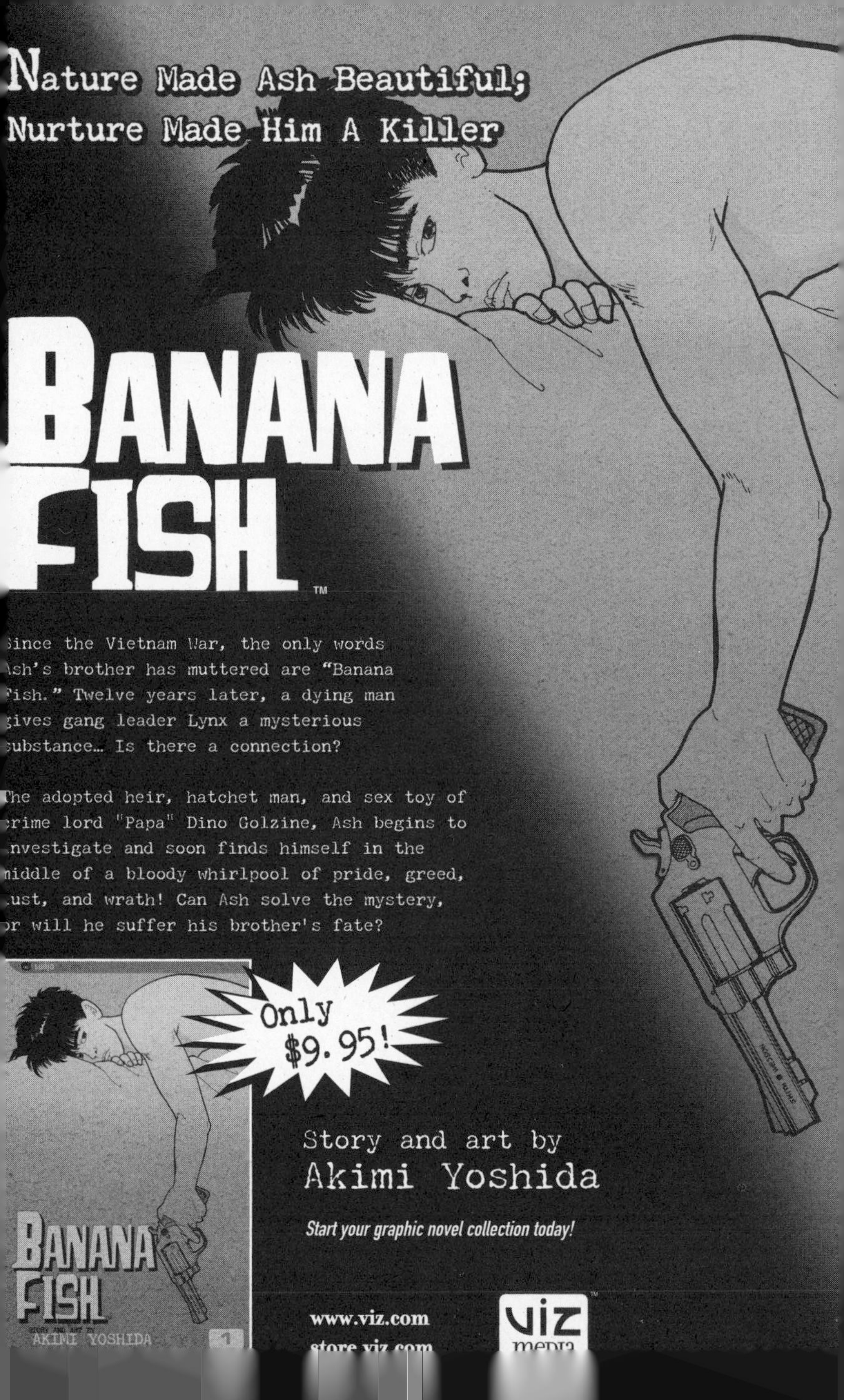

Nature Made Ash Beautiful;
Nurture Made Him A Killer
BANANA FISH™
Since the Vietnam War, the only words Ash's brother has muttered are "Banana Fish." Twelve years later, a dying man gives gang leader Lynx a mysterious substance… Is there a connection?
The adopted heir, hatchet man, and sex toy of crime lord "Papa" Dino Golzine, Ash begins to investigate and soon finds himself in the middle of a bloody whirlpool of pride, greed, lust, and wrath! Can Ash solve the mystery, or will he suffer his brother's fate?
BANANA FISH
AKIMI YOSHIDA
1
Only $9.95!
Story and art by
Akimi Yoshida
Start your graphic novel collection today!
www.viz.com
store.viz.com
viz media™

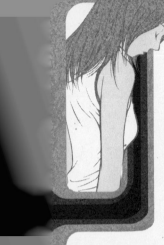
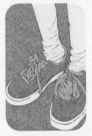
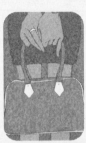

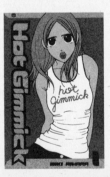
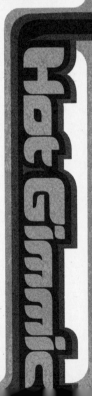

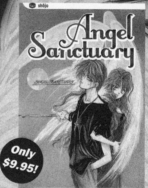

A Beauty Who Feels Like a Beast!

To overcome an embarrassing past, teenage Ai gets a makeover and attends a new high school. Soon, the hottest guy at school is chatting her up! But beauty is only skin deep, and Ai learns that fresh makeup and new clothes can't hide her insecurities or doubts.

A tale of high school neurosis at its finest—start your graphic novel collection today!

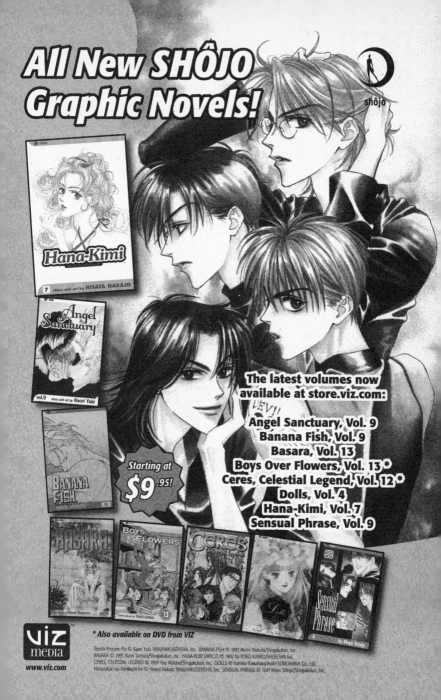

LOVE SHOJO? LET US KNOW!

☐ Please do NOT send me information about VIZ Media products, news and events, special offers, or other information.

☐ Please do NOT send me information from VIZ' trusted business partners.

Name: _____

Address: _____

City:_____ State:_____ Zip:_____

E-mail:_____

☐ Male ☐ Female Date of Birth (mm/dd/yyyy): ___/___/___ (Under 13? Parental consent required)

What race/ethnicity do you consider yourself? (check all that apply)

☐ White/Caucasian ☐ Black/African American ☐ Hispanic/Latino

☐ Asian/Pacific Islander ☐ Native American/Alaskan Native ☐ Other:_____

What VIZ shojo title(s) did you purchase? (indicate title(s) purchased)

_____

_____

What other shojo titles from other publishers do you own? _____

_____

Reason for purchase: (check all that apply)

☐ Special offer ☐ Favorite title / author / artist / genre

☐ Gift ☐ Recommendation ☐ Collection

☐ Read excerpt in VIZ manga sampler ☐ Other_____

Where did you make your purchase? (please check one)

☐ Comic store ☐ Bookstore ☐ Mass/Grocery Store

☐ Newsstand ☐ Video/Video Game Store

☐ Online (site:_____) ☐ Other_____

How many shojo titles have you purchased in th[barcode sticker] **?**
(please check one from each column)

SHOJO MANGA	VIZ SHOJO MANGA
☐ None	☐ None
☐ 1 – 4	☐ 1 – 4
☐ 5 – 10	☐ 5 – 10
☐ 11+	☐ 11+

What do you like most about shojo graphic novels? **(check all that apply)**

☐ Romance
☐ Drama / conflict
☐ Fantasy
☐ Comedy
☐ Real-life storylines
☐ Relatable characters
☐ Other ______________________________

Do you purchase every volume of your favorite shojo series?

☐ Yes! Gotta have 'em as my own
☐ No. Please explain: ______________________________

Who are your favorite shojo authors / artists? ______________________________

____

What shojo titles would like you translated and sold in English? ______________________________

____

THANK YOU! Please send the completed form to:

VIZ media

NJW Research
ATTN: VIZ Media Shojo Survey
42 Catharine Street
Poughkeepsie, NY 12601

Your privacy is very important to us. All information provided will be used for internal purposes only and will not be sold or otherwise divulged.